NOVELISTS ON THE NOVEL

NOVELISTS

ON

THE NOVEL

by

MIRIAM ALLOTT

LONDON: Routledge and Kegan Paul
NEW YORK: Columbia University Press

First published 1959

Published as a Routledge paperback 1965, 1968 and 1973
by Routledge and Kegan Paul Ltd
Broadway House, 68–74 Carter Lane, London EC4V 5EL

Printed in Great Britain by
Fletcher & Son Ltd, Norwich

ISBN 0 7100 4648 0

CONTENTS

CONTENTS

II. THE NOVEL AS A PORTRAIT OF LIFE

III. THE ETHICS OF THE NOVEL

CONTENTS

CONTENTS

Part Two THE GENESIS OF A NOVEL

I The Novelist's Approach and Equipment
II Germination
III At Work: Effort and Inspiration

CONTENTS

III. THE NOVELIST AT WORK: EFFORT AND INSPIRATION

Part Three THE CRAFT OF FICTION

I *Structural Problems*
   Unity and Coherence
   Plot and Story
   The Time-Factor

II *Narrative Technique*

III *Characterization*

IV *Dialogue*

V *Background*

VI *Style*

CONTENTS

CONTENTS

CONTENTS

TO THE MEMORY OF
MY FATHER

PREFACE

ONLY the practitioner can speak with final authority about the problems of his art. In this book I have gathered together discussions about the nature and craft of fiction by novelists, believing that these are the most likely people to clear up the confusions of novel criticism. In reading what they have to say, with due allowance made for variations of temperament and historical background, their general agreement on essential issues is striking. In a sense, then, their commentaries can be said to contribute to a recognized 'working' aesthetic of the novel. I should, of course, have liked to represent the views of many more English and foreign novelists, especially contemporaries, but my selections are limited by space and matters of copyright. I have included one writer, Mrs. Anna Barbauld, who is not a novelist, for her admirable and too much neglected editorial work in her series, *British Novelists*, which appeared in 1810. In arranging my materials and in the editorial introductions to the three parts of the book—The Nature of Prose Fiction, The Genesis of a Novel and The Craft of Fiction —I have aimed at a chronological order, hoping that readers will feel as I do the interest of following from the beginning the gradual evolution of a literary form.

I must not end without expressing my gratitude to everyone who has helped me to prepare this book for the press. I should like especially to thank Professor Kenneth Muir of the Department of English Literature at Liverpool University for various helpful suggestions and for reading the book in proof; my mother for advice in translating from the French; and my husband who has done his best to see that my text is accurate and my prose readable, and who has helped me all along in more ways than can be easily acknowledged here. I must also thank warmly Miss Eda Whelan of the Harold Cohen Library (University of Liverpool) for going to so much trouble to obtain books for me, and Miss Margaret Burton, Departmental Secretary, who typed parts of the manuscript.

M. A.

Liverpool, April 1959

Part One

THE NATURE OF
PROSE FICTION

... the real, if unavowed, purpose of fiction is to give pleasure by gratifying the love of the uncommon in human experience ...

The writer's problem is, how to strike the balance between the uncommon and the ordinary so as on the one hand to give interest, on the other to give reality.

In working out the problem, human nature must never be made abnormal, which is introducing incredibility. The uncommonness must be in the events, not in the characters; and the writer's art lies in shaping that uncommonness while disguising its unlikelihood, if it be unlikely.

The whole secret of fiction and the drama—in the constructional part—lies in the adjustment of things unusual to things eternal and universal. The novelist who knows exactly how exceptional, and how non-exceptional, his events should be made, possesses the key to the art.

THOMAS HARDY.

INTRODUCTION

I The Novel and the Marvellous

THERE IS plenty of support from other novelists for Hardy's account of the 'real, if unavowed, purpose of fiction'—that is, 'to give pleasure by gratifying the love of the uncommon in human experience'—and for his argument that this purpose will be best realized when the novelist persuades the reader of the 'truth' of his characters. The novelist's natural desire to indulge our sense of wonder is modified by his knowledge that he must also compel our assent—'we must first *believe* before we can be *affected*', says Hurd in his *Letters on Chivalry*[1]—and so, whenever he is drawn into a discussion about the question of probability, a harassing problem troubling the artistic conscience ever since Aristotle, the novelist's argument usually proceeds from the value of 'the marvellous' to the necessity of maintaining verisimilitude and consistency in his characters' behaviour. He gives special emphasis to these ideas when he is conscious of evolving a new kind and is not yet quite certain of where he stands in relation to existing forms of narrative such as Epic or Romance.

'Every writer may be permitted to deal with the wonderful as much as he pleases', says Fielding, provided the actions of his characters are 'within the compass of human agency' and 'likely for the very actors and characters themselves to have performed'.[2] A Märchen element survives in all his own stories; the poor boy makes good, the foundling turns out to be the Squire's nephew, the hard-pressed family comes into a fortune. Regret that modern fiction seemed 'to stoop with disenchanted

---

[1] *Letters on Chivalry and Romance* (1762), Letter x.
[2] See below, p. 60.

3

wings to truth' compelled many of Fielding's successors in the eighteenth century to heighten the element of 'the marvellous' in their stories. Horace Walpole is an early example, but, as he tells us in his preface to *The Castle of Otranto* (1765), he is anxious to avoid the implausible characterization of the old romances, where people were given absurd dialogue to speak and seemed 'to lose their senses' whenever they witnessed marvellous happenings. He tries, without perhaps much success, to persuade his readers of the truth of his characters by making them behave 'as it might be supposed mere men and women would do' when confronted with a giant in armour or a statue bleeding at the nose. His admirer, Clara Reeve, seeks to follow his example in *The Old English Baron: A Gothic Tale* (1778).[1] Another eighteenth-century novelist, Richard Cumberland, believes that the author may travel a good distance into 'the fields of fancy' for his own and his reader's enjoyment, but he tries not to make his characters behave unnaturally: although events 'closely bordering on the marvellous' call for heightened effects in character-drawing, there are limits which are not to be transgressed.[2]

Many novelists other than the Gothic romancers came to feel that their best means of reconciling 'the uncommon and the ordinary' was to set their stories in the past. Scott explains his choice of the reign of James I as a setting for *The Fortunes of Nigel* (1822) on the grounds that this period seemed distant enough in time to allow him to introduce incidents which are 'marvellous and improbable' but was also near enough to the present for the behaviour of his characters to carry conviction for his modern readers.[3] Hawthorne, with the greater meticulousness of a later age, explains that *The House of the Seven Gables* (1851) must come 'under the Romantic definition' because in attempting 'to connect a bygone time with the very present that is flitting away from us' it dispenses with complete fidelity to the possible and probable.[4] He is careful to add that even a Romance 'sins unpardonably so far as it may swerve aside from the truth of the human heart'. He himself prefers to 'mingle the Marvellous rather as a slight, delicate and evanescent flavour, than as any portion of the dish offered to the public', but an author 'can

---

[1] See below, p. 45.   [2] See below, pp. 47–8.
[3] See below, p. 50.   [4] See below, pp. 50–1.

hardly be said . . . to commit a literary crime even if he disregard this caution'.[1] Novelists who do not write about the past but are nevertheless haunted by it often 'mingle the Marvellous' in their stories by introducing elements of fantasy and the supernatural which leave us with the impression that their 'ordinary world . . reaches back'. The phrase is used by E. M. Forster in connection with Dostoevsky,[2] and in Mr. Forster's own novels the presence of Pan may upset an English party of sightseers in Italy or Greece, or a ghost cause a car to swerve on an Indian highroad. Henry James, whose novels and stories are filled with his 'sense of the past', encourages his imagination to conjure up ghosts and presences, believing that these best serve the storyteller's fundamental appeal to wonder.[3] But his ghosts, no less than the people whom they haunt, must behave as we might reasonably expect them to behave—Ralph Pendrel in *The Sense of the Past* (1917), for example. When James's novels are not dealing directly with the supernatural, they are still accompanied by overtones of fantasy; his figures are 'natural' in motivation but legendary in their extravagant wealth, beauty, intelligence or doom—what else is Milly Theale (she is often called a Princess by her friends) but a victim of evil enchantment straight out of a fairy-tale? Conrad recognizes a double allegiance to 'the uncommon' and 'the ordinary' by calling himself 'a romantic realist'.[4] Although, as both he and James agree, what is remote and unfamiliar is not necessarily wonderful in itself,[5] his stories of the sea and of distant continents derive some of their power from the sense of the supernatural which they evoke. If Conrad's own feeling for the fascination of 'the uncommon' gives us at one extreme *The Arrow of Gold* (1919), a story so falsified by sentimentality that it forfeits almost all claim to consideration as a serious work of art, at the other it produces such compelling achievements as 'The Heart of Darkness' (1902), *Nostromo* (1904), 'The Secret Sharer' (1910) and *Victory* (1915).

Novelists, then, have continued to gratify 'our love of the uncommon in human experience' in spite of firmly distinguishing their own species of fiction as different in kind from 'the

[1] Ibid.   [2] See E.M. Forster, *Aspects of the Novel* (1927), Chapter vii.
[3] See below, pp. 56–7.   [4] See below, pp. 54–5.
[5] See below, pp. 54–6.

Romance'. 'What a duce,' writes Richardson in 1762, 'do you think I am writing a Romance? Don't you see that I am copying Nature?' [1] More than a century later, James still recognizes this difference, although he is more acutely conscious of the difficulties of definition. In his view, the romance deals with 'experience liberated, so to speak, experience disengaged, disembroiled, disencumbered, exempt from the conditions that we usually know to attach to it'. [2] The novelist knows that 'the balloon of experience is in fact tied to the earth' and he keeps it that way, however long his cable may be: but 'the art of the necromancer is, "for the fun of it", insidiously to cut the cable'. It says much for the natural imaginative gifts of our earlier novelists that they kept the cable as long as possible, and sometimes cut it, in spite of a certain amount of confusion about the real nature of their 'new species of writing'.

In fact their attempts to understand their new kind, and to relate it, however mistakenly, to earlier forms of fiction, may have done much to keep their sense of wonder alive. As long as they were occupied in sorting out the complicated relationships connecting their own art to classical epic and heroic or pastoral romance, they were unlikely to remain completely insulated from the imaginative appeal of these narratives. Brooding over the old stories, the eighteenth-century novelist could however be certain of one thing; whatever the degree of his personal response to 'the marvellous', his finished work was concerned, as little previous fiction had been, with 'natural' behaviour and 'real' people. Sometimes he explained his preference for this realism on moral grounds. Characters who are a convincingly natural mixture of good and bad, he argued, are more likely to provide useful examples than those who are extraordinarily wicked or virtuous; moreover extravagance of any kind misleads the reader and unfits him for ordinary life. Since he was happier with classical support he sometimes tried to claim a precedent in Greek and Roman epic, but this did not really fortify his position. For one thing, the behaviour of the characters in the classical epic did not accord with the notions which a polite age entertained about the ideal way to conduct oneself in society. In *The History of Sir Charles Grandison* (1754), Richardson makes Lady Charlotte expand his own

[1] See below, p. 41.   [2] See below, p. 56.

views, already expressed to Lady Bradshaigh, about the epic's
'savage spirit' and the 'infinite mischief' it had done 'for a
series of ages'.[1] Lady Charlotte blames 'the poetical tribe' for
encouraging men and women in the deceptions which they
practise on each other:

> With regard to *epics*, would Alexander, madman as he was, have
> been so *much* a madman, had it not been for Homer? Of what
> violence, murder, depredations, have not the epic poets been the
> occasion, by propagating false honours, false glory, and false
> religion?[2]

Defoe felt that the siege of Troy was for nothing other than
'the rescue of a Whore'.[3] The peculiar numinousness surrounding the epic also helped to place it at a remote distance from
the preoccupations of a rational, ordered society. 'The *Marvellous* and *Wonderful* is the Nerve of the Epic Strain; But what
marvellous things happen in a well-ordered state . . .?' asks
Blackwell wistfully in *An Enquiry into the Life and Writings of
Homer* (1735).[4] Blackwell has some community of feeling with
Voltaire in the second chapter of his *Essai sur la Poésie Epique*
(1727): '*Il faut peindre avec des couleurs vraies comme les anciens, mais
il ne faut pas peindre les mêmes choses*'.[5]

Such doubts about the contemporary relevance of the heroic
poem were fairly common throughout the eighteenth century, as
Ian Watt demonstrates in *The Rise of the Novel* (1957),[6] but
they provide evidence of the strength of the classical position
generally. Homer and Virgil, as Clara Reeve points out in *The
Progress of Romance* (1785), were among 'the School books, that
generally make a part of the education of young men'.[7] Men
'of sense, and of learning' continued 'to venerate' them.[8] Clara
Reeve does not blame this taste in itself (although she is
troubled about effects on the sexual morality of the young:
'Virgil . . . informs them of many things they had better be
ignorant of.—As a woman I cannot give this argument its full

---

[1] *Correspondence* (1804), Vol. IV, p. 287.
[2] *The History of Sir Charles Grandison*, Anna Barbauld's edn. of 1810,
Vol. VI, Letter xlv.
[3] See *The Felonious Treaty* (1711), p. 17.   [4] P. 26.
[5] *Œuvres Complètes* (1883–5), Vol. VIII, Chapter i, p. 313.
[6] See Chapter viii.   [7] Vol. II, p. 81.
[8] Vol. I, pp. 17, 21.

weight.—But a hint is sufficient . . .' [1]). What seems to her to be absurd is that people who 'venerate the epic' should at the same time 'decry the romance'.[2] The fables 'of the old classic Poets' are often 'far more wild and extravagant, and infinitely more incredible'.[3] In her view, the romance continued a tradition of fantasy and heroic adventure which the epic had begun. She herself was attracted by the inventive imagination of this tradition, although she admitted its frequent extravagance, and she thought too that on the whole it inculcated high standards of virtue and honour.

Those eighteenth-century novelists who continued to lean on the epic reserved their disapproval for the romance, refusing to identify the one kind with the other and, unlike Clara Reeve, failing to see any inconsistency in enjoying 'the marvellous' when it was 'classical' and suspecting it when it was not. Fielding may have been aware that the apparent inconsistency needed some thinking out, but he is expert at leaving his reader in two minds about his real meaning. As his novels testify on almost every page, he went through the 'grand old fortifying curriculum' at Eton. We expect him to be among those whom Clara Reeve describes as 'venerating the epic' while they 'decry the romance', and he seems to come up to expectation in the 'Author's Preface' to *Joseph Andrews* (1742). He places this work with Archbishop Fénelon's *Télémaque* (1699) in the same category as the *Odyssey* because, metre aside, these two narratives contain all the epic's 'other parts' as enumerated by Aristotle, i.e. 'fable, action, characters, sentiments and diction'. It is 'fairer and more reasonable' to relate *Joseph Andrews* to the epic 'from which it differs only in a single instance than to confound it with . . . the voluminous works, commonly called Romances, namely Clelia, Cleopatra, Astraea, Cassandra, the Grand Cyrus, and innumerable others, which contain, as I apprehend, very little instruction or entertainment'.[4]

It is quite possible that Fielding is having as much fun at Aristotle's expense as he is at the expense of the romancers. It is hard indeed to think of any narrative which does *not* contain 'fable, action, characters, sentiments and diction'. What is certain, however, is that Fielding expresses a general feeling about

[1] Vol. II, p. 82.   [2] Vol. I, p. 17.
[3] Vol. I, p. 21.   [4] See below, pp. 59–60.

the *romans de longue haleine* composed in the preceding century which even the upholders of the romantic tradition show no hesitation in sharing. These voluminous works kept their enormous popularity in England and France until late in the seventeenth century, when they fell into the neglect from which they have never since recovered. Of Fielding's list of titles, the earliest is 'Astraea', written by Honoré D'Urfé (1567–1625), the first part appearing in 1607, the fifth and last, which was never completed, in 1627. The full title of the book is *L'Astrée, ou par plusieurs histoires et sous personnes de bergers et d'autres sont déduits les divers effets de l'honnête amitié*—which may explain why it took so long to write. The story of the chequered loves of the shepherd Celadon and the shepherdess Astrée in the fifth century A.D. is told diffusely in a tiresome number of episodes, but then the narrative is no more than a framework for interminable discussions on the theme of virtuous love (*l'honnête amitié*). Although *L'Astrée* is strictly the only pastoral fiction, all the other books mentioned by Fielding derive from the same 'Arcadian' tradition, as Dunlop points out in his agreeable *History of Fiction* (1814).[1] The sentimental analysis and episodic structure recur in La Calprenède's (1614–63) *Cassandre* (1642–63) and *Cléopatre* (1646–57). Both are set in heroic antiquity and *Cassandre*, with Alexander the Great as its hero, runs to ten volumes. The two remaining books are by the most popular romancer of all, Mademoiselle Madeleine de Scudéry (1607–1701). *Clélie* (1654–60) is an 'histoire romaine', and *Artamène, ou le Grand Cyrus* (1649–53), another ten-volume novel, which rivalled in its enormous following even d'Urfé's *L'Astrée*, is set in the fifth century B.C. and deals with the wooing in disguise of the Princess of the Medes by the Persian conqueror, Cyrus. The English translation attracted hordes of enthusiastic readers, including Mrs. Pepys, whose husband reproved her for narrating 'long stories out of *Grand Cyrus*, which she would tell, though nothing to the purpose, nor in any good manner'.[2] 'These were the books that pleased our grandmothers', says Clara Reeve, speaking in the

---

[1] He seems to feel, however, that many of their elements originate in 'anterior and more spirited compositions': this is why he also relates them to the 'heroic' romance. See John Dunlop, *The History of Fiction* (1814), Chapter x.

[2] See *The Diary of Samuel Pepys*, 12 May 1666.

person of Euphrasia in *The Progress of Romance*, adding that now (1785) such romances have 'become the lumber of a bookseller's shop, and are frequently seen to wrap a pound of sugar from the grocer's'.[1]

It is obvious that *Joseph Andrews* has little in common with these works, from which Fielding seemingly derived so much less 'instruction and entertainment' than from 'the epic kind'. But 'instruction and entertainment' are not peculiar to the epic. An enthusiast for fiction like Dunlop is able to find 'a powerful instrument of virtue and happiness' in every kind of narrative from *Theagenes and Chariclea* to the novels of Mrs. Radcliffe. *Joseph Andrews* is, in fact, as far from the *Aeneid* as it is from *L'Astrée*. As we have no evidence of what Homer's 'comic epic', the *Margites*, was really like, Fielding's fiction is to all intents and purposes just what he says it is: 'a new species of writing'. He runs counter to the Romance here in his first novel—written, as he tells us on his title-page, 'in imitation of the manner of Cervantes'—by making his characters not of high degree but of 'inferior rank and consequently of inferior manners', and the 'sentiments and diction' not 'sublime' but 'ludicrous'. On the other hand, when he glances at the epic, he does so, as so often in his later novels, in order to make fun of it. Various mock-heroic elements which are repeated in the pseudo-Virgilian similes and battle-pieces of *Jonathan Wild* (1743) and *Tom Jones* (1749), seem to indicate Fielding's amusement at epical extravagance quite as much as his humorous recognition that the prevailing temper of modern society is profoundly unheroic. Sometimes his play of irony suggests an even stronger feeling. In the first chapter of his moral fable, *Jonathan Wild*—indeed in the whole book—he indicts all heroic stories more ruthlessly even than Defoe or Richardson for propagating 'false honours, false glory and false religion'. Of course Fielding's irony points in various directions and this particular significance is not a primary one. There is, in any case, evidence throughout Fielding's fiction of a progressive movement away from burlesque and satire towards a different kind of art. *Joseph Andrews* soon ceases to be a simple parody of *Pamela*; the second version of *Jonathan Wild* tones down the direct political satire and humanizes the theme; *Tom Jones*, experimental and tentative as

[1] See *The Progress of Romance*, Vol. I, p. 70.

it so often appears, is nevertheless more closely organized than the picaresque, episodic *Joseph Andrews*; while *Amelia* (1751) brings us face to face with an altogether new type of structure. Here Fielding seems to have passed beyond his preoccupation with literary 'kinds' and, even if he intends us to hear Virgilian echoes, as George Sherburn suggested in 1936,[1] his interest is now concentrated on the interplay of characters within a domestic setting. He is, in fact, beginning to depict 'such familiar things as pass every day before our eyes'—which Clara Reeve felt to be the true subject-matter of 'the Novel'—and he gratifies his 'love of the uncommon in human experience' simply by heightening the feeling in certain episodes and contriving a happy ending for the trials of the faithful Amelia and her wavering husband, Captain Booth.

A more clear-cut attitude to romance and epic is apparently taken up by Tobias Smollett in his preface to *Roderick Random* (1748) where he gives a rapid sketch, as highly coloured as it is ferocious, of three phases in the evolution of prose fiction.[2] In this moral fable, 'the Ancients' represent excellence, the writers of the romances are the villains, and Cervantes and his imitators come to the rescue. Since 'the Ancients . . . had seen so many remarkable events celebrated in verse by their best poets', there was at first little demand for prose fiction. Then came the dark ages, 'when the minds of men were debauched, by the imposition of priestcraft, to the utmost pitch of credulity'. In this depraved age, 'the authors of romance arose'.[3] Unable to match the ancient poets in point of genius they tried to excel them in invention and lost sight of probability. They appealed 'to the wonder rather than the judgment of their readers'. Instead of making their heroes 'dignified in sentiment and practice' they distinguished them by 'their bodily strength, activity and extravagance of behaviour'. Deplorable as the Romances were, people enjoyed reading them. At last Cervantes appeared and with one blow,

[1] 'Fielding's *Amelia*: An Interpretation', *ELH*, Vol. III, pp. 1–14.

[2] See below, pp. 43–4.

[3] Warton in his 'A Stricture on Romantic Literature' also connects the rise of romance with the susceptibilities of a 'superstitious' age. See Warton's *History of Poetry*, ed. W. Carew Hazlitt (1871), Vol. I, *Of the Origin of Romantic Fiction in Europe*, pp. 247–8. See also Thomas Holcroft's preface to *Alwyn: the Gentleman Comedian* (1780), below, pp. 46–7.

by an inimitable piece of ridicule, reformed the taste of mankind, representing chivalry in the right point of view, and converting romance to purposes far more useful and entertaining, by making it assume the sock, and point out the follies of ordinary life.[1]

Cervantes, Smollett goes on, was followed 'by other Spanish and French authors', especially 'Monsieur le Sage', whose *Gil Blas de Santillane* (1715–35) he gave the first English translation of in 1749.

Yet in spite of the simplifications of this account, Smollett himself is as far from being a simple didactic realist as Cervantes or Le Sage.[2] His journalistic talents produce fiction which is sprawling, savage and often wildly fantastic in its comic invention. He frequently 'loses sight of probability', he certainly does not appeal more to the reader's 'judgment' than to his sense of 'wonder', and his characters are notorious for their 'extravagance of behaviour'. When we read in *Peregrine Pickle* of Commodore Trunnion's ride to his wedding on horseback we recognize at once the nature of Smollett's appeal for Dickens.[3] He did not attempt 'to strike a balance between the ordinary and the uncommon', but let invention rip. There may even be a distorted romanticism behind his cruelty and disgust. 'He writes like a man with a skin too few', is Walter Allen's comment in *The English Novel* (1954).[4]

It may come as a surprise after reading Fielding's and Smollett's attempts to distinguish between different kinds of storytelling to find Thomas Holcroft, twenty or so years later, claiming in the preface to *Alwyn: or the Gentleman Comedian* (1780) that 'modern writers use the word Romance to signify a fictitious history of detached and independent adventures', and 'under that idea, call the Telemaque of Fenelon, and the Cyrus of Ramsay,[5] Romances'. Holcroft goes even further. Although

---

[1] See below, p. 44.

[2] Cervantes hints at the limitations of his own anti-romanticism in the sixth chapter of *Don Quixote*.

[3] See *The Adventures of Peregrine Pickle*, Vol. I, Chapter viii.

[4] P. 65.

[5] i.e., Andrew Michael Ramsay, *A New Cyropaedia or The Travels of Cyrus* (1727). See also the same author's *A Discourse upon Epic Poetry*, printed as preface to Archbishop Fénelon's *The Adventures of Telemachus, the Son of Ulysses*, Ozell's translation, 1720.

they belong to 'a different species' from *Le Grand Cyrus* and *Télémaque* both *Gil Blas* and *Roderick Random* 'come under the same denomination'. In this judgment all are Romances. Smollett would have been astonished at this opinion. But if we do not allow the term 'Romance' to lead us astray, Holcroft's argument as a whole makes sense. He places these books together not because they resemble each other in their fantasy but because they are all guilty of one kind of extravagance. They all lack unity and coherence of design. As long as their incidents are 'related with spirit, the intention is answered'; their adventures 'pass before the view for no other purpose than to amuse by their peculiarity', and they need not affect 'the main story' —'if there should be one', Holcroft pointedly adds. A Novel, on the other hand, is 'another kind of work. Unity of design is its character.' Its incidents are 'entertaining in themselves' but they are combined in a special way and 'made to form a whole'. 'An unnecessary circumstance becomes a blemish' because it may detract 'from the simplicity which is requisite to exhibit the whole to advantage'. This is subtler and more helpful than Smollett's description of a novel, in the preface to *Ferdinand, Count Fathom* (1753), as 'a large diffused picture' which depends on 'a principal personage to attract the attention, unite the incidents, unwind the clue of the labyrinth and at last close the scene by virtue of his own importance'. But we should notice that it is not its 'epic regularity' which Holcroft has in mind when he separates 'the Novel' from 'the Romance'. Holcroft, like Fielding, had written plays and he found what he needed in the necessities of dramatic structure.

Thus, as in dramatic works, those circumstances which do not tend either to the illustration or the forwarding of the main story, or, which do not mark some character, or person in the drama, are to be esteemed unnecessary.

Hence it appears that the Novel is a work much more difficult than the Romance, and justly deserves to be ranked with those dramatic works whose utility is generally allowed.[1]

Holcroft, the associate of Godwin, translator of Goethe's *Hermann und Dorothea* (1801) and composer of the *Memoirs* which Hazlitt was to complete and edit after his death, heralds an age

[1] See below, p. 47.

which was to look with a more dispassionate eye on Epic and Romance and was gradually to become familiar with the idea that a novel could be an organized structure, different in kind from either. There is still little sign of this equilibrium in Clara Reeve's *The Progress of Romance*, published five years after *Alwyn*, but she uses 'the Novel' as a term indicating a particular literary kind with a fresh note of confidence:

The Novel is a picture of real life and manners, and of the times in which it is written. The Romance in lofty and elevated language, describes what never happened nor is likely to happen. The Novel gives a familiar relation of such things as pass every day before our eyes. . . .[1]

Clara Reeve's discussion of the 'Progress of Romance' reflects a mood that makes itself increasingly felt throughout the later eighteenth century. Her study owes a good deal, as she admits, to earlier commentators. Hurd, Beattie, Percy and Mallet are all acknowledged or drawn on and it is obviously of importance to her that these writers, in their enthusiasm for the 'romantic', seek to establish the continuity of romantic fantasy from the classical stories and the Eastern tales to the days of chivalry and beyond. Without their specialized knowledge, she nevertheless makes a brave effort to cut her own path through the tangled undergrowth of story-telling from Homer to her own times, enlivening her argument by casting it into the form of a dialogue between three characters. The chief of these, Euphrasia, who speaks for the author, maintains that

Homer was the parent of Romance; where ever his works have been known, they have been imitated by the Poets and Romance writers. —I look upon Virgil as the most successful of his Imitators.[2]

Hortensius, who represents a more orthodox view, objects that 'this is what I call degrading both these divine men',[3] but Euphrasia is undeterred. 'I venerate Homer as much as one un-learned in his own language can do', she allows, but roundly claims that there is little to choose between him and the author of Sinbad the Sailor's adventures. Both show 'variety of charac-ters', both relate 'marvellous adventures', and in the history of

[1] See below, p. 47.
[2] See *The Progress of Romance*, Vol. I, p. 19.
[3] Ibid.

Sinbad 'we have most of the adventures that Ulysses meets with in the *Odyssey*'. In short, 'Epic Poetry is the parent of Romance'.[1]

Clara Reeve, then, in direct contrast to Smollett, is openly attracted by medieval and renaissance romances. It is 'modern' romances which, in common with her contemporaries, she finds less pleasing. The tales of D'Urfé and Madeleine de Scudéry were superior to the old romances in some ways, particularly, perhaps, because 'they were written with more regularity, and brought nearer to probability'—what she objected to in them was that they mixed truth and fact insidiously, building 'fictitious stories' on 'obscure parts of true history' so that young people 'imbibed such absurd ideas of facts and persons, as were very difficult to be rectified'.[2] But in spite of her sense of the perils of extravagance and her strait-laced concern for the morals of 'the young person', she remains cool about novels whose simple ambition it is to show vice punished and virtue rewarded.[3] She wants, as she explains in the preface to her own novel, *The Old English Baron*, 'to unite the various merits and graces of the ancient Romance and modern Novel'.[4] To achieve this end, she says,

there is required a sufficient degree of the marvellous to excite attention; enough of the manners of real life to give an air of probability to the work; and enough of the pathetic to engage the heart in its behalf.[5]

It is left to Scott finally to tidy up the novelist's remaining confusions about epic, romance and the novel. In Clara Reeve's definitions of the novel and the romance he would not perhaps have found much with which to disagree. Romance, as he describes it in his essay on the subject, is 'a fictitious narrative in prose or verse: the interest of which turns upon marvellous and uncommon incidents', while a novel is 'a fictitious narrative, differing from the Romance, because the events are accommodated to the ordinary train of human events, and the modern state of society'.[6] There may be compositions 'which it is difficult to assign precisely or exclusively to the one class or the other; and which in fact, partake of the nature of both'. As an

---

[1] Vol. I, pp. 19, 22–5. [2] Vol. I, pp. 64–5.
[3] Vol. II, pp. 41–2. [4] See below, p. 45.
[5] Ibid. [6] See below, p. 49.

article on Madame Cottin's *Amelie Mansfield* had already put it in 1809, novels are, after all, 'often *"romantic"*, not indeed by the relation of what is obviously miraculous or impossible, but by deviating, though perhaps insensibly, beyond the bounds of probability or consistency'.[1] It is with certain underlying assumptions in studies like Clara Reeve's *The Progress of Romance*, Hurd's *Letters on Chivalry* or Percy's and Ritson's introductions to their various anthologies, that Scott is in real disagreement and in discussing this difference he shows his usual common sense. He dissents in particular from their 'levelling proposition' that Epic and Romance belong ultimately to the same class. He recognizes, as Addison, Voltaire and Blackwell recognized before him, the irreducible difference in quality between 'the marvellous' of the earliest heroic poems and the fantasy of their successors in the romantic kind. The feeling, which was made familiar to a later age by W. P. Ker, that 'Epic' implies some weight and massiveness while 'Romance means nothing if it does not convey some notion of mystery and fantasy',[2] had been experienced by Addison: speaking of the epic's power to combine astonishment and belief, he goes on, 'if the fable is only probable, it differs nothing from a true history, if it is only marvellous, it is no better than a romance'.[3] The feeling is again conveyed through Blackwell's regretful admissions that 'polishing diminishes a Language . . . it coops a Man up in a Corner . . .' and that Ariosto and Tasso

quitting life, betook themselves to Aerial Beings and Utopian Characters, and filled their Works with Charms and Visions, the modern Supplements of the Marvellous and the Sublime.[4]

For similar reasons, Voltaire sets Lucian's treatment of the enenchanted wood in the *Pharsalia* far above Tasso's portrayal of a kindred subject in the eighteenth book of the *Gerusalemme Liberata*.[5] Like these writers, Scott recognizes the supernatural grandeur of the epic, while responding to the pleasing appari-

---

[1] See below, pp. 49–50.
[2] See W. P. Ker, *Epic and Romance* (1897), Chapter i.
[3] *Spectator*, No. 315.
[4] *An Enquiry into the Life and Writings of Homer* (1735), pp. 58–9, 68–9.
    'Essai sur la Poésie Epique', Chapter viii, *Œuvres Complètes* (1883–5), Vol. VIII, pp. 343–6.

tions of the romance. He knows that in some works there are properties belonging to each kind which may be almost equally balanced, but

our taste and habits readily acknowledge as complete and absolute a difference between the Epopeia and Romance, as can exist betwixt two distinct species of the same generic class.[1]

The preoccupation of eighteenth-century novelists with the real relationship of the novel, the epic and the romance had its uses. It kept the creative imagination exposed to the 'appeal to wonder' of the old story-tellers, even in the teeth of the disapproval of reason or the moral sense with their allied demands that probability should be strictly kept. Yet this tug of war of allegiances had obvious disadvantages between 1760 and 1790. Attracted on the one hand by the literary possibilities of 'a familiar relation of such things as pass every day' and, on the other, by the appeal of 'nature strongly featured and probability closely bordering on the marvellous',[2] the novelists of these years only too easily fell into the trite or the extravagant, 'the Scylla and Charybdis of those who deal in fiction', as Coleridge puts it in his review of Mrs. Radcliffe's *The Mysteries of Udolpho* (1794).[3] The work of the earlier novelists of the eighteenth century has a drive and coherence from their excitement at realizing the congenial possibilities of the 'new species of writing'. They were pioneers. In the novels of Defoe, Fielding and Sterne the tastes and sensibility of their authors are everywhere felt. But the flood of fiction which poured into English bookshops and circulating libraries in the last thirty-five years of the eighteenth century shows little of their distinction. We find that novelists who commented interestingly on the nature of the novel did not themselves produce outstanding novels. Clara Reeve's *The Old English Baron* (1777), Holcroft's *Alwyn* (1785) and Richard Cumberland's *Henry* (1795) are patchy at best. Nor did the sentimental humanitarians, Henry Mackenzie and

---

[1] See his 'Essay on Romance', *Miscellaneous Prose Works* (1882), Vol. VI, pp. 138-9. He makes a similar distinction between Epic and Romance in the preface to *The Bridal of Triermain* (1813).

[2] See Clara Reeve and Richard Cumberland, below, pp. 47-8.

[3] First published in *The Critical Review*, August 1794; reprinted in *Coleridge, Select Poetry and Prose* (1933), ed. Stephen Potter, pp. 203-4.

Henry Brooke, much remedy matters with *The Man of Feeling* (1771) and *The Fool of Quality* (1766–70). Signs of improvement appear with Godwin's *Caleb Williams* (1795)—perhaps the most original novel in the later eighteenth century—and with the books of Fanny Burney and Maria Edgeworth, whom Jane Austen praised in her famous defence of the novel in the fifth chapter of *Northanger Abbey* (1818). A nice equilibrium of all its elements does not in fact appear in the English novel before Jane Austen, who wins a triumph for the Augustan virtues of propriety and proportion without in the least refusing to gratify our 'love of the uncommon'. Of Jane Austen's five novels, three are 'Cinderella' stories in which the heroine rises through love-attachments from some lowly or humiliating social position to pride of place and fortune. Jane Austen transposes the pleasurably 'romantic' into the key of ordinary everyday experience, making her transformation of fortune appear, to use Clara Reeve's words, 'such as may happen to our friend or to ourselves'.[1] When she subjects Mrs. Radcliffe and the sensational novelists to her ridicule, she does so because they fail to 'strike the balance between the uncommon and the ordinary', not because they dare to deal in the 'uncommon' itself. If it were otherwise, she would hardly have taken to story-telling on her own account.

But the discrimination of her art is very different in kind from later attempts to 'strike the balance'. These are often the result of a new tendency, quite alien to the eighteenth-century novel, to probe the nature of this human desire for 'the uncommon' and 'the exceptional' and its connection with 'such things as may pass every day'. The impulse to indulge a longing for the uncommon is of course encouraged by certain forces at work in the nineteenth century and this indulgence is clearly evident in George Sand's early novels and Charlotte Brontë's *Jane Eyre* (1847) and *Villette* (1853). Stendhal, however, is the best example of the self-critical artist who sets out to portray in his fictional characters what happens when this longing for 'the exceptional' conflicts with the demands of contemporary society. Stendhal, in one sense, belongs to that long French tradition which extends from Madame de Lafayette to Proust and favours the minute analysis of every aspect of *amitié*, *honnête* or other-

---

[1] See below, p. 51.

wise. His original contribution to this tradition is the self-consciousness which enables him to do justice, especially in *Le Rouge et le Noir* (1831), to the *logique* which he admired and the *espagnolisme* which fascinated him. Like his creator, Stendhal's Julien Sorel—to use phrases which Flaubert applied to himself[1] —is 'a lover of great eagle flights', of 'sonority', of the *panache* and glory of the heroic, which are epitomized for him in the person of Napoleon. This passionate attachment to the heroic and the grandiose of course runs counter to the unheroic values of bourgeois society. To this society Sorel wishes to stand in the relationship of a conqueror. He goes into battle wearing a priest's cassock instead of a scarlet cloak and carrying a copy of Molière's *Tartuffe*.

Here 'the uncommon' and 'the ordinary' comment obliquely on each other—the criticism of society in the novel is as illuminating as the analysis of Sorel's romantic attachment to 'the exceptional' (and, one may add, as devastating in its irony). The more finished the artist, the more conscientiously he tries to heighten the effect of this commentary. Flaubert is an obvious example and so is Conrad, who deliberately explores in his characters human attitudes which his own 'romantic feeling of reality' helps him to understand. This feeling

may be a curse but when disciplined by a sense of personal responsibility and a recognition of the hard facts of existence shared with the rest of mankind becomes but a point of view from which the very shadows of life appear endowed with an internal glow. . . . It is none the worse for the knowledge of the truth. . . .[2]

The reader may be just as strongly affected by the counterpoint of 'the ordinary' and 'the uncommon' when they are handled by a less self-conscious artist. Henry James found that 'in the men of the largest responding imagination before the human scene'—he mentions Scott, Balzac and 'the coarse, comprehensive, prodigious Zola'—the imaginative current remains 'extraordinarily rich and mixed, washing us successively with the warm wave of the near and familiar and the tonic shock . . . of the far and strange'.[3] Maupassant agrees with James about Zola:

. . . child of romanticism that he is, and himself a romantic in

---

[1] See below, p. 51.   [2] See below, p. 54.   [3] See below, p. 55.

method, he has a tendency to the lyrical, a need to exalt, to enlarge
. . . Moreover he is well aware of this tendency in himself and fights
it unremittingly only to succumb again and again.[1]

The harshness which Zola uses in portraying contemporary
society—a harshness which was to be largely responsible for a
belief that 'realism' was necessarily incompatible with 'idealism'
in art—can indeed be felt as an expression of sour romanticism.

When they tried to incorporate 'the marvellous' into their
fiction, what the primitive novelists sensed and the great artists
have always succeeded in showing us is that a certain kind of
fantasy is a necessary and a valuable ingredient in fiction. This
fantasy does not provide a means of escape into a world of fixed
ideals—the world conjured up by so many heroic and chival-
rous romances—but, in Shelley's words, it 'quickens and en-
larges the mind'. The novel furthers this quickening process by
attempting to realize the wonderful and strange in terms of the
near and familiar.

II   The Novel as a Portrait of Life

IN ORDER to create the illusion of 'reality' while gratifying our
'love of the uncommon in human experience', the novelist, as
we have seen, holds to the Aristotelian view that he must make
us believe in the 'probability' of his characters and events.
'Every good author will confine himself within the bounds of
probability', writes Fielding.[2] He is at one with Richardson in
holding that the novelist should avoid, if possible, extremes of
virtue and vice in his characters together with such happenings as 'sudden conversions', which, Richardson says emphatically, have 'neither *art*, nor *nature*, nor even *probability*, in them'.[3]
'There is required . . . enough of the manners of real life to give
an air of probability to the work', says Clara Reeve when she
comments on Horace Walpole's attempt 'to unite the various
merits and graces of the ancient Romance and modern Novel'.[4]
In 'the fields of fancy, *sunt certi denique fines*', maintains Richard
Cumberland, and 'it requires a nice discernment to find them
out, and a cautious temper not to step beyond them'.[5] Accord-

[1] See below, p. 53.   [2] See below, p. 61.   [3] See below, p. 61.
[4] See below, p. 45.   [5] See below, p. 48.

ing to Hawthorne's definition, a novel 'is presumed to aim at a very minute fidelity, not merely to the possible, but to the probable and ordinary course of man's experience'.[1] Maupassant, who is opposed to the theories of scientific realism, emphasizes nevertheless that the principal effect which the novelist seeks is 'the feeling of simple reality'.[2] Some novelists who seem to stray beyond 'the bounds of probability' take care to explain that they are not really doing so at all. Dickens decides that such 'accidents' as Madame Defarge's death in *A Tale of Two Cities* (1859) are 'inseparable from the passion and action of the character' and 'consistent with the entire design'.[3] Dostoevsky implies that it is our own notions of probability which are at fault if we find his events 'exceptional'.[4] To Trollope, the distinction which some Victorian readers made between his own 'realistic' work and the 'sensational' stories of 'my friend Wilkie Collins' seemed artificial. 'I do not know that a novel can be too sensational', he says, provided that 'truth of description, truth of character, human truth as to men and women' are maintained.[5]

Recent commentators on the novel have helped us to understand more clearly than before some of the reasons which first made story-tellers wish to include in their fiction 'enough of the manners of real life to give an air of probability to the work'. Ian Watt, for example, in *The Rise of the Novel*, draws an interesting parallel between the new procedures of investigation adopted by the great seventeenth-century innovators of philosophical realism—notably Descartes and Locke—and the narrative methods which the first novelists employed in their 'new species of writing'. Arnold Kettle, on the other hand, in *An Introduction to the English Novel* (1951) examines the effects on literature of the social changes which were the consequences of the break-down of feudalism. 'The impulse towards realism in prose literature', he tells us, 'was part and parcel of the breakdown of feudalism and of the revolution that transformed the feudal world.'[6] He reminds us of the upsurge of courageous enterprise and creative energy in those crucial periods of 'revolutionary transformation', the sixteenth and seventeenth

---

[1] See below, p. 51.
[2] See below, p. 70.
[3] See below, p. 60.
[5] See below, pp. 67–8.
[4] See below, p. 68.
[6] Vol. I, p. 25

centuries. In these centuries it is in poetry that men give the fullest expression to the moving spirit of the age, but 'in the eighteenth century it is in prose'. The task of such writers as Fielding

was not so much to adapt themselves to a revolutionary situation as to cull and examine what the revolution had produced.[1]

Their task was to 'take stock', to try to give an 'objective controlled and conscious view of reality', and they used prose because of its capacity to 'make coherent some facet of outer reality already apprehended'. In doing so they were furthering

an advanced, subtle, precise form of human expression, presupposing a formidable self-consciousness, a delicacy of control which it has taken human beings untold centuries to acquire.[2]

This seems to be a reasonable view to take, even if Arnold Kettle also emphasizes the quickened fantasy which in Rabelais' *Gargantua and Pantagruel* (1532–5) and in Cervantes' *Don Quixote* (1605) begins to replace the less stimulating invention of some of the cruder medieval romances where 'a static, idealist moral code' is imposed upon 'the actual movement and complexity of human behaviour'. But it is difficult to avoid over-simplification in discussing a subject so complex as the nature of realism in fiction, and Arnold Kettle's final statement of the problem why the novel arose when it did is perhaps too general to be completely satisfactory. 'Why did the medieval romance not continue to satisfy the needs of the men and women of the bourgeois revolution?' he asks, and finds 'at bottom' that 'the bourgeoisie, in order to win its freedom from the feudal order, had to tear the veil of romance from the face of feudalism'.[3] In 'bourgeois man', he adds,

every need and instinct urged him to expose and undermine feudal standards and sanctities. Unlike the feudal ruling class he did not feel himself immediately threatened by revelations of the truth about the world and so he was not afraid of realism.[4]

Ian Watt rightly stresses that the 'issue which the novel raises more sharply than any other literary form' is 'the problem of the correspondence between the literary work and the reality

---

[1] Vol. I, pp. 37–8. [2] Ibid.
[3] Ibid. [4] Ibid.

which it imitates'.[1] Because 'this is essentially an epistemological problem' he feels that

the nature of the novel's realism, whether in the early eighteenth century or later, can best be clarified by the help of those professionally concerned with the analysis of concepts, the philosophers.[2]

Philosophy is one thing and literature another, but Ian Watt's analysis places a useful emphasis on the shift in literature and life from the 'objective, social and public orientation of the classical world' to an orientation which is more 'subjective, individualistic and private'[3]—the transition period being the eighteenth century itself. The philosophical tendency to regard 'the pursuit of truth as a wholly individual matter' has a parallel in the novel's rejection of the traditional plots of classical and renaissance epic:

Defoe and Richardson are the first great writers in our literature who did not take their plots from mythology, history, legend or previous literature. In this they differ from Chaucer, Spenser, Shakespeare and Milton . . .[4]

Individual experience begins 'to replace collective tradition as the ultimate arbiter of reality'.[5] Again, the methods of characterization of the eighteenth-century novelists run parallel with the new philosophical emphasis on the supreme importance of individual consciousness and identity. Ian Watt is interested in the names which early novelists choose to give their characters. The type-name survives in Fielding (Allworthy, Heartfree, Thwackum) but Fielding also finds names (Western, Amelia Booth, Mrs. Waters) which suggest that characters are to be regarded as 'particular individuals in the contemporary social environment'.[6] Certainly, it is the individual peculiarities of temperament, the Shandy-ism, so to speak, of human nature, which increasingly attracts the novelist's attention. He makes it more and more his business 'to number the streaks of the tulip', disregarding the views of Shaftesbury and Johnson alike, both of whom felt that it was not the business of artists to deal in

---

[1] See *The Rise of the Novel*, p. 11.
[2] Ibid.
[3] P. 176.
[4] P. 14.
[5] Ibid.
[6] Pp. 18–21.

particulars, or to become, as Shaftesbury says, 'mere' face-painters and historians.[1] The novelist brings the same particularizing tendencies, logically enough, to his treatment of place and time. Locke's 'principle of individuation', Ian Watt reminds us,

> was that of existence at a particular locus in space and time: since, as he wrote, 'ideas become general by separating from them the circumstances of time and place,' so they become particular only when both these circumstances are specified. In the same way the characters of the novel can only be individualized if they are set in a background of particularized time and place.[2]

Thus the novelist sets his scene with care, describing it with increasing minuteness of detail, and he chooses a particular period in time for the unfolding of his supposed events. The novelists' management of these elements will be discussed at greater length in a subsequent chapter dealing with his craftsmanship. In this context it is enough to add that almost every narrative technique which he uses has behind it the same intentions which have been noticed here. The autobiographical memoir, the epistolary method, the 'dramatized consciousness', the withdrawal of the author from the scene, the stream of consciousness; all these methods are designed to heighten the desired effect of authenticity and verisimilitude by locating experience in the individual consciousness, and by making that consciousness operate in a particular place at a particular time.

These tendencies helped to encourage that effect of 'Dutch minuteness' in the novel which even the earliest critics of eighteenth-century fiction recognized as its most characteristic 'novelty'. Mrs. Barbauld discovers in Richardson 'the accuracy and finish of a Dutch painter . . . content to produce effects by the patient labour of minuteness',[3] and Scott echoes this when he compares Richardson's art with 'paintings which have been very minutely laboured'.[4] Mario Praz in *The Hero in Eclipse in Victorian Fiction* (1956) tends to overlook the eighteenth-century

---

[1] See Samuel Johnson, *Rasselas* (1759), Chapter x, and Shaftesbury, *Essay on the Freedom of Wit and Humour* (1709), Part IV, section iii.

[2] *The Rise of the Novel*, p. 21.

[3] See below, Part III, p. 309.

[4] See below, Part III, pp. 266-7.

literary origins of this care for detail, but his study demonstrates the support it found from Romanticism. He shows, for example, that George Eliot's admiration for the 'rare, precious quality of truthfulness' which she finds in Dutch paintings is representative of a general Victorian taste for a photographic or more than photographic accuracy and for humble domestic subjects.[1] The psychological reasons which George Eliot gives for her preference for certain Dutch paintings are to the point here. She recognizes that the artist's inborn delight in elaboration needs to be disciplined in the interests of truth:

The pencil is conscious of a delightful felicity in drawing a griffin —the longer the claws and the larger the wings, the better; but that marvellous felicity which we mistook for genius is apt to forsake us when we want to draw a real unexaggerated lion. Examine your words well, and you will find that even when you have no motive to be false, it is a very hard thing to say the exact truth, even about your own immediate feelings—much harder than to say something fine about them which is *not* the exact truth.[2]

In its care for precision in the statement of feeling this reminds us of Stendhal's letter to his sister, Pauline, about the difficulty which the writer experiences in saying 'exactly' what he intends without falsification or inflation of any kind.[3] But in addition to the delight afforded to her by the 'rare, precious quality of truthfulness' in many Dutch paintings, George Eliot finds

a source of delicious sympathy in these faithful pictures of a monotonous, homely existence, which has been the fate of so many more among my fellow-mortals than a life of pomp and of absolute indigence, of tragic suffering or of world-stirring action.[4]

George Eliot is expressing here the interest in the ordinary or 'Bedford' level of society which was one of the distinctive characteristics of the nineteenth-century novelist, whether in England, France or Russia. The effects of this interest, whether good or bad, on the quality of fiction were far-reaching. They extended the novel's range of subject-matter and added to the importance of its social comment. But they were also to be responsible for some damaging misconceptions about the nature

---

[1] Pp. 322–7.   [2] *Adam Bede* (1859), Book Second, Chapter xvii.
[3] See Part II below, pp. 127–8.   [4] *Adam Bede*, loc. cit.

of 'realism', in particular the notion that by 'realism' is meant an exclusive concern with 'low' subjects and the seamier side of human life. From this position it is a short distance to the fallacy that 'the real' and 'the ideal' are incompatible in art.[1]

The repercussions of this social interest were first felt in France in the art of Balzac and Stendhal (Balzac's enthusiastic salute to the otherwise neglected Stendhal is very largely a gesture of sympathetic recognition[2]). In England, they were felt in the vigorous social novels of the 1840's and the early 1850's—in, for instance, Dickens's *Dombey and Son* (1846–8), *Bleak House* (1852–3) and *Hard Times* (1854), Mrs. Gaskell's *Mary Barton* (1848) and *North and South* (1854–5), and Charles Kingsley's *Yeast* (1848) and *Alton Locke* (1850). In Russia, the novel may be said to have come into being as a direct result of this social concern. Gogol is a pioneer and Dostoevsky's remark, 'We have all come from under Gogol's Greatcoat', acknowledges the originality in Russia of the portrayals of humble life in *The Greatcoat* and *Dead Souls* (both of 1842).

It was in France that writers were to allow this new range of subject-matter to lead them to some damaging theories about the function of the novel. Balzac's grandiose scheme to leave behind a complete record of every aspect of his own life and times is itself an extraordinary project, and so is the conception on which it is based: that human beings who make up society can be 'scientifically' classified. There is, however, a tremendous imaginative vitality which lifts individual novels in Balzac's *Comédie Humaine* above the limitations of his programme. Zola's scientific programme is a more serious matter since it is more ruthlessly followed. Zola really believed that Balzac had successfully proved the novelist's obligation to carry out 'experiments' which would illustrate the laws of heredity and environment—he cites *La Cousine Bette* (1846) as an example[3]—and he tried to put his own theories into practice in the huge *Rougon-Macquart* series (1871–93). This brings us to the windy and pro-

[1] See Stevenson's discussion of this problem below, pp. 72–3.

[2] See H. de Balzac, 'Etude sur M. Beyle', *Œuvres Complètes* (1873), Vol. XXIII, pp. 687–738. Reprinted, with Stendhal's reply, as preface to C. K. Scott-Moncrieff's translation of Stendhal's *The Charterhouse of Parma*, Phoenix Library, 1931.

[3] See below, pp. 68–9.

longed controversy over Realism and Naturalism, of which Zola's own *Le Roman Expérimental* (1880) is one of the key documents. It is difficult now to believe in the bitterness released by these controversies, in the 'telegrams and anger' which they produced. The nature of the attacks which the Realists had to endure can be judged by their major principles of defence. They asserted that the final unflattering impression of humanity left by their fantastic accumulation of detail—detail in Balzac 'of every physical feature and material object that the novelist could lay hands on', in Zola of physiological processes 'to the point of nausea' [1] was the effect of an observation more dispassionately truthful than any that fiction had hitherto attempted. They then hedged, asserting defensively that this 'scientific' observation was not 'simply photographic'.[2]

In fact, of course, their practice was very often much at odds with their theory. Balzac, having laid down a principle of scientific investigation, 'then elaborated a picture so violently coloured that the reason must reject it, though the imagination may accept it'. He writes about his characters 'with an intense excitement'.[3] On the fascinating romanticism of 'the coarse, comprehensive, prodigious Zola' we have already discovered Maupassant and Henry James in agreement. Even Zola himself has to admit in the end that it is the artist's individual sensibility and not his systematic accumulation of realistic social detail that gives value to his work.[4] In fact it is impossible for the artist to confine himself in the strait-waistcoat of any kind of 'scientific realism'. It is for this reason that so many novelists dislike insignificant detail. Tolstoy ridicules the total recall of

the appearances, faces, garments, gestures, sounds, apartments of the acting persons . . .[5]

Dostoevsky takes a similar attitude—

Arid observation of every day trivialities I have long since ceased to regard as realism.[6]

---

[1] See Geoffrey Brereton, *A Short History of French Literature* (1954), pp. 215–16, 225.
[2] See, for example, Zola's defence, quoted below, p. 70.
[3] *A Short History of French Literature*, p. 218.
[4] See below, p. 70.
[5] See below, pp. 74–5.   [6] See below, p. 68.

Instead of relying on these 'trivialities' he gives us situations which 'most people regard as fantastic and lacking in universality' but which, he tells us, '*I* hold to be the inmost essence of truth'.[1] The vivid impression left by his work does not derive solely from the use it makes of violent acts which were suggested to him by 'real' newspaper reports or by stories which he heard from his fellow-prisoners in Siberia. It owes as much to those strange elements—the hallucinations, nightmares and legends—which contribute to the feeling that his characters and events stand for more than themselves, that, as Mr. Forster says, 'infinity attends them', that their 'ordinary world reaches back'.[2] A similar enlarging effect is obtained in the novels of Hardy, Emily Brontë, Melville, Conrad and Mr. Forster himself, where, at certain moments, things perceived are given a special significance which transforms them into symbols of universal value.

The genius for 'particularity' to which the English novel owes much of its vitality and richness of texture is again a gift of the poetic imagination rather than the effect of dispassionate and 'scientific' observation. This is as apparent in the impressionism of Richardson's descriptive method in *Pamela* and *Clarissa* as it is in the verbal fantasy of Dickens's Mrs. Gamp, an achievement which cannot be explained as the 'Beiedermeier' art of Professor Praz's thesis. It is true that the English novelist's resistance to literary formulas and his slow development as a self-conscious artist have usually protected this inventiveness at the expense of his acquiring valuable formal disciplines. Many of his novels are indeed 'large, loose, baggy monsters', and his unaristocratically lavish display can be distasteful, especially when his social conscience tells him to load his detail with pathetic or moral significance. Even so, our first great self-conscious artists in the novel, Conrad and James—neither of whom, as it happens, is English by birth—do not allow their distaste for this excess and their admiration for the French novelist's sense of form to blind them to the fact that the French Realist doctrines stultify imagination and interfere with poetic truth. The immediate successors of James and Conrad, however, were less discriminating in following French example. They belonged to the

---

[1] See below, p. 68.
[2] *Aspects of the Novel*, p. 173.

28

age of H. G. Wells—Virginia Woolf felt that to 'complete' their novels it was necessary 'to join a society, or, more desperately, to write a cheque' [1]—and they found support for their social documentation in Realist fiction of the 'School' of Médan. So we find Arnold Bennett in his *Clayhanger* trilogy[2] and George Moore in *Esther Waters* (1894) swamping their imaginative talents in the accumulation of social detail.

It is not surprising that Flaubert explodes with rage when he is proclaimed High Priest of the Naturalists and Realists. 'There is no Truth, there are only ways of seeing', he writes to Zola's disciple, Léon Hennique. 'Down with Schools, whatever they are, down with empty words',[3] and again, to his congenial brother-artist, Turgenev:

It isn't enough merely to observe; we must order and shape what we have seen. Reality . . . ought to be no more than a spring-board . . . This materialism makes my blood boil . . .[4]

In England, Hardy, Conrad and James agree with him. 'Realism is an unfortunate, an ambiguous word', says Hardy and he calls for the exercise of 'the Daedalian faculty for selection and cunning manipulation'.[5] Life is all 'inclusion and confusion', says Henry James, and art 'all discrimination and selection'.[6] 'Liberty of the imagination' should be the artist's 'most precious possession', maintains Conrad, indignantly repudiating 'the human perverseness' which discovers in 'the free work' of great artists 'the fettering dogmas of some romantic, realistic or naturalistic creed'.[7] The same impatience with literary formulas gives us Virginia Woolf's acid essay on 'Mr. Bennett and Mrs. Brown'[8] and Lawrence's scornful dismissal of 'Kodak' fiction.[9] The transfiguring function of art which all these writers uphold is given its best description in 1881, in Maupassant's intelligent preface to his novel, *Pierre et Jean:*

. . . The realist, if he is an artist, will seek to give us not a banal

---

[1] See Virginia Woolf, 'Mr. Bennett and Mrs. Brown', 1924; first printed in *The Captain's Death Bed* (1950).
[2] *Clayhanger* (1910), *Hilda Lessways* (1911), *These Twain* (1916).
[3] See René Dumesnil, *Le Réalisme et le Naturalisme* (1955), p. 367.
[4] See below, p. 69.   [5] See below, p. 73.
[6] See below, p. 75.   [7] See Part II below, pp. 132-3.   [8] Loc. cit.
[9] See 'Art and Morality' (1925); reprinted in *Phoenix* (1936).

photographic representation of life, but a vision of it that is fuller, more vivid and more compellingly truthful than even reality itself . . .[1]

This is akin to Conrad's 'form of imagined life clearer than reality' whose verisimilitude 'puts to shame the pride of documentary history'.[2] It expresses the same spirit which to-day compels François Mauriac to assert that the real novelist is 'not an observer but a creator',[3] and which makes André Gide declare through the character of his novelist, Edouard, in *Les Faux Monnayeurs* (1925), that the novel 'has always clung to reality with such timidity'.[4] But we have to agree that Edouard recognizes the novelist's most crippling dilemma when he declares that he would like to write a novel which might be at the same time 'true' and 'far from reality', 'particular' and 'general' and whose subject might be precisely the struggle between 'what reality offers' and 'what he himself desires to make of it'. [5]

III The Ethics of the Novel

IN THE struggle between 'what reality offers' and 'what he himself desires to make of it', the novelist's sense of moral purpose plays an important part. 'Thumbs off the scale', cries D. H. Lawrence, announcing as firmly as Turgenev or Flaubert a belief in the artist's impersonality and justice.[6] Yet his work, unlike theirs, remains unabashedly subjective and didactic. The novelist's theory and practice are most likely to part company whenever his anxiety to grind some special axe urges the preacher to take over from the artist. In general, the novelist's desire to emphasize the *utile* at the expense of the *dulce* has usually had damaging effects on his adjustment of 'the uncommon' and 'the ordinary', interfering with the effect of verisimilitude which it is important for him to achieve and also impairing his purity of vision. This is particularly the case in the English novel, which has suffered acutely in the past from the didactic zeal of middle-class Puritanism: it is only with the advent of Hardy,

---

[1] See below, p. 71.   [2] See below, p. 76.
[3] See below, p. 80.   [4] See below, p. 78.
[5] See below, p. 79.   [6] See below, pp. 101–2.

Conrad and James in the later nineteenth century that the question of the ethics of the novel is posed more subtly. The simplicity and persistence of the earlier view may be indicated by setting Richardson's eighteenth-century pronouncement

Instruction, Madam, is the pill; amusement is the gilding . . .

beside Trollope's explanation to his Victorian readers,

I have ever thought of myself as a preacher of sermons and my pulpit as one which I could make both salutary and agreeable to my audience . . .

—the audience in both cases being predominantly middle-class and containing many susceptible Young Persons.[1] Richardson wishes to 'turn young people into a course of reading different from the pomp and parade of romance-writing', substituting for 'the improbable and marvellous' such stories as 'might tend to promote the cause of religion and virtue'.[2] 'Let him never touch a romance or a novel', is Goldsmith's advice to his brother concerning his son's reading: 'they teach the youthful mind to sigh after beauty and happiness which never existed'.[3] There is much debate on the éffects of reading Rousseau's novels. *La Nouvelle Héloise*, says Euphrasia in *The Progress of Romance*, is

a dangerous book to put into the hands of youth, it awakens and nourishes those passions which it is the exercise of Reason, and of Religion also, to regulate, and to keep within their true limits.[4]

She proposes abridgement and alteration of the two first volumes so as

to give a different turn to the story, and to make the two Lovers, stop short of the *act*, that made it criminal in either party to marry another, for were they not *actually wedded* in the sight of Heaven?[5]

Euphrasia seems to have ignored Rousseau's own contribution to the discussion. In the preface to the 1762 edition he rounds on his attackers and, pushed into extreme views perhaps by their antagonism, declares that the very idea of making literature 'useful to the young' is nonsense. Much more important is that a good example should be set to young people by the behaviour

[1] See below, p. 90, 87.   [2] See below, p. 85.
[3] See below, p. 87.   [4] See below, p. 86.   [5] Ibid.

and actions of their parents. If mothers behave circumspectly, then their daughters will too.[1] Scott is more openly an entertainer than Rousseau. He is liberal enough to believe that an obvious moral tagged on to a novel is as incongruous as a beggar limping at the end of a procession. Nevertheless he feels that there is some 'advantage to a young person' in a tale which calls upon him 'to attend to the voice of principle and self-denial.'[2] Trollope congratulated himself on his certainty

that no girl has risen from my pages less modest than she was before . . . that no youth has been told that in falseness and flashness is to be found the road to manliness . . .[3]

Dickens makes fun of Podsnap's notion that 'the Young Person's' susceptibilities should provide the criterion for literary excellence, but he was careful to avoid anything in his own work that might shock conventional moral susceptibilities.[4] In the present century the novelist may still be troubled by the problem of the Young Person. François Mauriac knows that there are certain important limits to the novelist's responsibility for what he writes—he must be true to his inner vision and he must realize that there are incalculable elements in all creation[5]—but this should not blind him to the dangerous effects that his fiction may have on young imaginations. He tells us that

a boy once sent me a photograph with the words: 'To the man who nearly made me kill my grandmother.' In the accompanying letter he explained that the old lady resembled the heroine of *Genetrix* to such an extent that he had been on the very verge of strangling her during her sleep. How can readers like that be protected?[6]

In the eighteenth century and in the nineteenth century down to late Victorian times English novelists were usually willing to make some sacrifice of probability on moral grounds. Richardson plunges the Harlowe family into swift, wholesale repentance after Clarissa's death in spite of disliking the improbability of 'sudden conversions'.[7] Fielding presents us with Blifil and Amelia (although Amelia, after all, is charming) in spite of his sensible belief that characters in novels should be a plausible mixture of good and bad.[8] Even Jane Austen's sense

[1] See below, pp. 85-6.   [2] See below, pp. 92, 87.
[3] See below, pp. 87-8.   [4] See below, p. 88.
[5] See below, pp. 106-8.   [6] See below, p. 89.
[7] See below, p. 61.   [8] See below, p. 91.

of proportion is upset by this didacticism. Most of us feel that the *utile* lugubriously overshadows the *dulce* in *Mansfield Park*. The *utile* clogs George Eliot's intelligent, compassionate novels with stodgy sermons and impairs their integrity by seeing to it that wrongdoers are always made to suffer for their sins. Lawrence, middle-class morality's most spectacular victim, packs his books with angry puritan exhortations and punishes behaviour which he dislikes, in spite of assuring us that art, although 'moral', should not be didactic. It says a good deal for the creative exuberance of our novelists that they have frequently managed to overcome the worst effects of their own didacticism. They often 'bounce' us into acceptance of their characters and events by the sheer strength of their invention.

Nineteenth-century social conventions are partly responsible for hindering the development of the English novelist's understanding of his moral responsibilities as an artist. The Victorian attitude to sex was particularly hampering. Charlotte Brontë seems to rebel against some of its conventions when she shows her plain heroines tormented by passion, but it is obvious that she has a less independent spirit than her sister, Emily, who is unique among nineteenth-century English novelists. Thackeray, whom Charlotte idolized until they met, is very conscious of crippling moral and social pressures. The irritable frustration detected in his apology for introducing 'a little more frankness than is customary' into *Pendennis* helps to account for some of the ambiguity which blurs his character-drawing.[1] Amelia Sedley, for example, lacks the confident definition of Dora Copperfield and Ada Clare largely because Thackeray is less at ease than Dickens in creating the simplified moral universe which satisfied and reassured so vast a proportion of the Victorian reading public. But Thackeray looks back to the vigorous satire of eighteenth-century novelists rather than forward to the subtler discriminations of the later nineteenth century. He envies without daring to emulate the bolder attack and broader humanity of his great model, Fielding. Eighteenth-century attitudes and influences, lingering on from Fielding's day (the Regency period acts as a preservative), do something to enliven the political and social novels of the 1830's and 1840's by warding off, temporarily, the more suffocating encroachments of Victorianism.

[1] See below, pp. 93–4.

Even so, a novel like Mrs. Gaskell's *Ruth* (1853) demonstrates the pitiful constriction on ethical grounds of the valuable Victorian impulse to stiffen the texture of the novel and extend its range of social reference.

To turn from the mid-nineteenth-century English novel to the French or Russian novel of the same period is to enter a world which may be less rich in invention but is certainly governed by a more sensible conception of the *utile*. It is a world more freely and vividly illuminated by general ideas and often more truthful in feeling. English fiction in the 1830's gained from the freshness and originality of Dickens's *Pickwick Papers* (1836–7), *Oliver Twist* (1837–8) and *Nicholas Nickleby* (1838–9) but the moral assumptions behind these tales make them embarrassingly naïve when they are set beside Stendhal's achievement in *Le Rouge et le Noir* (1831) and *La Chartreuse de Parme* (1839), and Gogol's in *The Memoirs of a Madman* and *Nevsky Prospect* (both of 1835). The contrast is not greatly lessened when the English novel reaches a maturer art with Dickens's *Bleak House* (1852–3) and *Our Mutual Friend* (1864–5); George Eliot's first full-length novel, *Adam Bede* (1859); and Thackeray's *Vanity Fair* (1847–8) and *Pendennis* (1848–50). In these years Tolstoy and Dostoevsky were transforming the novel into a form more serious and powerful than it had ever seemed likely to become, while Flaubert and Turgenev were increasing enormously its subtlety of texture. *War and Peace* (1862–9) and *Crime and Punishment* (1866), both contemporary with *Our Mutual Friend*, are obviously achievements of quite a different order. *War and Peace*, setting aside its wider range, is a more valuable work than *Our Mutual Friend* if only because Tolstoy is more honest and more intelligent about the nature of ordinary human experience than Dickens. Dostoevsky, of course, depicts in *Crime and Punishment*, as in his other novels, regions of spiritual suffering which are outside Dickens's conception. Turgenev's novels, *A Nest of Gentlefolk* (1858) and *On the Eve* (1859), together with Flaubert's *Madame Bovary* (1857), belong to the same period as George Eliot's *Adam Bede*, but these French and Russian novels have a sensitivity to moral complexity which is beyond George Eliot at this stage of her career. It is only with *Middlemarch* (1872) that the English novel begins to stand comparison with French and Russian fiction. Among its other qualities, George Eliot's masterpiece is remarkable for the revelation —so unwelcome to Anglo-Saxondom—that good intentions are not enough and that sympathetic understanding of human relations, which are affairs of some complexity, is also a function of intelligence.

It is easy to distinguish the more adult sense of moral responsibility in French and Russian contributions to 'The Ethics of the Novel'. Whether it is Flaubert, Turgenev or Tolstoy who speaks, it is the author's responsibility to the truth of his vision which is stressed, and only when the English writer has broken out of his insularity and his provincialism late in the nineteenth century into their fresher cosmopolitan air do we hear him echoing their plea for responsible impartiality. In the case of the Russian, this freedom is connected with the state of Russian society at the time—the 'Asiatic' freedom from the pressure towards uniformity of customary opinion which Tocqueville and John Stuart Mill had discovered in Western societies. With the Frenchman, it is much more a matter of his recognized seriousness about being an artist. How far this takes him from more blatant 'art for art's sake' simplifications is suggested when we contrast impassioned pronouncements by Flaubert or Maupassant with Oscar Wilde's tripping statement in the preface to *The Picture of Dorian Gray* (1891):

There is no such thing as a moral or an immoral book. Books are well-written or badly written.[1]

Even if he writes, as François Mauriac says, 'in fear and trembling under the eye of the Trinity',[2] the French novelist recognizes that the validity of his writing must depend on its truth to his own vision as an artist. (Failure to recognize this accounts for the falsity of tone in much Victorian expression of religious sentiment.) Mauriac, who is perhaps this age's greatest novelist, naturally rejects outright Jacques Maritain's Zola-like comparison of 'a novelist bending over the human heart with a physiologist over a frog or a guinea-pig'.[3] In taking into account the 'mysterious, unforeseeable and inevitable elements' in artistic creation, and in emphasizing the artist's need to 'purify the source', he acknowledges the strength of these elements and

[1] See below, p. 108.   [2] See below, p. 106.
[3] See below, p. 80.

35

also their close identity with the genuine creative self.[1] It will be seen that Mauriac's explanation of his position as a Catholic novelist is compatible with a Chekhovian view of artistic detachment, i.e. that the artist 'must set the question, not solve it'. Chekhov says of the artist that he

> observes, selects, guesses, combines—these in themselves presuppose questions; if from the very first he had not put a question to himself there would be nothing to divine nor to select . . . in 'Anna Karenin' and in 'Onyeguin' not a single problem is solved, but they satisfy completely because all the problems are set correctly.[2]

Perhaps it is the French novelist's intellectual curiosity which has most consistently protected him from narrow forms of didacticism. It has certainly stood him in good stead in his resistance to middle-class prejudices, which can be far stuffier in provincial France than almost anywhere else. While Dickens was entertaining his middle-class readers and encouraging their cosier prejudices (his narrative vivacity carried them safely past the dangerous areas in his satire), the voices of Stendhal, Flaubert and Zola were almost drowned by the clamour of an outraged *bourgeoisie*. Nevertheless these writers persisted in exposing the *esprit belge* of middle-class society with a ruthlessness undreamed of in Victorian England. The penetrating analysis of Stendhal's Gina de Sanséverina in *La Chartreuse de Parme*, a superb manifestation of this truthful spirit, is inconceivable in any Victorian novel—indeed it has no parallel in English fiction until the time of Miss Ivy Compton-Burnett: without his melancholy, Gina has much in common with Octave de Malivert, the hero of Stendhal's first novel, *Armance* (1827), who admits to Madame de Bonnivet,

> I have no *conscience*. I find no trace in me of what you call a *sens intime*, no *instinctive* repugnance for crime. When I abhor vice it is quite simply as the result of a rational process and because I find it harmful.[3]

Stendhal has not the slightest intention of punishing his apparently amoral Duchess, and his novel is vivified by her intelligence and her irrepressible charm. When he makes her tell her lover that she will not be gay 'for a month' after her 'sacri-

[1] See below, pp. 107–8. [2] See below, p. 99.
[3] *Armance*, Chapter vi.

fice' to the youthful prince,[1] he makes us gloomily conscious of Little Emily's different fate and reminds us by contrast of the muddle about sex which hangs like a miasma over almost the entire English novel.

The nineteenth-century Russian novelist is as far as his French contemporaries from regarding the relationships between human beings as a matter for simple moral condemnation or approval. The characters in all Dostoevsky's novels react to each other with the nakedness of feeling which reveals in the individual conflicting impulses of pride and submission, hatred and love. Turgenev establishes the relationship between pairs of friends and lovers with an impartial tenderness which does not depend on the art of understatement alone for the avoidance of sentimentality. The friendship between the angular, aggressive Nihilist, Bazarov, and his unassailably gentle disciple, Arkady, in *Fathers and Sons* (1861) is handled with the same delicacy and insight as the love-affair between Liza and Lavretzky in *A Nest of Gentlefolk*. Tolstoy recognizes as dispassionately as Flaubert that such victims of adulterous passion as his own Anna Karénina are doomed to suffer, but he enters into their situation with an intelligent compassion which relegates Lady Dedlock and Edith Dombey to the world of *East Lynne* and the penny novelette. No female characters comparable in stature or truth with Anna Karénina or Emma Bovary appear in the English novel until James describes tormented creatures like Charlotte Stant or Madame de Vionnet —and even then, as his *Notebooks* reveal, he had to contort plot and story in order not to offend English susceptibilities by making 'the adulterine element' over-explicit.[2] Even if the Russian novelist has not had to contend until quite recently with the same public prejudices as English and French novelists (there is perhaps a parallel to be drawn between his difficulties now and their difficulties a hundred years ago), he has always been subjected to the strain provided by the very preoccupations—social, moral, religious—which stimulated him to write. All that one can finally say is that in the nineteenth century in Russia the strain was not too much for him.

[1] *La Chartreuse de Parme*, Chapter xxvii.

[2] See *The Notebooks of Henry James* (1947), ed. F. O. Matthiessen and Kenneth B. Murdock, pp. 187–8, 170.

Until late in his history, the English novelist has to substitute for such French and Russian gifts the splendid inventiveness which is the 'gilding' for his moral pill. But invention fails to ensure that his art will be, as Maupassant desires, 'compellingly truthful' as well as 'vivid'. As their contributions in 'The Ethics of the Novel' reveal, our later nineteenth-century novelists are only too conscious of this shortcoming in their predecessors. Envious of the freedom of their fellow-writers abroad and anxious for the dignity and integrity of their own art, their pleading sometimes betrays an edge of desperation. In 1881 we find Stevenson urging that 'it must always be foul to tell what is false; and it can never be safe to suppress what is true'.[1] Seven years later Hardy re-states the case, arguing that novels 'without a moral purpose' are more valuable in the end because 'the didactic novel is generally so devoid of *vraisemblance* as to teach nothing but the impossibility of tampering with natural truth to advance dogmatic opinions'.[2] Looking back to the eighteen-eighties from the first decade of the twentieth century, Henry James remembered that even then the only questions which mattered to him in considering the moral significance of a work of art were, 'Is it valid . . . is it genuine, is it sincere, the result of some direct impression or perception of life?'[3]

The intense seriousness with which these later novelists sometimes discuss their art may take us by surprise. We expect a sombre sense of vocation from the acknowledged 'sage' (George Eliot) or the religiously committed writer (François Mauriac), but the so-called 'pure' novelist can display an even more exalted sense of responsibility. Conrad, for example, tells us that the artist must make 'many acts of faith', the greatest being 'the cherishing of undying hope', which involves 'all the piety of effort and renunciation'.[4] He defines the novelist's art as 'rescue work carried out in darkness against cross gusts of wind swaying the action of a great multitude'. It is the

snatching of vanishing phrases of turbulence, disguised in fair words, out of the native obscurity into a light where the struggling forms may be seen, seized upon, endowed with the only possible form of permanence in this world of relative values—the permanence of

---

[1] See below, pp. 97–8.　　　[2] See below, p. 98.
[3] See below, p. 99.　　　[4] See below, p. 100.

memory. And the multitude feels it obscurely too; since the demand of the individual to the artist is, in effect, the cry, 'take me out of myself!' meaning really, out of my perishable activity into the light of imperishable consciousness.[1]

A confession of faith of this kind is unlikely to appear in England, France or any other country much before the end of the nineteenth century, although there are signs of a similar mood being implicit earlier in the sensitive, sceptical utterances of such artists as Flaubert and Turgenev. George Eliot betrays a sufficient trace of an analogous feeling for one of her Victorian critics to express uneasiness about the 'profoundly melancholy' implications of *Middlemarch*,[2] but, in intention at least, she is as anxious as her Victorian predecessors and contemporaries to subdue troubled speculation about the dark side of the moon. Conrad's confession belongs to an age when her 'meliorism' finally loses its efficiency. It looks pale among the dark colours of the tragic universe experienced by Michael Henchard and Jude the Obscure. Paradoxically, it is in this context of doubt and scepticism that the novel acquires its most potent supernatural ambience—we are particularly aware of it in the novels of Hardy, James and Conrad, where it is associated with a vivid sense of hostile or evil forces at work in the world. This mood of pessimism approximates the later nineteenth-century novel more closely than at any other time in its history to a recognizable tragic form. The nineteenth-century Russian novel, of course, with its profound feeling for religious conflict is remarkable for its powerful interpretation of tragic dilemma— the central book of *The Brothers Karamazov* containing the legend of the Grand Inquisitor is perhaps its greatest achievement in this respect. The French novel has had to wait longer for such qualities to appear, perhaps because of the very intellectual gifts which bring it to its early maturity: it has had to wait, in fact, until Proust prepared it formally to accommodate the new dimensions of spiritual conflict explored by Mauriac, Sartre and Camus.

Joyce exemplifies how the serious twentieth-century novelist

---

[1] See below, p. 101.
[2] See R. H. Hutton, 'George Eliot as Author', *Essays on Some of the Modern Guides of English Thought in Matters of Faith* (1887).

may feel called upon to purify his art in the service of a perplexed and rudderless human consciousness. Such writers pursue their vocation with dedicated passion:

Welcome, O life! I go to encounter for the millionth time the reality of experience and to forge in the smithy of my soul the uncreated conscience of my race. . . . Old father, old artificer, stand me now and ever in good stead.[1]

And so their writing becomes an act of faith, their art a form of religion. In the rhythms of Stephen Dedalus's peroration, as in James's invocation to his muse[2] and Conrad's description of 'wrestling with the Lord' about *Nostromo*,[3] we hear the chant of the high priest inaugurating a ritual of great complexity and sacredness. What has happened is that art as religion finds power to resist moral views external to itself. It now strikes 'a balance between the ordinary and the uncommon' and adjusts 'things unusual to things eternal and universal' according to its own terms of moral reference.

[1] James Joyce, *A Portrait of the Artist as a Young Man* (1916), concluding paragraphs.
[2] See Part II below, pp. 156–7.
[3] See Part II below, pp. 151–2.

TEXT

I   *The Novel and the Marvellous*

REJECTING ROMANTIC IMPROBABILITY

(i)

... What a duce, do you think I am writing a Romance? Don't you see that I am copying Nature ...

> Samuel Richardson. *Letter to Miss Mulso* (*5 October 1752*), Correspondence (*1804*).

(ii)

... there were very few novels and romances that my lady would permit me to read; and those I did, gave me no great pleasure; for either they dealt so much in the *marvellous* and *improbable*, or were so unnaturally *inflaming* to the *passions*, and so full of *love* and *intrigue*, that most of them seemed calculated to *fire* the *imagination*, rather than to *inform* the *judgment*. Titles and tournaments, breaking of spears in honour of a mistress, engaging with monsters, rambling in search of adventures, making unnatural difficulties, in order to shew the knight-errant's prowess in overcoming them, is all that is required to constitute the *hero* in such pieces. And what principally distinguishes the character of the *heroine* is, when she is taught to consider her father's house as an enchanted castle, and her lover as the hero who is to dissolve the charm, and to set her at liberty from one confinement, in order to put her into another, and, too probably, a worse: to instruct her how to climb walls, leap precipices, and do twenty other extravagant things, in order to show the mad strength of a passion she ought to be ashamed of; to make parents and guardians pass for tyrants, the voice of reason to be drowned in that of indiscreet love, which exalts the other sex, and debases her own. And what is the instruction that can be gathered from such pieces, for the conduct of common life?

> *Samuel Richardson.* Pamela, or Virtue Rewarded (*1740*), Part II, Letter cii.

A CAUTION AGAINST THE SUPERNATURAL

. . . I think it may very reasonably be required of every writer, that he keeps within the bounds of possibility; and still remembers that what it is not possible for man to perform, it is scarce possible for man to believe he did perform. This conviction perhaps gave birth to many stories of the ancient heathen deities (for most of them are of poetical original). The poet, being desirous to indulge a wanton and extravagant imagination, took refuge in that power, of the extent of which his readers were no judges, or rather which they imagined to be infinite, and consequently they could not be shocked at any prodigies related of it. This hath been strongly urged in defence of Homer's miracles; and it is perhaps a defence; not, as Mr. Pope would have it, because Ulysses told a set of foolish lies to the Phaeacians, who were a very dull nation; but because the poet himself wrote to heathens, to whom poetical fables were articles of faith. For my own part, I must confess, so compassionate is my temper, I wish Polypheme had confined himself to his milk diet, and preserved his eye; nor could Ulysses be much more concerned than myself, when his companions were turned into swine by Circe, who showed, I think, afterwards, too much regard for man's flesh to be supposed capable of converting it into bacon. I wish, likewise, with all my heart, that Homer could have known the rule prescribed by Horace, to introduce supernatural agents as seldom as possible. We should not then have seen his gods coming on trivial errands, and often behaving themselves so as not only to forfeit all title to respect, but to become the objects of scorn and derision. A conduct which must have shocked the credulity of a pious and sagacious heathen; and which could never have been defended, unless by agreeing with a supposition to which I have sometimes almost inclined, that this most glorious poet, as he certainly was, had an intent to burlesque the superstitious faith of his own age and country.

But I have rested too long on a doctrine which can be of no use to a Christian writer; for as he cannot introduce into his works any of that heavenly host which make a part of his creed, so it is horrid puerility to search the heathen theology for any of those deities who have been long since dethroned from their immortality. Lord Shaftesbury observes that nothing is more cold than the invocation of a muse by a modern; he might have added, that nothing can be more absurd. A modern may with much more elegance invoke a ballad, as some have thought Homer did, or a mug of ale, with the author of Hudibras; which latter may perhaps have inspired more poetry, as well as prose, than all the liquors of Hippocrene or Helicon.

The only supernatural agents which can in any manner be allowed to us moderns, are ghosts; but of these I would advise an author to be extremely sparing. These are indeed, like arsenic, and other dangerous drugs in physic, to be used with the utmost caution; nor would I advise the introduction of them at all in those works, or by those authors, to which, or to whom, a horse-laugh in the reader would be any great prejudice or mortification.

As for elves and fairies, and other such mummery, I purposely omit the mention of them, as I should be very unwilling to confine within any bounds those surprising imaginations, for whose vast capacity the limits of human nature are too narrow; whose works are to be considered as a new creation; and who have consequently iust right to do what they will with their own.

Man, therefore, is the highest subject (unless on very extra-ordinary occasions indeed) which presents itself to the pen of our historian, or of our poet; and in relating his actions, great care is to be taken that we do not exceed the capacity of the agent we describe.

Henry Fielding. The History of Tom Jones, a Foundling (*1749*)
Book VIII, Chapter i.

ROMANCE REFORMED BY THE NOVELIST

It is no wonder that the ancients could not relish a fable in prose, after they had seen so many remarkable events celebrated in verse by their best poets. But when the minds of men were debauched, by the imposition of priestcraft, to the utmost pitch of credulity, the authors of romance arose, and, losing sight of probability, filled their performances with the most monstrous hyperboles. If they could not equal the ancient poets in point of genius, they were resolved to excel them in fiction, and apply to the wonder rather than the judg-ment of their readers. Accordingly they brought necromancy to their aid, and instead of supporting the character of their heroes by dignity of sentiment and practice, distinguished them by their bodily strength, activity, and extravagance of behaviour. Although nothing could be more ludicrous and unnatural than the figures they drew, they did not want patrons and admirers, and the world actually began to be infected with the spirit of knight-errantry, when

Cervantes, by an inimitable piece of ridicule, reformed the taste of mankind, representing chivalry in the right point of view, and converting romance to purposes far more useful and entertaining, by making it assume the sock, and point out the follies of ordinary life.

The same method has been practised by other Spanish and French authors, and by Monsieur Le Sage, who, in his Adventures of Gil Blas, has described the knavery and foibles of life, with infinite humour and sagacity.

Tobias Smollett. Preface to Roderick Random (*1748*).

PLEASING DELUSIONS

From the same taste of being acquainted with the various surprising incidents of mankind, arises our insatiable curiosity for novels or romances; infatuated with a sort of knight-errantry, we draw these fictitious characters into a real existence; and thus, pleasingly deluded, we find ourselves as warmly interested, and deeply affected by the imaginary scenes of *Arcadia*, the wonderful achievements of Don Quixote, the merry conceits of *Sancho*, rural innocence of a Joseph Andrews, or the inimitable virtues of *Sir Charles Grandison*, as if they were real, and these romantic heroes had experienced the capricious fortunes attributed to them by the fertile invention of the writers.

Performances of this kind have indeed one advantage, that, as they are the works of fancy, the author, like a painter, may so colour, decorate, and embellish them, as most agreeably to flatter our humour, and most highly promise to entertain, captivate and enchant the mind.

Sarah Fielding. Introduction to The Lives of Cleopatra and Octavia (*1757*)

LA BELLE NATURE

N. . . . These letters are not letters, this novel is not a novel: your characters are people from another world.

R. I'm sorry for this world then.

N. Don't worry; there are plenty of mad people here too. Your characters, however, are not to be found in nature.

R. . . . Why make up your mind about them in this way? Do you really claim to know just how far men can differ from each other, how much characters vary, or to just what extent customs and prejudices alter with time, place and period? Who dares to set precise limits to nature and say: man can go as far as this, but no further?

N. By that remarkable reasoning, unheard-of monsters, giants, pygmies, fantasies of every kind, could all be admitted as parts of the natural order and portrayed. We should no longer possess any common standard. I repeat, in representations of human nature, everyone must be able to distinguish the human being.

R. I agree with that, provided that one also knows how to distinguish what makes for differences of type from what is essential to the species. What would you think of people who could only recognize members of our own species when they are dressed as Frenchmen?

N. What would you think of the man who, without describing form or feature, sets about portraying a human being with a veil for clothing? Wouldn't one have the right to ask him where the human being was?

R. Without describing form or feature? Are you being fair? That there are no perfect people—that is the really unlikely thing . . . I must ask you to look once more at the inscription on the copy.

N. *Les Belles Ames!* Fine sounding words!

R. O philosophy, what pains you are at to shrivel human hearts and make men paltry.

N. But the romantic spirit exalts and deceives . . .

Jean-Jacques Rousseau. Preface (1762) to La Nouvelle Héloïse (*1760*).

COMBINING THE MARVELLOUS AND THE PROBABLE

The business of Romance is, first, to excite the attention; and secondly, to direct it to some useful, or at least innocent end. Happy the writer who attains both these points, like Richardson; and not unfortunate, or undeserving praise, he who gains only the latter, and furnishes out an entertainment for the reader.

Having in some degree opened my design, I beg leave to conduct my reader back again till he comes within view of *The Castle of Otranto*; a work which, as already has been observed, is an attempt to unite the various merits and graces of the ancient Romance and modern Novel. To attain this end, there is required a sufficient degree of the marvellous to excite attention; enough of the manners of real life to give an air of probability to the work; and enough of the pathetic to engage the heart on its behalf.

Clara Reeve, Preface to The Old English Baron (*1778*).

ROMANCE LACKS UNITY OF DESIGN

In the dark ages, when bigotry and zeal had, almost, obliterated every trace of ancient literature, the only writings, meant for amusement, were the legends of saints; in which the marvellous was, alone, predominant. Secure from criticism, by the tremendous alliance between their works and THE FAITH, the more improbable the story, the greater was its merit, with this species of writers. Their imaginations thus emancipated, their saints became warriors, the extravagant fables of the old poets were outdone, and the champions of Christendom rivalled the worthies of Greece. They overcame monsters and giants; pursued necromancers through lakes of fire; till by their prowess, and prayers, they sent the enchanters, blaspheming through the air, on the backs of fiery dragons, and made their castles vanish. These authors seem to have had a confused idea of the Grecian fables: a similarity to the Cyclops, Hydras, Minotaurs, Syrens and Circes, may easily be traced. The Phoenicians, Egyptians, Libyans, Grecians, Gauls, each had a Hercules, who performed wonderful, and impossible things. The monks invented one for the Christians; only they called him St. George. But as he was, more particularly, the hero of England, by being its tutelary saint, each powerful state was allotted a champion. One of these, St. Denis for France, Voltaire has made a principal personage in the machinery of his Henriade.

These miraculous tales were succeeded by romances of voluminous magnitude, in which the passion of love was drawn in the most hyperbolical manner; such were Clelia, the grand Cyrus, etc. A sameness of character, of incident, of language, pervaded the whole. Plot they had none, and but one moral distributed through the endless pages of endless volumes: yet these were the entertainment of the gay and the politic; and were held in estimation so late as at the end of the last century.

Modern writers use the word Romance, to signify a fictitious history of detached and independent adventures; and under that idea call the Telemaque of Fenelon, and the Cyrus of Ramsay, Romances. Le Sage's Gil Blas, and Smollett's Roderick Random, though of a different species, come under the same domination. A Novel is another kind of work. Unity of design is its character. In a Romance, if the incidents be well marked and related with spirit, the intention is answered; and adventures pass before the view for no other purpose than to amuse by their peculiarity, without, perhaps, affecting the main story, if there should be one. But in a Novel, a combination of incidents, entertaining in themselves, are made to form a whole; and an unnecessary circumstance becomes a blemish, by detaching from the simplicity which is requisite to exhibit that whole to advantage. Thus, as in dramatic works, those circumstances which do not tend, either to the illustration or the forwarding the main story, or, which do not mark some character, or person in the drama, are to be esteemed unnecessary.

Hence it appears that the legitimate Novel is a work much more difficult than the Romance, and justly deserves to be ranked with those dramatic pieces whose utility is generally allowed.

Thomas Holcroft. Preface to Alwyn: or
The Gentleman Comedian (*1780*)

THE DIFFERENCE BETWEEN THE NOVEL AND THE ROMANCE

Euphrasia. . . . The word *Novel* in all languages signifies something new. It was first used to distinguish these works from Romance, though they have lately been confounded together and are frequently mistaken for each other.

Sophronia. But how will you draw the line of distinction, so as to separate them effectually, and prevent further mistakes?

Euphrasia. I will attempt this distinction, and I presume if it is properly done it will be followed,—If not, you are but where you were before. The Romance is an heroic fable, which treats of fabulous persons and things.—The Novel is a picture of real life and manners, and of the times in which it is written. The Romance in lofty and elevated language, describes what never happened nor is likely to happen.—The Novel gives a familiar relation of such things, as pass every day before our eyes, such as may happen to our friend, or to ourselves; and the perfection of it, is to represent every scene, in so easy and natural a manner, and to make them appear so probable, as to deceive us into a persuasion (at least while we are reading) that all is real, until we are affected by the joys or distresses, of the persons in the story, as if they were our own.

Clara Reeve. The Progress of Romance (*1785*),
Vol. I, Evening vii.

SUNT CERTI DENIQUE FINES

(i)

To represent scenes of familiar life in an elegant and interesting manner, is one of the most difficult tasks an author can take in hand;

for of these every man is a critic: Nature is in the first place to be attended to, and probability is not to be lost sight of; but it must be nature strongly featured, and probability closely bordering on the marvellous; the one must touch upon extravagance, and the other be highly seasoned with adventures—for who will thank us for a dull and lifeless journal of insipid facts? Now every peculiarity of humour in the human character is a strain upon nature, and every surprising incident is a degree of violence to probability. How far shall we go then for our reader's amusement, how soon shall we stop in consideration of ourselves? There is undoubtedly a land-mark in the fields of fancy, *sunt certi denique fines*, but it requires a nice discernment to find them out, and a cautious temper not to step beyond them.

Richard Cumberland. Henry (*1795*),
Book the Fourth, Chapter i.

(ii)

Would that, like the monster Briareus, I could strike a hundred blows in the same instant, and that all the vampers of romance, who merit annihilation, were in my presence!—they are the vermin of literature—their spawn creep to our firesides, and cover our tables, our chairs, our sofas and our mantel pieces. . . .

Those who read many romances are, I imagine, insensible to the inconsistencies which I am unfortunate enough to detect, even in works written by men of talents and genius; and thus I am deprived of that interest in the perusal of them, which others enjoy to an intense degree. Sometimes I notice incongruities that the most accommodating and indulgent critic would be at a loss to reconcile: sometimes I read a picturesque description that turns nature into a second state of chaos; and sometimes I meet with an author who does all he can to make the human shape more than divine. Thus is the spell dissolved, nor can it be wondered at if I throw the book from me in disgust.

Mrs. Sarah Green. '*Literary Retrospection*', Romance Readers
and Romance Writers, A Satirical Novel (*1810*).

AN EPIC IN PROSE?

. . . A good novel is an epic in prose, with more of character and less (indeed in modern novels nothing) of the supernatural machinery.

Anna Laetitia Barbauld. '*On the origin and progress of Novel-
writing*', The British Novelists (*1810*), *Vol. I.*

NOVEL: ROMANCE: EPIC

Dr. Johnson has defined Romance in its primary sense, to be 'a military fable of the middle ages; a tale of wild adventures in love and chivalry.' But although this definition expresses correctly the ordinary idea of the word, it is not sufficiently comprehensive to answer our present purpose. A composition may be a legitimate romance, yet neither refer to love nor chivalry—to war nor to the middle ages. The 'wild adventures' are almost the only absolutely essential ingredient in Johnson's definition. We would be rather inclined to describe a *Romance* as 'a fictitious narrative in prose or verse; the interest of which turns upon marvellous and uncommon incidents;' thus being opposed to the kindred term *Novel*, which Johnson has described as 'a smooth tale, generally of love'; but which we would rather define as 'a fictitious narrative, differing from the Romance, because the events are accommodated to the ordinary train of human events, and the modern state of society.' Assuming these definitions, it is evident, from the nature of the distinction adopted, that there may exist compositions which it is difficult to assign precisely or exclusively to the one class or the other; and which, in fact, partake of the nature of both. But, generally speaking, the distinction will be found broad enough to answer all general and useful purposes.

Sir Walter Scott. 'Essay on Romance' (1824); reprinted in Miscellaneous Prose Works (*1882*), *Vol. VI.*

The *epic* poem and the *romance of chivalry* transport us to the world of wonders, where supernatural agents are mixed with human characters, where the human characters themselves are prodigies, and where events are produced by causes widely and manifestly different from those which regulate the course of human affairs. With such a world we do not think of comparing our actual situation; to such characters we do not presume to assimilate ourselves or our neighbours; from such a concatenation of marvels we draw no conclusions with regard to our expectations in real life. But real life is the very thing which *novels* affect to imitate; and the young and inexperienced will sometimes be too ready to conceive that the picture is true, in those respects at least in which they wish it to be so. Hence both their temper, conduct, and happiness may be materially injured. For novels are often *romantic*, not indeed by the relation of what is obviously miraculous or impossible, but by deviating, though perhaps insensibly, beyond the bounds of probability or consistency.

> *Review of Madame Cottin's* Amélie Mansfield *(1809)*,
> Quarterly Review, *Vol. I; reprinted as a footnote to Sir
> Walter Scott's 'Essay on Romance'*, Miscellaneous Prose
> Works *(1882), Vol. VI.*

THE HISTORICAL ROMANCE COMBINES THE MARVELLOUS AND THE PROBABLE

(i)

It appeared likely, that out of this simple plot I might weave something attractive; because the reign of James I, in which George Heriot flourished, gave unbounded scope to invention in the fable, while at the same time it afforded greater variety and discrimination of character than could, with historical consistency, have been introduced, if the scene had been laid a century earlier. Lady Mary Wortley Montague has said, with equal truth and taste, that the most romantic region of every country is that where the mountains unite themselves with the plains or lowlands. For similar reasons, it may be in like manner said, that the most picturesque period of history is that when the ancient rough and wild manners of a barbarous age are just becoming innovated upon, and contrasted, by the illumination of increased or revived learning, and the instructions of renewed or reformed religion. The strong contrast produced by the opposition of ancient manners to those which are gradually subduing them, affords the lights and shadows necessary to give effect to a fictitious narrative; and while such a period entitles the author to introduce incidents of a marvellous and improbable character, as arising out of the turbulence, independence and ferocity, belonging to old habits of violence, still influencing the manners of a people who had been so lately in a barbarous state; yet, on the other hand, the characters and sentiments of many of the actors may, with the utmost probability, be described with great variety of shading and delineation, which belongs to the newer and more improved period, of which the world has but lately received the light.

> *Sir Walter Scott. Introduction (1831) to*
> The Fortunes of Nigel *(1822).*

(ii)

When a writer calls his work a Romance, it need hardly be observed that he wishes to claim a certain latitude, both as to its fashion and material, which he would not have felt himself entitled to assume had he professed to be writing a Novel. The latter form of composition is presumed to aim at a very minute fidelity, not merely to the possible, but to the probable and ordinary course of man's experience. The former—while, as a work of art, it must rigidly subject itself to laws, and while it sins unpardonably so far as it may swerve aside from the truth of the human heart—has fairly a right to present that truth under circumstances, to a great extent, of the writer's own choosing or creation. If he thinks fit, also, he may so manage his atmospherical medium as to bring out or mellow the lights and deepen and enrich the shadows of the picture. He will be wise, no doubt, to make a very moderate use of the privileges here stated, and, especially, to mingle the Marvellous rather as a slight, delicate, and evanescent flavour, than as any portion of the actual substance of the dish offered to the public. He can hardly be said, however, to commit a literary crime even if he disregard this caution.

In the present work, the author has proposed to himself—but with what success, fortunately, it is not for him to judge—to keep undeviatingly within his immunities. The point of view in which this tale comes under the Romantic definition lies in the attempt to connect a bygone time with the very present that is flitting away from us. It is a legend prolonging itself, from an epoch now gray in the distance, down into our own broad daylight, and bringing along with it some of its legendary mist, which the reader, according to his pleasure may either disregard, or allow it to float almost imperceptibly about the characters and events for the sake of a picturesque effect. The narrative, it may be, is woven of so humble a texture as to require this advantage, and, at the same time, to render it the more difficult of attainment.

Nathaniel Hawthorne. Preface to The House of the Seven Gables (*1851*).

THE NOVELIST'S SENSE OF CONFLICT

(i)

. . . There are in me, from the literary point of view, two distinct personalities: one who is fascinated by bombast, lyricism, great eagle flights, all the sonorities of style and the high summits of ideas; another who burrows and digs for the truth, excavating as much as he can, who likes to give the humble detail as much emphasis as the grandiose, who wants you to feel the things he represents with an almost physical immediacy; this person likes to laugh and enjoys the animal side of man's nature. . . .

> Gustave Flaubert. *Letter to Louise Colet* (*16 January 1842*), Correspondence (*1900*).

. . human life is a sad show, undoubtedly: ugly, heavy and complex. The only object of Art, for men of feeling, is 'to make all disagreeables evaporate' [1] . . .

> Gustave Flaubert. *Letter to Amélie Bosquet* (*July 1864*), Correspondence (*1900*).

(ii)

Brought up in the atmosphere of romanticism, saturated with its masterpieces, carried away by lyrical flights, at first we experience the enthusiastic phase which is the period of initiation. But however beautiful it may be, one literary form can become fatally monotonous, particularly for those whose only concern is with literature, who make it from morning to night and live by it. Then a strange need for change grows in us; even the greatest of the wonders which we so passionately admire turn us against them, because we know only too well how they are produced: we belong, as they say, to that fraternity. So we look out for something else, or, rather, we turn back to something else; but we seize on this 'something else', re-cast it, add to it and make it our own: and then we believe, sometimes quite sincerely, that we have invented it ourselves. . . .

Zola, in this sense then, is a revolutionary. But he is a revolutionary brought up to admire what he now wishes to destroy, like a priest who forsakes the altar . . . this novelist, who has described himself as a naturalist, in spite of his consistently violent attacks on the romantics, uses the same methods of amplification as they do, though he applies them in a different way.

His theory goes like this: life is our only model since we cannot conceive anything beyond our senses; consequently to distort life is to produce a bad work of art, since it would be a work of falsification.

Horace has defined the imagination in this way:

> Humano capiti cervicem pictor equinam
> Jungere si velit, et varias inducere plumas
> Undique collatis membris, ut turpiter atrum
> Desinat in piscem mulier formosa superne . . .

---

[1] '. . . escamoter le fardeau et l'amertume.'

This is to say that the strongest effort of imagination can do no more than set the head of a beautiful woman on the body of a horse, cover the creature with feathers, and give it a hideous fish's tail: in fact, produce a monster.

Conclusion: everything which isn't exactly true is deformed, in other words, becomes a monster. This is not far from saying that imaginative literature can produce nothing other than monsters . . .

For Zola, then, truth alone can produce works of art. We are not to use our imagination, we are to observe and describe meticulously what we have seen. . . .

However, child of romanticism that he is, and himself a romantic in method, he has a tendency to the lyrical, a need to exalt, to enlarge, to make symbols of beings and objects. Moreover he is well aware of this tendency in himself and fights it unremittingly only to succumb again and again. His theory and his practice are perpetually in conflict.

> Guy de Maupassant. 'Emile Zola', Les Célébrités
> Contemporaines (*1883*).

THE QUALITY OF ROMANCE

To come at all at the nature of this quality of romance, we must bear in mind the peculiarity of our attitude to any art. No art produces illusion; in the theatre we never forget that we are in the theatre; and while we read a story, we sit wavering between two minds, now merely clapping our hands at the merit of the performance, now condescending to take an active part in fancy with the characters. This last is the triumph of romantic story-telling: when the reader consciously plays at being the hero, the scene is a good scene. Now in character-studies the pleasure that we take is critical; we watch, we approve, we smile at incongruities, we are moved to sudden heats of sympathy with courage, suffering or virtue. But the characters are still themselves, they are not us; the more clearly they are depicted, the more widely do they stand away from us, the more imperiously do they thrust us back into our place as a spectator. I cannot identify myself with Rawdon Crawley or with Eugène de Rastignac, for I have scarce a hope or fear in common with them. It is not character but incident that woos us out of our reserve. Something happens as we desire to have it happen to ourselves; some situation, that we have long dallied with in fancy, is realized in the story with enticing and appropriate details. Then we forget the characters; then we push the hero aside; then we plunge into the table in our own person and bathe in fresh experience;

and then, and then only, do we say we have been reading a romance. It is not only pleasurable things that we imagine in our day-dreams; there are lights in which we are willing to contemplate even the idea of our own death; ways in which it seems as if it would amuse us to be cheated, wounded or calumniated. It is thus possible to construct a story, even of tragic import, in which every incident, detail and trick of circumstance shall be welcome to the reader's thoughts. Fiction is to the grown man what play is to the child; it is there that he changes the atmosphere and tenor of his life; and when the game so chimes with his fancy that he can join in it with all his heart, when it pleases him with every turn, when he loves to recall it and dwells upon its recollection with entire delight, fiction is called romance.

Robert Louis Stevenson. 'A Gossip on Romance' (1882);
reprinted in Memories and Portraits (1887).

A ROMANTIC REALIST

I have not sought for special imaginative freedom or a larger play of fancy in my choice of characters and subjects. The nature of the knowledge, suggestions or hints used in my imaginative work has depended directly on the conditions of my active life. It depended more on contacts, and very slight contacts at that, than on actual experience; because my life as a matter of fact was far from being adventurous in itself. Even now when I look back on it with a certain regret (who would not regret his youth?) and positive affection, its colouring wears the sober hue of hard work and exacting calls of duty, things which in themselves are not much charged with a feeling of romance. If these things appeal strongly to me even in retrospect it is, I suppose, because the romantic feeling of reality was in me an inborn faculty. This in itself may be a curse but when disciplined by a sense of personal responsibility and a recognition of the hard facts of existence shared with the rest of mankind becomes but a point of view from which the very shadows of life appear endowed with an internal glow. And such romanticism is not a sin. It is none the worse for the knowledge of truth. It only tries to make the best of it, hard as it may be; and in this hardness discovers a certain aspect of beauty.

I am speaking here of romanticism in relation to life, not of romanticism in relation to imaginative literature, which, in its early days, was associated simply with medieval subjects sought for in a remote past. My subjects are not medieval and I have a natural right to them because my past is very much my own. If their course lie out of the beaten path of organized social life, it is, perhaps, because I myself did in a short break away from it early in obedience to an impulse which must have been very genuine since it has sustained me through all the dangers of disillusion. But that origin of my literary work was very far from giving a larger scope to my imagination. On the contrary, the mere fact of dealing with matters outside the general run of everyday experience laid me under the obligation of a more scrupulous fidelity to the truth of my own sensations. The problem was to make unfamiliar things credible. To do that I had to create for them, to reproduce for them, to envelop them in their proper atmosphere of actuality. This was the hardest task of all and the most important, in view of that conscientious rendering of truth in thought and fact which has always been my aim.

Joseph Conrad. Preface to Within the Tides *(1915).*

CUTTING THE CABLE

By what art or mystery, what craft of selection, omission or commission, does a given picture of life appear to us to surround its theme, its figure and images, with the air of romance while another picture close beside it may affect us as steeping the whole matter in the element of reality? It is a question, no doubt, on the painter's part, very much more of perceived effect, effect *after* the fact, than of conscious design . . . and I doubt if any novelist, for instance, ever proposed to commit himself to one kind or the other with as little mitigation as we are sometimes able to find for him. The interest is greatest—the interest of his genius, I mean, and of his general wealth—when he commits himself in both directions; not quite at the same time or to the same effect, of course, but by the need of performing his whole possible revolution, by the law of some rich passion for extremes.

Of the men of largest responding imagination before the human scene, of Scott, of Balzac, even of the coarse, comprehensive, prodigious Zola, we feel, I think, that the deflexion toward either quarter has never taken place; that neither the nature of the man's faculty nor the nature of his experience has ever quite determined it. His current remains therefore extraordinarily rich and mixed, washing us successively with the warm wave of the near and the familiar and the tonic shock, as may be, of the far and strange. (In making which opposition I suggest not that the strange and far are at all necessarily romantic: they happen to be simply the unknown,

which is quite a different matter. The real represents to my perception the things we cannot possibly *not* know, sooner or later, in one
way or another; it being but one of the accidents of our hampered
state, and one of the incidents of their quality and number, that
particular instances have not yet come our way. The romantic
stands, on the other hand, for the things that, with all the facilities
in the world, all the wealth and all the courage and all the wit and
all the adventure, we never *can* directly know; the things that can
reach us only through the beautiful circuit and subterfuge of our
thought and desire). . . .

The only *general* attribute of projected romance that I can see,
the only one that fits all cases, is the fact of the kind of experience
with which it deals—experience liberated, so to speak, experience
disengaged, disembroiled, disencumbered, exempt from the conditions that we usually know to attach to it and, if we so wish to put
the matter, drag upon it, and operating in a medium which relieves
it, in a particular interest, of the inconvenience of a *related*, a measur-
able state, a state subject to all our vulgar communities. The greatest
intensity may so be arrived at evidently—when the sacrifice of
community, of the 'related' sides of situations, has not been too
rash. It must to this end not flagrantly betray itself; we must even
be kept if possible, for our illusion, from suspecting any sacrifice at
all. The balloon of experience is in fact of course tied to the earth,
and under that necessity we swing, thanks to a rope of remarkable
length, in the more or less commodious car of the imagination; but
it is by the rope we know where we are, and from the moment that
cable is cut we are at large and unrelated; we only swing apart from
the globe—though remaining as exhilarated, naturally, as we like,
especially when all goes well. The art of the necromancer is, 'for the
fun of it,' insidiously to cut the cable, to cut it without our detecting
him. What I have recognized then in *The American*, much to my
surprise and after long years, is that the experience here presented
is the disconnected and uncontrolled experience—uncontrolled by
our general sense of 'the way things happen'—which romance alone
more or less successfully palms off on us.

> *Henry James. Preface to* The American *(1877); first printed
> in the New York edition of the* Novels and Stories *(1907–17),
> Vol. II.*

GHOST STORIES

. . . since the question has ever been for me but of wondering and,
with all achievable adroitness, of causing to wonder, so the whole

fairy-tale side of life has used, for its tug at my sensibility, a cord all its own. When we want to wonder there's no such good ground for it as the wonderful—premising indeed always, by an induction as prompt, that this element can but be at best, to fit its different cases, a thing of appreciation. . . . The ideal, obviously, on these lines, is the straight fairy-tale, the case that has purged in the crucible all its *bêtises* while keeping all its grace. It may seem odd, in a search for the amusing, to try to steer wide of the silly by hugging close to the 'supernatural'; but one man's amusement is at the best (we have surely long had to recognize) another's desolation; and I am prepared with the confession that the 'ghost-story', as we for convenience call it, has ever been for me the most possible form of the fairy-tale. . . .

. . The moving accident, the rare conjunction, whatever it be, doesn't make the story—in the sense that the story is our excitement, our amusement, our thrill and our suspense; the human emotion and the human attestation, the clustering human conditions we expect presented, only make it. The extraordinary is most extra-ordinary in that it happens to you and me, and it's of value (of value for others) but so far as visibly brought home to us. At any rate, odd though it may sound to pretend that one feels on safer ground in tracing such an adventure as that of the hero of 'The Jolly Corner' than in pursuing a bright career among pirates or detectives, I allow that composition to pass as the measure or limit, on my own part, of any achievable comfort in the 'adventure-story'; and this not because I may 'render'—well what my poor gentleman attempted and suffered in the New York house—better than I may render detectives or pirates or other splendid desperadoes, though even here too there would be something to say; but because the spirit engaged with the forces of violence interests me most when I can think of it as engaged most deeply, most finely and most 'subtly' (precious term!). For then it is that, as with the longest and firmest prongs of consciousness, I grasp and hold the throbbing subject; *there* it is above all that I find the steady light of the picture.

Henry James. Preface to The Altar of the Dead; *first printed in the New York edition of the* Novels and Stories *(1907–17), Vol. XVII.*

ADJUSTING THE EXCEPTIONAL AND THE NON-EXCEPTIONAL

The real, if unavowed, purpose of fiction is to give pleasure by gratifying the love of the uncommon in human experience, mental or corporeal.

This is done all the more perfectly in proportion as the reader is illuded to believe the personages true and real like himself.

Solely to this latter end a work of fiction should be a precise transcript of ordinary life: but,

The uncommon would be absent and the interest lost, Hence,

The writer's problem is, how to strike the balance between the uncommon and the ordinary so as on the one hand to give interest, on the other to give reality.

In working out this problem, human nature must never be made abnormal, which is introducing incredibility. The uncommonness must be in the events, not in the characters; and the writer's art lies in shaping that uncommonness while disguising its unlikelihood, if it be unlikely.

> *Thomas Hardy. Notebook entry (July 1881) from* The Early Life of Thomas Hardy, 1840–1891 *(1928), Chapter xi.*

A story must be exceptional enough to justify its telling. We tale-tellers are all Ancient Mariners, and none of us is warranted in stopping Wedding Guests (in other words, the hurrying public) unless he has something more unusual to relate than the ordinary experience of every average man and woman.

The whole secret of fiction and the drama—in the constructional part—lies in the adjustment of things unusual to things eternal and universal. The writer who knows exactly how exceptional, and how non-exceptional, his events should be made, possesses the key to the art.

> *Thomas Hardy. Notebook entry (23 February 1893) from* The Later Years of Thomas Hardy, 1892–1928 *(1930), Chapter ii.*

II The Novel as a Portrait of Life

A NEW SPECIES OF WRITING

As it is possible the mere English reader may have a different idea of romance from the author of these little volumes, and may consequently expect a kind of entertainment not be found, nor which was even intended, in the following pages, it may not be improper to premise a few words concerning this kind of writing, which I do not remember to have seen hitherto attempted in our language.

The EPIC, as well as the DRAMA, is divided into tragedy and comedy. HOMER, who was the father of this species of poetry, gave us a pattern of both these, though that of the latter kind is entirely lost; which Aristotle tells us, bore the same relation to comedy which his Iliad bears to tragedy. And perhaps, that we have no more instances of it among the writers of antiquity, is owing to the loss of this great pattern, which, had it survived, would have found its imitators equally with the other poems of this great original.

And farther, as this poetry may be tragic or comic, I will not scruple to say it may be likewise either in verse or prose: for though it wants one particular, which the critic enumerates in the constituent parts of an epic poem, namely metre; yet, when any kind of writing contains all its other parts, such as fable, action, characters, sentiments, and diction, and is deficient in metre only, it seems, I think, reasonable to refer it to the epic; at least, as no critic hath thought proper to range it under any other head, or to assign it a particular name to itself.

Thus the Telemachus of the archbishop of Cambray appears to me of the epic kind, as well as the Odyssey of Homer; indeed, it is much fairer and more reasonable to give it a name common with that species from which it differs only in a single instance, than to confound it with those which it resembles in no other. Such are those voluminous works, commonly called Romances, namely, Clelia, Cleopatra, Astraea, Cassandra, the Grand Cyrus, and innumerable others, which contain, as I apprehend, very little instruction or entertainment.

Now, a comic romance is a comic epic poem in prose; differing from comedy, as the serious epic from tragedy: its action being more extended and comprehensive; containing a much larger circle of incidents, and introducing a greater variety of characters. It differs from the serious romance in its fable and action in this; that as in the one these are grave and solemn, so in the other they are light and ridiculous: it differs in its characters by introducing persons of inferior rank, and consequently, of inferior manners, whereas the grave romance sets the highest before us: lastly, in its sentiments and diction; by preserving the ludicrous instead of the sublime. In the diction, I think, burlesque itself may be sometimes admitted; of which many instances will occur in this work, as in the description of the battles, and some other places, not necessary to be pointed out to the classical reader, for whose entertainment those parodies or burlesque imitations are chiefly calculated.

> *Henry Fielding. Preface to* The History of the Adventures of Joseph Andrews (*1742*).

THE BOUNDS OF PROBABILITY

... the actions should be such as may not only be within the compass of human agency, and which human agents may probably be supposed to do; but they should be likely for the very actors and characters themselves to have performed; for what may be only wonderful and surprising in one man, may become improbable, or indeed impossible, when related of another.

This last requisite is what the dramatic critics call conversation of character; and it requires a very extraordinary degree of judgment, and a most exact knowledge of human nature.

It is admirably remarked by a most excellent writer, that zeal can no more hurry a man to act in direct opposition to itself, than a rapid stream can carry a boat against its own current. I will venture to say, that for a man to act in direct contradiction to the dictates of his nature, is, if not impossible, as improbable and as miraculous as anything which can well be conceived. Should the best parts of the story of M. Antoninus be ascribed to Nero, or should the worst incidents of Nero's life be imputed to Antoninus, what would be more shocking to belief than either instance? whereas both these being related of their proper agent, constitute the truly marvellous.

Our modern authors of comedy have fallen almost universally into the error here hinted at; their heroes generally are notorious rogues, and their heroines abandoned jades, during the first four acts; but in the fifth, the former become very worthy gentlemen, and the latter women of virtue and discretion: nor is the writer often so kind as to give himself the least trouble to reconcile or account for this monstrous change and incongruity. . . .

Within these few restrictions, I think, every writer may be permitted to deal as much in the wonderful as he pleases; nay, if he thus keeps within the rules of credibility, the more he can surprise the reader the more he will engage his attention, and the more he will charm him. As a genius of the highest rank observes in his fifth chapter of the 'Bathos', 'The great art of all poetry is to mix truth with fiction, in order to join the credible with the surprising.'

For though every good author will confine himself within the bounds of probability, it is by no means necessary that his characters, or his incidents, should be trite, common, or vulgar; such as happen in every street, or in every house, or which may be met with in the home articles of a newspaper. Nor must he be inhibited from showing many persons and things, which may possibly have never fallen within the knowledge of great part of his readers. If the writer strictly observes the rules above-mentioned, he hath discharged his part; and is then entitled to some faith from his reader, who is indeed guilty of critical infidelity if he disbelieves him.

> *Henry Fielding.* The History of Tom Jones, a Foundling (*1749*)
> *Book VIII, Chapter i.*

NO 'SUDDEN CONVERSIONS'

But whatever were the fate of his work, the author was resolved to take a different method. He always thought that *sudden conversions*, such especially as were left to the candour of the reader to *suppose* and *make out*, had neither *art*, nor *nature*, nor even *probability*, in them; and that they were moreover of very *bad* example. To have a Lovelace, for a series of years, glory in his wickedness, and think that he had nothing to do, but as an act of grace and favour to hold out his hand to receive that of the best of women, whenever he pleased, and to have it thought that marriage would be a sufficient amends for all his enormities to others as well as to her—he could not bear that.

> *Samuel Richardson.* Postscript *to* Clarissa, or The History of a
> Young Lady . . . (*1747–8*).

TRUTH TO BE KEPT IN SIGHT

I know that the privileges of the novelist are more than can well be defined, and his range wider than that portion of created nature which is known to us; yet I do not meditate to stretch my flight so far, nor shall I put my privileges to their full exertion: it is not my ambition to run truth out of sight, or put credulity out of breath by following me; I do not propose to make any demands upon my hero that he cannot reasonably fulfil, or press him into streights from which virtue, by its native energy, cannot extricate herself with ease; I shall require of him no sacrifices for the sake of public fame, no pedantic ostentatious apathy, for his lot is humble, and his feelings natural; I shall let him swim with the current, and not strive to tow him against the stream of probability.

I know that I could play my puppets after my own fancy, for the wires are in my hand; that I could make them declaim like heroes in a tragedy, or gabble like a gang of gypsies under a hedge; that I could weave my fable as the Turks do carpets, without counterfeiting the likeness of any one thing in earth, sea, or air; produce beings out of nature, that no sober author ever dreamt of, and force beings into nature, that no well-bred reader ever met with: but I have lived long enough to see wonderful revolutions effected by an intemperate abuse of power, and shall be cautious how I risk privileges so precious upon experiments so trivial.

I am not sure that I shall make my leading characters happy enough to satisfy the sanguine, serious enough to suit the sentimental, or beautiful enough to warm the imagination of the animated reader. Some may think I have not been sufficiently liberal to them in point of fortune, others may wish I had favoured them with a few more casualties and misadventures.

Richard Cumberland. Henry (*1795*), *Book First, Chapter i*

THE OFFSPRING OF NATURE

Let me . . . prepare for disappointment those who . . . entertain the gentle expectation of being transported to the fantastic regions of Romance, where Fiction is coloured by all the gay tints of luxurious Imagination, where Reason is an outcast, and where the sublimity of the marvellous, rejects all aid from sober Probability. The heroine of these memoirs, young, artless, and inexperienced, is

No faultless Monster, that the world ne'er saw,

but the offspring of Nature, and of Nature in her simplest attire.

Fanny Burney. Preface to Evelina (*1778*).

THE PATHS OF COMMON LIFE: JANE AUSTEN'S 'EMMA'

... the author of novels was, in former times, expected to tread pretty much in the limits between the concentric circles of probability and possibility; and as he was not permitted to transgress the latter, his narrative, to make amends, almost always went beyond the bounds of the former. Now, although it may be urged that the vicissitudes of human life have occasionally led an individual through as many scenes of singular fortune as are represented in the most extravagant of these fictions, still the causes and personages acting on these changes have varied with the progress of the adventurer's fortune, and do not present that combined plot, (the object of every skilful novelist,) in which all the more interesting individuals of the dramatis personae have their appropriate share in the action and in bringing about the catastrophe. Here, even more than in its various and violent changes of fortune, rests the improbability of the novel. The life of man rolls forth like a stream from the fountain, or it spreads out into tranquillity like a placid or stagnant lake. In the latter case, the individual grows old among the characters with whom he was born, and is contemporary,—shares precisely the sort of weal and woe to which his birth destined him,—moves in the same circle,—and, allowing for the change of seasons, is influenced by, and influences the same class of persons by which he was originally surrounded. The man of mark and of adventure on the contrary, resembles, in the course of his life, the river whose mid-current and discharge into the ocean are widely removed from each other, as well as from the rocks and wild flowers which its fountains first reflected; violent changes of time, of place, and of circumstances, hurry him forward from one scene to another, and his adventures will usually be found only connected with each other because they have happened to the same individual. Such a history resembles an ingenious, fictitious narrative, exactly in the degree in which an old dramatic chronicle of the life and death of some distinguished character, where all the various agents appear and disappear as in the page of history, approaches a regular drama, in which every person introduced plays an appropriate part, and every point of the action tends to one common catastrophe.

We return to the second broad line of distinction between the novel, as formerly composed, and real life,—the difference, namely, of the sentiments. The novelist professed to give an imitation of nature, but it was, as the French say, *la belle nature*. Human beings, indeed, were presented, but in the most sentimental mood, and with minds purified by a sensibility which often verged on extravagance.

In the serious class of novels, the hero was usually

> 'A knight of love, who never broke a vow.'

And although, in those of a more humorous cast, he was permitted a license, borrowed either from real life or from the libertinism of the drama, still a distinction was demanded even from Peregrine Pickle, or Tom Jones; and the hero, in every folly of which he might be guilty, was studiously vindicated from the charge of infidelity of the heart. The heroine was, of course, still more immaculate; and to have conferred her affections upon any other than the lover to whom the reader had destined her from their first meeting, would have been a crime against sentiment which no author, of mode ate prudence, would have hazarded, under the old *régime*.

Here, therefore, we have two essential and important circumstances, in which the earlier novels differed from those now in fashion, and were more nearly assimilated to the old romances. And there can be no doubt that, by the studied involution and extrication of the story, by the combination of incidents new, striking and wonderful beyond the course of ordinary life, the former authors opened that obvious and strong sense of interest which arises from curiosity; as by the pure, elevated, and romantic cast of the sentiment, they conciliated those better propensities of our nature which loves to contemplate the picture of virtue, even when confessedly unable to imitate its excellencies.

But strong and powerful as these sources of emotion and interest may be, they are, like all others, capable of being exhausted by habit. The imitators who rushed in crowds upon each path in which the great masters of the art had successively led the way, produced upon the public mind the usual effect of satiety. The first writer of a new class is, as it were, placed on a pinnacle of excellence, to which, at the earliest glance of a surprized admirer, his ascent seems little less than miraculous. Time and imitation speedily diminish the wonder, and each successive attempt establishes a kind of progressive scale of ascent between the lately deified author, and the reader, who had deemed his excellence inaccessible. The stupidity, the mediocrity, the merit of his imitators, are alike fatal to the first inventor, by shewing how possible it is to exaggerate his faults and to come within a certain point of his beauties.

Materials also (and the man of genius as well as his wretched imitator must work with the same) become stale and familiar. Social life, in our civilized days, affords few instances capable of being painted in the strong dark colours which excite surprise and horror; and robbers, smugglers, bailiffs, caverns, dungeons, and madhouses, have been all introduced until they ceased to interest. And thus in the novel, as in every style of composition which appeals to the public taste, the more rich and easily worked mines being exhausted, the adventurous author must, if he is desirous of success, have recourse to those which were disdained by his predecessors as unproductive, or avoided as only capable of being turned to profit by great skill and labour.

Accordingly a style of novel has arisen, within the last fifteen or twenty years, differing from the former in the points upon which the interest hinges; neither alarming our credulity nor amusing our imagination by wild variety of incident, or by those pictures of romantic affection and sensibility, which were formerly as certain attributes of fictitious characters as they are of rare occurrence among those who actually live and die. The substitute for these excitements, which had lost much of their poignancy by the repeated and injudicious use of them, was the art of copying from nature as she really exists in the common walks of life, and presenting to the reader, instead of the splendid scenes of an imaginary world, a correct and striking representation of that which is daily taking place around him.

In adventuring upon this task, the author makes obvious sacrifices, and encounters peculiar difficulty. He who paints from *le beau idéal*, if his scenes and sentiments are striking and interesting, is in a great measure exempted from the difficult task of reconciling them with the ordinary probabilities of life: but he who paints a scene of common occurrence, places his composition within that extensive range of criticism which general experience offers to every reader. The resemblance of a statue of Hercules we must take on the artist's judgment; but every one can criticize that which is presented as the portrait of a friend, or neighbour. Something more than a mere sign-post likeness is also demanded. The portrait must have spirit and character, as well as resemblance; and being deprived of all that, according to Bayes, goes 'to elevate and surprize,' it must make amends by displaying depth of knowledge and dexterity of execution. We, therefore, bestow no mean compliment upon the author of Emma, when we say that, keeping close to common incidents, and to such characters as occupy the ordinary walks of life, she has produced sketches of such spirit and originality, that we never miss the excitation which depends upon a narrative of uncommon events, arising from the consideration of minds, manners, and sentiments greatly above our own. In this class she stands almost alone; for the scenes of Miss Edgeworth are laid in higher life, varied by more romantic incident, and by her remarkable power of embodying and illustrating national character. But the author of Emma confines herself chiefly to the middling classes of society; her most distinguished characters do not rise greatly above well-bred country gentlemen and ladies: and those which are sketched with most originality and precision, belong to a class rather below that standard. The narrative of all her novels is composed of such common occurrences as may have fallen under the observation of most folks; and her dramatis personae conduct themselves upon the motives and principles which the readers may recognize as ruling their own and that of most of their acquaintances. The kind of moral, also, which these novels inculcate, applies equally to the paths of common life . . .

> Sir Walter Scott. Review of Jane Austen's Emma (*1815*), Quarterly Review, *Vol. XIV.*

ACCIDENTS ADMISSIBLE?

. . . I am not clear, and I never have been clear, respecting the canon of fiction which forbids the interposition of accident in such a case as Madame Defarge's death. Where the accident is inseparable from the passion and action of the character; where it is strictly consistent with the entire design, and arises out of some culminating proceeding on the part of the individual which the whole story has led up to; it seems to me to become, as it were, an act of divine justice.

> Charles Dickens. *John Forster*, The Life of Charles Dickens (*1874*), *Vol. III.*

DICKENS DEFENDS FANTASY

It does not seem to me to be enough to say of any description that tt is the exact truth. The exact truth must be there; but the merit or art in the narrator, is the manner of stating the truth. As to which thing in literature, it always seems to me that there is a world to be done. And in these times, when the tendency is to be frightfully literal and catalogue-like—to make the thing, in short, a sort of sum in reduction that any miserable creature can do in that way —I have an idea (really founded on the love of what I profess), that the very holding of popular literature through a kind of popular dark age, may depend on such fanciful treatment.

> Charles Dickens. *Letter to John Forster* (1859). *See John Forster,* The Life of Charles Dickens (*1874*), *Vol. III.*

THE ART OF NOVELS IS TO REPRESENT NATURE

I think Mr. Dickens has in many things quite a divine genius so to speak, and certain notes in his song are so delightful and admirable, that I should never think of trying to imitate him, only hold my tongue and admire him. I quarrel with his Art in many respects: which I don't think represents Nature duly ... the Art of Novels *is* to represent Nature: to convey as strongly as possible the sentiment of reality—in a tragedy or a poem or a lofty drama you aim at producing different emotions; the figures moving, and their words sounding, heroically: but in a drawing-room drama a coat is a coat, and a poker a poker; and must be nothing else according to my ethics, not an embroidered tunic, nor a great red-hot instrument like the Pantomime weapon.

William Makepeace Thackeray. Letter to David Masson (6 May 1851), Letters *(1945).*

REALISM COMPATIBLE WITH SENSATIONALISM

Among English novels of the present day, and among English novelists, a great division is made. There are sensational novels and anti-sensational, sensational novelists and anti-sensational; sensational readers and anti-sensational. The novelists who are considered to be anti-sensational are generally called realistic. I am realistic. My friend Wilkie Collins is generally supposed to be sensational. The readers who prefer the one are supposed to take delight in the elucidation of character. They who hold by the other are charmed by the construction and gradual development of a plot. All this is, I think, a mistake,—which mistake arises from the inability of the imperfect artist to be at the same time realistic and sensational. A good novel should be both, and both in the highest degree. If a novel fail in either, there is a failure in Art. Let those readers who believe that they do not like sensational scenes in novels think of some of those passages from our great novelists which have charmed them most:—of Rebecca in the castle with Morton; of the mad lady tearing the veil of the expected bride, in *Jane Eyre*; of Lady Castlewood as, in her indignation, she explains to the Duke of Hamilton Henry Esmond's right to be present at the marriage of his Grace with Beatrix;—may I add of Lady Mason, as she makes her confession at the feet of Sir Peregrine Orme? Will any one say that the authors of these passages have sinned in being over-sensational? No doubt, a string of horrible incidents, bound together without truth in details, and told as affecting persons without character,—wooden blocks, who cannot make themselves known to the reader as men and women,—does not instruct or amuse, or even fill the mind with awe . . . No novel is anything, for purposes either of comedy or tragedy, unless the reader can sympathize with the characters whose names he finds upon the page. Let an author so tell his tale as to touch his reader's heart and draw his tears, and he has, so far, done his work well. Truth let there be,—truth of description, truth of character, human truth as to men and women. If there be such truth, I do not know that a novel can be too sensational.

Anthony Trollope. Autobiography (*1883*), *Chapter xii.*

TRUTH LIES IN THE 'EXCEPTIONAL'

. . . I have my own idea about art, and it is this: What most people regard as fantastic and lacking in universality, *I* hold to be the inmost essence of truth. Arid observation of everyday trivialities I have long since ceased to regard as realism—it is quite the reverse. In any newspaper one takes up, one comes across reports of wholly authentic facts, which nevertheless strike one as extraordinary. Our writers regard them as fantastic, and take no account of them; and yet they are the truth, for they are facts. But who troubles to observe, record, describe them? They happen every day and every moment, therefore they are not 'exceptional' . . .

Feodor Dostoevsky. Letter to Nikolay Strachov (26 February 1869), Letters (*1914*), *transl. Ethel Colburn Mayne.*

SCIENTIFIC REALISM

. . . we can easily see that the novelist is equally an observer and an experimentalist. The observer in him gives the facts as he has observed them, suggests the point of departure, displays the solid earth on which his characters are to tread and the phenomena to develop. Then the experimentalist appears and introduces an experiment, that is to say, sets his characters going in a certain story so as to show that the succession of facts will be such as the requirements of the determinism of the phenomina under examination call for. Here it is nearly always an experiment 'pour voir', as Claude Bernard calls it. The novelist starts out in search of a truth. I will take as an example the character of the Baron Hulot in *Cousine Bette*, by Balzac. The general fact observed by Balzac is the ravages that the amorous temperament of a man brings about in his home, in his family, and in society. As soon as he has chosen his subject he starts from known facts; then he makes his experiment, and exposes Hulot to a series of trials, placing him amid certain surroundings in order to exhibit how the complicated machinery of his passions works. It is then evident that there is not only observation there, but that there is also experiment: Balzac does not remain satisfied with photographing the facts collected by him, but interferes in a direct way to place his character in certain conditions, and of these he remains the master. The problem is to know what such a passion, acting in such a surrounding and under such circumstances, would produce from the point of view of an individual and of society; and an experimental novel, *Cousine Bette*, for example, is simply the report of the experiment that the novelist conducts before the eyes of the public. In fact the whole operation consists in taking facts from nature, then in studying the mechanism of these facts, acting upon them, by the modification of circumstance and surroundings, without deviating from the laws of nature. Finally, you possess knowledge of the man, scientific knowledge of him, in both his individual and social relations.

> *Emile Zola*. '*Du Roman Expérimental*', *Chapter i*, Le Roman Expérimental (*1880*), *transl. Belle M. Sherman* (*New York, 1893*).

REALITY ONLY A SPRING-BOARD

I think exactly as you do about the *Nabab*. It's unequal. It isn't enough merely to observe; we must order and shape what we have seen. Reality, in my view, ought to be no more than a spring-board. Our friends believe that to it alone belongs the Kingdom! This materialism makes my blood boil, and nearly every Monday I feel a wave of anger as I read old Zola's literary articles. After the Realists, we have the Naturalists and the Impressionists. What progress! A gang of humbugs trying to make themselves believe, and us with them, that they have discovered the Mediterranean. . . .

> *Gustave Flaubert. Letter to Ivan Tourgenev (8 November 1877)*, Correspondance (*1930*).

Like you I've read a few bits of *L'Assommoir*. They annoyed me. Zola is becoming a 'Précieuse' in reverse . . . He has Principles which are shrivelling his brain. If you read his articles on Mondays you will see how he thinks he has discovered 'Naturalism'. As for poetry and style, which are the two eternal principles, he never mentions them at all. Question our friend Goncourt likewise. If he is honest he will declare to you that French literature did not exist before Balzac. That's where the misuse of intelligence and the fear of not being original gets us.

> Gustave Flaubert. Letter to Ivan Tourgenev (*14 November 1876*), Correspondance (*1930*).

THE NATURALIST MODIFIES NATURE

. . . A contemptible reproach which they heap upon us naturalistic writers is the desire to be simply photographic. We have in vain declared that we admit the necessity of an artist's possessing an individual temperament and a personal expression; they continue to reply to us with these imbecile arguments, about the impossibility of being strictly true, about the necessity of arranging facts to produce a work of art of any kind. Well, with the application of the experimental method to the novel that quarrel dies out. The idea of experiment carries with it the idea of modification. We start, indeed, from the true facts, which are our indestructible basis; but to show the mechanism of these facts it is necessary for us to produce and direct the phenomena; this is our share of invention, here is the genius in the book. Thus without having recourse to questions of form and style, which I shall examine later, I maintain even at this point that we must modify nature, without departing from nature, when we use the experimental method in our novels. If we bear in mind this definition, that 'observation indicates and experiment teaches', we can even now claim for our books this great lesson of experiment.

> Emile Zola. '*Du Roman Expérimental*', Chapter i, Le Roman Expérimental (*1880*), transl. Belle M. Sherman (*New York, 1893*)

REALISTS ARE ILLUSIONISTS

To sum up, whereas the novelist of yesterday selected for his narrative life's crises, the most intense experiences of soul and heart, the novelist of to-day writes of the heart, the soul and the intelligence in their normal state. To produce the effect he wants, that is to say the feeling of simple reality, and to emphasize the artistic doctrine that he wants to draw from it—that is, the revelation of what is truly the contemporary human being before his eyes—he must use only those actions whose truth is constant and unassailable.

But in putting the point of view of these realistic artists it is necessary to examine and discuss their theory, which can be summed up simply in these words: 'The whole truth and nothing but the truth.'

Since their intention is to bring out the philosophy of certain unchanging everyday facts, they will often have to alter events for the benefit of verisimilitude but at the expense of truth, for 'truth may sometimes seem improbable'.

The realist, if he is an artist, will seek to give us not a banal photographic representation of life, but a vision of it that is fuller, more vivid and more compellingly truthful than even reality itself.

To give an account of everything would be impossible, for we should need at least one volume for each day in order to record the multitude of insignificant incidents that fill our lives.

Selection is therefore necessary,—and that is the first blow to the theory of 'the whole truth'

Life, moreover, is made up of elements that are utterly different from each other, of things utterly unexpected, contrary and incongruous; it is harsh, inconsequent, incoherent, and filled with disasters which, inexplicable, illogical and contradictory as they are, must be gathered together under the heading 'sundry happenings'.

That is why the artist, having made his choice of subject, should select from this life, crowded as it is with accidents and trivialities, only those characteristic details that are useful for his theme; all the rest, all the incidentals, he must reject.

Here is one example from a thousand:

The number of people in this world who die accidentally every day is considerable. But can we, in the middle of a narrative, allow a tile to fall on the head of a central character, or throw him under the wheels of a carriage, on the pretext that we must do justice to the part played by accident?

Again, life treats everything on the same level, precipitating events or letting them drag on indefinitely. Art, on the other hand, consists in contriving precautions and preparations, managing cunning, concealed transitions, bringing essential events into a strong light by the skill of the writing alone, and affording all the others the degree of emphasis appropriate to their relative importance, and all this in order to produce that profound impression of the special truth one wants to reveal.

To make true, then, one must give a complete illusion of truth by following the ordinary logic of events and not by slavishly transcribing them in the haphazard way they come.

From all this I conclude that Realists of talent ought rather to be called Illusionists.

> *Guy de Maupassant. 'Le Roman', Introduction to*
> Pierre et Jean (*1888*).

REPRESENTATIVE ART BOTH REALISTIC
AND IDEAL

In literature (from which I must draw my instances) the great change of the past century has been effected by the admission of detail. It was inaugurated by the romantic Scott; and at length, by the semi-romantic Balzac and his more or less wholly unromantic followers, bound like a duty on the novelist. For some time it signified and expressed a more ample contemplation of the conditions of man's life; but it has recently (at least in France) fallen into a merely technical and decorative stage, which it is, perhaps, still too harsh to call survival. With a movement of alarm, the wiser or more timid begin to fall a little back from these extremities; they begin to aspire after a more naked, narrative articulation; after the succinct, the dignified and the poetic; and as a means to this, after a general lightening of this baggage of detail. After Scott we beheld the starveling story—once, in the hands of Voltaire, as abstract as a parable—begin to be pampered upon facts. The introduction of these details developed a particular ability of hand; and that ability, childishly indulged, has led to the works that now amaze us on a railway journey. A man of the unquestionable force of M. Zola spends himself on technical successes. To afford a popular flavour and attract the mob, he adds a steady current of what I may be allowed to call the rancid. That is exciting to the moralist; but what more particularly interests the artist is this tendency of the extreme of detail, when followed as a principle, to degenerate into mere *feux-de-joie* of literary tricking. The other day even M. Daudet was to be heard babbling of audible colours and visible sounds.

This odd suicide of one branch of the realists may serve to remind us of the fact which underlies a very dusty conflict of the critics. All representative art, which can be said to live, is both realistic and ideal; and the realism about which we quarrel is a matter purely of externals. It is no especial cultus of nature and veracity, but a mere whim of veering fashion, that has made us turn our back upon the larger, more various, and more romantic art of yore. A photographic exactitude in dialogue is now the exclusive fashion; but even in the ablest hands it tells us no more—I think it even tells us less—than Molière, wielding his artificial medium, has told to us and to all time of Alceste or Orgon, Dorine or Chrysale. The historical novel is forgotten. Yet truth to the conditions of man's nature and the conditions of man's life, the truth of literary art, is free of the ages. It may be told us in a carpet comedy, in a novel of adventure, or a fairy-tale. The scene may be pitched in London, on the sea-coast of Bohemia, or away on the mountains of Beulah. And by an odd and luminous accident, if there is any page of literature calculated to awaken the envy of M. Zola, it must be that *Troilus and Cressida* which Shakespeare, in a passion of unmanly anger with the world, grafted on the heroic story of the siege of Troy.

This question of realism, let it then be clearly understood, regards not in the least degree the fundamental truth, but only the technical method, of a work of art. Be as ideal or as abstract as you please, you will be none the less veracious; but if you be weak, you run the risk of being tedious and inexpressive; and if you be very strong and honest, you may chance upon a masterpiece.

> *Robert Louis Stevenson. 'A Note on Realism' (1883);*
> *reprinted in* The Art of Writing (*1919*).

THE NOVEL 'AN ARTIFICIALITY DISTILLED FROM THE FRUITS OF OBSERVATION'

The most devoted apostle of realism, the sheerest naturalist, cannot escape, any more than the withered old gossip over her fire, the exercise of Art in his labour or pleasure of telling a tale. Not until he becomes an automatic reproducer of all impressions whatsoever can he be called purely scientific, or even a manufacturer on scientific principles. If in the exercise of his reason he select or omit, with an eye to being more truthful than truth (the just aim of Art), he transforms himself into a technicist at a move.

As this theory of the need for the exercise of the Daedalian faculty for selection and cunning manipulation has been disputed, it may be worth while to examine the contrary proposition. That it should ever have been maintained by such a romancer as M. Zola, in his work on the *Roman Expérimental*, seems to reveal an obtuseness to the disproof conveyed in his own novels which, in a French writer, is singular indeed. To be sure that author—whose powers in story-telling, owing to the fact that he is not a critic—does in a measure concede something in the qualified counsel that the novel should keep as close to reality *as it can*; a remark which may be interpreted with infinite latitude, and would no doubt have been cheerfully accepted by Dumas *père* or Mrs. Radcliffe. It implies discriminative choice; and if we grant that we grant all. But to maintain in theory what he abandons in practice, to subscribe to rules and to work by instinct, is a proceeding not confined to the author of *Germinal* and *La Faute de l'Abbé Mouret*.

The reasons that make against such conformation of story-writing to scientific processes have been set forth so many times in examining the theories of the realist, that it is not necessary to recapitulate them here. Admitting the desirability, the impossibility of reproducing in its entirety the phantasmagoria of experience with infinite and atomic truth, without shadow, relevancy, or subordination, is not the least of them. The fallacy appears to owe its origin to the just perception that with our widened knowledge of the universe and its forces, and man's position therein, narrative, to be artistically convincing, must adjust itself to the new alignment, as would also artistic works in form and colour, if further spectacles in their sphere could be presented. Nothing but the illusion of truth can permanently please, and when the old illusions begin to be penetrated, a more natural magic has to be supplied.

Creativeness in its full and ancient sense—the making a thing or situation out of nothing that ever was before—is apparently ceasing to satisfy a world which no longer believes in the abnormal—ceasing at least to satisfy the van-couriers of taste; and creative fancy has accordingly to give more and more place to realism, that is, to an artificiality distilled from the fruits of closest observation.

This is the meaning deducible from the work of the realists, however stringently they themselves may define realism in terms. Realism is an unfortunate, an ambiguous word, which has been taken up by literary society like a view-halloo, and has been assumed in some places to mean copyism, and in others pruriency, and has led to two classes of delineators being included in one condemnation.

Thomas Hardy. 'The Science of Fiction' (1891);
reprinted in Life and Art *(1925).*

IMITATION CANNOT SERVE AS A STANDARD

[A] second method which gives a semblance of art is what I called imitation. The essence of this method consists in rendering the details which accompany that which is described or represented. In the literary art this method consists in describing, down to the minutest details, the appearance, faces, garments, gestures, sounds, apartments of the acting persons, with all those incidents which occur in life. Thus, in novels and stories, they describe, with every speech of the acting person, in what voice he said it, and what he did then. And the speeches themselves are not told so as to make the best sense, but as incoherently as they are in life, with interruptions and abrupt endings . . .

Imitation cannot serve as a standard of the value of art, because, if the chief property of art is the infection of others with the sensation described by the artist, the infection with the sensation not only does not coincide with the description of the details of what is being conveyed, but for the most part is impaired by a superabundance of details. The attention of him who received artistic impressions is distracted by all these well-observed details, and on account of them the author's feeling, if he has any, is not communicated.

It is just as strange to value the production of art by the degree of its realism and truthfulness of details communicated, as it is to judge of the nutritive value of food by its appearance. When we define the value of a production by its realism, we merely show by this that we are not speaking of a production of art, but of an imitation of it.

Leo Tolstoy. *'What is art?'* (*1897*), Complete Works (*1904*), Vol. *XXII, transl. Leo Werner.*

ART 'ALL DISCRIMINATION AND SELECTION'

. . . Life being all inclusion and confusion, and art being all discrimination and selection, the latter, in search of the hard latent *value* with which alone it is concerned, sniffs round the mass as instinctively and unerringly as a dog suspicious of some buried bone. The difference here, however, is that, while the dog desires his bone but to destroy it, the artist finds *his* tiny nugget, washed free of awkward accretions and hammered into a sacred hardness, the very stuff for a clear affirmation, the happiest chance for the indestructible. It at the same time amuses him again and again to note how, beyond the first step of the actual case, the case that constitutes for him his germ, his vital particle, his grain of gold, life persistently blunders and deviates, loses herself in the sand. The reason is of course that life has no direct sense whatever for the subject and is capable, luckily for us, of nothing but splendid waste. Hence the opportunity for the sublime economy of art, which rescues, which saves, and hoards and 'banks', investing and reinvesting these fruits of toil in wondrous useful 'works' and thus making up for us, desperate spendthrifts that we all naturally are, the most princely of incomes. It is the subtle secrets of that system, however, that are meanwhile the charming study, with an endless attraction above all, in the question—endlessly baffling indeed—of the method at the heart of the madness; the madness, I mean, of a zeal, among the reflective sort, so disinterested. If life, presenting us the germ, and left merely to herself in such a business, gives the case away, almost always, before we can stop her, what are the signs for our guidance, what the primary laws for a saving selection, how do we know when and where to intervene, where do we place the beginnings of the wrong or the right deviation? Such would be the elements of an enquiry upon which, I hasten to say, it is quite forbidden me here to embark: I but glance at them in evidence of the rich pasture that at every turn surrounds the ruminant critic. The answer may be after all that mysteries here elude us, that general considerations fail or mislead, and that even the fondest of artists need ask for no wider range than the logic of the particular case. The particular case, or in other words his relation to a given subject, once the relation is established, forms in itself a little world of exercise and agitation. Let him hold himself perhaps supremely fortunate if he can meet half the questions with which the air alone may swarm.

> *Henry James. Preface to* The Spoils of Poynton (*1897*); *first printed in the New York edition of the* Novels and Stories (*1907–17*), *Vol. XV.*

IMAGINED LIFE CLEARER THAN REALITY

What is it that Novalis says? 'It is certain my conviction gains infinitely the moment another soul will believe in it.' And what is a novel if not a conviction of our fellow-men's existence strong enough to take upon itself a form of imagined life clearer than reality and whose accumulated verisimilitude of selected episodes puts to shame the pride of documentary history?

> *Joseph Conrad.* A Personal Record (*1912*), *Chapter i.*

IS LIFE LIKE THIS?

Admitting the vagueness which afflicts all criticism of novels, let us hazard the opinion that for us at this moment the form of fiction most in vogue more often misses than secures the thing we seek. Whether we call it life or spirit, truth or reality, this, the essential thing, has moved off, or on, and refuses to be confined any longer in such ill-fitting vestments as we provide. Nevertheless, we go on perseveringly, conscientiously, constructing our two and thirty chapters after a design which more and more ceases to resemble the vision in our minds. So much of the enormous labour of proving the solidity, the likeness to life, of the story is not merely labour thrown away but labour misplaced to the extent of obscuring and blotting out the light of the conception. The writer seems constrained, not by his own free will but by some powerful and unscrupulous tyrant who has him in thrall, to provide a plot, to provide comedy, tragedy, love, interest, and an air of probability embalming the whole so impeccable that if all his figures were to come to life they would find themselves dressed down to the last button of their coats in the fashion of the hour. The tyrant is obeyed; the novel is done to a turn. But sometimes, more and more often as time goes by, we suspect a momentary doubt, a spasm of rebellion, as the pages fill themselves in the customary way. Is life like this? Must novels be like this?

Look within and life, it seems, is very far from being 'like this'. Examine for a moment an ordinary mind on an ordinary day. The mind receives a myriad impressions—trivial, fantastic, evanescent, or engraved with the sharpness of steel. From all sides they come, an incessant show of innumerable atoms; and as they fall, as they shape themselves into the life of Monday or Tuesday, the accent falls differently from of old; the moment of importance came not here but there; so that, if a writer were a free man and not a slave, if he could write what he chose, not what he must, if he could base his work upon his own feeling and not upon convention, there would be no plot, no comedy, no tragedy, no love interest or catastrophe in the accepted style, and perhaps not a single button sewn on as the Bond Street tailors would have it. Life is not a series of gig lamps symmetrically arranged; life is a luminous halo, a semi-transparent envelope surrounding us from the beginning of consciousness to the end. Is it not the task of the novelist to convey this varying, this unknown and uncircumscribed spirit, whatever aberration or complexity it may display, with as little mixture of the alien and external as possible? We are not pleading merely for courage and sincerity; we are suggesting that the proper stuff of fiction is a little other than custom would have us believe it.

Virginia Woolf. 'Modern Fiction' (1919); reprinted in
The Common Reader (*1925*)

REALISM IMPAIRS THE SENSE OF TRAGEDY

. . . Most books that live, live in spite of the author's laying it on thick. Think of *Wuthering Heights*. It is quite as impossible to an Italian as even *I Malavoglia* is to us. But it is a great book.

The trouble with realism—and Verga was a realist—is that the writer, when he is a truly exceptional man like Flaubert or like Verga, tries to read his own sense of tragedy into people much smaller than himself. I think it is a final criticism against *Madame Bovary* that people such as Emma Bovary and her husband Charles simply are too insignificant to carry the full weight of Gustave Flaubert's sense of tragedy. Emma and Charles Bovary are a couple of little people. Gustave Flaubert is not a little person. But, because he is a realist and does not believe in 'heroes', Flaubert insists on pouring his own deep and bitter tragic consciousness into the little skins of the country doctor and his uneasy wife. The result is a discrepancy. *Madame Bovary* is a great book and a very wonderful picture of life. But we cannot help resenting the fact that the great tragic soul of Gustave Flaubert is, so to speak, given only the rather commonplace bodies of Emma and Charles Bovary. There's a misfit. And to get over the misfit you have to let in all sorts of seams of pity. Seams of pity which won't be hidden.

The great tragic soul of Shakespeare borrows the bodies of kings and princes—not out of snobbism, but out of natural affinity. You can't put a great soul into a commonplace person. Commonplace persons have commonplace souls. Not all the noble sympathy of Flaubert or Verga for Bovarys and Malavoglias can prevent the said Bovarys and Malavoglias from being commonplace persons. They were chosen because they *were* commonplace and not heroic. The authors insisted on the treasure of the humble. But they had to lend the humble by far the best part of their own treasure, before the said humble could show any treasure at all.

D. H. Lawrence. 'Giovanni Verga', Phoenix (1922).

REALISM AND STYLIZATION

'Is it because the novel, of all literary *genres*, is the freest, the most *lawless*,' held forth Edouard, ' . . . is it for that very reason, for fear of that very liberty (the artists who are always sighing after liberty are often the most bewildered when they get it), that the novel has always clung to reality with such timidity? And I am not speaking only of the French novel. It is the same with the English novel; and the Russian novel, for all its throwing off of constraints, is a slave to resemblance. The only progress it looks to is to get still nearer to nature. The novel has never known that "formidable erosion of contours," as Nietzsche calls it; that deliberate avoidance of life, which gave style to the works of the Greek dramatists, for instance, or to the tragedies of the French seventeenth century. Is there anything more perfectly and deeply human than these works? But that's just it—they are human only in their depths; they don't pride themselves on appearing so—or, at any rate, on appearing real. They remain works of art . . .

'Well, I should like a novel which should be at the same time as true and as far from reality, as particular and at the same time as general, as human and as fictitious as *Athalie*, or *Tartuffe* or *Cinna*.'

'And . . . the subject of this novel?'

'It hasn't got one,' answered Edouard brusquely, 'and perhaps that's the most astonishing thing about it. My novel hasn't got a subject. Yes, I know, it sounds stupid. Let's say, if you prefer it, it hasn't got *one* subject . . . "a slice of life," the naturalist school said. The great defect of that school is that it always cuts its slice in the same direction; in time, lengthwise. Why not in breadth? Or in depth? As for me I should like not to cut at all. Please understand; I should like to put everything into my novel. I don't want any cut of the scissors to limit its substance at one point rather than at another. For more than a year now that I have been working at it, nothing happens to me that I don't put into it—everything I see, everything I know, everything that other people's lives and my own teach me . . .'

'And the whole thing stylized into art?' said Sophroniska, feigning the most lively attention, but no doubt a little ironically. Laura could not suppress a smile. Edouard shrugged his shoulders slightly and went on:

'And even that isn't what I want to do. What I want is to represent reality on the one hand, and on the other that effort to stylize it into art of which I have just been speaking.'

'My poor dear friend, you will make your readers die of boredom,' said Laura; as she could no longer hide her smile, she had made up her mind to laugh outright.

'Not at all. In order to arrive at this effect—do you follow me? —I invent the character of a novelist, whom I make my central figure; and the subject of the book, if you must have one, is just that very struggle between what reality offers him and what he himself desires to make of it.'

> *André Gide*. Les Faux Monnayeurs (*1925*), *Part II, Chapter iii,*
> *transl. Dorothy Bussy* (*1952*).

TRUTH STRANGER THAN FICTION

'But it can't be too queer,' said Philip. 'However queer the picture is, it can never be half so odd as the original reality. We take it all for granted; but the moment you start thinking, it becomes queer. And the more you think, the queerer it grows. That's what I want to get in this book—the astonishingness of the most obvious things. Really any plot or situation would do. Because everything's implicit in anything. The whole book could be written about a walk from Piccadilly Circus to Charing Cross . . .

Aldous Huxley. Point Counter Point (*1928*), *Chapter xiv.*

NOT AN OBSERVER, BUT A CREATOR

'The essential point . . . is not to know whether a novelist may or may not portray a given aspect of evil. The essential point is to know at what altitude he is when he makes this portrayal and whether his art and his soul are pure enough and strong enough to make it without conniving at it. The more the modern novel plunges into human misery, the more are superhuman virtues demanded from the novelist. For example, to write the work of a Proust as it should be written would require the interior light of a Saint Augustine. Unfortunately, it is just the opposite that has happened, and we see the observer and the thing observed—the novelist and his subject—rivalling one another in degradation.'

This is what Jacques Maritain says, and everyone will agree that he puts the question very well: everyone, that is, except the novelist. However, he does not take into account the real point, since he neglects to consider the fundamental laws of novel-creation. He mentions the 'observer and the thing observed'. In fact he compares a novelist bending over the human heart with a physiologist over a frog or a guinea-pig. According to Maritain, the novelist is detached from his subject in the way the man in the laboratory is detached from the animal whose stomach he is deliberately dissecting. I, however, hold that the operation of the novelist is utterly different from that of the experimentalist. As far as the novel is concerned, Jacques Maritain has stopped at the old naturalistic ideas. It is a condition of art that the novelist should connive at the subject of his creation, in spite of Maritain's warning, for the real novelist is not an observer, but a creator of fictitious life. It is not his function to observe life, but to create it. He brings living people into the world; he does not observe them from some lofty vantage point. He even confuses and, in a way, loses his own personality in the subject of his creation, and his identification with it is pushed so far that he actually becomes his creation.

François Mauriac. God and Mammon (*first published 1929; English translation 1936*), *Chapter v.*

A DISCUSSION ABOUT CATEGORIES OF FICTION

(i) *Henry James dismisses them*

There is an old-fashioned distinction between the novel of character
and the novel of incident, which must have cost many a smile to the
intending romancer who was keen about his work. It appears to
me as little to the point as the equally celebrated distinction between
the novel and the romance—to answer as little to any reality. There
are bad novels and good novels, as there are bad pictures and good
pictures; but that is the only distinction in which I see any meaning,
and I can as little imagine speaking of a picture of character. When
one says picture, one says of character, when one says novel, one
says of incident, and the terms may be transposed. What is character
but the determination of incident? What is incident but the illustration of character? What is a picture or a novel that is *not* of character?
What else do we seek in it and find in it? It is an incident for a
woman to stand up with her hand resting on a table and look out
at you in a certain way; or if it be not an incident, I think it will be
hard to say what it is. At the same time it is an expression of character. If you say you don't see it (character in *that—allons donc!*)
this is exactly what the artist who has reasons of his own for thinking
he *does* see it undertakes to show you. When a young man makes up
his mind that he has not faith enough to enter the Church, as he
intended, that is an incident, though you may not hurry to the end
of the chapter to see whether perhaps he doesn't change once more.
I do not say that these are extraordinary or startling incidents. I
do not pretend to estimate the degree of interest proceeding from
them, for this will depend upon the skill of the painter. It sounds
almost puerile to say that some incidents are intrinsically much
more important than others, and I need not take this precaution
after having professed my sympathy for the major ones in remarking
that the only classification of the novel that I can understand is into
the interesting and the uninteresting.

The novel and the romance, the novel of incident and that of
character—these separations appear to me to have been made by
critics and readers for their own convenience, and to help them out
of some of their difficulties, but to have little reality or interest for
the producer, from whose point of view it is, of course, that we are
attempting to consider the art of fiction. . . The French, who have
brought the theory of fiction to remarkable completeness, have but
one word for the novel, and have not attempted smaller things in it,
that I can see, for that. I can think of no obligation to which the

'romancer' would not be equally held with the novelist; the standard of execution is equally high for each. . . .

. . . I have just been reading, at the same time, the delightful story of *Treasure Island*, by Mr. Robert Louis Stevenson, and the last tale from M. Edmond de Goncourt, which is entitled *Chérie*. One of these works treats of murders, mysteries, islands of dreadful renown, hairbreadth escapes, miraculous coincidences and buried doubloons. The other treats of a little French girl who lived in a fine house in Paris and died of wounded sensibility because no one would marry her. I call *Treasure Island* delightful, because it appears to me to have succeeded wonderfully in what it attempts; and I venture to bestow no epithet upon *Chérie*, which strikes me as having failed in what it attempts—that is, in tracing the development of the moral consciousness of a child. But one of these productions strikes me as exactly as much of a novel as the other; and having a 'story' quite as much. The moral consciousness of a child is as much a part of life as the islands of the Spanish Main.

> Henry James. '*The Art of Fiction*' (*1884*); reprinted in
> Partial Portraits (*1888*).

(ii) STEVENSON REMONSTRATES

The life of man is not the subject of novels, but the inexhaustible magazine from which subjects are to be selected; the name of these is legion; and with each new subject—for here again I must differ by the whole width of heaven from Mr. James—the true artist will vary his method and change the point of attack. That which was in one case excellence, will become a defect in another; what was the making of one book, will in the next be impertinent or dull. First each novel, and then each class of novels, exists by and for itself. I will take, for instance, three main classes, which are fairly distinct: first the novel of adventure, which appeals to certain almost sensual and quite illogical tendencies in man; second, the novel of character, which appeals to our intellectual appreciation of man's foibles and mangled and inconstant motives; and third, the dramatic novel, which deals with the same stuff as the serious theatre, and appeals to our emotional nature and moral judgment.

And first for the novel of adventure. Mr. James refers, with singular generosity of praise, to a little book about a quest for hidden treasure . . . in this elementary novel of adventure, the characters need to be presented with but one class of qualities—the warlike and formidable. So as they appear insidious in deceit and fatal in combat, they have served their end. Danger is the matter with which this class of novel deals; fear, the passion with which it idly trifles; and the characters are portrayed only so far as they realize the sense of danger and provoke the sympathy of fear. To add more traits, to be too clever, to start the hare of moral or intellectual interest while we are running the fox of material interest, is not to enrich but to stultify your tale. The stupid reader will only be offended, and the clever reader lose the scent.

The novel of character has this difference from all the others: that it requires no coherency of plot, and for this reason, as in the case of *Gil Blas*, it is sometimes called the novel of adventure. It turns on the humours of the persons represented; these are, to be sure, embodied in incidents, but the incidents themselves, being tributary, need not march in a progression; and the characters may be statically shown. As they enter, so may they go out; they must be consistent, but they need not grow. Here Mr. James will recognize the note of his own work: he treats, for the most part, the statics of character, studying it at rest or only gently moved; and, with his usual delicate and just artistic instinct, he avoids those stronger passions which would deform the attitudes he loves to study, and change his sitters from the humorists of ordinary life to the brute forces and bare types of more emotional moments. In his recent *Author of Beltraffio*, so just in conception, so nimble and neat in workmanship, strong passion is indeed employed; but observe that it is not displayed. Even in the heroine the working of the passion is suppressed; and the great struggle, the true tragedy, the *scène à faire*, passes unseen behind the panels of a locked door. The delectable invention of the young visitor is introduced, consciously or not, to this end: that Mr. James, true to his method, must avoid the scene of passion. I trust no reader will suppose me guilty of undervaluing this little masterpiece: I mean merely that it belongs to one marked class of novel, and that it would have been very differently conceived and treated had it belonged to that other marked class, of which I now proceed to speak.

I take pleasure in calling the dramatic novel by that name, because it enables me to point out a strange and peculiarly English misconception. It is sometimes supposed that the drama consists of incident. It consists of passion, which gives the author his opportunity; and that passion must progressively increase, or the actor, as the piece proceeded, would be unable to carry the audience from a lower to a higher pitch of interest and emotion. A good serious play must therefore be founded on one of the passionate *cruces* of life, where duty and inclination come nobly to the grapple; and the same is true of what I call, for that reason, the dramatic novel. I will instance a few worthy specimens, all of our own day and language: Meredith's *Rhoda Fleming*, that wonderful and painful book, long out of print and hunted for at bookstalls like an Aldine; Hardy's *Pair of Blue Eyes*; and two of Charles Reade's, *Griffith Gaunt* and *The Double Marriage*, originally called *White Lies* and founded (by an accident quaintly favourable to my nomenclature) on a play by Maquet, the partner of the great Dumas. In this kind of novel the closed door of *The Author of Beltraffio* must be broken open; passion must appear upon the scene and utter its last word; passion is the be-all and end-all, the plot and the solution, the protagonist and the *deus ex machinâ* in one. The characters may come anyhow upon the stage: we do not care; the point is that, before they leave it, they shall become transfigured and raised out of themselves by passion. It may be part of the design to draw them with detail; to depict a full-length character, and then behold it melt and change in the furnace of emotion. But there is no obligation of the sort; nice portraiture is not required; and we are content to accept more abstract types, so they be strongly and sincerely moved. A novel of this class may even be great, and yet contain no individual figure; it may be great, because it displays the workings of the perturbed heart and the impersonal utterance of passion; and with an artist of the second class it is, indeed, even more likely to be great, when the issue has been thus narrowed and the whole force of the writer's mind directed to passion alone. Cleverness again, which has its fair field in the novel of character, is debarred all entry upon this more solemn theatre. A far-fetched motive, an ingenious evasion of the issue, a witty instead of a passionate turn, offend us like insincerity. All should be plain, all straightforward to the end. Hence it is that, in *Rhoda Fleming*, Mrs. Lovel raises such resentment in the reader; her motives are too flimsy, her ways are too equivocal, for the weight and strength of her surroundings. Hence the hot indignation of the reader when Balzac, after having begun the *Duchesse de Langeais* in terms of strong if somewhat swollen passion, cuts the knot by the derangement of the hero's clock. Such personages and incidents belong to the novel of character; they are out of place in the high society of the passions; when the passions are introduced into art at their full height, we look to see them, not baffled and impotently striving, as in life, but towering above circumstance and acting substitutes for fate.

Robert Louis Stevenson. 'A Humble Remonstrance' (1884); reprinted in Memories and Portraits *(1887).*

III The Ethics of the Novel

THE NOVELIST AND THE YOUNG PERSON

(i)

... I thought the story, if written in an easy and natural manner, suitable to the simplicity of it, might possibly introduce a new species of writing, that might possibly turn young people into a course of reading different from the pomp and parade of romance-writing, and dismissing the improbable and marvellous, with which novels generally abound, might tend to promote the cause of religion and virtue.

> *Samuel Richardson. Preface to* Clarissa, the History of a Young Lady ... (*1747–8*).

(ii)

R. ... A decent young girl doesn't read love stories. If any such girl reads this one, in spite of its title, she is not to grumble about the harm it will have done her: she will be deceiving herself. The harm was done already; she has nothing left to risk.

N. Wonderful! Erotic writers all, welcome to the school-room. Here you are all completely vindicated.

R. Yes, so they are, if it is by their own heart and by the purpose of their writings.

N. Well, are you vindicated according to these conditions?

R. I have too much pride to answer that; but Julie[1] made a rule of her own for judging books. If you find it a good one, use it to judge this book by.

People have wanted to make novel-reading useful to the young; I can't think of anything more senseless: it's like setting fire to the house so that the fire-brigade can be called out. According to this nonsensical notion, instead of aiming the lesson of this kind

---

[1] The heroine of *La Nouvelle Héloise*.

of work at its true object, people aim the lesson at young girls,[1] not realizing that young girls play no part in the irregularities which they deplore. In general, their behaviour is regular, even if their hearts are unsound. They obey their mothers, waiting meanwhile until they can imitate them. When grown women do their duty, be sure that young girls won't fail in theirs.

Jean-Jacques Rousseau. Preface (1762) to
La Nouvelle Héloise (*1760*).

(iii)

Hortensius . . . If Rousseau intended by this work to give a check to this shameful intercourse of the sexes, so frequently practised on the Continent, under the specious name of gallantry, he is to be commended; and if it produced effects he did not forsee, he ought to be excused.

Euphrasia. I am sure Rousseau is much obliged to your sensible and polite apology for his *Eloise*. But after all the objections remain. It is a dangerous book to put into the hands of youth, it awakens and nourishes those passions, which it is the exercise of Reason, and of Religion also, to regulate, and to keep within their true limits. On this account I have often wished that the two first Volumes of *Eloise*, could be abridged and altered, so as to render them consistent with the unexceptionable morals of the two last.— I thought it might be possible to give a different turn to the story, and to make the two Lovers, stop short of the *act*, that made it criminal in either party to marry another, for were they not *actually wedded* in the sight of heaven? and could *Eloise* with any pretension to virtue, or to delicacy, give herself to another man?

If this insuperable objection was removed; then might the Lovers renew their friendship with honour and dignity on both sides, then might the husband in full confidence in his wife's principles, invite her friend, and even leave them together without appearing so justly-ridiculous in his conduct as he now does to impartial judges.

Hortensius. I like your plan, and advise you to make this alteration yourself.

Euphrasia. You must excuse me Sir,—I have not yet the presumption to attempt it, or to think myself able to do justice to Rousseau in such an alteration.—It must remain as it is, it has done all the mischief in its power to the youth of this generation; and the worst

[1] This applies only to modern English novels [Rousseau's footnote].

part of it is, that those who write only for depraved and corrupted minds, dare appeal to Rousseau as a precedent.

> *Clara Reeve.* The Progress of Romance (*1785*),
> *Vol. II, Evening ix.*

(iv)

Above all things let him[1] never touch a romance or a novel; these paint beauty in colours more charming than nature; and describe happiness that man never tastes. How delusive, how destructive are those pictures of consummate bliss. They teach the youthful mind to sigh after beauty and happiness which never existed; to despise the little good which fortune has mixed in our cup, by expecting more than she ever gave; and in general, take the word of a man who has studied nature more by experience than precept; take my word for it that books teach us very little of the world.

> *Oliver Goldsmith. Letter to the Reverend Henry Goldsmith (no date),*
> Miscellaneous Works (*1801*), *Vol. I.*

(v)

. . . I am, I own, no great believer in the moral utility to be derived from fictitious compositions; yet, if in any case a word spoken in season may be of advantage to a young person, it must surely be when it calls upon him to attend to the voice of principle and self-denial, instead of that of precipitate passion.

> *Sir Walter Scott. Introduction (1831) to*
> The Fortunes of Nigel (*1822*).

(vi)

There are many who would laugh at the idea of a novelist teaching either virtue or nobility,—those, for instance, who regard the reading of novels as a sin, and those also who think it to be simply an idle pastime. They look upon the tellers of stories as among the tribe of those who pander to the wicked pleasures of a wicked world. I have regarded my art from so different a point of view that I have ever thought of myself as a preacher of sermons, and my pulpit as one which I could make both salutary and agreeable to my audience. I do believe that no girl has risen from the reading of my pages less modest than she was before, and that some may have learned from them that modesty is a charm worth preserving. I

---

[1] i.e. Goldsmith's young nephew.

think that no youth has been taught that in falseness and flashness is to be found the road to manliness; but some may perhaps have learned from me that it is to be found in truth and a high but gentle spirit. Such are the lessons I have striven to teach; and I have thought that it might best be done by representing to my readers characters like themselves,—or to which they might liken themselves.

Anthony Trollope. An Autobiography (*1883*), *Chapter viii*.

(vii)

A certain institution in Mr. Podsnap's mind which he called 'the young person' may be considered to have been embodied in Miss Podsnap, his daughter. It was an inconvenient and exacting institution, as requiring everything in the universe to be filed down and fitted to it. The question about everything was, would it bring a blush into the cheek of the young person? And the inconvenience of the young person was, that, according to Mr. Podsnap, she seemed liable to burst into blushes when there was no need at all. There appeared to be no line of demarcation between the young person's excessive innocence, and another person's guiltiest knowledge. Take Mr. Podsnap's word for it, and the soberest tints of drab, white, lilac, and grey, were all flaming red to this troublesome Bull of a young person.

Charles Dickens. Our Mutual Friend (*1860*), *Chapter xi*.

(viii)

By what it shall decide to do in respect to the 'young' the great prose fable will, from any serious point of view, practically see itself stand or fall. What is clear is that it has, among us, veritably never chosen—it has, mainly, always obeyed an unreasoning instinct of avoidance in which there has often been much that was felicitous. While society was frank, was free about the incidents and accidents of the human constitution, the novel took the same robust ease as society. The young then were so very young that they were not table-high. But they began to grow, and from the moment their little chins rested on the mahogany, Richardson and Fielding began to go under it. There came into being a mistrust of any but the most guarded treatment of the great relation between men and women, the constant world-renewal which was the conspicuous sign that whatever the prose picture of life was prepared to take upon itself, it was not prepared to take it on itself not to be superficial. Its position became very much: 'There are other things don't you know? For heaven's sake let *that* one pass!' And to this wonderful propriety of letting it pass the business has been for these so many years—with the consequences we see to-day—largely devoted.

> Henry James. '*The Future of the Novel*', The International Library of Famous Literature, *Vol. XIV; reprinted in* The Future of the Novel (*New York, 1956*), *ed. Léon Edel.*

(ix)

Of all the compliments that can be paid to a writer, there is one especially that will make him glow with pleasure, namely: 'You are admired so much among the younger generation.' Then his head positively swells, for though he may seem to be detached, what he wants above all things is to get the attention of the younger generation, and if he does not do this he considers he has failed in his mission. Nothing matters to him except that. He has got to reach others, and particularly he has got to reach those who are still capable of being influenced and dominated, the younger mentalities which are hesitating and unformed. He wants to leave his mark on this living wax and imprint all that is best in him on those who are going to survive him. It is not enough for the writer who writes so as not to be alone merely to reach other people; he wants to make them replicas of himself: he wants his own image and likeness to be resurrected in them when he himself is in the grave. . . .

Unfortunately, readers who have attained the age of reason are often more dangerously disturbed by books than other readers. It is probably better to be read by little girls who have tea in the nursery and who do not know what evil is than by young people in full flush of youth. It would be difficult to imagine the sort of letters a writer can receive. After reading a book of mine called *Genetrix*, a boy once sent me a photograph with the words: 'To the man who nearly made me kill my grandmother.' In an accompanying letter he explained that the old lady resembled the heroine of *Genetrix* to such an extent that he had been on the very verge of strangling her during her sleep. How can readers like that be protected? Father Bethléem himself cannot do anything. The reading of imaginative literature should be forbidden to adults rather than to children.

> *François Mauriac.* God and Mammon (*first published, 1929; English translation, 1936*), *Chapter v.*

REFORMING THE WICKED READER

Every wicked reader will here be encouraged to a change, and it will appear that the best and only good end of a wicked mispent life is repentance; that in this, there is comfort, peace, and often-times hope, and that the penitent shall be returned like the prodigal, *and his latter end be better than his beginning.*

While these things, and such as these, are the ends and designs of the whole book, I think I need not say one word more as an apology for any part of the rest, no, nor for the whole; if discouraging every-thing that is evil, and encouraging everything that is virtuous and good; I say, if these appear to be the whole scope and design of the publishing this story, no objection can lie against it, neither is it of the least moment to inquire whether the colonel hath told his own story true or not; if he has made it a history or a parable, it will be equally useful, and capable of doing good; and in that it recom-mends itself without any other introduction.

> *Daniel Defoe. Preface to* The History and Remarkable Life of the Truly Honourable Colonel Jacque (*1722*).

GILDING THE PILL

In this general depravity, when even the pulpit has lost great part of its weight, and the clergy are considered as a body of *interested* men, the author thought he should be able to answer it to his own heart, be the success what it would, if he threw in his mite towards introducing a reformation so much wanted: and he imagined, that if in an age given up to diversion and entertainment, he could *steal in*, as may be said, and investigate the great doctrines of Christianity under the fashionable guise of an amusement, he should be most likely to serve his purpose; remembering that of the poet:

> A verse may find him who a sermon flies,
> And turn delight into a sacrifice . . .

> *Samuel Richardson. Post-script to* Clarissa, the History of a Young Lady . . . (*1747-8*).

. . . instruction without entertainment (were I capable of giving the best) would have but few readers. Instruction, Madam, is the pill; amusement is the gilding. Writings that do not touch the passions of the light and airy, will hardly ever reach the heart. Perhaps I have in mine been too copious on that subject; but it is a subject in which, at one time or another of their lives, all men and all women are interested, and more liable than in any other to make mistakes, not seldom fatal ones.

> *Samuel Richardson. Letter to Lady Elchin (22 September 1755*), Correspondence (*1804*).

USEFUL EXAMPLES PROVIDED

... nor do I, indeed, conceive the good purposes served by inserting characters of such angelic perfection, or such diabolical depravity, in any work of invention; since, from contemplating either, the mind of man is more likely to be overwhelmed with sorrow and shame than to draw any good uses from such patterns; for in the former instance he may be both concerned and ashamed to see a pattern of excellence in his nature, which he may reasonably despair of ever arriving at; and in contemplating the latter he may be no less affected with those uneasy sensations, at seeing the nature of which he is a partaker degraded into so odious and detestable a creature.

In fact, if there be enough of goodness in a character to engage the admiration and affection of a well-disposed mind, though there should appear some of those little blemishes *quas humana parum cavit natura,* they will raise our compassion rather than our abhorrence. Indeed, nothing can be of more moral use than the imperfections which are seen in examples of this kind; since such form a kind of surprise, more apt to affect and dwell upon our minds than the faults of very vicious and wicked persons. The foibles and vices of men, in whom there is great mixture of good, become more glaring objects from the virtues which contrast them and show their deformity; and when we find such vices attended with their evil consequence to our favourite characters, we are not only taught to shun them for our own sake, but to hate them for the mischiefs they have already brought on those we love.

Henry Fielding. Tom Jones (*1749*), *Book X, Chapter i.*

EXEMPLARY AMBITIONS ACHIEVED

If I have not succeeded in my endeavours to unfold the mysteries of fraud, to instruct the ignorant, and entertain the vacant; if I have failed in my attempts to subject folly to ridicule, and vice to indignation; to arouse the spirit of mirth, wake the soul of compassion, and touch the secret springs that move the heart; I have, at least, adorned virtue with honour and applause, branded iniquity with reproach and shame, and carefully avoided every hint or expression which could give umbrage to the most delicate reader. ...

Tobias Smollett. Preface to The Adventures of Ferdinand Count Fathom (*1753*).

NO POLITICS?

(i)

All that I am bound to do as a story-maker is, to make a story; I am not bound to reform the constitution of my country in the same breath, nor even (Heaven be thanked!) to overturn it, though that might be the easier task of the two, or, more properly speaking, one and the same thing in its consequences. Nature is my guide; man's nature, not his natural rights: the one ushers me by the straight avenue to the human heart, the other bewilders me in a maze of metaphysics.

Richard Cumberland. Henry (*1795*), *Book the Sixth, Chapter i.*

(ii)

Politics in a work of literature are like a pistol-shot in the middle of a concert, something loud and vulgar and yet a thing to which it is not possible to refuse one's attention.

Stendhal. La Chartreuse de Parme (*1839*), *Chapter xxiii,* transl. *C. K. Scott Moncrieff* (*1926*).

THE READER UNINTERESTED IN THE MORAL

The professed moral of a piece is usually what the reader is least interested in; it is like the mendicant, who cripples after some gay procession, and in vain solicits the attention of those who have been gazing upon it. Excluding from consideration those infamous works, which address themselves directly to awakening the grossest passions of our nature, we are inclined to think, the worst evil to be apprehended from the perusal of novels is, the habit is apt to generate an indisposition to real history, and useful literature; and that the best which can be hoped is, that they may sometimes instruct the youthful mind by real pictures of life, and sometimes awaken their better feelings and sympathies by strains of generous sentiment, and fictitious woe. Beyond this point they are a mere elegance, a luxury contrived for the amusement of polished life, and the gratification of that half love of literature which pervades all ranks in an advanced stage of society, and are read much more for amusement, than with the best hope of deriving instruction from them.

Sir Walter Scott. 'Fielding', Lives of the Novelists (*1827*).

ON NOT IMPALING THE BUTTERFLY

Many writers lay very great stress upon some definite moral purpose, at which they profess to aim their works. Not to be deficient in this particular, the author has provided himself with a moral,—the truth, namely, that the wrong-doing of one generation lives into the successive ones, and, divesting itself of every temporary advantage, becomes a pure and uncontrollable mischief; and he would feel it a singular gratification if this romance might effectually convince mankind—or, indeed, any man—of the folly of tumbling down an avalanche of ill-gotten gold, or real estate, on the heads of an unfortunate posterity, thereby to maim and crush them, until the accumulated mass shall be scattered abroad in its original atoms. In good faith, however, he is not sufficiently imaginative to flatter himself with the slightest hope of this kind. When romances do really teach anything, or produce any effective operation, it is usually through a far more subtle process than the ostensible one. The author has considered it hardly worth his while, therefore, relentlessly to impale the story with its moral as with an iron rod,—or, rather, as by sticking a pin through a butterfly,—thus at once depriving it of life, and causing it to stiffen in an ungainly and unnatural attitude. A high truth, indeed, fairly, finely, and skilfully wrought out, brightening at every step, and crowning the final development of a work of fiction, may add an artistic glory, but is never any truer, and seldom any more evident, at the last page than at the first.

> *Nathaniel Hawthorne. Preface to* The House of the Seven Gables (*1851*).

TRUTH IS BEST

Even the gentlemen of our age—this is an attempt to describe one of them, no better nor worse than most educated men—even these we cannot show as they are, with the notorious foibles and selfishness of their lives and their education. Since the author of Tom Jones was buried, no writer of fiction among us has been permitted to depict to his utmost power a man. We must drape him, and give him a certain conventional simper. Society will not tolerate the Natural in our Art. Many ladies have remonstrated and subscribers left me, because in the course of the story, I described a young man resisting and affected by temptation. My object was to say, that he had the passions to feel, and the manliness and generosity to overcome them. You will not hear—it is best to know it—what moves the real world, what passes in society, in the clubs, colleges, mess-rooms,—what is the life and talk of your sons. A little more frankness than is customary has been attempted in this story; with no bad desire on the writer's part, it is hoped, and with no ill consequence to any reader. If truth is not always pleasant; at any rate truth is best. . . .

William Makepeace Thackeray. Preface to Pendennis *(1850)*.

THE WRITER'S RESPONSIBILITY

But man or woman who publishes writings inevitably assumes the office of teacher or influencer of the public mind. Let him protest as he will that he only seeks to amuse, and has no pretension to do more than while away an hour of leisure or weariness—'the idle singer of an empty day'—he can no more escape influencing the moral taste, and with it the action of the intelligence, than a setter of fashions in furniture and dress can fill the shops with his designs and leave the garniture of persons and houses unaffected by his industry.

For a man who has a certain gift of writing to say, 'I will make the most of it while the public likes my wares—as long as the market is open and I am able to supply it at a money profit—such profit being the sign of liking'—he should have a belief that his wares have nothing akin to the arsenic green in them, and also that his con-tinuous supply is secure from a degradation in quality which the habit of consumption encouraged in the buyers may hinder them from marking their sense of by rejection; so that they complain, but pay, and read while they complain. Unless he has that belief, he is on a level with the manufacturer who gets rich by fancy-wares coloured with arsenic green. He really cares for nothing but his income. He carries on authorship on the principle of the gin-palace.

And bad literature of the sort called amusing is spiritual gin.

George Eliot. 'Leaves from a Note-book: Authorship',
The Impressions of Theophrastus Such *(1879)*.

AN ARGUMENT ABOUT ARTISTIC DETACHMENT

. . . I do not recognize my right to accuse anyone. I don't even think that the novelist should express his own opinion of the things of this world. He may communicate it, but I don't want him to state it. (This is part of my own particular aesthetic doctrine.) And so I limit myself to revealing things as they appear to me, and to explain-ing that which seems to me to be the truth. Never mind the con-

sequences! Rich or poor, victors or vanquished, I admit none of all
that. I want neither love, nor hate, nor pity, nor anger. As for
sympathy, that's different: one can never have enough of it . . .

Isn't it time to bring Justice into Art? The impartiality of painting
would then reach the majesty of the law,—and the precision of
science!

> Gustave Flaubert. Letter to George Sand (*10 August 1868*),
> Correspondance (*1903*).

I know you disapprove of the intervention of personal doctrine in
literature. Are you right? Isn't this lack of conviction rather than
aesthetic principle? One can't have any real philosophy without it
coming to light. I haven't any literary advice to give you. I've no
judgment to pass on your friends, the writers of whom you speak. I
told Goncourt myself all I thought; as for the others I firmly believe
that they have more learning and talent than I. Only I think there
is wanting in them, and in you especially, a sufficiently decided and
extensive vision of life. Art isn't simply painting. True painting,
moreover, is full of the spirit that moves the brush. Art isn't only
criticism and satire: criticism and satire paint only one aspect of
truth . . .

> George Sand. Letter to Gustave Flaubert (*18–19 December, 1875*),
> Correspondance (*1892*).

One must write for all those who long to read and who can profit
by good reading. So one must go straight to the highest morality
that one can find in oneself and make no mystery about the valuable
moral sense in one's work. People have found *Madame Bovary*
immoral. If one part of the public set up an outraged clamour, the
other better-balanced and more extensive part found in the book
a harsh and striking lesson directed at the woman without conscience or loyalty, and at vanity, ambition, unreason. They pitied
her, compelled by your art; but the lesson was still clear, and it
would have been so even more, it would have been clear to *everyone*,
if you had really wanted it to be, had you brought out more
definitely the opinion you held, and which ought to be held, of the
heroine, her husband, her lovers . . .

The reader turns away from a book where all the characters are
good without shades or weakness; he knows very well that this isn't
human. I believe that art, this special art of story-telling, is valueless
without conflict of character; but in that struggle I want to see good
triumph; that events may crush the upright man I allow, but he

must be neither dishonoured nor diminished, and go to the stake conscious that he is happier than his executioners.

George Sand. Letter to Gustave Flaubert (12 January 1876),
Correspondance (*1892*),

As to making known my own opinion about the characters I produce, no, no, a thousand times no! I cannot see that I have any right to do it. If the reader can't find in a book the moral that is to be found there, then either the reader is a fool or else the book is *false* in its exactness. For once anything is true, then it is good. Even obscene books are only immoral in that they are deficient in truth. Things don't happen 'like that' in real life.

And note that I loathe what it is fashionable to call 'realism' even though they set me up as one of its High Priests.

Gustave Flaubert. Letter to George Sand (6 February 1876),
Correspondance (*1900*).

HIGH MORAL PURPOSE OF THE NATURALISTS

They accuse us of immorality, we writers of the naturalist school; and they are right: we lack the morality of mere words. Our morality is what Claude Bernard has so precisely defined: 'The modern morality searches out the causes, desires to explain and act upon them; in a word, to master the good and the evil; to bring forth the one and develop it; to battle against the other, extirpate and destroy it.' The high and stern philosophy of our naturalistic works is admirably summed up in those few lines. We are looking for the causes of social evil; we study the anatomy of classes and individuals to explain the derangements which are produced in society and in man. This often necessitates our working on tainted subjects, our descending into the midst of human follies and miseries. But we obtain the necessary data so that by knowing them one may be able to master the good and the evil. Lo! here is what we have seen, observed and explained in all sincerity. Now it remains for the legislators to bring the good and develop it. No work can be more moralizing than ours, then, because it is upon it that the law should be based. How far are we from the tirades in favour of virtue which interest no one? Our virtue does not consist of words, but of acts; we are the active labourers who examine the building, point out the rotten girders, the interior crevices, the loosened stones, all the ravages which are not seen from the outside, and which can at any moment undermine the entire edifice. Is not this a work more truly useful, more serious and more worthy than that of placing oneself

96

on a rock, a lyre in one's hand, and striving to encourage men by a hullabaloo of deep-sounding words? Ah! what a parallel I could draw between the works of the romantics and the works of the naturalists! The ideal is the root of all dangerous reveries. The moment that you leave the solid ground of truth you are thrown into all kinds of monstrosities. Take the novels and the dramas of the romantic school; study them from this point of view; you will find there the most shameful subtleties of the *débauché*, the most stupefying insanities of mind and body. Without doubt these bad places are magnificently draped; they are infamous alcoves before which is drawn a silken curtain; but I maintain that these veils, these hidden infamies offer a much greater peril, insomuch that the reader may dream over them at his ease, enlarge upon them, and abandon himself to them as a delicious and permissible recreation. With the naturalistic writings this hypocrisy is impossible. These works may frighten, but they do not corrupt. Truth misleads no one. If it is forbidden to children it is the prerogative of men, and whoever makes himself familiar with it desires a certain profit therefrom. All this is a simple and irrefutable matter upon which all the world should agree. They call us corrupters; nothing can be more foolish. The corrupters are the idealists who lie.

> *Emile Zola. 'Lettre à la Jeunesse', Le Roman Expérimental (1880), transl. Belle M. Sherman (New York, 1893).*

FOUL TO TELL WHAT IS FALSE: UNSAFE TO SUPPRESS WHAT IS TRUE

There are two duties incumbent upon any man who enters on the business of writing: truth to the fact and a good spirit in the treatment. In every department of literature, though so low as hardly to deserve the name, truth to the fact is of importance to the education and comfort of mankind, and so hard to preserve, that the faithful trying to do so will lend some dignity to the man who tries it. Our judgments are based upon two things: first, upon the original preferences of our soul; but, second, upon the mass of testimony to the nature of God, man, and the universe which reaches us, in divers manners, from without. For the most part these divers manners are reducible to one, all that we learn of past times and much that we learn of our own reaching us through the medium of books or papers, and even he who cannot read learning from the same source at second-hand and by the report of him who can. Thus the sum of the contemporary knowledge or ignorance of good and evil is, in large measure, the handiwork of those who write. Those who write have to see that each man's knowledge is, as near as they can make it, answerable to the facts of life; that he shall not suppose himself an angel or a monster; nor take this world for a hell; nor be suffered to imagine that all rights are concentred in his own caste or country, or all veracities in his own parochial creed. Each man should learn what is within him, that he may strive to mend; he must be taught what is without him, that he may be kind to others. It can never be wrong to tell him the truth; for, in his disputable state, weaving as he goes his theory of life, steering himself, cheering or reproving others, all facts are of the first importance to his conduct; and even if a fact shall discourage or corrupt him, it is still best that he should know it; for it is in this world as it is, and not in a world made easy by educational suppressions, that he must win his way to shame or glory. In one word, it must always be foul to tell what is false; and it can never be safe to suppress what is true.

> *Robert Louis Stevenson. 'The Morality of the Profession of Letters'*
> *(1881); reprinted in* The Art of Writing *(1919).*

NATURAL TRUTH BETTER THAN DIDACTICISM

It may seem something of a paradox to assert that the novels which most conduce to moral profit are likely to be among those written without a moral purpose. But the truth of the statement may be realized if we consider that the didactic novel is so generally devoid of *vraisemblance* as to teach nothing but the impossibility of tampering with natural truth to advance dogmatic opinions. Those, on the other hand, which impress the reader with the inevitableness of character and environment in working out destiny, whether that destiny be just or unjust, enviable or cruel, must have a sound effect, if not what is called a good effect, upon a healthy mind.

Of the effects of such sincere presentation on weak minds, when the courses of the characters are not exemplary, and the rewards and punishments ill adjusted to deserts, it is not our duty to consider too closely. A novel which does moral injury to a dozen imbeciles, and has bracing results upon a thousand intellects of normal vigour, can justify its existence; and probably a novel was never written by the purest-minded author for which there could not be found some moral invalid or other whom it was capable of harming.

> *Thomas Hardy. 'The Profitable Reading of Fiction' (1888);*
> *reprinted in* Life and Art *(1925).*

THE ARTIST MUST SET THE QUESTION, NOT SOLVE IT

Specialists exist for special questions; it is their business to judge of the commune, the future of capitalism, the evil of drink, of boots, of the diseases of women . . . An artist must judge only of what he understands; his sphere is as limited as that of any other specialist—this I repeat and on this I always insist. That in his sphere there are no questions but merely answers can only be maintained by the man who has never written and knows nothing about imaginative work. An artist observes, selects, guesses, combines—these in themselves presuppose questions; if from the very first he had not put a question to himself, there would be nothing to divine nor to select. To be brief, I'll finish with psychiatry; to deny that artistic creation involves problems and purposes would be to admit that an artist creates without premeditation, without design, under a spell. Therefore if an artist boasted to me of having written a story without a previously settled design, but by inspiration, I should call him a lunatic.

You are right in demanding that an artist should take a conscious attitude to his work, but you confuse two conceptions: *the solution of a question and the correct setting of a question.* The latter alone is obligatory for the artist. In 'Anna Karenin' and in 'Onyeguin' not a single problem is solved, but they satisfy completely because all the problems are set correctly. It is for the judge to put the questions correctly; and the jurymen must decide, each one according to his taste.

> *Anton Chekhov. Letter to A. S. Souvorin (27 October 1888),*
> Life and Letters *(1925), transl. and ed. S. S. Koteliansky and Philip Tomlinson.*

IS IT GENUINE, IS IT SINCERE?

. . . Recognizing so promptly the one measure of the worth of a given subject, the question about it that, rightly answered, disposes of all others—is it valid, in a word is it genuine, is it sincere, the result of some direct impression or perception of life?—I had found small edification, mostly, in a critical pretension that had neglected from the first all delimitation of ground and all definition of terms. The air of my earlier time shows, to memory, as darkened, all round, with that vanity—unless the difference to-day be just in one's own final impatience, the lapse of one's attention. There is, I think, no more nutritive or suggestive truth in this connexion than that of the perfect dependence of the 'moral' sense of a work of art on the amount of felt life concerned in producing it. The question comes back thus, obviously, to the kind and degree of the artist's prime sensibility, which is the soil out of which his subject springs. The quality and capacity of that soil, its ability to 'grow' with due freshness and straightness any vision of life, represents, strongly or weakly, the projected morality. That element is but another name for the more or less close connexion of the subject with some mark made on the intelligence, with some sincere experience. By which, at the same time, of course, one is far from contending that this enveloping air of the artist's humanity—which gives the last touch to the worth of the work—is not a widely and wondrously varying element; being on one occasion a rich and magnificent medium and on another a comparatively poor and ungenerous one. Here we get exactly the high price of the novel as a literary form—its power not only, while preserving that form with closeness, to range through all the differences of the individual relation to its general subject-matter, all the varieties of outlook on life, of disposition to reflect and project, created by conditions that are never the same from man to man (or, so far as that goes, from man to woman), but positively to appear more true to its character in proportion as it strains, or tends to burst, with a latent extravagance its mould.

> Henry James. *Preface to* The Portrait of a Lady (*1881*); *first printed in the New York edition of the* Novels and Stories (*1907–17*), *Vol. IV.*

CHERISHING UNDYING HOPE

It must not be supposed that I claim for the artist in fiction the freedom of moral Nihilism. I would require from him many acts of faith of which the first would be the cherishing of an undying hope; and hope, it will not be contested, implies all the piety of effort and renunciation. It is the God-sent form of trust in the magic force and inspiration belonging to the life of this earth. We are inclined to forget that the way of excellence is in intellectual, as distinguished from emotional, humility. What one feels so hopelessly barren in declared pessimism is just its arrogance. It seems as if the discovery made by many men at various times that there is much evil in the world were a source of proud and unholy joy unto some of the modern writers. That frame of mind is not the proper one in which to approach seriously the art of fiction. It gives an author—goodness only knows why—an elated sense of his own superiority. And there is nothing more dangerous than such an elation to that absolute loyalty towards his feelings and sensations an author should keep hold of in his most exalted moments of creation.

To be hopeful in an artistic sense it is not necessary to think that the world is good. It is enough to believe that there is no impossibility of its being made so.

Joseph Conrad. 'Books' (1905); reprinted in Notes on Life and Letters (1921).

Action in its essence, the creative art of a writer of fiction may be compared to rescue work carried out in darkness against cross gusts of wind swaying the action of a great multitude. It is rescue work, this snatching of vanishing phrases of turbulence, disguised in fair words, out of the native obscurity into a light where the struggling forms may be seen, seized upon, endowed with the only possible form of permanence in this world of relative values—the permanence of memory. And the multitude feels it obscurely too; since the demand of the individual to the artist is, in effect, the cry 'Take me out of myself!' meaning really, out of my perishable activity into the light of imperishable consciousness.

Joseph Conrad. 'Henry James, An Appreciation' (1905); reprinted in Notes on Life and Letters (1921).

THUMBS OFF THE SCALE

If we think about it, we find that our life *consists* in this achieving of a pure relationship between ourselves and the living universe about us. This is how I 'save my soul' by accomplishing a pure relationship between me and another person, me and other people, me and a nation, me and a race of men, me and the animals, me and the trees or flowers, me and the earth, me and the skies and sun and stars, me and the moon: an infinity of pure relations, big and little, like the stars of the sky: that makes our eternity, for each one of us, me and the timber I am sawing, the lines of force I follow; me and the dough I knead for bread, me and the very motion with which I write, me and the bit of gold I have got. This, if we knew it, is our life and our eternity: the subtle perfected relation between me and my whole circumambient universe.

And morality is that delicate, for ever trembling and changing *balance* between me and my circumambient universe, which precedes and accompanies a true relatedness.

Now here we see the beauty and the great value of the novel. Philosophy, religion, science, they are all of them busy nailing things down, to get a stable equilibrium. Religion, with its nailed-down One God, who says *Thou shalt, Thou shan't,* and hammers home every time; philosophy, with its fixed ideas; science with its 'laws': they, all of them, all the time, want to nail us on to some tree or other.

But the novel, no. The novel is the highest example of subtle inter-relatedness that man has discovered. Everything is true in its own time, place, circumstance, and untrue outside of its own place, time, circumstance. If you try to nail anything down, in the novel, either it kills the novel, or the novel gets up and walks away with the nail.

Morality in the novel is the trembling instability of the balance. When the novelist puts his thumb in the scale, to pull down the balance to his own predilection, that is immorality.

The modern novel tends to become more and more immoral, as the novelist tends to press his thumb heavier and heavier in the pan: either on the side of love, pure love: or on the side of licentious 'freedom'.

The novel is not, as a rule, immoral because the novelist has any dominant *idea*, or *purpose*. The immorality lies in the novelist's helpless, unconscious predilection. Love is a great emotion. But if you set out to write a novel, and you yourself are in the throes of the great predilection for love, love as the supreme, the only emotion worth living for, then you will write an immoral novel.

> *D. H. Lawrence. 'Morality and the Novel' (1925); reprinted in* Phoenix *(1936).*

BEST TO BE WITHOUT ANY VIEWS

With the novel you can do anything: you can inquire into every department of life, you can explore every department of the world of thought. The one thing you cannot do is to propagandize, as an author, for any cause . . .

It is obviously best if you can contrive to be without any views at all: your business with the world is rendering, not alteration. You have to render life with such exactitude that more specialized beings than you, learning from you what are the secret needs of humanity, may judge how many white-tiled bathrooms are, or to what extent parliamentary representation is, necessary to the happiness of men and women. If, however, your yearning to amend the human race is so great that you cannot possibly keep your fingers out of the watchsprings there is a device that you can adopt.

Let us suppose that you feel tremendously strong views as to sexual immorality or temperance. You feel that you must express these, yet you know that, like, say, M. Anatole France, who is also a propagandist, you are a supreme novelist. You must then invent, justify, and set going in our novel a character who can convincingly express your views. If you are a gentleman you will also invent, justify and set going characters to express views opposite to those you hold . . .

> Ford Madox Ford. Joseph Conrad, A Personal Remembrance (*1924*), *Part III, Chapter ii.*

I have always had the greatest contempt for novels written with a purpose. Fiction should render, not draw morals. But when I sat down to write that series of volumes [i.e. the Tietjens novels] I sinned against my gods to the extent of saying that I was going —to the level of the light vouchsafed me—to write a work that should have for its purpose the obviating of all future wars.

> Ford Madox Ford. It Was the Nightingale (*1934*), *Part II, Chapter ii.*

HOW TO PRESENT IDEAS IN A NOVEL

(i)

. . . The introduction of the dramatic element, of the image, the picture, of description, of dialogue, seems to me indispensable in modern literature. Let us confess frankly that *Gil Blas* is wearisome as form: in the piling up of events and ideas there is something sterile. The idea personified in a character, shows a finer intelligence. Plato cast his psychological ethics in the form of dialogue.

> Honoré de Balzac. '*Etude sur H. Beyle*' (*1840*); *reprinted in* The Charterhouse of Parma (*1931*), *transl. C. K. Scott Moncrieff.*

(ii)

. . . All through my career as a writer, I have never taken *ideas* but always *characters* for my starting point.

> Ivan Turgenev. Letter to Leonid Polonsky (*27 February 1869*). See David Magarshack, Turgenev (*1954*), *Part III.*

. . . I must confess that I never attempted to 'create a character' if in the first place I had in mind an idea and not a living person.

> Ivan Turgenev. '*Concerning Fathers and Sons*' (*1868?*). *Ibid.*

(iii)

... Because a novel is a microcosm, and because man in viewing the universe must view it in the light of a theory, therefore every novel must have the background or the structural skeleton of some theory of being, some metaphysic. But the metaphysic must always subserve the artistic purpose beyond the artist's conscious aim. Otherwise the novel becomes a treatise.

> D. H. Lawrence. 'Study of Thomas Hardy', Chapter ix, Phoenix (1936).

(iv)

Never present *ideas* except in terms of temperaments and characters.

> André Gide. Logbook of The Coiners (1927), p. 2, transl. Justin O'Brien.

(v)

Novel of ideas. The character of each personage must be implied, as far as possible, in the ideas of which he is the mouthpiece. In so far as theories are rationalizations of sentiments, instincts, dispositions of soul, this is feasible. The chief defect of the novel of ideas is that you must write about people who have ideas to express —which excludes all but about ·01 per cent. of the human race. Hence the real, the congenital novelists don't write such books. But then I never pretended to be a congenital novelist.

The great defect of the novel of ideas is that it's a made-up affair. Necessarily; for people who can reel off neatly formulated notions aren't quite real; they're slightly monstrous. Living with monsters becomes rather tiresome in the long run.

> Aldous Huxley. Point Counter Point (1928), Chapter xxii.

POETIC JUSTICE

M. J. What is odd, but of course it isn't serious criticism, is the recoil of some reviewers from what they call 'the sorry spectacle of adult human nature' presented in your novels, as if they were a board examining the degrees of moral turpitude among a group of immigrants. Yours are not the *only* doubtful characters in fiction! And when characters are accepted, even the *New Statesman* 'violently hoped for a quite different, a more vindictive ending of *Elders and*

Betters.' Is it the old demand for what was called 'poetic justice', the calling in the world of fiction to redress the balance of the real world?

I. C. B. I should have said that there were a good many good people in my books, and this may mean that I hardly see eye-to-eye with the reviewers.' But I think that life makes great demand on people's characters, and gives them, and especially used to give them, great opportunity to serve their own ends by the sacrifice of other people. Such ill-doing may meet with little retribution, may indeed be hardly recognized, and I cannot feel so surprised if people yield to it.

I have been told that I treat evil-doing as if it were normal, and am not normally repelled by it, and this may be putting my own words in another form. As you say, there are many doubtful characters in other fiction. Something must happen in a novel, and wrong-doing makes a more definite picture or event. Virtue tends to be more even and less spectacular, and it does not command so much more sympathy, as is proved by the accepted tendency of the villain to usurp the hero's place.

The *New Statesman* wanted wickedness to be punished, but my point is that it is not punished, and that is why it is natural to be guilty of it. When it is likely to be punished, most of us avoid it. I do not think this desire is the old demand for poetic justice, any more than the normal demand for actual justice. In a book there hardly seems to be any difference.

> *Ivy Compton-Burnett. 'A Conversation Between I. Compton-Burnett and M. Jourdain',* Orion (*1945*).

MORAL TRAGEDY

There is a kind of tragedy, it seems to me, which has hitherto almost entirely eluded literature. The novel has dealt with the contrariness of fate, good or evil fortune, social relationships, the conflicts of passions and of characters—but not with the very essence of man's being.

And yet, the whole effect of Christianity was to transfer the drama on to the moral plane. But properly speaking there are no Christian novels. There are novels whose purpose is edification; but that has nothing to do with what I mean. Moral tragedy—the tragedy, for instance, which gives such terrific meaning to the Gospel text: 'If the salt have lost his flavour wherewith shall it be salted?'—that is the tragedy with which I am concerned.

> *André Gide. Les Faux Monnayeurs, Part I, Chapter xiii (1925), transl. Dorothy Bussy (1952).*

THE CHRISTIAN NOVELIST

If there is one dogma which has gained the support of the majority of writers in this century and the last, it is the dogma of the absolute independence of the artist. It seems to be agreed, once and for all, that a work of art has no object outside itself. It only counts in so far as it is gratuitous or useless: or anything written to prove a point or to be of use is disqualified from the realm of art. Gide says that 'the moral issue for the artist is not that he should present an idea that is useful but that he should present an idea well'.

But we can be sure that this would not have to be said so persistently and so often by some writers if it were not vigorously contradicted by others. In fact, from the other end of the literary world comes a ceaseless protest against the pretensions to absolute independence on the part of the artist. For example, when Ernest Psichari proclaims that one must write with fear and trembling under the eye of the Trinity, he is being the mouthpiece of all those who believe in the immortality of each individual soul, and therefore believe in the extreme importance of their writings as affecting each immortal destiny.

Then, between these two opposing camps, there is the huge crowd of novelists who fluctuate and hesitate. On the one hand they admit that their work is valuable only inasmuch as it apprehends living men in their completeness, in their heights and in their depths—the human creature as he is. They feel that any intervention in the unfolding of their characters—even to prove the truth of what they believe—is an abuse. They feel a sincere revulsion against falsifying life. On the other hand, they know that they are treading on dangerous ground, and that their intense desire to depict human emotions and passions may have an incalculable and permanent effect on the lives of many people.

Every novelist worthy of the name and every playwright who is a born Christian suffers from the torment of this dilemma. . . .

This question then emerges: Must one stop writing even if one feels deeply that writing is one's vocation and that literary creation is as natural as breathing? Perhaps some doctor holds the key to the enigma; perhaps somebody somewhere knows the way in which a scrupulous novelist can escape from these choices—these three choices of either changing the object of his observation or falsifying life or running the risk of spreading scandal and misery among his fellow-creatures.

We may as well admit that a writer who is torn by this problem is hardly ever taken seriously. On his left there is only mockery and shrugging of shoulders—a refusal to admit that such a problem really exists. People deny that an artist has any other duty than to realize and achieve a beautiful piece of work, or that he can have any other care than to approach as near as possible to psychological truth. On his right there is an even greater misunderstanding. There is a total ignorance of the fact that he has scruples or high motives at all. It is difficult not to have a choking feeling the first time pious reviewers treat you as a pornographer and accuse you of writing obscenity for the sake of making money. When I was young and naïve I felt an insuperable desire to pour out my heart to some distinguished and holy people about all these difficulties, but as soon as I had begun I realized that they made no essential distinction between me and, for instance, the author of the *Revue des Folies Bergères*. I am not really shocked by their attitude, for I can understand perfectly well that people who are specifically in charge of souls are faced with an infinite number of problems which are far more urgent to them than the aesthetic problem, and it would be ludicrous for me to feel indignant with them on the grounds that they do not consider aesthetics to be as important as I do. . . .

Bossuet said that there was no greater difference than the difference between living according to nature and living according to grace. If the novelist is religious he suffers from this divergence, which upsets all Christians, in an especially sharp and tragic way. How could he consent to silence? And if he cannot come to a solution on this point we must remember to take into account the poor and sordid motives which attach a man to his job—especially when his job, as with the job of literature, flatters his vanity and his liking for a halo and at the same time brings him various sorts of advantages. But the necessity which obliges a genuine man of letters to write must not be forgotten. He cannot not write. He follows a deep and imperative need. We cannot smother the restless and importunate germs inside us; they demand life and we cannot know beforehand what sort of souls they will have. Our sincerest critics ought to ponder and try to understand Goncourt's affirmation: 'One does not write the book one wants to.' No, we do not write the book we want to write; alas, we write the book we deserve to write. Our judges come down on us as though our work were entirely dependent on our own free will, as if we made a deliberate decision to write a good or a bad book, tell an edifying story or a scandalous one. They do not seem to have the remotest idea of the mysterious, unforeseeable and inevitable elements in all creative novel-writing. The urge to write in a man of letters ends up by becoming a monster-like necessity which cannot be frustrated. Some time ago there was an amusing drawing that a hat manufacturer used as an advertisement: it consisted of a machine with a live rabbit going into it at one end and hats coming out of it at the other. It is in this way that life, with all its hopes and sorrows, is engulfed by the novelist, and nothing can prevent a book emerging from this per-petual receiving of impressions. Even if he withdraws from the world and shuts his eyes and stops up his ears, his most distant past will begin to ferment. His childhood and youth alone is enough to provide a born novelist with an immense amount of literary nourishment. Nobody can stop the flow of the river which flows from us.

There is no doubt that our books have a deep resemblance to ourselves, and we can quite rightly be judged and condemned by them. Novalis' axiom, 'Character is destiny', has often been repeated. And so, just as there is a close bond between a man's character and what happens to him during his life, so there is a similar relationship between a novelist's character and the creatures and events brought into being by his imagination. This is not to say that he is any more the absolute master of these creatures and events than he is of the course of his own fate.

People of my calibre complicate the 'drama of the Catholic novelist'. The humblest priest would tell me, like Maritain: 'Be pure, become pure, and your work too will have a reflection in heaven. Begin by purifying the source and those who drink of the water cannot be sick . . .' And I give the last word to the priest.

> *François Mauriac.* God and Mammon (*first published, 1929;* *English translation, 1936*), *Chapter v.*

TAILPIECE

There is no such thing as a moral or an immoral book. Books are well written or badly written.

> *Oscar Wilde.* Preface *to* The Picture of Dorian Gray (*1891*).

Part Two

THE GENESIS OF A NOVEL

INTRODUCTION

AS WE HAVE SEEN, the novelist's search for the objectivity which he values is complicated by 'the struggle between what reality offers him and what he himself desires to make of it'.[1] It is further complicated by the fact that once he begins to create he has to contend with elements in his art which are outside the conscious control of the will. François Mauriac insists in *God and Mammon* that these elements limit the novelist's moral responsibility for what he writes:

Our judges come down on us as though our work were entirely dependent on our own free will, as if we made a deliberate decision to write a good or a bad book, tell an edifying story or a scandalous one. They do not seem to have the remotest idea of the mysterious, unforeseeable and inevitable elements in all creative novel-writing.[2]

M. Mauriac's discussion implies that the serious artist is bound to identify such incalculable impulses with his genuine creative self, and so do many of the comments which appear in this chapter under the following headings:

I The Novelist's Approach and Equipment
II Germination
III At Work: Effort and Inspiration

What is said in the last of these three sections briefly makes clear the conscious effort which the novelist's task requires, but it is left to the next (and lengthiest) chapter, 'The Craft of Fiction', to illustrate in detail the crucial importance of deliberate contrivance. The concern of the present commentary is with the novelist's more instinctive creative self and with his desire to preserve its integrity.

[1] See above, pp. 30, 79.   [2] See above, p. 108.

I   The Novelist's Approach and Equipment

OBVIOUSLY the novelist starts from experience, from 'some direct impression or perception of life', but it is only a degree less obvious that for experience to be of any use to him he must find some way of distancing it. Thus he is obscurely tempted both to live actively and variously and to stand aside and become a mere spectator; the one alternative increasing the experience available to him as an artist, but only at the risk of swamping and clogging the filter through which the experience eventually has to pass: the other alternative reducing the amount of experience in the interests of composure and proportion, but at the risk of threatening the vitality of the work in which the experience is to be embodied. The apparent dilemma exists for every creative writer but it especially concerns the novelist, in whose art 'the problem of the correspondence between the literary work and the reality which it imitates' is felt more starkly.[1] Of course the dilemma is more apparent than real because a particular novelist will incline one way or the other in accordance with his temperament, and the extent to which he can consciously modify a temperamental attitude to experience is limited.

This forking to left or right as directed by psychological disposition is noticed throughout the whole course of the novel's history, separating in their respective 'comprehensiveness' and 'exclusiveness' the novels of Fielding and Richardson, Scott and Jane Austen, Balzac and Flaubert, Tolstoy and Turgenev, H. G. Wells and Henry James. The sensitive discriminating art of such novelists as Jane Austen, Flaubert, Turgenev and Henry James—whether protected with unremitting vigilance in the respective fastnesses of Chawton, Croisset, Spasskoye or Rye—deliberately limits and excludes experience because its first concern is with order, harmony and pattern. On the other hand, Fielding and Smollett, Dickens and Balzac, Dostoevsky and Tolstoy, novelists who readily commit themselves to what Johnson's Imlac calls 'the current of life', crowd their canvases with character and incident, description and comment, risking incoherence and loss of intensity because in the end they care

---

[1] See above, pp. 22–3.

more for content and variety than for matters of style and 'form'.

The largely inborn predilections of a novelist in this matter are easily recognized in his work, but many novelists are quite explicit about where they stand. Fielding adds to the qualities which he invokes 'to direct my pen' a wide and immediate knowledge of every kind of human being

from the minister at his levee, to the bailiff in his sponging-house; from the duchess at her drum, to the landlady behind her bar. From thee only can the manners of mankind be known; to which the recluse pedant, however great his parts or extensive his learning may be, hath ever been a stranger.[1]

But the 'exclusive' writer is afraid that this degree of involvement may jeopardize his artistic vision by turning him into a 'victim of life'. Flaubert uses the phrase in his argument with his mother about the novelist's contact with actuality. 'If one gets mixed up with life,' he says, 'one cannot see it clearly: one suffers too much or enjoys it too much.'[2] The attitude expressed by George Sand when she writes about the artist's need 'to live according to his nature'—

for the man who likes strife, warfare; for the man who likes women, love; for someone old who likes nature as I do, travel, flowers, rocks, vast landscapes, children . . . everything that stirs one, that combats moral decline. . . .[3]

—is answered by Flaubert with the belief that

you will depict wine, women, love, war, glory on condition . . . that you will not be a drunkard, a lover, a husband or a soldier of the line.[4]

Turgenev, whom Flaubert greatly admired—'For a long time I have regarded you as my master', he wrote in 1863[5]—is ultimately in sympathy with this view, all the more perhaps because of his many distracting emotional entanglements. It was in his years of isolation at Spasskoye that he produced three of his best books, *A Nest of Gentlefolk* (1858), *On the Eve* (1859) and *Fathers and Sons* (1861). When he came away to live in the

---

[1] See below, p. 125.   [2] See below, p. 126.
[3] See below, pp. 126–7.   [4] See below, p. 126.
[5] See David Magarshack, *Turgenev* (1954), p. 237.

fashionable resort of Baden-Baden he wrote very little during his eight years there; what he did produce included *Enough: A Fragment from the Diary of a Dead Artist* (1864), which contained the passage,

. . . Stop rushing about, stop striving – it is time you shrank into yourself: it is time you took your head into your hands and told your heart to be still. . . .[1]

The Russian novelists usually insist on more direct contact with society than Flaubert needed. This is true even of Turgenev. In his 1852 review of *The Niece*, a novel by Countess Salias, he assures us that the greatest genius 'is always in touch with life in general' since a novel is 'a reflection of the elements of social life'.[2] His fellow-countryman, Dostoevsky, is 'driven to the conviction' that the artist must 'make himself acquainted, down to the smallest detail' with every aspect of 'that reality which he designs to show forth', and he believes that the only writer in Russia 'who is really remarkable in that respect' is Tolstoy.[3] Dostoevsky's French model 'in that respect' is Victor Hugo, a writer whom Flaubert once passionately admired and then bitterly rejected in a private statement to Madame Roger de Genettes, written in July 1862.

George Sand is right, of course, but she does not tell us much when she says that the artist should live 'according to his nature'. Fielding lives 'according to his nature' by mixing with all kinds of men: and Flaubert does so by remaining an observer, withdrawn, sceptical and more or less disengaged. The justification of both types of novelist is in their finished work, and different kinds of success are reached through the exuberance of the one and the fastidiousness of the other. Failures are equally characteristic. The inclusive writer forgets that his creative imagination is not equally stimulated by everything that happens to him, while the exclusive writer is in danger of cutting out experience until his private emotions and personal conflicts are his only remaining source of inspiration. Such an inclusive writer as Dickens, for instance, damages the fabric of his fantasy-world by attempting to portray the behaviour of the aristocracy, the feelings of ordinary people in

[1] Op. cit., p. 222. [2] Op cit., p. 143.
[3] See below, p. 127.

love, or the real ills of a changing society, subjects which do not call out his best gifts—indeed they emphasize his emotional and intellectual weaknesses and distract attention from the brilliance of his comic invention and creation of atmosphere. Flaubert, the 'exclusive' novelist, paralysed by his obsession with the 'two distinct personalities' which he discovers in himself (the Romantic and the encyclopaedic scientist), produces the sad, flat-toned, nerveless biography of Frédéric Moreau, the man to whom, as to James's hero in 'The Beast in the Jungle', 'nothing on earth was to happen'.

Yet it must be said that when the exclusive writer 'spins his web from his own inwards' his artistic conscience provides some safeguard against the unbalancing dangers of auto-biography. Such bitter little satires as Henry James's 'The Death of the Lion' or 'The Next Time', which mourn unrecognized talent and express their author's deep personal disappointment during the 1890's, are preserved by their artistic tact from the embarrassing subjectivity which distorts such wishful fantasies as Lawrence's *Aaron's Rod* (1922) and *The Plumed Serpent* (1926), or Rolfe's *Hadrian VII* (1904) and *The Desire and Pursuit of the Whole* (1934). So, too, *L'Education Sentimentale* can rise above its own *ennui* to the poignancy and universality of its memorable conclusion. Stendhal recognizes the value of a similar artistic scrupulousness when he tells his sister that a writer who wishes to express things which he feels to be profoundly important must practise the art of understatement, so that he seems to be 'trying to get them by unnoticed'.[1] His own novels owe their extraordinary effect of vigour and clarity to their strenuously disciplined expression of personal themes.

In spite of this it would be wrong to say that a novelist's impeccable technique is enough by itself to 'cut the umbilical cord binding the author to his work'. *Madame Bovary* is a superbly composed novel, but writers as diametrically opposed as James and Lawrence unite in recognizing that Flaubert has overburdened his heroine with significance.[2] Flaubert describes the book as 'pure invention' in a letter which also asserts that art should rise above personal feeling and emotional

---

[1] See below, p. 128.

[2] See above, pp. 77–8, and also Henry James, 'Gustave Flaubert', *Notes on Novelists* (1914).

susceptibility.[1] But he sets excessively narrow limits to his heroine's probable range of experience, stripping her of almost all ordinary human dignity and finally destroying her horribly, because he wants to emphasize the dangers inherent in a particular kind of romantic sensibility which he recognizes as a part of his own personality. '*Madame Bovary c'est moi*' is almost literally true, even if, in another sense, it indicates the belief which Flaubert expresses to George Sand:

We must, by an effort of the mind, go over to our characters, as it were, not make them come over to us.[2]

Even so, it is a measure of Flaubert's excellence as a novelist—some of its qualities are noticed in Maupassant's tribute[3]—that although Madame Bovary is portrayed as shallow and ignoble almost beyond belief, her story remains, in its controlled pity and pain, such a remarkable achievement.

Flaubert's compassionate insight is one of the personal disciplines which the novelist consciously seeks for the purification of his creative self. Personal involvement of some kind is unavoidable, even essential; therefore the perils of autobiographical feeling must be held in check. Not all novelists would agree with everything said by Tolstoy in the passage which I have headed 'The Voice of True Feeling',[4] but his belief that 'whatever the artist depicts . . . we see and seek only the soul of the artist himself' is echoed by writers remote from the missionary zeal which more and more informs his own theory and practice. For Stevenson 'the author's attitude' always comes first[5] and Henry James's description of 'the house of fiction'—one of the finest we have—draws our attention to the truth that neither subject nor literary form can have any significance without the presence of 'the watcher at the window' whose consciousness works on all it sees and presents to us its own version of reality.[6] It is for this reason that Tolstoy recommends the novelist to cultivate 'a clear, fresh view of the universe'[7] and Stevenson urges him to keep his mind 'supple, charitable and bright'.[8] James's writings are instinct with a particularly sensitive appre-

---

[1] See below, Part III, p. 271.
[2] See below, Part III, p. 271.
[3] See below, Part III, p. 272.
[4] See below, pp. 128-9.
[5] See below, p. 129.
[6] See below, pp. 131-2.
[7] See below, p. 131.
[8] See below, p. 129.

ciation of the values of compassion, charity and sympathy. Sayings of Hardy and Conrad emphasize the freely-playing sympathies of an imagination unfettered by fixed prejudices, while Arnold Bennett notes in his diary that the essential characteristic of the really great novelist is 'a Christ-like all-embracing compassion'.[1] In *A Treatise on the Novel* Mr. Liddell sets out Mr. T. S. Eliot's 'Eight Points of Humanism' and adds a ninth point of his own, which places Justice and Mercy among the essential virtues of the novelist.[2]

The cultivation of what may be called the more professional gifts of the novelist also requires self-discipline. 'Talent is a long patience' is the text from Buffon which Flaubert holds up before his young disciple, Maupassant.[3] Maupassant himself stresses how long and attentively the artist should look at everything around him.

Everything contains some element of the unexplored because we are accustomed to use our eyes only with the memory of what other people before us have thought about the object we are looking at. The least thing has a bit of the unknown in it. Let us find this. In order to describe a fire burning or a tree in a field, let us stand in front of that fire and that tree until they no longer look to us like any other fire or any other tree.[4]

Flaubert seems to think that the practice of self-discipline can create talent. 'If you have originality,' he told Maupassant, 'you must bring it out. If you haven't any, then you must acquire some.'[5] There are in fact novelists who by sheer hard work and concentrated application have turned themselves into craftsmen of more than ordinary competence. 'You have wit, description and philosophy—these go a good way towards the production of a novel,' G. H. Lewes told George Eliot in 1856. 'It is worth while for you to try the experiment.'[6] All that she then lacked, they both felt, was 'the highest quality of fiction—dramatic presentation' (this anticipates the self-exhortation which appears again and again in James's *Notebooks*: 'Dramatize! Dramatize!'[7]). As it turned out, George Eliot possessed

---

[1] See below, p. 133.   [2] See *A Treatise on the Novel*, pp. 53–61.
[3] See below, pp. 130–1.   [4] Ibid.   [5] Ibid.   [6] See below, p. 136.
[7] See, for example, *The Notebooks of Henry James*, p. 197, where James explores the possibilities of 'dramatizing' by 'illustrative action' the '*déchéance* of the aristocracy through its own want of imagination, of nobleness, of delicacy. . . .'

this power too. She and Lewes were right about its importance. Dramatic presentation is the one method by which the novelist can hope to objectify his experience successfully. In so far as it is a skill it may be acquired, but only by those who begin with a certain sympathetic receptiveness, a quality which in 'dedicated' novelists is close to the lack of individuality of Keats's 'chameleon poet'.

If there is any novelist likely to combine fullness of experience with artistic fastidiousness it is the man or woman who comes to novel-writing in later years after leading an active life; like Conrad, for example, or, among our recent contemporaries, the late Mr. Joyce Cary. Whether he is the form-worshipping artist in his lonely tower or the shoulder-rubbing producer of what James calls 'fluid puddings' with the 'strong rank quality' of experience,[1] the novelist, unlike the poet, has nothing to lose and everything to gain by starting late. As Auden says, any novelist

> Must struggle out of his boyish gift and learn
> How to be plain and awkward, how to be
> One after whom none think it worth to turn.
>
> For to achieve his lightest wish, he must
> Become the whole of boredom, subject to
> Vulgar complaints like love, among the Just
>
> Be just, among the Filthy, filthy too,
> And in his own weak person if he can
> Must suffer dully all the wrongs of man.[2]

II Germination

THE PRACTICE of the art of fiction offers the novelist two main sources of consolation and delight. There is the excitement of the process of 'germination' when the creative imagination is fertilized by the 'wind-blown particle;[3] and there is the subse-

---

[1] See below, Part III, p. 235.

[2] W. H. Auden, *Collected Shorter Poems*, 1930–44 (1950), p. 54.

[3] A novelist of course may seek and find a congenial subject, or decide to work up a background with which he is already familiar, but such work

quent elation of the inspirational self—George Eliot calls it the 'not-self', so different is it from normal experience[1]—descending on the artist to enable him to compose whole scenes and episodes apparently without taking thought. These moments when the novelist experiences the exhilaration of uncovenanted power compensate for the long intervals of dull, arduous toil, the mental and physical exhaustion of writing thousands of words 'in the best order'.

What novelists tell us about the 'germination' of a novel shows that most of them cannot explain exactly what has happened. Dickens's unenlightening 'I thought of Mr. Pickwick' recalls Richardson's 'Hence sprung Pamela'.[2] The moment came for Dickens while he was devising narratives for a series of sporting sketches and for Richardson while he was compiling a volume of letters on etiquette; but neither occupation explains why such picturesque abstractions as Pickwick and Pamela should present themselves to their creators. Turgenev's experience, as described by Henry James, seems to have been of a similar ultimately mysterious kind. Figures offered themselves spontaneously to his imagination as '*disponibles*'.[3] Already well defined in, let us say, appearance and gesture, they haunted him until he evolved on their behalf situations and circumstances in which they could fully come alive. James interprets him as saying,

. . . As for the origins of one's wind-blown germs themselves, who shall say, as you ask, where *they* come from? We have to go too far back, too far behind to say. Isn't it all we can say that they come from every quarter of heaven, that they are *there* at almost every turn of the road? They accumulate, and we are always picking them over, selecting among them. They are the breath of life—by which I mean that life, in its own way, breathes them upon us.[4]

James himself talks of

the merest grain, the speck of truth, of beauty, of reality, scarce visible to the common eye,[5]

only prepares for the real germination when the author is 'surprised' by his subject.

[1] See below, p. 155.   [2] See below, pp. 134-5.
[3] See Part III below, pp. 286-7.   [4] Ibid.
[5] See below, pp. 138-9.

which provides the novelist with his 'germ'. Conrad tells us that 'the first hint for *Nostromo*' came to him 'in the shape of a vagrant anecdote, completely destitute of valuable details'.[1] The mysterious moment is full of delight. At the touch of the starched napkin on his mouth Proust is transported to the Balbec of his youth and experiences a moment of pure joy, 'the instant to which my whole life has doubtless aspired'.[2] 'What is it to be?' asks Virginia Woolf, an adventurer about to embark on *The Waves*: 'Anything may be out of the window—a ship— a desert—London.'[3] We are reminded here of the unpredictability of the course followed by the novelist's imagination once it has been stimulated. *The Waves* grew out of images of moths mingling with 'the ship, the night, etc., all flowing together' while 'A man and a woman are to be sitting at a table talking', but these images have altogether vanished from the finished work.[4] Another classic example is, of course, Henry James's *The Spoils of Poynton*, a novel which illustrates how the imagination can transform a piece of trivial gossip into a subtle statement about destructive pride released by great possessions.[5] But it also shows how mercilessly the novelist's constructive and imaginative powers can be subjugated by a limiting type of experience. James's exodus from London and settlement at Rye was an admission that regular attendance at the dinner-tables of late-Victorian high society was no way of safeguarding the best in his creative self or of placing that self where it might receive the most valuable 'wind-blown particles'. His finest work was written in the seclusion of Rye, and it is significant that the real inspiration of such books as *The Wings of the Dove*, *The Ambassadors* and *The Ivory Tower* was rooted in his past life and in long memories of the distant American scene.

[1] See below, pp. 139–40.
[2] See below, pp. 141–2.   [3] See below, pp. 142–3.
[4] See Virginia Woolf, *A Writer's Diary* (1953), pp. 108, 142–3, 146, 148–9, 157–9, 162, 163–6, 169.
[5] See below, pp. 138–9, and *The Notebooks of Henry James*, pp. 81, 136–8, 198–200, 207–12, 214–20, 247–56.

III At Work: Effort and Inspiration

ONCE THE NOVELIST settles to the serious task of composition, his initial delight is likely to fade. Flaubert describes the artist as a 'monstrosity, something outside nature',[1] and as we listen to him describing the anguish of writing, an anguish often prolonged for weeks and months, we find it easy to agree. Flaubert's entire correspondence exhales the atmosphere of a 'harsh existence, devoid of all outward joy', an existence in which he is sustained only by his 'rage' of composition and by some twenty-five satisfactory pages finally achieved after six weeks of unremitting toil.[2] We find Dostoevsky describing himself as working 'nervously with pain and travail of soul' and Tolstoy telling us that he leaves 'a piece of flesh in the inkpot' every time he dips his pen.[3] Conrad takes 'twenty months, neglecting the common joys of life' to wrestle with *Nostromo*:

. . . it is difficult to characterize otherwise the intimacy and the strain of a creative effort in which mind and will and conscience are engaged to the full, hour after hour, day after day, away from the world, and to the exclusion of all that makes life really lovable and gentle. . . .[4]

It is not only the meticulous stylists and fastidious craftsmen who suffer like this. Even Richard Cumberland thinks of himself in his 'darker intervals' as 'a carrier's horse, whose slow and heavy pace argues the load he draws, and the labour he endures'.[5] The business-like Trollope feels imprisoned by his desk as he produces his merciless '250 words every quarter of an hour'.[6] Dickens is driven nearly to breaking-point to meet the demands of serial publication.[7]

Then unpredictably the god descends again to relieve the inhuman strain and the writer recaptures some of the joy of his

[1] See below, p. 126.   [2] See below, pp. 148–9.
[3] See below, pp. 149–50.   [4] See below, p. 152.
[5] See below, p. 145.   [6] See below, pp. 147–8.
[7] See, for example, John Forster, *The Life of Charles Dickens* (1872–4), Vol. II, Chapter xiii.

original conception. James expresses a typical rush of gratitude and relief:

... the prospect clears and blushes, and my poor blest old Genius pats me so admirably and lovingly on the back that I turn, I screw round and bend my lips to passionately in my gratitude kiss its hand ...[1]

George Eliot writes the interview between Dorothea and Rosamund in *Middlemarch* without

alteration or erasure, in an intense state of excitement and exaltation, feeling herself entirely possessed by the feelings of the two women.[2]

Because these visitations are so much outside the ordinary range of experience Flaubert is at pains to distinguish 'inner vision' from what is ordinarily termed 'hallucination'. 'I know both states very well', he tells the critic, Taine:

In a state of hallucination properly so called there is always terror ... In the poetic vision, on the contrary there is joy; it is something that enters into you. ...[3]

Yet possession by the inspirational self may be disquieting. Charlotte Brontë speaks of the creative gift as something which the writer may be unable to master, 'something that, at times, strangely wills for itself'. When it takes command it rejects uncongenial rules and restrictions; it will

no longer consent to 'harrow the valleys, or be bound with a band in the furrow'.[4]

Charlotte Brontë is thinking uneasily of the power which impelled her sister to create Heathcliff, a figure to her so strange and so unaccountable. But Emily Brontë possessed a constructive power and a gift for organization which usually secured for her the direction of her 'inner vision', and she knew that in the end the inspirational self had to be trusted. 'What interests me', writes Virginia Woolf as she looks back over the final stages of composition of *The Waves*, is

the freedom and boldness with which my imagination picked up,

---

[1] See below, p. 157.   [2] See below, p. 155.
[3] See below, p. 155.   [4] See below, p. 154.

used and tossed aside all the images, symbols which I had prepared.
I am sure that this is the right way of using them—not in set pieces
· .. Thus I hope to have kept the sound of the sea and the birds,
dawn and garden subconsciously present, doing their work
underground. ....[1]

This quotation may be read side by side with E. M. Forster's
account of 'rhythm' and 'pattern', which appears in the next
chapter as part of the novelist's discussion about his structural
problems.[2] Both passages show a distrust of mechanical
systems of organization and set the same kind of value on the
uncalculated, compulsive movements of the individual
imagination. 'What about the creative state?' asks Mr. Forster
on another occasion:

In it a man is taken out of himself. He lets down as it were a bucket
into his subconscious and draws up something which is normally
beyond his reach. He mixes this thing with his normal experiences,
and out of the mixture he makes a work of art. ... And when the
process is over, when the picture or symphony or lyric or novel (or
whatever it is) is complete, the artist, looking back on it, will wonder
how on earth he did it. And indeed he did not do it on earth.[3]

This exaggerates by slighting the work that must go into the
studied shaping of what luck gives the artist-creator—but the
exaggeration may be pardoned if it brings out the importance
for the novelist of 'possession' by his own imagination.

[1] See below, pp. 157–8.   [2] See Part III below, pp. 237–40.
[3] See below, p. 158.

TEXT

I The Novelist's Approach and Equipment

INVOKING ASSISTANCE

. . . whose assistance shall I invoke to direct my pen?

First, Genius; thou gift of Heaven; without whose aid in vain we struggle against the stream of nature . . .

And thou, almost the constant attendant on true genius, Humanity, bring all thy tender sensations . . . From these alone proceed the noble, disinterested friendship, the melting love, the generous sentiment, the ardent gratitude, the soft compassion, the candid opinion; and all those strong energies of a good mind, which fill the moistened eyes with tears, the glowing cheeks with blood, and swell the heart with tides of grief, joy and benevolence.

And thou, O Learning! (for without thy assistance nothing pure, nothing correct, can genius produce) do thou guide my pen . . .

Lastly, come Experience, long conversant with the wise, the good, the learned, and the polite. Nor with them only, but with every kind of character, from the minister at his levée, to the bailiff in his sponging-house; from the duchess at her drum, to the landlady behind her bar. From thee only can the manners of mankind be known; to which the recluse pedant, however great his parts or extensive his learning may be, hath ever been a stranger.

Come all these, and more, if possible; for arduous is the task I have undertaken; and, without all your assistance, will, I find, be too heavy for me to support.

> *Henry Fielding.* The History of Tom Jones, A Foundling *(1749), Book XIII, Chapter i.*

IN THE DESTRUCTIVE ELEMENT IMMERSE?

(i)

Whenever anyone—however unimportant or great—wants to concern himself with the works of God he must begin, if only for reasons

125

of health, by putting himself in a position where he cannot be their victim. You will depict wine, love, women, glory, on condition, my good fellow, that you will not be a drunkard, a lover, a husband, or a soldier of the line. If one gets mixed up with life, one cannot see it clearly; one suffers too much, or enjoys it too much. The artist, in my opinion, is a monstrosity, something outside nature. All the misfortunes with which Providence overwhelms him derive from his stubborn attempt to deny this axiom. He suffers from it, and makes others suffer too. Ask women who have loved poets about this, and men who have loved actresses. So (this is the conclusion) I am resigned to living as I have done till now, alone, with a host of great men for society, with my bear's skin, being myself a bear, etc. I don't give a damn for the world, for the future, for what people say, for any settled establishment whatever, even for literary fame—which once upon a time made me spend so many sleepless nights imagining it. There, that's how I am; such is my character.

> *Gustave Flaubert. Letter to his mother (15 December 1850),*
> Correspondance (*1900*).

(ii)

In a week or so, I go to New York, to bury myself in a third-story room, and work and slave on my 'whale' while it is driving through the press. *That* is the only way I can finish it now,—I am so pulled hither and thither by circumstances. The calm, the coolness, the silent grass-growing mood in which a man *ought* always to compose, —that, I fear, can seldom be mine. Dollars damn me; and the malicious Devil is forever grinning in upon me, holding the door ajar. My dear Sir, a presentiment is upon me,—I shall at last be worn out and perish, like an old nutmeg-grater, grated to pieces by the constant attrition of the wood, that is, the nutmeg. What I feel most moved to write, that is banned,—it will not pay. So the product is a final hash, and all my books are botches.

> *Herman Melville. Letter to Nathaniel Hawthorne (June 1851).*
> *See Julian Hawthorne,* Nathaniel Hawthorne and his Wife,
> A Biography (*1885*), *Vol. I.*

(iii)

I believe that the artist must live as much as possible according to his nature. For the man who likes strife, warfare; for the man who likes women, love; for someone old who likes nature, as I do, travel, flowers, rocks, vast landscapes, children too, a family—everything that stirs one, that combats moral decline.

I believe that art needs a palette always overflowing with colour, soft or violent according to the subject of the painting; that the artist is an instrument on which everything must play before he can play on others; but all this is perhaps not applicable to a mind like yours, which has acquired so much and has nothing further to do but sort it all out. I shall insist only on this: that physical well-being is essential to moral well-being, and I dread on your behalf a decline of health that will force you to hold up your work and let it grow cold.

> *George Sand. Letter to Gustave Flaubert (31 December 1867),* Correspondance (*1892*).

(iv)

. . . I have been driven to the conviction that an artist is bound to make himself acquainted, down to the smallest detail, not only with the technique of writing, but with everything—current no less than historical events—relating to that reality which he designs to show forth. We have only one writer who is really remarkable in that respect: it is Count Leo Tolstoy. Victor Hugo whom I extraordinarily admire as a novelist (only think: Tchutchev, who is now dead, once got positively angry with me on account of this view of Hugo, and said that my 'Raskolnikov' was much greater than Hugo's 'Misérables')—is certainly prone to be too long-winded in his description of details, but he gives us most marvellous effects of observation, which would have been lost to the world but for him. As I am now purposing to write a very big novel, I must devote myself most especially to the study of actuality: I don't mean, actuality in the literal sense, for I am fairly well versed in that but certain peculiarities of the present moment . . .

> *Feodor Dostoevsky. Letter to Madame Ch. D. Altschevsky* (*9 April 1876*), Letters (1914), *transl. Ethel Colburn* *Mayne.*

THE VOICE OF TRUE FEELING

(i)

The more one delves into one's soul, the more one dares to express the most secret thought, then the more one shrinks when it is written down, it seems so strange, and it is this strangeness which is its merit. It is for this reason that it is original, and if it is true as well, if your words really indicate what you feel, then it is sublime. Write me exactly what you feel.

There is a risk in this habit which one has to take. One may not find it in oneself to write just what one feels, and following this principle, one behaves as if one did not believe it. This is a mistake; we must write it coolly at all times. For example, I was never less inclined to write than at this moment. I've worked like a demon all morning copying out letters vilely garbled in thought and style; then for a quarter of an hour I read a horribly turgid book (that is, a book where the expression exaggerated the thoughts and feelings of the writer).[1] This fault is the worst of all in my view; it is the one that most blunts the sensibility. One should not write unless one has important or profoundly beautiful things to say, but then one must say them with the utmost simplicity, as though one were trying to get them by unnoticed. This is the opposite of what all the fools of this century do, but it is what all great men accomplish.

> *Stendhal. Letter to his sister, Pauline (20 August 1805),* Correspondance (*1908*).

(ii)

For my work on art I diligently and with much labour read this winter the famous novels and stories which are praised by all of Europe, those by Zola, Bourget, Huysmans, Kipling. At the same time I came across a story in a children's periodical, by an entirely unknown writer, which told of the preparations which were being made for Easter in a widow's poor family. The story tells with what difficulty the mother obtained some white flour, which she spread on the table, in order to knead it, after which she went to fetch some yeast, having told the children not to leave the room and to watch the flour. The mother went away, and the neighbouring children ran with a noise under the window, inviting them to come out into the street to play. The children forgot their mother's command, ran out into the street, and engaged in a game. The mother returns with yeast; in the room a hen is on the table, scattering on the earth floor the last of the flour to her chicks, which pick it out of the dust. The mother in despair scolds the children, the children yell. And the mother pities her children; but there is no white flour left, and, to find help out of the calamity, the mother decides that she will bake Easter bread out of sifted black flour, smearing it with the white of an egg, and surrounding it with eggs.

[1] Madame de Staël, *De l'influence des Passions sur le Bonheur* (1796).

'Black bread—the white loaf's grandfather,' the mother quotes the proverb to the children to console them for not having an Easter bread baked of white flour. And the children suddenly pass from despair to joyous raptures, and in different voices repeat the proverb and with greater merriment wait for the Easter bread.

Well? The reading of the novels and stories by Zola, Bourget, Huysmans, Kipling, and others, with the most pretentious of subjects, did not move me for a moment; I was, however, all the time annoyed at the authors, as one is annoyed at a man who considers you so naïve that he does not even conceal that method of deception with which he wishes to catch you. From the very first lines you see the intention with which the story is written, and all the details become useless, and you feel annoyed. Above all else, you know that the author has no other feeling than the desire to write a story or a novel, and that he never had any other feeling. And so you receive no artistic impression whatever; but I could not tear myself away from the story of the unknown author about the children and the chicks, because I was at once infected by the sensation which obviously the author had gone through, experienced, and conveyed.

Leo Tolstoy. 'What is Art?' (1897), Complete Works (1904), Vol. XXII, transl. Leo Weiner.

ONLY ONE TOOL IN THE WORKSHOP

In all works of art, widely speaking, it is first of all the author's attitude that is narrated, though in the attitude there be implied a whole experience and a theory of life. An author who has begged the question and reposes in some narrow faith cannot, if he would, express the whole or even many of the sides of this various existence; for, his own life being maim, some of them are not admitted in his theory, and were only dimly and unwillingly recognized in his experience. Hence the smallness, the triteness, and the inhumanity in works of merely sectarian religion; and hence we find equal although unsimilar limitation in works inspired by the spirit of the flesh or the despicable taste for high society. So that the first duty of any man who is to write is intellectual. Designedly or not, he has so far set himself up for a leader of the minds of men; and he must see that his own mind is kept supple, charitable and bright. Everything but prejudice should find a voice through him; he should see the good in all things; where he has even a fear that he does not wholly understand, there he should be wholly silent; and he should recognize from the first that he has only one tool in his workshop, and that tool is sympathy.

> Robert Louis Stevenson. '*The Morality of the Profession of Letters*' (*1881*); *reprinted in* The Art of Writing (*1919*).

LEARNING THE LESSON OF THE MASTER

... Flaubert, whom I used to see sometimes, took a liking to me. I plucked up courage to submit some essays to him. He read them kindly and said: 'I don't know whether you will have any talent. What you brought me shows a certain intelligence, but don't you forget this, young man: talent—as Buffon says—is nothing other than a long patience. Work.'

I worked, and often I went back to see him, realising that I pleased him because he began to call me, humorously, his disciple.

For seven years I wrote verse, I wrote short tales, I wrote *nouvelles*, I even wrote an execrable play. None of these survive. The master read them all, and then at dinner on the following Sunday he would expand his critical comments, strengthening in me, bit by bit, two or three principles which summarise his long and patient teaching. 'If you have any originality,' he would say, 'you must bring it out. If you haven't any, then you must acquire some.'

—Talent is a long patience.—It involves looking at everything one wants to describe long enough, and attentively enough, to find in it some aspect that no one has yet seen or expressed. Everything contains some element of the unexplored because we are accustomed to use our eyes only with the memory of what other people before us have thought about the object we are looking at. The least thing has a bit of the unknown in it. Let us find this. In order to describe a fire burning or a tree in a field, let us stand in front of that fire and that tree until they no longer look to us like any other fire or any other tree.

That is how one becomes original.

Having stated this truth, that in the entire world there are no two grains of sand, no two flies, no two hands or noses, exactly alike— he would then make me describe, in a few sentences, a being or an object in such a way as to particularise it distinctly and to distinguish it from all other beings, or all other objects, of the same race or kind.

He would say to me, 'When you pass a grocer sitting at his door, or a concierge smoking his pipe, or a cab-stand, you must show me that grocer and that concierge, their attitude, their whole physical appearance, including as well—indicated by the aptness of your image—their entire moral nature, in such a way that I shan't confuse them with any other grocer or any other concierge; and you must make me see, with a single word, in what way one cab-horse is totally unlike fifty others that go before and after it.'

I have dealt elsewhere with his ideas on style. They are very closely connected with the theory of observation that I have just set down. . . .[1]

Guy de Maupassant. 'Le Roman', Preface to
Pierre et Jean (*1888*).

THE SOUL OF THE ARTIST

People little sensitive to art often think that a work of art possesses unity when the same personages act in it from beginning to end, when all is built on one and the same fundamental plan of incidents, or when the life of one and the same man is described. This is mistaken; and the unity appears true only to the superficial observer. The cement which binds together every work of art into a whole and thereby produces the effect of life-like illusion, is not the unity of persons and places, but that of the author's independent moral relation to the subject. In reality, when we read or examine the art-work of a new author, the fundamental questions which arise in our mind are always of this kind: 'Well, what sort of a man are you? What distinguishes you from all the people I know, and what information can you give me, as to how we must look upon our life.' Whatever the artist depicts, whether it be saints or robbers, kings or lackeys, we seek and see only the soul of the artist himself. And if he be an established writer, with whom we are already acquainted, the question is no longer: 'Who are you?' but 'Well, what more can you tell me that is new? From what standpoint will you now illuminate life for me?' Therefore, a writer who has not a clear, definite and fresh view of the universe, and especially a writer who does not even consider this necessary, cannot produce a work of art. He may write much and beautifully, but a work of art will not result So it was with Maupassant and his novels.

Leo Tolstoy. Preface to Nikirov's Russian translation of Maupassant;
reprinted in the English translation as Guy de Maupassant (*1896*).

THE WATCHER AT THE WINDOW

The house of fiction has in short not one window, but a million—a number of possible windows not to be reckoned, rather; every one

---

[1] See below, Part III, pp. 317–18.

of which has been pierced, or is still pierceable, in its vast front, by the need of the individual vision and by the pressure of the individual will. These apertures, of dissimilar shape and size, hang so, all together, over the human scene that we might have expected of them a greater sameness of report than we find. They are but windows at the best, mere holes in a dead wall, disconnected, perched aloft; they are not hinged doors opening straight upon life But they have this mark of their own that at each of them stands a figure with a pair of eyes, or at least with a field-glass, which forms, again and again for observation, a unique instrument, insuring to the person making use of it an impression distinct from every other. He and his neighbours are watching the same show, but one seeing more where the other sees less, one seeing black where the other sees white, one seeing big where the other sees small, one seeing coarse where the other sees fine. And so on, and so on; there is fortunately no saying on what, for the particular pair of eyes, the window may *not* open; 'fortunately' by reason, precisely, of this incalculability of range. The spreading field, the human scene, is the 'choice of subject'; the pierced aperture, either broad or balconied or slit-like and low-browed, is the 'literary form'; but they are, singly or together, as nothing without the posted presence of the watcher—without, in other words, the consciousness of the artist. Tell me what the artist is, and I will tell you of what he has *been* conscious. Thereby I shall express to you at once his boundless freedom and his 'moral' reference.

> *Henry James. Preface to* The Portrait of a Lady (*1881*); *first printed in the New York edition of the* Novels and Stories (*1907–17*), *Vol. III.*

THE BUSINESS OF THE NOVELIST

The business of the poet and novelist is to show the sorriness underlying the grandest things, and the grandeur underlying the sorriest things.

> *Thomas Hardy. Notebook entry (19 April 1885) from* The Early Life of Thomas Hardy, 1840–1891 (*1928*), *Chapter xiii.*

THE NOVELIST'S MOST PRECIOUS POSSESSION

Liberty of the imagination should be the most precious possession of a novelist. To try voluntarily to discover the fettering dogmas of some romantic, realistic, or naturalistic creed in the free work of its own inspiration, is a trick worthy of human perverseness which, after inventing an absurdity, endeavours to find for it a pedigree of distinguished ancestors. It is a weakness of inferior minds when it is not the cunning device of those who, uncertain of their talent, would seek to add lustre to it by the authority of a school. Such, for instance, are those who have proclaimed Stendhal for a prophet of Naturalism. But Stendhal himself would have accepted no limitation of his freedom. Stendhal's mind was of the first order. His spirit above must be raging with a peculiarly Stendhalesque scorn and indignation. For the truth is that more than one kind of intellectual cowardice hides behind the literary formulas. And Stendhal was pre-eminently courageous. He wrote his two great novels, which so few people have read, in a spirit of fearless liberty.

> *Joseph Conrad. 'Books' (1905); reprinted in*
> Notes on Life and Letters (*1921*).

THE NOVELIST'S ESSENTIAL CHARACTERISTIC

Essential characteristic of the really great novelist: a Christ-like, all-embracing compassion.

> *Arnold Bennett. Notebook entry (15 October 1896),*
> The Journals of Arnold Bennett (*1931*).

THE NOVELIST'S RAISON D'ÊTRE

... I am far from sharing Gide's opinion that good literature cannot be made out of fine sentiments, and that the worse the characters are the better the book. Nevertheless, it certainly is not easy to make good literature with only good sentiments, and it is almost impossible to isolate the good from the bad so as to make an edifying portrayal. The ambition of the modern novelist is to apprehend the whole of human nature, including its shifting contradictions. In the world of reality you do not find beautiful souls in the pure state—these are only to be found in novels and in bad novels at that. What we call a beautiful character has become beautiful at the cost of a struggle against itself, and this struggle should not stop until the bitter end. The evil which the beautiful character has to overcome in itself and from which it has to sever itself, is a reality which the novelist must account for. If there is a reason for the existence of the novelist on earth it is this: to show the element which holds out against God in the highest and noblest characters—the innermost evils and dissimulations; and also to light up the secret source of sanctity in creatures who seem to us to have failed.

> *François Mauriac. God and Mammon (1929;*
> *English translation, 1936), Chapter v.*

II Germination

'HENCE SPRUNG PAMELA'

Two booksellers, my particular friends, entreated me to write for them a little volume of letters, in a common style, on such subjects as might be of use to those country readers who were unable to indite for themselves. Will it be any harm, said I, in a piece you want to be written so low, if we should instruct them how they should think & act in common cases, as well as indite? They were the more urgent with me to begin the little volume, for this hint. I set about it, & in the progress of it, writing two or three letters to instruct handsome girls, who were obliged to go out to service, as we phrase it, how to avoid the snares that might be laid against their virtue; the above story recurred to my thought; and hence sprung Pamela.

> *Samuel Richardson. Letter to Johannes Stinstra (2 June 1753),* Correspondance (*1804*).

'I THOUGHT OF MR. PICKWICK'

. . . The idea propounded to me was that the monthly something should be a vehicle for certain plates to be executed by Mr. Seymour; and there was a notion, either on the part of that admirable humorous artist, or of my vistitor, that a NIMROD CLUB, the members of which were to go out shooting, fishing, and so forth, and getting themselves into difficulties through their want of dexterity, would be the best means of introducing these. I objected, on consideration, that although born and partly bred in the country I was no great sportsman, except in regard to all kinds of locomotion; that the idea was not novel, and had already been much used; that it would be infinitely better for the plates to arise naturally out of the text: and that I would like to take my own way, with a freer range of English scenes and people, and was afraid I should ultimately do so in any case, whatever course I might prescribe to myself at starting. My views being deferred to, I thought of Mr. Pickwick, and wrote the first number; from the proof sheets of which Mr. Seymour made his drawing of the club and his happy portrait of its founder. I connected Mr. Pickwick with a club, because of the original suggestion; and I put in Mr. Winkle expressly for the use of Mr. Seymour.

> *Charles Dickens. John Forster*, The Life of Charles Dickens *(1874), Vol. I, Chapter v.*

MARY ANN EVANS INTO GEORGE ELIOT

September 1856 made a new era in my life, for it was then that I began to write fiction. It had always been a vague dream of mine that some time or other I might write a novel; and my shadowy conception of what the novel was to be, varied of course, from one epoch of my life to another. But I never went further towards the actual writing of the novel than an introductory chapter describing a Staffordshire village and the life of the neighbouring farm-houses; and as the years passed on I lost any hope that I should ever be able to write a novel, just as I desponded about everything else in my future life. I always thought I was deficient in dramatic power, both of construction and dialogue, but I felt I should be at ease in the descriptive parts of a novel. My 'introductory chapter' was pure description, though there were good materials in it for dramatic presentation. It happened to be among the papers I had with me in Germany, and one evening at Berlin something led me to read it to George.[1] He was struck with it as a bit of concrete description, and it suggested to him the possibility of my being able to write a novel, though he distrusted—indeed disbelieved in—my possession of any dramatic power. Still, he began to think that I might as well try some time what I could do in fiction; and by-and-by, when we came back to England, and I had greater success than he ever expected in other kinds of writing, his impression that it was worth while to see how far my mental power would go, towards the production of a novel, was strengthened. He began to say very positively, 'You must try and write a story,' and when we were at Tenby he urged me to begin at once. I deferred it, however, after my usual fashion, with work that does not present itself as an absolute duty. But one morning as I was thinking what should be the subject of my first story, my thoughts merged themselves into a dreamy doze, and I imagined myself writing a story, of which the title was 'The Sad Fortunes of the Reverend Amos Barton.' I was soon wide awake again and told G. He said, 'Oh, what a capital title!' and from that time I had settled it in my mind that this should be my

[1] i.e. George Henry Lewes.

first story. George used to say, 'It may be a failure—it may be that you are unable to write fiction. Or perhaps it may be just good enough to warrant you trying again.' Again, 'You may write a *chef-d'oeuvre* at once—there's no telling.' But his prevalent impression was, that though I could hardly write a *poor* novel, my effort would want the highest quality of fiction—dramatic presentation. He used to say, 'You have wit, description, and philosophy—those go a good way towards the production of a novel. It is worth while for you to try the experiment.'

> *George Eliot.* George Eliot's Life as related in her Letters and Journals (*1884*), ed. *J. W. Cross, Chapter vii.*

A SCARLET LETTER

But the object that most drew my attention, in the mysterious package, was a certain affair of fine red cloth, much worn and faded. There were traces about it of gold embroidery, which, how-ever, was greatly frayed and defaced; so that none, or very little, of the glitter was left. It had been wrought, as was easy to perceive, with wonderful skill of needlework; and the stitch (as I am assured by ladies conversant with such mysteries) gives evidence of a now forgotten art, not to be recovered even by the process of picking out the threads. This rag of scarlet cloth,—for time and wear and a sacrilegious moth had reduced it to little other than a rag,—on careful examination, assumed the shape of a letter. It was the capital letter A. By an accurate measurement, each limb proved to be pre-cisely three inches and a quarter in length. It had been intended, there could be no doubt, as an ornamental article of dress; but how it was to be worn, or what rank, honour, and dignity, in by-past times, were signified by it, was a riddle which (so evanescent are the fashions of the world in these particulars) I saw little hope of solving. And yet it strangely interested me. My eyes fastened themselves upon the old scarlet letter, and would not be turned aside. Certainly, there was some deep meaning in it, most worthy of interpretation, and which, as it were, streamed forth from the mystic symbol, subtly communicating itself to my sensibilities, but evading the analysis of my mind.

> *Nathaniel Hawthorne. 'The Custom House',* The Scarlet Letter (*1850*).

THE BEGINNING OF BARCHESTER

In the course of this job[1] I visited Salisbury, and whilst wandering

[1] For the General Post Office.

there on a midsummer evening round the purlieus of the cathedral I conceived the story of *The Warden*,—from whence came that series of novels of which Barchester, with its bishops, deans, and archdeacon, was the central site. I may as well declare at once that no one at their commencement could have had less reason than myself to presume himself to be able to write about clergymen. I have been often asked in what period of my early life I had lived so long in a cathedral city as to have become intimate with the ways of a Close. I never lived in any cathedral city,—except London, never knew anything of any Close, and at that time had enjoyed no particular intimacy with any clergyman. My archdeacon, who has been said to be life-like, and for whom I confess that I have all a parent's fond affection, was, I think, the simple result of an effort of my moral consciousness. It was such as that, in my opinion, that an archdeacon should be,—or, at any rate, would be with such advantages as an archdeacon might have; and lo! an archdeacon was produced who has been declared by competent authorities to be a real archdeacon down to the very ground. And yet, as far as I can remember, I had not then ever spoken to an archdeacon. I have felt the compliment to be very great. The archdeacon came whole from my brain after this fashion;—but in writing about clergymen generally, I had to pick up as I went whatever I might know or pretend to know about them. But my first idea had no reference to clergy in general. I had been struck by two opposite evils,—or what seemed to me to be evils,—and with an absence of all art-judgement in such matters, I thought that I might be able to expose them, or rather to describe them, both in one and the same tale. The first evil was the possession by the Church of certain funds and endowments which had been intended for charitable purposes, but which had been allowed to become incomes for idle Church dignitaries. There had been more than one such case brought to public notice at the time, in which there seemed to have been an egregious malversation of charitable purposes. The second evil was its very opposite. Though I had been much struck by the injustice above described, I had also often been angered by the undeserved severity of the newspapers towards the recipients of such incomes, who could hardly be considered to be the chief sinners in the matter. When a man is appointed to a place it is natural that he should accept the income allotted to that place without much inquiry. It is seldom that he will be the first to find out that his services are overpaid. Though he be called upon only to look beautiful and to be dignified upon State occasions, he will think £2000 a year little enough for such beauty and dignity as he brings to the task. I felt that there had been some tearing to pieces which might have been spared. But I was altogether wrong in supposing that the two things could be combined. . . .

Nevertheless I thought much about it, and on the 29th July 1852, —having been then two years without having made any literary effort,—I began *The Warden*, at Tenbury in Herefordshire.[1] It was then more than twelve months since I had stood for an hour on the little bridge in Salisbury, and had made out to my own satisfaction the spot on which Hiram's hospital should stand. Certainly no other work that I ever did took up so much of my thoughts.

Anthony Trollope. An Autobiography (*1883*), *Chapter v.*

HENRY JAMES IS INOCULATED

It was years ago, I remember, one Christmas Eve when I was dining with friends: a lady beside me made in the course of talk one of those allusions that I have always found myself recognising on the spot as 'germs'. The germ, wherever gathered, has ever been for me the germ of a 'story', and most of the stories straining to shape under my hand have sprung from a single small seed, a seed as minute and wind-blown as that casual hint for 'The Spoils of Poynton' dropped unwittingly by my neighbour, a mere floating particle in the stream of talk. What above all comes back to me with this reminiscence is the sense of the inveterate minuteness, on such happy occasions, of the precious particle—reduced, that is, to its mere fruitful essence. Such is the interesting truth about the stray suggestion, the wandering word, the vague echo, at touch of which the novelist's imagination winces as at the prick of some sharp point: its virtue is all in its needle-like quality, the power to penetrate as finely as possible. This fineness it is that communicates the virus of suggestion, anything more than the minimum of which spoils the operation. If one is given a hint at all designedly one is sure to be given too much; one's subject is in the merest grain, the speck of truth, of beauty, of reality, scarce visible to the common eye—since, I firmly hold, a good eye for a subject is anything but usual. Strange and attaching, certainly, the consistency with which the first thing to be done for the communicated and seized idea is to reduce almost to nought the form, the air as of a mere disjoined and lacerated lump of life, in which we may have happened to meet it. . . .

So it was, at any rate, that when my amiable friend, on the

---

[1] 'Herefordshire' is the emended reading of *The Oxford Trollope* (1950). The 1883 edition has 'Worcestershire'.

Christmas Eve, before the table that glowed safe and fair through the brown London night, spoke of such an odd matter as that a good lady in the north, always well looked on, was at daggers drawn with her only son, ever hitherto exemplary, over the ownership of the valuable furniture of a fine old house just accruing to the young man by his father's death, I instantly became aware, with my 'sense for the subject', of the prick of inoculation; the *whole* of the virus, as I have called it, being infused by that single touch. There had been but ten words, yet I recognised in them, as in a flash, all the possibilities of the little drama of my 'Spoils,' which glimmered then and there into life; so that when in the next breath I began to hear of action taken . . . I saw Life again at her stupid work. For the action taken, and on which my friend, as I knew she would, had already begun all complacently and benightedly further to report, I had absolutely, and could have, no scrap of use; one had been so perfectly qualified to say in advance: 'It's the perfect little workable thing, but she'll strangle it in the cradle, even while she pretends, all so cheeringly, to rock it; wherefore I'll stay her hand while yet there's time.' I didn't, of course, stay her hand—there never *is* in such cases 'time'; and I had once more the full demonstration of the fatal futility of Fact . . . It was not, however, that this in the least mattered, once the seed had been transplanted to richer soil. . . .

> Henry James. *Preface to* The Spoils of Poynton (*1897*); *first printed in the New York edition of the* Novels and Stories (*1907–17*), *Vol. X*.

THE INCEPTION OF 'NOSTROMO'

. . . the first hint for *Nostromo* came to me in the shape of a vagrant anecdote completely destitute of valuable details.

As a matter of fact in 1875 or '6, when very young, in the West Indies, or rather in the Gulf of Mexico, for my contacts with land were short, few, and fleeting, I heard the story of some man who was supposed to have stolen single-handed a whole lighter-full of silver, somewhere on the Tierra Firme seaboard during the troubles of a revolution.

On the face of it this was something of a feat. But I heard no details, and having no particular interest in crime *qua* crime I was not likely to keep that one in my mind. And I forgot it till twenty-six or seven years afterwards I came upon the very thing in a shabby volume picked up outside a second-hand bookshop. It was the life story of an American seaman written by himself with the assistance of a journalist. In the course of his wanderings that American sailor worked for some months on board of a schooner, the master and owner of which was the thief of whom I had heard in my very young days. I have no doubt of that because there could hardly have been two exploits of that peculiar kind in the same part of the world and both connected with a South American revolution.

The fellow had actually managed to steal a lighter with silver, and this, it seems, only because he was implicitly trusted by his employers, who must have been singularly poor judges of character. In the sailor's story he is represented as an unmitigated rascal, a small cheat, stupidly ferocious, morose, of mean appearance, and altogether unworthy of the greatness this opportunity had thrust upon him. What was interesting was that he would boast of it openly.

He used to say: 'People think I make a lot of money in this schooner of mine. But that is nothing. I don't care for that. Now and then I go away quietly and lift a bar of silver. I must get rich slowly—you understand.'

There was also another curious point about the man. Once in the course of some quarrel the sailor threatened him: 'What's to prevent me reporting ashore what you have told me about that silver?'

The cynical ruffian was not alarmed in the least. He actually laughed. 'You fool, if you dare talk like that on shore about me you will get a knife stuck in your back. Every man, woman, and child in that port is my friend. And who's to prove the lighter wasn't sunk? I didn't show you where the silver is hidden. Did I? So you know nothing. And suppose I lied? Eh?'

Ultimately the sailor, disgusted with the sordid meanness of that impenitent thief, deserted from the schooner. The whole episode takes about three pages of his autobiography. Nothing to speak of; but as I looked them over, the curious confirmation of the few casual words heard in my early youth evoked the memories of that distant time when everything was so fresh, so surprising, so venturesome, so interesting; bits of strange coasts under the stars, shadows of hills in the sunshine, men's passions in the dusk, gossip half forgotten, faces grown dim. . . . Perhaps, perhaps, there still was in the world something to write about. Yet I did not see anything at first in the mere story. A rascal steals a large parcel of a valuable commodity— so people say. It's either true or untrue; and in any case it has no value in itself. To invent a circumstantial account of the robbery did not appeal to me, because my talents not running that way I did not think that the game was worth the candle. It was only when it dawned upon me that the purloiner of the treasure need not necessarily be a confirmed rogue, that he could be even a man of character, an actor and possibly a victim in the changing scenes of a revolution, it was only then that I had the first vision of a twilight country which was to become the province of Sulaco, with its high shadowy Sierra and its misty Campo for mute witnesses of events flowing from the passions of men short-sighted in good and evil.

Such are in very truth the obscure origins of *Nostromo*—the book. From that moment, I suppose, it had to be. Yet even then I hesitated, as if warned by the instinct of self-preservation from venturing on a distant and toilsome journey into a land full of intrigues and revolutions. But it had to be done.

Joseph Conrad. Preface to Nostromo *(1904).*

PROUST RECAPTURES THE PAST

. . . One might have said that the portents which that day were to rescue me from my discouragement and give me back faith in litera-ture, were determined to multiply themselves, for a servant, a long time in the service of the Prince de Guermantes, recognised me and, to save me going to the buffet, brought me some cakes and a glass of orangeade into the library. I wiped my mouth with the napkin he had given me and immediately, like the personage in the *Thousand and One Nights* who unknowingly accomplished the rite which caused the appearance before him of a docile genius, invisible to others, ready to transport him far away, a new azure vision passed before my eyes; but this time it was pure and saline and swelled into shapes like bluish udders. The impression was so strong that the moment I was living seemed to be one with the past and . . . I believed that the servant had just opened the window upon the shore and that everything invited me to go downstairs and walk along the high sea-wall at high tide; the napkin upon which I was wiping my mouth had exactly the same kind of starchiness as that with which I had attempted with so much difficulty to dry myself before the window the first day of my arrival at Balbec and within the folds of which, now, in that library of the Guermantes mansion, a green-blue ocean spread its plumage like the tail of a peacock. And I did not merely rejoice in those colours, but in that whole instant which produced them, an instant towards which my whole life had doubtless aspired, which a feeling of fatigue or sadness had prevented my ever experiencing at Balbec but which now, pure, disincarnated and freed from the imperfections of exterior perceptions, filled me with joy. . . . I noted that there would be great difficulties in creating the work of art I now felt ready to undertake without its being consciously in my mind, for I should have to construct each of its successive parts out of a different sort of material. The material which would be suitable for memories at the side of the sea would be quite different from those of afternoons at Venice which would demand a material of its own, a new one, of a special transparency and sonority, compact, fresh and pink, different again if I wanted to describe evenings at Rivebelle where, in the dining-room open upon the garden, the heat was beginning to disintegrate, to descend and come to rest on the earth, while the rose-covered walls of the restaurant were lighted up by the last ray of the setting sun, and the last water-colours of day-light lingered in the sky. I passed rapidly over all these things, being summoned more urgently to seek the cause of that happiness with its peculiar character of insistent certainty, the search for which I had formerly adjourned. And I began to discover the cause by comparing those varying happy impressions which had the common quality of being felt simul-taneously at the actual moment and at a distance in time, because of which common quality the noise of the spoon upon the plate, the unevenness of the paving-stone, the taste of the madeleine, imposed the past upon the present and made me hesitate as to which time I was existing in. Of a truth, the being within me which sensed this impression, sensed what it had in common in former days and now, sensed its extra-temporal character, a being which only appeared when through the medium of the identity of present and past, it found itself in the only setting in which it could exist and enjoy the essence of things, that is, outside Time.

> *Marcel Proust*. Time Regained (*1927*), *Chapter iii, transl. Stephen Hudson (1931*).

WHAT IS IT TO BE?

Tuesday, May 28th (1929).

Now about this book, *The Moths*.[1] How am I to begin it? And what is it to be? I feel no great impulse; no fever; only a great pressure of difficulty. Why write it then? Why write at all? Every morning I write a little sketch, to amuse myself. I am not saying, I might say, that these sketches have any relevance. I am not trying to tell a story. Yet perhaps it might be done in that way. A mind thinking. They might be islands of light—islands in the stream that I am trying to convey; life itself going on. The current of the moths flying strongly this way. A lamp and a flower pot in the centre. The flower can always be changing. But there must be more unity between each scene than I can find at present. Autobiography it

---

[1] This became *The Waves* (1931).

might be called. How am I to make one lap or act, between the coming of the moths, more intense than another; if there are only scenes? One must get the sense that this is the beginning; this is the middle; that the climax—when she opens the window and the moth comes in. I shall have the two different currents—the moths flying along; the flower upright in the centre; a perpetual crumbling and renewing of the plant. In its leaves she might see things happen. But who is she? I am very anxious that she should have no name. I don't want a Lavinia or a Penelope: I want 'she'. But that becomes arty, Liberty greenery yallery somehow: symbolic in loose robes. Of course I can make her think backwards and forwards; I can tell stories. But that's not it. Also I shall do away with exact place and time. Anything may be out of the window—a ship—a desert—London.

Virginia Woolf. A Writer's Diary (1953).

NO NOTEBOOKS

M. J. I don't think you have the note-book habit, I mean the collection of unrelated notes of things seen and heard. Katherine Mansfield filled note-books with memoranda and worked these up into what she called vignettes, or into her stories. She also made notes of phrases and sentences for as she said, 'one never knows when a little tag like that may come in useful to round off a paragraph.' I like to know how people work.

I. C. B. I daresay you do, but the people themselves are not always quite sure. I have not the note-book habit; that is, I do not watch or listen to strangers with a view to using the results. They do not do or say things that are of any good. They are too indefinite and too much alike and are seldom living in anything but the surface of their lives. Think how rarely we should ourselves say or do anything that would throw light on our characters or experience.

But as I have already said, some sort of starting-point is useful; and I get it almost anywhere; and I doubt if Katherine Mansfield really got more help than this from what she saw and heard. You say she worked it up, and I am sure she must have done so.

I cannot understand her noting phrases and sentences for future use, and find it hard to believe that they served any purpose. Rounding off a paragraph, occurring in the normal course of writing, by a tag overheard and stored up, seems to me too unnatural to be possible. She said that she never knew when such things would come in useful, and I suspect that she never found out.

Ivy Compton-Burnett. 'A Conversation Between I. Compton-Burnett and M. Jourdain', Orion (1945).

III   The Novelist at Work: Effort and Inspiration

RICHARDSON IN DIFFICULTIES

I am a very irregular writer: can form no plan; nor write after what I have preconceived. Many of my friends wonder at this: but so it is. I have not therefore that encouragement to proceed, that those have, who, forming an agreeable plan, write within its circle, and go on step by step with delight, knowing what they drive at. Execution is all they have to concern themselves about, having the approbation of their friends of their plan, and perhaps helped by those friends to incidents or enlargement. But I often compare myself to a poor old woman, who having no bellows, lays herself down on her hearth, and with her mouth endeavours to blow up into a faint blaze a little handful of sticks, half green, half dry, in order to warm a mess of pottage, that, after all her pains, hardly keeps life and soul together. This stick lights, that goes out; and she is often obliged to have recourse to her farthing candle, blinking in its shove-up socket; the lighter up of a week's fires. Excellent housewife, from poverty.

> *Samuel Richardson. Letter to Lady Bradshaigh (probably between April and December 1751), Correspondence (1804).*

I am at a part, that it is four chances to one I shall not be able to get over. You cannot imagine how many difficult situations I have involved myself in. Entanglement, and extrication, and re-entanglement, have succeeded each other, as the day the night; and now the few friends who have seen what I have written, doubt not but I am stuck fast. And, indeed, I think so myself.

> *Samuel Richardson. Letter to Lady Bradshaigh (23 February 1752), Correspondence (1804).*

A CARRIER'S HORSE

I hope the candid reader now and then calls to mind how much more nimbly he travels over these pages than the writer of them did. When our dullness is complained of, it would be but charity in him to reflect how much pains that same dullness has cost us; more, he may be assured, than our brighter intervals, where we sprung nimbly forward with an easy weight, instead of toiling like a carrier's horse, whose slow and heavy pace argues the load he draws, and the labour he endures. . . .

'Tis hard indeed to toil, as we sometimes do, to our own loss and disappointment; to sweat in the field of fame, merely to reap a harvest of chaff, and pile up reams of paper for the worm to dine upon. It is a cruel thing to rack our brains for nothing, run our jaded fancies to a stand-still, and then lie down at the conclusion of our race, a carcase for the critics.

Richard Cumberland. Henry (*1795*), *Book the Seventh, Chapter i.*

WHOM THE DEVIL DRIVES

Author. . . . I think there is a demon who seats himself on the feather of my pen when I begin to write, and leads it astray from the purpose. Characters expand under my hand; incidents are multiplied; the story lingers, while the materials increase; my regular mansion turns out a Gothic anomaly, and the work is closed long before I have attained the point I proposed.

Captain. Resolution and determined forbearance might remedy that evil.

Author. Alas! my dear sir, you do not know the force of paternal affection. When I light on such a character as Baillie Jarvie, or Dalgetty, my imagination brightens, and my conception becomes clearer at every step which I take in his company, although it leads me many a weary mile away from the regular road, and forces me to leap hedge and ditch to get back into the route again. If I resist the temptation, as you advise me, my thoughts become prosy, flat, and dull; I write painfully to myself, and under a consciousness of flagging which makes me flag still more; the sunshine with which fancy had invested the incidents, departs from them, and leaves every thing dull and gloomy. I am no more the same author I was in my better mood, than the dog in a wheel, condemned to go round and round for hours, is like the same dog merrily chasing his own tail, and gambolling in all the frolic of unrestrained freedom. In short, sir, on such occasions, I think I am bewitched.

Captain. Nay, sir, if you plead sorcery, there is no more to be said—
he must needs go whom the devil drives.

> *Sir Walter Scott. Introductory Epistle to*
> The Fortunes of Nigel (*1822*).

NO PLANNING

There was a time when I used to draw up plans for novels—for
Varina, for example; but drawing up plans freezes me stiff. I dictate
twenty-five or thirty pages, then it is evening and I need violent
distraction. It is necessary that by next morning I shall have forgotten everything. When I read three or four final pages of yesterday's chapter, to-day's chapter comes to me.

> *Stendhal. Letter to Balzac (30 October 1840), second draft,*
> Selected Letters (*1952*), transl. Norman Cameron.

WHAT, WHAT, WHAT! HOW, HOW, HOW!

Still there is something wanting to make an action for the story.
When Etherege appears, he should set some old business in motion,
that had been suspended ever since he was here before. What can
that be?—how can it appear as if dead men's business, that had
been buried with them, came to life again, and had to be finished
now? Truly this is hard;—here's the rub; and yet without it, the
story is meagre and barren.

This old man—what could he possibly be? The inheritor of some
peculiarity that has been known heretofore in the history of the
family, and the possession of which betrays itself in some of his
habits, or in his person. What? I can't make it out. Some physical
peculiarity?—'twon't do. Some mental or moral peculiarity? How?
The art of making gold? A peculiar kind of poison? An acquaintance
with wizard lore? Nothing of this. He is an eater of human flesh—
a vampire—a ghoul. He finds it necessary to eat a young child every
year, in order to keep himself alive. He shall have some famous
jewel, known for ages in the family annals—pah! He shall have
undertaken some investigation, which many members of his family
have been deluded into undertaking heretofore, and the nature of
which is to change their natures disastrously—'twon't do. He shall
have been to the Cave of Trophonious. He shall have been to Hell
—and I wish the Devil had kept him there. He shall have inherited
the Great Carbuncle, and shall be forbidden to show it to any
mortal. 'Twon't do. On account of some supposed hidden power
of his, the owner of the estate shall seek his aid. What, what, what!

How, how, how! When the heir was kidnapped to America, he carried this thing with him, which was the grand peculiarity of the family; and ever since there have [been] traditions about it, and a general secret inquest to find what has become of it. But what is it! Ah! Ah! He knows in what part of the castle something lies hidden; it shall be a rumour of a great treasure, [but] a treasure of gold— but on discovery, it shall prove to be only Evelyn's coffin, full of the golden hair into which she has been entirely changed. The story must not be founded at all on remorse or secret guilt—all that Poe wore out. Alas me! Some strange sort of a dreamer this old [man] might well be, who has brought down into this age some folly that belonged to that one—alchemy?—'twon't do. Some one of the Marquis of Worcester's century of inventions? Hardly, but I wish I knew what they were. The thing, though adorned with a deceitful splendour, shall be rather a curse than a blessing. A mystic of some kind. If I could but develop this rightly, it would be a good thing. A man aiming, the wrong way, [arrives] at some great good for his race. The first emigrant might have had the same tendency and suffered for it. A panacea for all ills. A friend of Swedenborg? A man with Medea's receipt? There is a latent something lying hereabouts, which, could I grip it, 'twould be the making of the story. A sort of apostle—a devoted, good man, but throwing himself away through some grand mistake! The example of the migrant was too much for him. So there shall be something strange and unworldly in the conduct of all who come to the knowledge of this man—they shall martyr themselves and their affections, give up the world, behave as if they were mad; though it shall really be the highest virtue and wisdom. I don't see any way yet, nor anything like it. But if I could get rid of any great crime on the part of the family, it would be better. Here, then, is a meek, patient, unpretending, wise old man, who develops peculiarities which draw the attention of profound observers upon him, though others see little that is remarkable in him. This is a better aspect than what I at first thought of. Follow out this clue stubbornly, stubbornly.

Nathaniel Hawthorne. Hawthorne's Dr. Grimshawe's Secret, *ed. Edward H. Davidson (1954), pp. 104-5.*

250 WORDS EVERY QUARTER OF AN HOUR

All those who have lived as literary men,—working daily as literary labourers,—will agree with me that three hours a day will produce as much as a man ought to write. But then, he should so have trained himself that he shall be able to work continuously during those three hours,—so have tutored his mind that it shall not be necessary for him to sit nibbling his pen, and gazing at the wall before him, till he shall have found the words with which he wants to express his ideas. It had at this time become my custom,—and it still is my custom, though of late I have become a little lenient with myself,—to write with my watch before me, and to require from myself 250 words every quarter of an hour. I have found that the 250 words have been forthcoming as regularly as my watch went. But my three hours were not devoted entirely to writing. I always began my task by reading the work of the day before, an operation which would take me half an hour, and which consisted chiefly in weighing with my ear the sound of the words and phrases. I would strongly recommend this practice to all tyros in writing. That their work should be read after it has been written is a matter of course,—that it should be read twice at least before it goes to the printers, I take to be a matter of course. But by reading what he has last written, just before he recommences his task, the writer will catch the tone and spirit of what he is then saying, and will avoid the fault of seeming to be unlike himself. This division of time allowed me to produce over ten pages of an ordinary novel volume a day, and if kept up through ten months, would have given as its results three novels of three volumes each in the year. . . .

I have never written three novels in a year, but by following the plan above described I have written more than as much as three volumes; and by adhering to it over a course of years, I have been enabled to have always on hand,—for some time back now,—one or two or even three unpublished novels in my desk beside me. Were I to die now there are three such,—besides *The Prime Minister*, half of which only has as yet been issued. One of these has been six years finished, and has never seen the light since it was first tied up in the wrapper which now contains it. I look forward with some grim pleasantry to its publication after another period of six years, and to the declaration of the critics that it has been the work of a period of life at which the power of writing novels has passed from me.

Anthony Trollope. An Autobiography (*1883*), *Chapter xv.*

MISERIES AND SPLENDOURS OF CREATION

If I haven't answered your doleful, discouraged letter before now it's because I have been in the middle of a great fit of work. The day before yesterday, I went to bed at 5 o'clock, and yesterday at 3. Since last Monday I've put everything else on one side, and all week I've been grinding away exclusively at my *Bovary*, exasperated at not getting ahead. I've got to my ball now, which I shall begin on Monday. I hope it will go better. Since you saw me I've written 25 clear pages (25 pages in six weeks). They've been difficult to get moving. I shall read them to Bouilhet tomorrow. As for me, I've so much worked them over, recopied them, altered them, handled them, that for the moment I can make neither head nor tail of them. But I think they stand up. You tell me of your discouragements: if only you could see mine! Sometimes I can't make out why my arms don't fall off my body with weariness, or why my brain doesn't turn to porridge. I lead a harsh existence, devoid of all outward joy, with nothing more to sustain me than a kind of everlasting rage that weeps sometimes for very powerlessness but is unceasing. I love my work with a frenzied perverted passion, as an ascetic loves the hair-shirt that scrapes his body. Sometimes, when I find myself empty, when expression won't come, when, after scribbling long pages, I find I haven't written a sentence, then I fall onto the couch and lie there, stupefied in an inward slough of despond.

I hate myself, and blame myself, for this frenzy of pride which makes me pant after mere imaginings. A quarter of an hour later, everything has altered; my heart is pounding for joy. Last Wednesday I had to get up to find my handkerchief: tears were running down my face. I had moved myself to tears in writing, revelling deliciously in the emotions of my own conception, in the sentence which rendered it, and in the pleasure of having found it. At least I think there were all these things in a state of feeling where nerves, after all, had more place than anything else. Of these moments there are some which are of the highest kind—those that have least to do with any element of the sensuous. They surpass virtue itself in their moral beauty, so detached are they from all personality and all human relationships. I have glimpsed sometimes (in my great days of sunlight) the glimmerings of a rapture which sends a shudder over my flesh, from my nails to the roots of my hair, a spiritual state thus far above life in which fame would be nothing and even happiness without point.

> *Gustave Flaubert. Letter to Louise Colet (24 April 1852)*,
> Correspondance (*1900*).

PAIN AND TRAVAIL OF SOUL

You simply can't imagine how frightfully busy I am, day and night; it is real hard labour! For I am now finishing the 'Karamazovs', and consequently summing up the entire work, which is personally very dear to me, for I have put a great deal of my inmost self into it. I work, in general, very nervously, with pain and travail of soul. Whenever I am writing, I am physically ill. And now I have to sum up all that I have pondered, gathered, set down, in the last three years. I must make this work good at all costs, or at least as good as *I* can. I simply don't know how anyone can write at great speed, and only for the money's sake. Now the time is come when I must wind up this novel, and that without delay. You will hardly believe me: many a chapter, for which I had been making notes all those three years, I was obliged, after finally setting it down, to reject, and write anew. Only separate passages, which were directly inspired by enthusiasm, came off at first writing; all the rest was hard work . . .

> *Feodor Dostoevsky. Letter to I. S. Aksakov (28 August 1880),*
> *Letters (1914), transl. Ethel Colburn Mayne.*

FLESH IN THE INK-POT

Tolstoi spoke on August 28th [1904] with exasperation about writing as a profession. I have rarely seen him so agitated.
He said:
'One ought only to write when one leaves a piece of one's flesh in the ink-pot each time one dips one's pen.'

1905, June 16th

'I always write in the morning. I was pleased to hear lately that Rousseau too, after he got up in the morning, went for a short walk and sat down to work. In the morning one's head is particularly fresh. The best thoughts most often come in the morning after waking, while still in bed or during the walk. Many writers work at night. Dostoevsky always wrote at night. In a writer there must always be two people—the writer and the critic. And, if one works at night, with a cigarette in one's mouth, although the work of creation goes on briskly, the critic is for the most part in abeyance, and this is very dangerous. . . .'

> *Leo Tolstoy. Talks with Tolstoi, ed. A. B. Goldenveizer (1922),*
> *transl. S. S. Koteliansky and Virginia Woolf (1923).*

COPIOUS PRELIMINARIES

. . . those wondrous and copious preliminary statements (of my fictions that are to be) don't really exist in any form in which they can be imparted. I think I know to whom you allude as having seen their semblance—and indeed their very substance; but in two exceptional (as it were) cases. In these cases what was seen was the statement drawn up on the basis of the serialization of the work—drawn up in one case with extreme detail and at extreme length (in 20,000 words!). Pinker saw that: it referred to a long novel, afterwards (this more than a year) written and finished, but not yet, to my great inconvenience, published; but it went more than two years ago to America, to the Harpers, and there remained and has probably been destroyed.[1] Were it here I would with pleasure transmit it to you; for, though I say it who should not, it *was*, the statement, full and vivid, I think as a statement could be, of a subject as worked out. Then Conrad saw a shorter one of the *Wings of the D.*—also well enough in its way, but only half as long and proportionately less developed. *That* had been prepared so that the book might be serialized in another American periodical, but this wholly failed (what secrets and shames I reveal to you!) and the thing (the book) was then written, the subject treated, on a more free and independent scale. But *that* synopsis too has been destroyed; it was returned from the U.S., but I had then no occasion to preserve it. And evidently no fiction of mine can or *will* now be serialized; certainly I shall not again draw up detailed and explicit plans for unconvinced and ungracious editors; so that I fear I shall have nothing of that sort to show. A plan for *myself*, as copious and developed as possible, I always do draw up—that is the two documents I speak of were based upon, and extracted from, such a preliminary *private* outpouring. But this latter voluminous effusion is, ever, so extremely familiar, confidential and intimate—in the form of an interminable garrulous letter addressed to my own fond fancy —that, though I always, for easy reference, have it carefully typed, it isn't a thing I would willingly expose to any eye but my own. And even *then*, sometimes, I shrink!

> Henry James. Letter to H. G. Wells (*15 November 1902*), The Letters of Henry James (*1920*).

WRESTLING WITH THE LORD

No ditch or wall encompassed my abode. The window was open; the door too stood open to that best friend of my work, the warm, still sunshine of the wide fields. They lay around me infinitely helpful, but truth to say I had not known for weeks whether the sun shone upon the earth and whether the stars above still moved on

---

[1] The project was for *The Ambassadors*; it was not destroyed. See *The Notebooks of Henry James* (1947), ed. F. O. Matthiessen and Kenneth B. Murdoch, p. 370.

their appointed courses. I was just then giving up some days of my allotted span to the last chapters of the novel *Nostromo*, a tale of an imaginary (but true) seaboard, which is still mentioned now and again, and indeed kindly, sometimes in connection with the word 'failure' and sometimes in connection with the word 'astonishing'. I have no opinion on this discrepancy. It's the sort of difference that can never be settled. All I know, is that, for twenty months, neglecting the common joys of life that fall to the lot of the humblest on this earth, I had, like the prophet of old, 'wrestled with the Lord' for my creation, for the headlands of the coast, for the darkness of the Placid Gulf, the light on the snows, the clouds on the sky, and for the breath of life that had to be blown into the shapes of men and women, of Latin and Saxon, of Jew and Gentile. These are, perhaps, strong words, but it is difficult to characterise otherwise the intimacy and the strain of a creative effort in which mind and will and conscience are engaged to the full, hour after hour, day after day, away from the world, and to the exclusion of all that makes life really lovable and gentle—something for which a material parallel can only be found in the everlasting sombre stress of the westward winter passage round Cape Horn. For that too is the wrestling of men with the might of their Creator, in a great isolation from the world, without the amenities and consolations of life, a lonely struggle under a sense of over-matched littleness, for no reward that could be adequate, but for the mere winning of a longitude. Yet a certain longitude, once won, cannot be disputed. The sun and the stars and the shape of your earth are the witnesses of your gain; whereas a handful of pages, no matter how much you have made them your own, are at best but an obscure and questionable spoil. Here they are. 'Failure'—'Astonishing': take your choice; or perhaps both, or neither—a mere rustle and flutter of pieces of paper settling down in the night, and indistinguishable, like the snowflakes of a great drift destined to melt away in sunshine.

Joseph Conrad. A Personal Record (*1912*), *Chapter v.*

FEATHERING ABOUT

Friday, April 30th (1926)
     . . . Yesterday I finished the first part of *To the Lighthouse*, and today began the second. I cannot make it out—here is the most difficult abstract piece of writing—I have to give an empty house, no people's characters, the passage of time, all eyeless and featureless with nothing to cling to; well, I rush at it, and at once scatter out two pages. Is it nonsense, is it brilliance? Why am I so flown with

words and apparently free to do exactly what I like? When I read a bit it seems spirited too; needs compressing, but not much else. Compare this dashing fluency with *Mrs. Dalloway* (save the end). This is not made up; it is the literal fact.

Friday, September 3rd (1926)

. . . The novel is now easily in sight of the end, but this, mysteriously, comes no nearer. I am doing Lily on the lawn; but whether it's her last lap, I don't know. Nor am I sure of the quality; the only certainty seems to be that after tapping my antennae in the air vaguely for an hour every morning I generally write with heat and ease till 12.30; and thus do my two pages. So 5th September it will be done, written over that is, in 3 weeks, I forecast, from today. What emerges? At this moment I'm casting about for an end. The problem is how to bring Lily and Mr. R. together and make a combination of interest at the end. I am feathering about with various ideas. The last chapter which I begin tomorrow is In the Boat: I had meant to end with R. climbing on to the rock. If so, what becomes of Lily and her picture? Should there be a final page about her and Carmichael looking at the picture and summing up R.'s character? In that case I lose the intensity of the moment. If this intervenes between R. and the lighthouse, there's too much chop and change, I think. Could I do it in a parenthesis? So that one had the sense of reading two things at the same time?

I shall solve it somehow, I suppose. Then I must go on to the question of quality. I think it may run too fast and free and so be rather thin. On the other hand, I think it is subtler and more human than *Jacob's Room* and *Mrs. Dalloway*. And I am encouraged by my own abundance as I write. It is proved, I think, that what I have to say is to be said in this manner. As usual, side stories are sprouting in great variety as I wind this up: a book of characters . . . but it is hopelessly undramatic. It is all in oratio obliqua. Not quite all; for I have a few direct sentences. The lyric portions of *To the Lighthouse* are collected in the 10-year lapse and don't interfere with the text so much as usual. I feel as if it fetched its circle pretty completely this time; and I don't feel sure what the stock criticism will be. Sentimental? Victorian?

Virginia Woolf. A Writer's Diary (1953).

THE NOVELIST INSPIRED

(i)

. . . Genius; thou gift of Heaven; without whose aid in vain we struggle against the stream of nature. Thou who dost sow the generous seeds which art nourishes, and brings to perfection. Do thou kindly take me by the hand, and lead me through all the mazes, the winding labyrinths of nature. Initiate me into all those mysteries which profane eyes never beheld. Teach me, which to thee is no difficult task, to know mankind better than they know themselves. Remove that mist which dims the intellect of mortals, and causes them to adore men for their art, or to detest them for their cunning, in deceiving others, when they are, in reality, the objects only of ridicule, for deceiving themselves. Strip off the thin disguise of wisdom from self-conceit, of plenty from avarice, and of glory from ambition. Come, thou that hast inspired thy Aristophanes, thy Lucian, thy Cervantes, thy Rabelais, thy Molière, thy Shakespeare, thy Swift, thy Marivaux, fill my pages with humour; till mankind learn the good-nature to laugh only at the follies of others, and the humility to grieve at their own.

> *Henry Fielding.* The History of Tom Jones, A Foundling
> (*1749*), *Book XIII, Chapter i.*

(ii)

Whether it is right or advisable to create beings like Heathcliff, I do not know: I scarcely think it is. But this I know; the writer who possesses the creative gift owns something of which he is not always master—something that, at times, strangely wills and works for itself. He may lay down rules and devise principles, and to rules and principles it will perhaps for years lie in subjection; and then, haply without any warning of revolt, there comes a time when it will no longer consent to 'harrow the valleys, or be bound with a band in the furrow'—when it 'laughs at the multitude of the city, and regards not the crying of the driver'—when, refusing absolutely to make ropes out of sea-sand any longer, it sets to work on statue-hewing, and you have a Pluto or a Jove, a Tisiphone or a Psyche, a Mermaid or a Madonna, as Fate or Inspiration direct. Be the work grim or glorious, dread or divine, you have little choice left but quiescent adoption. As for you—the nominal artist—your share in it has been to work passively under dictates you neither delivered nor could question—that would not be uttered at your prayer, nor suppressed nor changed at your caprice. If the result be attractive, the world will praise you, who little deserve praise; if it be repulsive, the same world will blame you, who almost as little deserve blame.

Charlotte Brontë. Preface to the 1850 edition of Wuthering Heights (*1847*).

(iii)

. . . She told me that, in all that she considered her best writing, there was a 'not herself' which took possession of her, and that she felt her own personality to be merely the instrument through which this spirit, as it were, was acting. Particularly she dwelt on this with regard to the scene in *Middlemarch* between Dorothea and Rosamond, saying that, although she always knew they had, sooner or later, to come together, she kept the idea resolutely out of her mind until Dorothea was in Rosamond's drawing-room. Then, abandoning herself to the inspiration of the moment, she wrote the whole scene exactly as it stands, without alteration or erasure, in an intense state of excitement and agitation, feeling herself entirely possessed by the feelings of the two women. Of all the characters she had attempted, she found Rosamond the most difficult to sustain. With this sense of 'possession', it is easy to imagine what the cost to the author must have been of writing books, each of which has its tragedy.

J. W. Cross. George Eliot's Life as related in her Letters and Journals (*1884*), *Chapter xix*.

(iv)

My imaginary characters take on my shape, they pursue me, or rather it is I who am in them. When I wrote about Emma Bovary's poisoning I had the *taste of arsenic so strongly in my mouth*, I was so thoroughly poisoned myself, that I gave myself two bouts of indigestion, one after another, two very real bouts since I vomited up my entire dinner . . .

Don't liken the artist's inner vision to that of the man who is genuinely suffering from hallucination. I know both states very well; there's a gulf between them. In a state of hallucination properly so called there is always terror; you feel your individuality slipping away from you; you feel you are going to die of it. In the poetic vision, on the contrary, there is joy; it is something that enters into you. It is no less true that you no longer know where you are . . . This vision often forms itself slowly, bit by bit, like the various parts of a *décor* one is setting up; but often again it is as swift and fugitive as hypnotic hallucinations. Something passes in front of your eyes; it is then that you have to fling yourself on to it, avidly . . .

> *Gustave Flaubert. Letter to H. A. Taine (1868?)*
> Correspondance (*1903*).

(v)

January 4th, 1910. I take this up again after an interruption—I in fact throw myself upon it this a.m. under the *secousse* of its being brought home to me even more than I expected that my urgent material reasons for getting settled at productive work again are of the very most imperative. *Je m'entends*—I have had a discomfiture (through a stupid misapprehension of my own, indeed); and I must now take up projected tasks—this long time *entrevus* and brooded over—with the firmest possible hand. I needn't expatiate on this—on the sharp consciousness of this hour of the dimly-dawning New Year, I mean; I simply invoke and appeal to all the powers and forces and divinities to whom I've ever been loyal and who haven't failed me yet—after all: never, never yet! Infinitely interesting—and yet somehow with a beautiful sharp poignancy in it that makes it strange and rather exquisitely formidable, as with an unspeakable deep agitation, the whole artistic question that comes up for me in the train of this idea of a new short serial for the Harpers, of the *donnée* for a situation that I began here the other day to fumble out. I mean I come back, I come back yet again and again, to my only seeing it in the dramatic way—as I can only see everything and anything now . . . Momentary sidewinds—things of no real authority—break in every now and then to put their inferior little questions to me; but I come back, I come back, as I say, I all throbbingly and yearningly and passionately, oh, *mon bon*, come back to this way that is clearly the only one in which I can do anything now, and that will open out to me more and more and that has overwhelming reasons pleading all beautifully in its breast. What really happens is that the closer I get to the problem of the application of it in any particular case, the more I get *into* that application, so the more doubts and torments fall away from me, the more I know where I am, the more everything spreads and shines and draws me on and I'm justified of my logic and my passion. . . . *Causons, causons, mon bon*—oh celestial, soothing, sanctifying process, with all the high sane forces of the sacred time fighting through it, on my side! Let me fumble it gently and patiently out—with fever and fidget laid to rest—as in all the old enchanted months! It only looms, it only shines and shimmers, *too* beautiful and too interesting;

it only hangs there too rich and too full and with too much to give and to pay; it only presents itself too admirably and too vividly, too straight and square and vivid, as a little organic and effective Action . . .

Thus just these first little wavings of the oh so tremulously passionate little old wand (now!) make for me, I feel, a sort of promise of richness and beauty and variety; a sort of portent of the happy presence of the elements. The good days of last August and even my broken September and better October come back to me with their gage of divine possibilities, and I welcome these to my arms, I press them with unutterable tenderness. I seem to emerge from these recent bad days—the fruit of blind accident (Jan. 1910)—and the prospect clears and blushes, and my poor blest old Genius pats me so admirably and lovingly on the back that I turn, I screw round, and bend my lips to passionately, in my gratitude, kiss its hand . . .

Henry James. The Notebooks of Henry James, *ed F. O. Matthiessen and Kenneth B. Murdock (1947).* .

(vi)

Saturday, February 7th (1931).

Here in the few minutes that remain, I must record, heaven be praised, the end of *The Waves*. I wrote the words O Death fifteen minutes ago, having reeled across the last ten pages with some moments of such intensity and intoxication that I seemed only to stumble after my own voice, or almost, after some sort of speaker (as when I was mad) I was almost afraid, remembering the voices that used to fly ahead. Anyhow it is done; and I have been sitting these 15 minutes in a state of glory, and calm, and some tears, thinking of Thoby and if I could write Julian Thoby Stephen 1881–1906 on the first page. I suppose not. How physical the sense of triumph and relief is! Whether good or bad it's done; and, as I certainly felt at the end, not merely finished, but rounded off, completed, the thing stated—how hastily, how fragmentarily I know; but I mean that I have netted that fin in the waste of water which appeared to me over the marshes out of my window at Rodmell when I was coming to an end of *To the Lighthouse*.

What interests me in the last stage was the freedom and boldness with which my imagination picked up, used and tossed aside all the images, symbols which I had prepared. I am sure that this is the right way of using them—not in set pieces, as I had tried at first, coherently, but simply as images, never making them work out; only suggest. Thus I hope to have kept the sound of the sea and the birds, dawn and garden subconsciously present, doing their work underground.

Virginia Woolf. A Writer's Diary (*1953*).

(vii)

What about the creative state? In it a man is taken out of himself. He lets down as it were a bucket into his subconscious, and draws up something which is normally beyond his reach. He mixes this thing with his normal experiences, and out of the mixture he makes a work of art. It may be a good work of art or a bad one—we are not here examining the question of quality—but whether it is good or bad it will have been compounded in this unusual way, and he will wonder afterwards how he did it. Such seems to be the creative process. It may employ much technical ingenuity and worldly knowledge, it may profit by critical standards, but mixed up with it is this stuff from the bucket, this subconscious stuff, which is not procurable on demand. And when the process is over, when the picture or symphony or lyric or novel (or whatever it is) is complete, the artist, looking back on it, will wonder how on earth he did it. And indeed he did not do it on earth.

E. M. Forster. 'The Raison d'Etre of Criticism in the Arts' (*1948*); *reprinted in* Two Cheers for Democracy (*1951*).

Part Three

THE CRAFT OF FICTION

INTRODUCTION

IT IS ON MATTERS of method and presentation that the artist is often found with the most illuminating things to say, and the novelist is no exception. Whether he considers characterization, narrative technique or the requirements of a good prose style, he is in fact making a statement about the nature of the novel, thus reminding us that form and substance are closely bound together. It may be added that the more successfully he performs his basic narrative function—'oh dear yes, the novel tells a story'—the more likely he is to drug our response to the 'finer growths' which make his work valuable and interesting.[1] How small a part 'story' plays in comparison with other elements in his craft appears in the subsequent discussion; the 'finer growths' are investigated under these general headings and sub-headings:

> I   Structural Problems
>   Unity and Coherence
>   Plot and Story
>   The Time-factor
> II   Narrative Technique
> III   Characterization
> IV   Dialogue
> V   Background
> VI   Style

[1] See E. M. Forster, *Aspects of the Novel*, Chapter ii.

I Structural Problems

UNITY AND COHERENCE

UNTIL THIS CENTURY, 'lay' criticism of the novel tended to concentrate on a limited number of elements, notably characterization, plot and, quite frequently, style. The principal criteria of
success for the first two were respectively verisimilitude and unexceptionable moral reference, for the third, correctness and
intelligibility. It is remarkable how obstinately and unenter-
prisingly these worthy but limited preoccupations persist
throughout the general run of nineteenth-century English
reviewing, no matter which of the major contemporary figures
is in question.[1] Even the more informed interest of some
French critics, notably of certain contributors to *Le Revue des
deux Mondes*, is fixed on general questions released by Realist
and Naturalist controversies rather than on genuine structural
analysis.[2] It is too much, perhaps, to expect interest in the
subtle interplay of the novel's various elements to appear so
soon. The conception of artistic structure has taken more than
a century to lay hold of the popular imagination, and in any
case the novel, still barely respectable even after two hundred
years, is the last form likely to command the appropriate kind
of critical interest and often has to do without it even to-day.
But one is a little surprised at the 'lay' failure to discuss some
of the more obvious 'finer growths', such as the handling of the
point of view from which the story is told or the management
of the time-factor, problems which had been exercising the
novelist's ingenuity for years and which have had such far-
reaching effects on his work. If early critics of *Wuthering Heights*

---

[1] See, for example, G. H. Ford, *Dickens and his Critics* (1955). For further
information I am also indebted to a doctoral thesis (Liverpool, 1958) by
R. J. Owens on George Eliot's critical reputation in the nineteenth century.

[2] See, among many others, Emile Montégut, 'Le Roman intime de la
littérature réaliste. *Fanny*, de M. E. Feydeau', *Revue des deux Mondes*,
1 November 1858; Saint-René Taillandier, 'Le Réalisme épique dans le
roman. *Salammbo* de M. G. Flaubert', *Revue des deux Mondes*, 15 February
1863; F. Brunetière, 'Le Roman réaliste contemporain': 'L'Esthétique
Naturaliste—Charles Bigot': 'Le Roman expérimental': 'Gustave Flaubert':
'Les Origines du Roman naturaliste', *Revue des deux Mondes*, 1 April 1875:
15 September 1879: 15 February 1880: 15 June 1880: 15 September 1881.

had considered Emily Brontë's treatment of these two factors alone, this great book might have been saved a good deal of incomprehension and neglect.

It has been left to a comparatively new kind of *littérateur* to stimulate this type of critical attention. I am speaking of the writer, faintly foreshadowed in the nineteenth century by people like G. H. Lewes and Théodore Bentzon, whose insight into the problems of prose fiction makes him a minor practitioner of some skill and imagination as well as a sensitive critical interpreter. Among the earliest of these is Sir Percy Lubbock, whose *The Craft of Fiction* (1921) breaks new ground by demonstrating that the novelist's choice of narrative method—the 'point of view' from which he tells his story—can vitally affect the unity, emphasis and coherence of his work. A later example is Mr. Robert Liddell, who has so far given us two studies of the novel, *A Treatise on the Novel* (1947) and *Some Principles of Fiction* (1953). Mr. Liddell encourages our fairly recent habit of approaching the novel as an organized and unified whole by recommending us—among other pieces of good advice— to combine the modern practice of isolating key passages for analysis with an extended variant of the older, so-called 'academic', examination of such elements as character and plot. Each method by itself is inadequate, but by combining them we may avoid the errors of distortion and so come to a better understanding of the artist's purpose and achievement.[1]

Before these critical developments took place, the conscious craftsman had long cried in the wilderness for some acknowledgment that his works might be skilfully unified structures. Henry James's prefaces and letters betray a Flaubert-like melancholy in their sorrowing admission that meticulous artistry in this respect is unlikely to be generally appreciated—Sir Percy Lubbock's study is, indeed, partly an act of piety by a Jamesian devotee anxious to render a hitherto unfulfilled service to the Master. But it must be recognized, too, that the least pretentious pot-boiling entertainer deserves credit for contriving in the interests of his design, even if this is no more than a simple adventure story, some interdependence of story, plot, character, dialogue and setting. Dickens, not perhaps either unpretentious or unambitious but at least a magnificent pot-boiling

[1] Robert Liddell, *A Treatise on the Novel*, pp. 21-9.

entertainer, is in the process nowadays of being exonerated from blame for failing to plan and organize his material; but the truth is that he would have been incapable of writing a single novel without some feeling for the relationship between character, setting and action, and without some elementary sense of structure and organization. 'Form *is* substance', as James says, 'to that degree that there is absolutely no substance without it.' [1]

Two factors are of importance in affecting the novelist's solution of his technical difficulties; his own temperament and the nature of his subject. 'Every great artist necessarily creates his own form', says Tolstoy in a statement which reads like a corollary to James's pronouncement about form and substance. [2] Stevenson adds, 'with each new subject . . . the true artist will vary his method and change the point of attack'. [3] This may superficially suggest that the novel is indeed as 'amorphous' as Mr. Forster says it is, [4] but it seems true to say that the novelist's 'subject', 'method' and 'point of attack' produce a limited number of recognizable 'kinds'. By the end of the eighteenth century it was already a commonplace that two essentially different kinds of fiction might be associated with the novelist's mode of solving basic technical problems. Johnson, Richard Cumberland, Mrs. Barbauld and Scott are among those who felt that the intrusive 'omniscient' author, his attention fixed on the 'dial-plate', was likely to produce a different type of novel from the man who tried to find out 'how a watch was made' and dramatized inner movements of feeling and thought with the help of the epistolary method, the autobiographical 'memoir', [5] or even the narrative 'going backwards' (Horace Walpole's description of *Tristram Shandy*[6]). Early novelists consciously separated themselves into opposite camps according to their method of approach. Fielding distinguished his kind from Richardson's, Sarah Fielding, allying herself with Richardson, distinguished hers from her brother's. [7] With the alterations in sensibility which took place in the nineteenth century, however, fresh forms of fiction appeared. The differences are obviously greater than the similarities when *Pride and Prejudice* is set beside

---

[1] See below, p. 235. [2] See below, p. 265.
[3] See Part I above, p. 82. [4] See *Aspects of the Novel*, pp. 14–15.
[5] See below, pp. 258–9. [6] See below, p. 257.
[7] See below, pp. 275–7.

Wuthering Heights or *Humphry Clinker* beside *Middlemarch*, while *Wuthering Heights* and *Middlemarch* themselves represent contrasting kinds of achievement. By the time of James it is becoming apparent that, according to his 'subject', 'method' and 'point of attack', the novelist will tend to produce one or other of four types of structure:

(i) As a commentator on the broad tendencies and attitudes of a society or an age, the novelist appears as the 'inclusive' panoramic author, whose portrait of life employs comedy, irony and satire as the instruments of its critical strategy. The fluency and inventiveness of this writer usually serve his story and his vivid presentation of surface attitudes at the expense of his sense of form and his insight into the hidden recesses of personality. Fielding and Dickens are examples and here, if anywhere, the reader may be able to abandon himself to the narrative, responding, without necessarily looking before and after, to the successions of crisis and resolution which make up the tale. (Even so, Fielding likes to remind us that memory and foreknowledge are needed to appreciate the workings of his plot and the full flavour of his comic irony.)[1]

(ii) As the analyst of individual feelings and emotions, the novelist appears as the sensitive 'exclusive' artist whose interpretation of life—especially in its exploration of hidden human conflict—is disciplined by a profounder irony and sometimes illuminates the nature of tragic experience. A certain technical fastidiousness is indissociable from this kind of writing; even when the nice discrimination of a Jane Austen or a Henry James is replaced by the 'dreadful fluidity of self-revelation' (as in *Jane Eyre* or Clarissa's letters) the novelist is still concentrating every ounce of his technical skill on the task of successfully dramatizing his chosen centre of consciousness. This kind of art demands a more complex response from the reader since memory and foreknowledge are indispensable for the full appreciation of, let us say, the extent and significance of Strether's illusions in *The Ambassadors* or the heroine's self-deceptions in *Emma*—or indeed, in the same novel, the full richness of Miss Bates's streams of consciousness, with their unwitting revelations about the Jane Fairfax–Frank Churchill situation.

[1] See, for example, *Tom Jones*, Book XVIII, Chap. ii, 'If the reader will please to refresh his memory by turning to the scene at Upton. . . .'

(iii) As 'sage' or 'prophet' the novelist tends to combine the inclusive writer's uneconomical prodigality and the exclusive writer's feeling for pattern. In the 'sage'—George Eliot or Tolstoy, for example—it is primarily an intellectual logic which shapes the pattern. Here again a certain strenuousness of critical response is demanded. In order to understand what George Eliot intends by her handling of the self-deceptions of Lydgate, Bulstrode or Dorothea herself—'our deeds determine us as much as we determine our deeds'—we need to pay as much attention to the interdependence of the various moments of moral crisis as we do when we read *Emma* or *The Ambassadors*. The same attention is needed if we are to grasp in Tolstoy the significant relationship between 'war' and 'peace', and between great historical events and the individual's personal experience of the passage of time.

(iv) For the novelist as 'prophet'—Dostoevsky, D. H. Lawrence or the late James—the shaping principle is less a matter of intellectual logic than of the poetic imagination expressing itself through symbols and sustained metaphors (which often provide overtones of the supernatural). Here a full response seems to demand an examination of the relationship between theme, image and the texture of the writing, as well as alertness to the interdependent sequences of crisis and resolution which contribute to the 'rhythm' of the whole work.

If the analogy between the novel and epic is insisted upon, it is possible to argue that of these various kinds the 'panoramic' approximates more closely than the others to the 'comic epic in prose' as defined by Fielding, while the writings of the 'sage' and 'prophet' more nearly approach the dimensions of the serious epic. But the usefulness of this analogy is doubtful. It was indicated in Chapter I that the novelist's attempt to relate his work to earlier forms of narrative was of value in keeping his imagination awake to the stimulus of fantasy. On the other hand, his conception of the classical epic as a form whose structural 'rules' necessarily established a precedent for his own work was not so helpful and on occasion could be inhibiting. In fact the novelist's *début* in a period interested in preserving the classical distinction of literary kinds placed him at a serious initial disadvantage and helped to prolong his period of experimental instability and self-consciousness. The novelist's natural independence and flexibility, his sense that it is his own personal vision which gives shape and meaning to his art, conflict with authoritarian efforts to tether him to 'rules' connected with 'the Unities' or to 'epic regularity'. Fielding's art, with its generous provision for tactical double-dealing, expresses an instinctive impatience with precedent, however strong his classical allegiances seem to be. As I have already pointed out, he leaves us plenty of room to believe that he is burlesquing the whole notion of following classical examples when he fathers his 'comic epic' on Homer's lost *Margites* or adopts Aristotle's enumeration of the epic's essential elements.[1] Even Fielding, however, frequently acknowledges the tendencies of his age without, apparently, any ambiguity of tone. In his favourable review of Charlotte Lennox's *The Female Quixote* (1752), he reaffirms the value of classical precedent:

here is a regular story, which, though possibly it is not pursued with that epic regularity which would give it the name of an Action, comes much nearer to that perfection than the loose unconnected Adventures in Don Quixote . . .[2]

In fact the concept of 'epic regularity' as a structural principle continues to haunt English writers as different from each other and as far apart in time as Richardson, Scott, Dickens, Trollope, Hardy and Conrad's disciple, Ford Madox Ford. As late as 1888 Hardy is still quoting Addison on the subject of the epic 'rules' which forbid digression and, in the same period, Fielding's 'Man of the Hill' episode is still a critical King Charles's Head.[3] Richard Cumberland, Mrs. Barbauld, Dickens and Trollope all refer to this interpolated story in *Tom Jones* with varying degrees of disapproval—and, possibly, envious irritation. 'It is thrust', grumbles Scott, 'unnecessarily and artificially' into the tale, 'in compliance with a custom introduced by Cervantes'.[4] Trollope argues that digressions

distract the attention of the reader, and always do so disagreeably. Who has not felt this to be the case even with 'The Curious Impertinent' and with the history of 'The Man of the Hill?'[5]

---

[1] See Part I above, pp. 59–60.
[2] See below, p. 227.
[3] See below, pp. 244, 233.
[4] See below, p. 231.
[5] See below, p. 233.

Dickens refers to digressions like these when he admits his own failure to make 'the blood of the whole book' circulate through 'The History of a Self-Tormentor' in *Little Dorrit*.[1]

But though they may affirm the value of 'regularity' in principle, English novelists do their best to circumvent its control. Their easy prodigality sometimes shocks the French artist. Flaubert could hardly get over his first encounter with *The Pickwick Papers*:

Some bits are magnificent; but what a defective structure! All the English writers are like that. Walter Scott apart, they lack composition. This is intolerable for us Latins.[2]

Moreover, English novelists thoroughly enjoy their freedom even while they pretend to apologize for it—indeed their exuberance seems to be heightened by the sense that their behaviour carries some flavour of the *enfant terrible*. Scott himself (Flaubert misjudges him) defends his 'scenes unlaboured and loosely put together' on the grounds of variety and entertainment, exclaiming with the Greek slave who brought a false report of victory, 'Am I to blame, O Athenians, who have given you one happy day?'[3] In *Tom Jones*, Fielding pretends to forestall pedantic strictures by telling 'any little reptile of a critic' to wait until the end of the story before condemning any of its incidents 'as impertinent and foreign to our main design'.[4] But it is Sterne who demonstrates with more vivacity than any other early writer that a novel can owe its coherence to something other than rules for epic regularity. His ingenious digressiveness, which is a complex and delightful outcome of an interest in Locke's theories about the association of ideas, his admiration for Swift and his own supple fantasy, expresses consistently his individual sensibility. He speaks no more than the truth about *Tristram Shandy* (1781) when he explains that digressions

incontestably, are the sunshine—they are the life, the soul of reading!—Take them out of this book, for instance—you might as well take the book along with them. . . .[5]

---

[1] See below, p. 231. [2] See below, p. 232.
[3] See below, pp. 229–30. [4] See below, p. 227.
[5] See below, p. 228.

The entire ordered disorder is given its focus by his personal slant on the freaks and oddities of life—'focus', as Tolstoy was to describe it more than a century later, is 'the most important thing in a work of art . . . the place in which all the rays meet or from which they issue', and it can be explained only 'by the work in its entirety'.[1]

Sterne's qualities of sensibility have persuaded some readers to think of him as an early precursor of Virginia Woolf,[2] but the comparison can be very misleading. Sterne's art has not finally freed itself from its age; its rebellion, after all, takes place within that age's system of values. Profounder modifications of sensibility have to occur before we find the novel responding to the more subtle rhythms of the poetic imagination. In England, the groundswell of romanticism affects the subject-matter of the novel long before Scott, as early indeed as Horace Walpole,[3] but it is not until Emily Brontë's *Wuthering Heights* (1848) that its full influence is felt in shape and structure and texture. The most finished art before *Wuthering Heights* had been Jane Austen's. Obedient to eighteenth-century notions of formal discipline, it is shaped by a rational, orderly temperament which dislikes waste and feels compelled to tidy up life's customary messiness. It marshals people and events with neatness and economy, firmly excludes unruly passions, and keeps comic freaks like Mr. Collins well in order. The whole design is in conformity with laws of reason and good sense which impose themselves, so to speak, from outside. In *Wuthering Heights*, on the other hand, an even more exacting sense of discipline has confronted powerful and complex emotions until the tension is felt everywhere in the book like a pulse. The movement of events, through cycles of crisis and calm, winter and summer, love and death, is governed by an interior dialectic which finally resolves itself in a tentative equilibrium. Elements are held together by an imaginative logic of the kind which a later 'poetic' novelist, E. M. Forster, attempts to analyse when he edges towards those 'aspects' of the novel which he calls 'pattern', 'rhythm', 'prophecy' and 'song'.[4]

[1] See below, p. 235.
[2] See, for example, E. M. Forster's comments in *Aspects of the Novel*, pp. 30–3.   [3] See Part I above, pp. 4, 17, 45.
[4] See below, pp. 237–40, and *Aspects of the Novel*, Chapter vii.

169

The most vital art produced in the novel by this type of sensibility appears when the novelist is emancipated from the closed morality of conventional beliefs and does not in any way lose his strong sense of concrete actuality. *Wuthering Heights* explores two violently opposed modes of being: on the one hand, the intimate experience of feeling, and on the other, the more orderly social virtues of life 'in the valley'. With the help of figures like Heathcliff and the Lintons and settings like the exposed house on the bare moortops and the sheltered Linton home below, Emily Brontë invests her conflicting allegiances with a local habitation and an authentic 'name'. Her book is a statement of emotional conflict in which various elements of character, setting and incident possess the force of metaphor without losing their 'solidity of specification'. A comparable effect distinguishes the writings of the French novelist, Stendhal. (It is in abstractifying his statement of conflict until almost all hold on the concrete is lost that the German novelist has differed so profoundly from his English, French and American counterparts.) In Stendhal, a romanticism reluctantly confessed is explored by a restless, incisive and obviously more worldly-wise intellect than Emily Brontë's.[1] The disciplinary function of his vigorous reasoning receives support from his classical sense of form, with the result that in *Le Rouge et le Noir* he achieves a superbly uncluttered and at the same time ruthlessly logical narrative sequence. But the texture of the whole book is given its richness and subtlety by emotions which find more than one level of significance in such objects as the 'walls' which Julien Sorel is continually obliged to scale, or in the 'scarlet' and the 'black' which recur at intervals to emphasize the nature of the conflicts dividing him. Similar qualities are discovered in *La Chartreuse de Parme*, which is less obedient to a feeling for economy but compensates for this by the poetic overtones which accompany the treatment of Fabrice's wandering and imprisonment, and by the vivacity which enlivens the interplay of passion and expediency in the novel's world of political intrigue.

At a later stage of its evolution in the history of the novel, this kind of sensibility more and more seeks the discipline of scrupulous aesthetic principles. A sign of this tendency is the

[1] See also Part I above, pp. 18–19.

novelist's increasing interest in matters of method and presentation. The effects of this interest are seen at their best in the finished art of 'pure' novelists like Henry James, Flaubert and Turgenev, writers who continue to record the conflicts of a particular kind of romanticism less as controversialists than as sensitive, compassionate suffering observers. Without the urgent disquiet of an Emily Brontë or a Stendhal, they employ a more patient, a more composed kind of analysis. Strictly speaking they are 'romantic' novelists only in the sense that their complexity has in it an irreducible surd element. Their art obeys instinctive and compulsive rhythms of feeling alien to a rational art like Jane Austen's, but they seek to control these rhythms by various devices, all of which increase aesthetic distance, especially the more or less deliberate arrangement of recurrent themes and objects in the manner of the *leit-motif*. Flaubert, for example, emphasizes the ebb and flow of feeling in *Madame Bovary* by introducing for the purposes of emotional contrast linked items such as the two wedding-bouquets, the luxurious carriage in Emma's honeymoon fantasy and the hansom-cab of her adulterous love-affair, and by emphasizing the divergent strains in the *comices agricoles*.[1] He also uses for the same ends the relentless march of the seasons and the blind beggar's song about summer and love—anticipating here Proust's use of the Vinteuil tune in *A la Recherche du Temps Perdu*. Later, Henry James makes the flawed *objet d'art* in *The Golden Bowl* the focus of his several themes and plays with images of innocence and cunning—especially the 'dove' and the 'serpent'—in *The Wings of the Dove*. Even if these craftsmen—who discuss various processes of composition in some detail—offer no hint of the symbols, sustained metaphors or 'patterns' of their work in progress and probably have to rely on 'a local impulse when the right interval is reached',[2] their devices obviously represent a more deliberately sustained search for aesthetic order than does the use of recurrences in *Wuthering Heights*. (Emily Brontë introduces, for example, a recurrent complex of elements

---

[1] See below, p. 240.

[2] There is no mention of the function of the Golden Bowl in any part of James's 'copious preliminaries'. See *The Notebooks of Henry James* (1947), ed. F. O. Mathiessen and Kenneth B. Murdoch, pp. 130–2, 187–9, 194, 228, 233, 234.

composed of Catherine Earnshaw's bed, the window, the tree outside and the suggestions of violence and the supernatural which accompany these things.[1])

The desire to be just by imposing this kind of aesthetic order on recalcitrant material is perhaps the most important single development in the evolution of the novel. The appearance of this new scrupulosity signalizes modes of feeling and thought altogether foreign to those which first brought the novel into being, and in many cases indicates a longing to transcend the impurities of a form which is rich in possibilities but somehow often apparently lacks congruity with the deeper needs of the artistic sense. The new approach lies behind Flaubert's desire to write a book 'about nothing' and his striving for symphonic effect in *Madame Bovary*,[2] Forster's need to believe that 'in music fiction is likely to find its nearest parallel'—a need felt by many other novelists of the early twentieth century, notably Proust, Aldous Huxley and André Gide[3]—and Virginia Woolf's combination of impressionism and poetic metaphor ('she is a poet who wants to write something as near to a novel as possible', says Forster[4]).

In reaching towards a method of reconciling the truths of individual observation with the part-abstractions of a wider realism these writers are served by their sense of form. The sensitive balance of their art is outside the range of both the 'sage' and such huge bardic novelists as Melville and Dostoevsky. The 'sage' sometimes gropes for similar devices in order to reinforce his argument. George Eliot seeks to underline the perils of moral indecision by placing her characters at hours of crisis near or on the drifting tides of rivers (Book Sixth, Chapter xiii in *The Mill on the Floss*; Book II, Chapter xvii in *Daniel Deronda*). But this kind of imagination is impelled towards metaphor by didactic zeal rather than aesthetic scruple (this is apparent in George Eliot's *The Spanish Gypsy* and helps to account for the work's total failure as a poem). Images and sustained metaphors in this case vivify the 'lesson' but do not indicate the feeling

[1] See my article, '*Wuthering Heights:* The rejection of Heathcliff?' *Essays in Criticism* (January 1958), pp. 27–47.

[2] See below, pp. 242, 240.

[3] See below, pp. 238–41.

[4] See E. M. Forster, *Virginia Woolf* (1942), p. 18.

for organic unity which accompanies poetic imagination. The feeling is detected in the 'prophetic' novelists even when they have difficulty in managing their material. Like the 'pure' novelists these writers also seek to transcend the novel's limitations, charging things perceived with the force of symbols, and striving to lift them, at various points, on to the level of universal significance. Dostoevsky has to admit that he cannot easily organize his loosely-knit, unwieldy material—his irritation with Turgenev springs in part from his envy of so finished an artist —but he does manage to swing the whole vast structure of *The Brothers Karamazov* on the pivotal themes of the tremendous 'Pro and Contra' sequence, where he employs fictional devices which borrow their effects from legend and allegory (the debate between Alyosha and Ivan includes the impressive 'Legend of the Grand Inquisitor'), and he enormously enriches his texture with the multiple levels of significance which he attaches to the various members of the Karamazov clan. In Melville, too, powerful feelings of anxiety which accompany the habit of metaphysical speculation find release in compulsive symbols of extraordinary impressiveness and appeal. The archetypal 'quest' pattern imposes a certain unity on *Moby Dick* which otherwise displays to an extreme degree the diffuseness and irregularity of the loose, comprehensive novel. Although D. H. Lawrence's preoccupations are of a totally different kind, his achievement similarly shows that the novelist's complete possession by his subject can force from him a series of connected images which will given an effect of coherence to his work. In *Women in Love* images of darkness and light, sun and snow, underline the novel's themes, while 'whiteness' acquires Melville-like connotations of danger, violence, sterility and destruction. But these writers also show us the dangerous failures of perspective in 'bardic' fiction: Melville in *Pierre*, for example, and—to be honest—Dostoevsky and Lawrence almost everywhere. When such breakdowns occur the reader may sigh for a little 'epic regularity' of the old-fashioned eighteenth-century kind.

PLOT AND STORY

The internal logic of the imagination and the emotions, however compulsive it may be, does not mean that the novelist can dispense with a narrative or a plot. These constitute the skeleton of his work, deplore it as he may. It is true that a lyrical talent like Virginia Woolf's in *The Waves* seems to make do with a skeleton of unprecedented fragility, but even here the narrative stands up sturdily on examination as one important means by which the work remains recognizably a novel. *The Waves* traces the development from childhood and early youth to troubled middle-age of six characters, Bernard, Louis, Neville, Rhoda, Susan and Jinny. These grow up together in the same nursery, school-room and garden. They go away to school, carrying with them the emotions, the fears and ambitions, which have already shaped their infancy. When their schooling is over, Neville and Bernard go on to a University, but Louis, the lonely Australian, finds employment as a clerk. Of the girls Jinny plunges into a life of pleasure, Susan sinks into placidity as the wife of a farmer and the mother of his children, and Rhoda, tormented by uncertainties and afraid of life, suffers from an unhappy love-affair with Louis, finally escaping from her anguish by suicide. Meanwhile, a young man named Percy, admired by the group and once in love with Susan, dies far away from them in India, heightening their sense of time, death and separation.

If this is not a narrative—and I have simplified it considerably—it is hard to say what is. It is also, if we examine it, a 'plot'. Novelists have not generally bothered a great deal to explain what difference is implied by the existence of the two terms, 'story' and 'plot'—indeed they often use them interchangeably. As an eighteenth-century critic said of the terms 'fable' and 'action', the terms 'seem not to be sufficiently distinguished'.[1] The blame for this lack of clarity must rest partly with the eighteenth-century neo-classicists, whose interpretations of classical 'rules' were often confused and contradictory, and partly with Aristotle himself, whose account of the relationship between $\mu\tilde{\upsilon}\theta o\varsigma$ and $\pi\rho\acute{\alpha}\gamma\mu\alpha\tau\alpha$ (i.e. 'plot' and 'the incidents, or things done' which combine to make up a narrative) leaves a good deal unanswered.[2] Few novelists have managed to be as helpful on the subject as Mr. Forster. 'Story', he

[1] Joseph Trapp, Preface to *Aeneis* (1718), *Works of Virgil* (1731).
[2] See, for example, H. Swedenberg, *The Theory of the Epic in England* (1944), p. 35, n. 8, pp. 166-8.

tells us, 'is a sequence of events unfolded in time.' As for 'plot', this is

> a narrative of events, the emphasis falling on causality. 'The king died and then the queen died' is a story. 'The king died and then the queen died of grief' is a plot.[1]

Obviously it is partly this causal connection which gives some of their significance to the 'sequences of events' in *The Waves*, since in the six characters thought, feeling and action are conditioned by the past and by the interplay of their contrasted personalities. If we give Mr. Forster's rudimentary situation another turn of the screw, we arrive moreover at an interesting complication of 'plot':

> 'The queen died, no one knew why, until it was discovered that it was through grief at the death of the king.' This is a plot with a mystery in it, a form capable of high development.[2]

The nature of this development becomes apparent, I think, if we turn from *The Moonstone* to *The Ambassadors*. 'Mystery' in the sense intended here is not, however, a device to be found in a novel like *The Waves*.

If we accept Mr. Forster's working definitions we find that many novelists who speak of 'story' are in fact referring to the basic type of 'plot', i.e. 'a narrative of events, the emphasis falling on causality'. So, Hardy insists that a 'story' should be an 'organism', and he quotes in support of his contention Addison's Aristotelian view of each of its events:

> nothing should go before it, or follow after it, that is not related to it[3]

—in other words, 'no digressions'. But then, by this definition, we should not be able to describe some of the tales in *The Arabian Nights* as 'stories' at all. Mr. Forster clears up a good deal of confusion when he attributes Scheherazade's success in keeping her head on her shoulders to her skill in unfolding 'a sequence of events' which takes little account of causality but is alert to the needs of the primitive instinct which asks 'what happens next'.[4] 'The sense of inevitability' which Ford Madox Ford—a writer who is at times something more than a conscientious technician—associates with 'story' is really a characteristic of 'plot'. 'What matters', maintains Ford, is 'your story,

---

[1] See below, p. 248. [2] Ibid.
[3] See below, p. 244. [4] See *Aspects of the Novel*, Chapter ii.

and then your story—and then your story', but he also refers to this essential element as the 'subject' and stresses that it must communicate a sense of inevitability, adding

a character may cry, 'If I had then acted differently, how different everything would now be.' The problem of the author is to make his then action the only action that character could have taken.[1]

By hinting at the novel's interdependence of 'character', 'action' and 'time', this passage leaves 'story'—the 'naked worm of time'—far behind and in fact makes a statement about a sequence of events where the emphasis falls on causality. The natural conclusion is, of course, that in the real novel there is always 'plot' and never simply 'story' in Mr. Forster's sense of these terms. (It is, after all, on the novelist's conception of cause and effect that the quality of his achievement ultimately depends.)

More often than not, the novelist's use of 'plot' as a term signifies exclusively 'a causal sequence complicated by a mystery'—with most of the emphasis on the 'mystery'—and as such it may become an aspect of his craft which he views understandably with some irritation ('conspiracy' or 'intrigue' as connotations of 'plot' may have an unconscious influence here). It is certainly 'plot' in this sense which George Eliot considers 'a vulgar coercion', and its connection in her mind with the merely sensational is indicated by her subsequent comment that readers prefer 'a murder in the middle distance', with a little light comedy to relieve it.[2] A similar identification of plot and sensationalism makes Trollope reject plot as an inferior thing, seen in its best light as a vehicle for 'real characters',[3] and Mary Mitford wish that novels might be written without any plot at all.[4] Mr. Forster, however, reserves his contempt for the 'story', a 'low atavistic form' appealing to no response more complex than a primitive curiosity. Plot, on the other hand, he reckons among the novel's 'finer growths', since it requires for its appreciation the exercise of intelligence and memory and can possess in its own right important aesthetic values.[5] Henry James's slightly acid reference to 'story' as 'the spoiled child

[1] See below, pp. 235, 245. [2] See below, pp. 247 8.
[3] See below, p. 247. [4] Ibid.
[5] See below, pp. 248–9.

176

of art' seems to derive from a similar sense of its essential naïveté.[1]

The novelist's impatience, whether it is aroused by the simplicities of story-telling or the latent sensationalism of plot in any but the most elevated sense of the word, is an effect of the recalcitrant nature of his material: 'art' being, as James puts it, 'all discrimination and selection', while 'life' is 'all inclusion and confusion'.[2] At a later stage of his development his impatience, as we have seen, is acute. But the novelist knows very well that he can never finally turn his back on the entertainer. If he rejects the fanciful invention of a Scheherazade in the interests of a more serious and 'significant' art, he must still retain his audience's interest and curiosity. It is here that comment is needed on the damaging effect of 'plot' conceived exclusively as a causal sequence requiring the complication of 'a mystery'. All depends, of course, on the interpretation given to the last phrase. It may signify no more than an understanding requiring to be completed, which is quite inoffensive. On the other hand it may mean the most tawdry sensationalism. In order to meet the demand for suspense and excitement the novelist frequently complicates with arbitrary and unnecessary 'mystifications' a sequence of events already shaped by the nature of his chosen themes. In *Middlemarch*, for example, the various degrees of self-deception, the clash of egotisms in the two principal marriages, the constant interplay of temperament and environment, are themes which illuminate and are in turn illuminated by the central conception of the moral life which sets in motion the real progression of events. Here is 'plot' enough, its sequence ordered by a particularly mature conception of the relationship between cause and effect: one which provides, moreover, plenty of entertainment for the reader who wants to know 'what happens next' (will Dorothea Casaubon discover her mistake? Will Lydgate marry Rosamond Vincy? Will Fred Vincy make good? etc.). Yet George Eliot yields to the 'vulgar coercion' and introduces the hocus-pocus about inheritance (the corresponding element is even worse in *Felix Holt*), which depends on coincidence and incongruous pseudo-Dickensian stock figures like Rigg and Raffles to prop it up. The irrelevant plotting may be justified to some extent in this

---

[1] See below, p. 245.   [2] See Part I above, p. 75.

instance because it provides George Eliot with the opportunity for her superb analysis of Bulstrode's stubborn self-delusion (he is morally guilty of Rigg's murder but is shown as still capable of keeping up his normal habits of prayer and devotion),[1] but there is plentiful analysis of this quality in the 'natural' progression of George Eliot's story: she does not need to plot elaborately in order to say what she has to say about various moral and psychological issues. Her own remarks about storytelling leave us with the feeling that she was not altogether satisfied with conventional techniques and might, with a little more imaginative independence, have made some interesting experiments of her own.[2]

But even Jane Austen admits 'mystery' into her plotting. As we expect, this is adroitly contrived to reinforce her ironic structure. 'Prejudice' delays Elizabeth's unravelling of the Darcy-Wickham situation, while 'pride' at first prevents Darcy from discussing Wickham's behaviour in detail as it finally compels him to speak out in his own defence. In *Emma*, the Jane Fairfax mystery provides a pointed comment on the gulf separating things as they appear to the deluded eyes of the egotist and things as they really are. Miss Bates's garrulity and Emma's self-deception—the one distracting attention from the relevant information which it offers, the other blunting perception—act admirably to preserve the surface mystery. But the exigences of 'a plot with a mystery in it' can betray even a Jane Austen occasionally into clumsy unravelling devices: the long explanatory letters from Darcy and Mrs. Gardiner in *Pride and Prejudice*, for example, or Mrs. Smith's 'confession' in *Persuasion* (this is Jane Austen's 'Man of the Hill' episode).[3]

Such clumsiness apart, Jane Austen does show that 'a plot with a mystery in it' is a form 'capable of high development'. Many of the great social satirists and comic entertainers tell in the opposite direction. Here mystery and concealment are valued merely as an easy way of keeping the story going; and probability in the treatment of cause and effect hardly comes into the question at all. When Fielding draws our attention to the ingenuity which delays his *dénouement* in *Tom Jones*, he is

---

[1] See *Middlemarch*, Book VII, Chapter lxx.
[2] See below, pp. 262–4.
[3] See *Pride and Prejudice*, Chapters xxi, lii, and *Persuasion*, Chapter xxi.

acknowledging with his usual humorous irony the artificiality of his own plot conventions. Accident and coincidence, blithely masquerading as a plausible sequence of causally connected events, keep Mrs. Waters and her revelations out of the way until he is ready to put an end to his tale.[1] Fielding is obviously drawing on the conventions of farce (as he had already done in his plays) but we cannot say that this is equally true of Dickens, especially in the 'serious' later novels. 'Intelligence and memory' are wasted in trying to follow his wildly improbable complications of accident, disguise, concealment and coincidence, because the relationships between these elements fail to illuminate what these books are really 'about'. How Little Dorrit, for example, comes to lose, regain and then re-lose a fortune matters less than the various effects of this process, which is primarily what Dickens is interested in; and the same can be said of the Chancery ramifications affecting almost all the characters in *Bleak House*. On the other hand, the 'mystification' in *Great Expectations* is entirely relevant to the causal sequence of events and has its own integral connection with the book's main theme. This is a more sophisticated use of 'a plot with a mystery in it' than is usual with Dickens. The extraordinary concealments and falsifications of identity in *Our Mutual Friend* are similarly ambitious, but here the conception is confused and melodramatic, and if anything the themes are obscured rather than clarified by the devices. Nevertheless, Dickens is attempting here to subtilize plot, and to make it play a meaningful part in a total design. A brilliant 'sensational' plot-maker like Wilkie Collins—whose mastery of 'the detective element' and whose firm, elementary structural sense certainly stung Dickens into a greater care for composition—does not try for similar significance. He starts with the avowed purpose of contriving a 'mystery' more or less for its own sake, using various legal anomalies for his material and working out his schemes with the skill of a good chess-player. His novels inaugurate the flourishing tradition of English (and American) detective fiction; and in his best books his firm, exciting 'plots'

[1] See *Tom Jones*, Books IX, X; Book XVIII, Chapters ii–xii. R. S. Crane in *Critics and Criticism* (1952) seems to suggest that Fortune and Chance are an integral part of Fielding's 'meaning': see 'The Concept of Plot and the plot of *Tom Jones*', *Critics and Criticism*, pp. 616–47.

THE CRAFT OF FICTION

provide admirable models, supported as they are by competent characterization, accurate special information and convincing evocation of background and atmosphere.

Plot, finally, can become aesthetically valuable as well as entertaining when it is made to serve, along with every other narrative device, the novelist's central conception of 'the way things happen'. Too often in the English novel it is manipulated by the preacher in order to demonstrate how things ought to happen. Even George Eliot's 'natural' sequences reveal this tendency—for example, in *Silas Marner* and *Daniel Deronda*. But a modern novelist, Miss Ivy Compton-Burnett, perhaps the most ruthless moralist of them all, demonstrates that the entire apparatus of melodrama can be used in the interests of the plot's aesthetic value, provided that this apparatus genuinely subserves the artist's vision of life. A firm believer in the structural importance of plot, Miss Compton-Burnett allows her characters to conceal, and then sometimes to uncover, every crime in the calendar from blackmail to incest and matricide, because she believes

there are signs that strange things happen, though they do not emerge. I believe it would go ill with many of us, if we were faced with a strong temptation, and I suspect that with some of us it does go ill.[1]

Her sense of hidden forms of violence and treachery beneath the superficial amenities of social intercourse gives her work its shapeliness and energy. For her, plot is altogether emancipated from the simple 'detective' formula and derives its importance from an artistic intention which is more serious and more imaginative than any elementary manipulation of curiosity and suspense. The complexity and subtlety of plot are greater still in such 'sequences of events, the emphasis falling on causality' as the process by which Strether's perplexity gradually yields to enlightenment, suffering and compassionate understanding in *The Ambassadors*; the complication and resolution of spiritual conflict in *Crime and Punishment* or *The Brothers Karamazov*; the means by which, in *Wuthering Heights*, passions of love, hatred and revenge work themselves towards a mood of equilibrium and reconciliation; or the turns of hostile destiny gradually

[1] See below, p. 249.

wearing down human endurance in *The Mayor of Casterbridge* or *Jude the Obscure*. The function of plot in such novels helps to distinguish the art of the 'poetic' novelist from, on the one hand, the limited if poised and sophisticated art of the rational 'exclusive' novelist like Jane Austen, and, on the other, the anecdotal and digressive expertise of the broad comic satirists like Fielding and Thackeray.

THE TIME-FACTOR

All novelists are bound alike by their allegiance to time. When Henry James warns his fellow-novelists that 'this eternal time-question is . . . always there and always formidable; always insisting on the *effect* of the great lapse and passage, of the "dark backward and abysm" ' [1] he is attaching himself to the distinction which most decidedly separates novelists from their predecessors in other literary forms. We sometimes speak of eighteenth-century literature as occupying itself primarily with generalities, but in fact the intellectual climate fostering the novel's growth is remarkable for its emphasis on the particular and the individual. The concept of individuality, which owes much to Lockeian and Cartesian influences, depends on particularity of place and time, and it is this precise spatial and temporal location of individual experience which is really the 'novel' aspect of fiction. The classical 'Unities', after all, sacrifice everything to singleness and force of impression, while the management of time in Elizabethan, and particularly Shakespearian, drama is endlessly and wantonly arbitrary. Three hundred years after the new attitude to the 'time-question' finally separated Defoe's narratives even from such 'realistic' fiction as Bunyan's or Nashe's, we find a modern novelist, E. M. Forster, reminding us that the novel faces one of its most exacting problems in its double allegiance to 'life by the clock' and 'life by values'. ('I only saw her for five minutes, but it was worth it', is his illustration of this difference.[2]) It is an allegiance from which there is no escape since in order to remain intelligible the novelist must always cling, 'however lightly', to 'the interminable tape-worm' of chronometrical time; and in order to make his selection of

---

[1] See below, p. 253. [2] Ibid.

events significant he must also concern himself unremittingly with 'life by values'.

It is easy to overlook the skill and patience demanded by the novelist's humble but necessary task of clinging to time 'by the clock' (we should certainly be disconcerted were he ever to let go). A good deal of his initial effort is spent in contriving an accurate chronological sequence for his events, selecting particular dates for the major occurrences in his characters' lives, and deciding the periods of time required for every sort of event from emotional recovery from a bereavement to a railway journey from, say, Lancaster to Clacton-on-Sea. Fielding, with the zeal of the pioneer, used an almanac for *Tom Jones*, so that it is even possible (should anyone be interested) to determine the phases of the moon during a particular period of the hero's wanderings.[1] Richardson's time-sequence is an example of phenomenally intricate and accurate contrivance and so, too, is Sterne's in *Tristram Shandy*. Emily Brontë, as different as possible from her predecessors in other ways, nevertheless shares their vigilant care for chronological accuracy, flawlessly interweaving the present of Lockwood's commentary with the past of Nellie Dean's narrative and firmly if unobtrusively establishing the relative ages of her characters—essential information in a story concerned with successive generations in two families—and in some cases even telling us the days and hours of their birth, marriage and burial. This is not to say that a good novelist will not make mistakes or that such mistakes are serious blemishes, but signs of this same care will be found in every kind of novelist, from the hugely comprehensive writers like Tolstoy and Balzac to the master craftsmen like James. Certainly the mysteriously shrouded events in *The Wings of the Dove* and *The Golden Bowl* are firmly tied to precise days and seasons (for example, it is in April, just four years and eight months after Prince Amerigo's marriage to Maggie Verver, that he and Charlotte finally go off to Gloucester together).

So far I have been speaking of chronology, of 'time by the clock'. Great differences emerge when we examine the novelist's

[1] See Homes Dudden, *Henry Fielding, His Life, Works and Times* (1952)' Vol. II, pp. 603–4. See also Robert Louis Stevenson's remarks, '. . . how troublesome the moon is! I have come to grief over the moon in *Prince Otto* . . .', below, p. 303.

handling of the relationship between 'time by the clock' and 'time by values'. Fielding certainly suggests that the distinction is important to him by declaring that some of his chapters will suggest 'only the time of a single day,' while others will 'comprise years':

> if whole years should pass without producing anything worthy . . . notice, we shall not be afraid of a chasm in our history, but shall hasten on to matters of consequence . . .[1]

But this is perhaps a dig at Richardson's minuteness of detail and his own tempo is regulated far more by complications of accident and adventure than by intensity of experience. Once he sets these adventures in motion he maintains a rapid pace which justifies references to his narrative skill. His Victorian admirer, Thackeray, deserves—and has lately received[2]—equal praise for a similar raciness when the narrative has to be impelled at speed. But no one would say that Fielding, Thackeray and Sterne (probably the first novelist to abandon chronological sequence for the sake of the individual's subjective commentary on experience) manage to dramatize the intense moment of personal experience in which it seems that ordinary 'time' is transcended, nor do these writers seek to convey any intimate sense of the relentless advance of 'time by the clock'. Of course this is partly a matter of the emotional climate of their age, and partly a matter of personal temperament. In *Vanity Fair*, the effects on a particular sensibility of an age more complex in its stresses and strains than Fielding's are felt in the faint aroma of melancholy emanating from Dobbin's middle-aged disenchantment and clinging so unmistakably to the novel's conclusion. But it is the more robust, less subtly constituted eighteenth-century affinities in Thackeray which render his Becky Sharp apparently as unaffected by the passage of time as she is by the workings of conscience. Richardson, of course, who so often has to stand as a remarkable exception, possesses a power astonishing in his period to capture movements of intense feeling at the very moment of experience: but in the end this quality brings him little nearer than Thackeray or Fielding to that sense of time wearing on remorselessly which gives moral and

---

[1] See below, p. 252.
[2] See Geoffrey Tillotson, *Thackeray the Novelist* (1954), Chapters iii, iv.

emotional significance to a novel like *Wuthering Heights*. Here the progress of the seasons, the cycle of the year, the alternations of summer warmth and winter violence, emphasize inevitable change to which even Catherine's emotional turbulence and Heathcliff's obdurate, destructive passions must submit. The very 'conclusion' is felt as a comment on this ceaseless process: at the moment when the ghosts begin to walk the moors, fresh forces, this time youthfully innocent and constructive, are inaugurating a further cycle of existence. Less complex, perhaps, but equally pervasive, a similar feeling for the passage of time conditions the whole texture of Tolstoy's *War and Peace*, where the bright promise of youth is gradually dulled into the commonplace attitudes of middle age; and this feeling also gives to Flaubert's *L'Education Sentimentale* the poignancy of its wonderful conclusion, where Frédéric Moreau and his friend Deslauriers, looking back from a disenchanted present to a moment of awkward adolescent embarrassment far away in the past, see it now as their one experience of genuine happiness. Even in *Persuasion*, Jane Austen's last novel (published the year after she died), the feeling creeps in—however distrustfully viewed by the author—and Anne Elliot's regret for 'youth, hope and spring, all gone together' causes us to think again about the limits of this novelist's anti-romanticism.[1]

It is only when his imagination is more than usually stimulated by time steadily and relentlessly moving on that the novelist is able to illuminate vividly for us the 'eternal moment' of intense experience: 'life by values' transcending 'life by the clock' and extending the boundaries of emotional experience as it does so. We enter into an experience of this order with Prince Andrew as he lies wounded on the battle-field of Austerlitz;[2] with Milly Theale as, at the height of her happiness, she gazes at the ominous Bronzino portrait—the beautiful girl of another age who is 'dead, dead, dead'—and sees its resemblance to herself;[3] with Lord Jim as he begins to understand the momentous effects of his leap over the ship's side into the little boat;[4] with Proust as he recaptures a whole life-time

[1] See *Persuasion*, Chapter x.
[2] Tolstoy, *War and Peace* (1868-9), Book III, Chapter xvi.
[3] Henry James, *The Wings of the Dove* (1902), Book Fifth, Chapter xi.
[4] Joseph Conrad, *Lord Jim* (1900), Chapters ix-x.

of experience during those moments spent in the Duchesse de Guermantes' anteroom;[1] with Mrs. Ramsay as she presides at her dinner-table and creates out of discordant elements a moment of composure and harmony.[2] For novelists of this century, the sense of time is heightened by the pressures of a discordant age as well as by new psychological and scientific discoveries. Already in the later nineteenth century the discordances are felt in 'the sick hurry and divided aims', while the break-up of accepted psychological concepts is signalled by the pre-Freudian theories of William James, who saw time as a constituting factor of personality and coined the phrase 'stream of consciousness' to explain a part of his meaning. Proust's *A la Recherche du Temps Perdu* (1913–1927), one of the masterpieces of this century, is directly inspired by that sense of 'the inseparableness of us from the past' which informs the Bergsonian theory of *durée*. As 'the eternal moment' of intense experience is taken more and more to be the factor shaping the present and future self, novelists resort to a whole new range of innovatory devices—including the abandonment of ordinary chronological sequence, as in Aldous Huxley's *Eyeless in Gaza* (1936) or William Faulkner's *The Sound and the Fury* (1929), as well as the stream-of-consciousness method, as in Virginia Woolf's *Mrs. Dalloway* (1925) or Joyce's *Ulysses* (1922)—in order to throw into relief these moments of heightened consciousness, these 'epiphanies', which seem to take place in a dimension outside the time registered by the clock on the wall. But these modern methods only give further emphasis to the fact that the sense of individuality depends on memory and that memory in turn depends on time. They remind us that moments of heightened awareness derive from all the moments of the past, that what we are depends on what we have been, and that in the art of the novel the sense of infinity is communicated most poignantly when we are aware of the steady ticking-away of time 'by the clock'.

[1] Marcel Proust, *Time Regained* (1927), Chapter iii.
[2] Virginia Woolf, *To the Lighthouse* (1927), Chapters i, xvii.

II Narrative Technique

THE DIFFERENCES in mood and tempo brought out by the novelist's handling of 'story', 'plot' and 'time' are emphasized further by his choice of narrative method. After *The Craft of Fiction* we can never again altogether ignore this aspect of the novelist's technique. 'The whole intricate question of method, in the craft of fiction,' says Sir Percy Lubbock, 'I take to be governed by the question of the point of view—the question of the relation in which the narrator stands to the story',[1] and he demonstrates with impressive authority and intelligence ways in which various types of writer have attempted to answer the question. And, although we may sympathize with Mr. Forster's demurring comments in *Aspects of the Novel*,[2] it seems true to say that the novelist, if not the reader, has always been very much alive to the importance of selecting the angle of vision from which he will best be able to illuminate and interpret his material and, most important of all, make it seem authentic. In the novel's earlier development, the choice, according to practice and theory alike, lay between the 'narrative or epic' manner, deriving from Cervantes and popularized by Le Sage in France and Fielding in England: the personal 'memoir', used by Marivaux and Smollett, and 'epistolary correspondence', which, combining features of the two other methods, was widely followed in France and was handled with astonishing resourcefulness and variety of effect by writers as different from each other in imaginative and moral vision as Choderlos de Laclos and Samuel Richardson. Most early narrative techniques derive ultimately from these methods, as Mrs. Barbauld indicates in her sensible commentary of 1804. 'The narrative or epic' method, she tells us, is 'the most common way' and has the advantage of flexibility because of the author's assumed omniscience. However, it must be diversified: the omniscient author's narrative

will not be lively, except he frequently drops himself and runs into

---

[1] See Percy Lubbock, *The Craft of Fiction*, Section xviii, and below, p. 268.

[2] See below, pp. 268-9.

dialogue: all good writers therefore have thrown as much as possible of the dramatic into their narrative.[1]

She reminds her readers that the method of 'memoirs' has also been adopted—'Smollett in his *Roderick Random* and Goldsmith, in his *Vicar of Wakefield*, have adopted this mode'—and that such first-person narrative has the advantage of 'the warmth and interest a person may be supposed to feel in his own affairs' (she cites Marivaux's *Marianne*, published 1731–41). Its limitations are such, however, that in the end she believes it to be 'the least perfect mode of any'. It is 'epistolary correspondence' which seems to her to unite 'in good measure the advantages of the other two'. One has to remember that Mrs. Barbauld's essay is written as an introduction to volumes commemorating Samuel Richardson, a master of epistolary art, but the reasons which she gives for this preference are perfectly sound. Playing down to some extent the awkward conventions of the epistolary novel, she emphasizes the dramatic vividness and immediacy of its impressions, its interesting varieties of personal style, and 'the peculiar way of thinking' displayed by its individual characters. Richardson's own account of his method also draws attention to its dramatic value.[2]

It says much for Mrs. Barbauld's perspicacity that subsequent novelists' views on narrative technique coincide at so many points with hers. For instance, they generally echo her misgivings about first-person narratives, in spite of the fact that it is a method which has helped to produce a good many masterpieces in its time (*Robinson Crusoe*, *The Vicar of Wakefield*, *Adolphe*, *Jane Eyre*, *Great Expectations*, *The Horse's Mouth*, *La Chute*, are all first-person narratives). It is usually criticized on aesthetic grounds and writers as different from each other as Trollope and Henry James reject it. Trollope prefers the omniscient manner of third-person narration because in his use of the third person, the author may make the 'I' of his narrative prone either to self-glorification or pretentious humility (was he thinking, one wonders, of *Bleak House*'s Esther Summerson?[3]) What appals James, however, is the 'terrible fluidity of self-revelation'.[4] (In Germany, where the whole purpose of the

---

[1] See below, p. 258.
[2] See below, pp. 256–7.
[3] See below, p. 260.
[4] See below, p. 261.

bildungsroman is to accommodate such self-revelation, we find that Goethe nevertheless attempts to check 'fluidity' in *The Sorrows of Werther*, 1774, by confining his first-person narrative to the epistolary convention and then breaking into this—as the much less economical Richardson also does—with editorial comment in the form of third-person narrative.[1]) Nowadays there are first-person narratives in English which are as taut and economical as James could have wished—but this may still be a sign, perhaps, of weakness rather than strength. Apart from such rare exceptions as Joyce Cary's Gully Jimson or Sara Monday, the 'I' becomes a de-personalized expression of the suffering modern sensibility. In order, perhaps, to control the 'fluidity' of their more exuberant egotism, earlier writers tend to use the story-within-a-story device, allowing the 'I' self-expression but confining it within the framework of an outer third-person narrative. Thus, in the 'narrative or epic' manner of the eighteenth century, first-person narrative is limited to digressions, either in the form of moral parables—Fielding allows Mrs. Wilson and the Man of the Hill their own words— or as author's commentary (although in the next century, if we take Thackeray as an instance, this can offer an irresistible temptation to moral homily). The story-within-a-story, whether couched in the first person or the third, has proved to be an enduring device, favoured by sophisticated craftsmen as well as the less self-conscious story-tellers. Fromentin uses a 'frame' for *Dominique* (1863), and it is interesting to find that when Henry James does employ first-person narrative, as in *The Turn of the Screw*, it is this method that he adopts. It is used to give perspective and variety as well as authenticity to their narratives by writers as different as Smollett, Scott, Dickens, Balzac and Conrad.

The epistolary method, as such, is virtually extinct. Its adoption as a narrative technique was one manifestation of the changing habit of mind which had helped to foster the novel itself: 'the transition from the objective, social and public orientation of the classical world to the subjective, individualist and private orientation of the life and literature of the last two hundred years'.[2] However, once the novelist had learnt from it every-

---

[1] See, for example the interpolated commentary on Werther's last days following Letter lxxxiv.   [2] See Ian Watt, *The Rise of the Novel*, p. 176.

thing it had to teach about the interpretation of private feeling and the power of individual self-expression, he began to evolve other narrative modes which took advantage of its valuable lessons while avoiding its diffuseness and clumsiness. Chekov was already calling it an 'antiquated affair' in 1886, although he thought it 'all right when the gist of the matters is in the letters themselves . . .' [1] It was handled best by French novelists —most devastatingly, perhaps, by Choderlos de Laclos in *Les Liaisons Dangereuses* (1782), where it served with splendid success his Gallic gift for the unflinching analysis of devious motive and perverse emotion. But in spite of the importance of French influences in English fiction, exercised in particular through the writings of Marivaux, Prévost and Rousseau, the French *expertise* in epistolary method was never really matched in England. After the appearance of *Pamela*—but, it must be stressed, before the publication of *Clarissa* which he praised with generous warmth[2]—Fielding had dismissed the method as unsuitable for a novel and in any case 'not used by the best writers of this kind'.[3] After experimenting both with this method and with omniscient narrative, Richard Cumberland in 1795 decided that the epistolary style was fun for the writer but 'the more usual way' was the one which the reader preferred.[4] Fanny Burney used it to good effect, but Jane Austen, in spite of admiring both her work and Richardson's, abandoned it altogether once the days of school-room squibs like *Love and Freindship* were over. She would probably have handled the form very successfully if we may judge by her masterly depiction of different shades of epistolary vulgarity in the letters of Isabella Thorpe, Lydia Bennet and Mr. Collins, and the nicely discriminated tone of injured and genuinely suffering dignity in Darcy's.[5] We might add that the *oratio obliqua* of her heroines' crucial moments of undeception if transposed into the first-person are creditable performances in the Richardsonian tradition of dramatized emotion. That the method can be made

[1] See below, p. 260.

[2] See E. L. McAdam, Jr., 'A New Letter from Fielding', *Yale Review* (1948), Vol. XXXVIII, and also *The Jacobite's Journal* (2 January 1748).

[3] See below, p. 256.   [4] See below, pp. 257–8.

[5] See *Northanger Abbey*, Chapter xxvii, and *Pride and Prejudice*, Chapters xiii, lvii, xlvii, xxxv.

to serve an instinct as fastidious as hers for economy in handling the comic interplay of incongruous characters is suggested by Henry James's success in the *nouvelle*, 'The Pension Beaurepas',[1] where people write home to their respective countries from a holiday pension in France and display in their letters some of those conflicting points of view which assist James with his 'international' theme. This *nouvelle* does not altogether satisfy Chekhov's requirement that 'the gist of the matter should be in the letters themselves', but as a sophisticated variation on the method used entertainingly in books like *Humphry Clinker, Love and Freindship, Camilla* and *Evelina* it does help to establish that in England—apart from Richardson—the method best serves light sentimental or social comedy rather than a more serious kind of analysis.

A certain indirection in the epistolary method suits the novelist's feeling for irony and 'pattern' better than the freer omniscient manner, but James draws attention to the advantages for his kind of vision of a method even more oblique and certainly more susceptible to disciplined economy and intensity of effect. To-day the choice seems to lie between this obliquity and the hard-wearing, panoramic, omniscient style of narration.

The latter in its picaresque form will probably always suit the social satirist: it has certainly done so from the days of the Spanish *picaro* to the days of Lucky Jim. Becky Sharp is a Victorian variant of the journeying hero/heroine, just as Moll Flanders is an eighteenth-century one. Becky Sharp, however, is the product of a more sophisticated social criticism, her journeys emphasizing a movement up and down the social ladder rather than to and fro along a country's high-roads. Stendhal's Julien Sorel is a not-so-distant relative and concurrently a forbear of various modern Angry Young Men in search of social success. But the conventions of omniscient panoramic narrative can serve with equal usefulness the altogether different vision of an artist who may be a 'seer' like Dostoevsky or a 'sage' like George Eliot. The method accommodates searching analysis of conscience and spiritual conflict as well as the depiction of large historical and social events. To the 'pure' novelist like James, however, the method seems dangerous. The 'strong,

[1] See 'The Pension Beaurepas' (1883); reprinted in *Lady Barbarina*, Macmillan ed. (1921-3), Vol. XIX.

rank quality of genius' can give it strength and substance, but its 'lack of composition, its defiance of economy and architecture' make it, in his view, a vicious model for general imitation.[1] In its place, he works out his own 'indirect and oblique view'. It is a method which—as he disarmingly admits—he elucidates in his prefaces and elsewhere 'even to extravagance'.[2]

What is the 'view'? It is a method of story-telling which tries to retain the vividness and immediacy, the 'warmth' as Mrs. Barbauld says, of self-revelation while insisting on a vigilant editorship to control its 'terrible fluidity'. It aims at concentration, subtlety, economy and intensity. It differs from epistolary and first-person methods by giving a third-person account of strictly selective impressions; from omniscient narrative by concentrating on the inner reactions to a given situation of a restricted number of characters (sometimes, indeed, confining itself almost exclusively to a single view-point); and from the 'stream of consciousness' by being less interested in the processes of ordinary undisciplined human consciousness than in illustrating the workings of this consciousness when it is directed to a particular end. It has, of course, its sometimes limiting conventions. Thus, if the novelist wishes to comment indirectly on aspects of his situation which seem to him important or significant, he often has to give special prominence to the meditations of characters endowed with a high degree of perceptiveness and self-expression. 'Having a consciousness highly susceptible of registration', says Henry James of his Prince in *The Golden Bowl*, 'he thus makes us see the things that most interest us. . . .'[3] However, in order to promote dramatic intensity, the recording character needs to be personally involved and, quite legitimately, may be perplexed as well as intelligent; the Prince, for all his perspicacity, is 'never a whit' the less 'a foredoomed, entangled, embarrassed agent in the general imbroglio'.[4]

The 'pure' novelist and the aesthetic writer value the method

---

[1] See below, p. 235.   [2] See below, p. 265.
[3] See below, p. 266.
[4] Ibid. These characteristics also distinguish certain kinds of modern first-person narratives. Thus the young boy who tells the story in J. D. Salinger's *The Catcher in the Rye* (1945) is unusually sensitive, perceptive and articulate (it is emphasized that English is the one subject in which he has satisfied his examiners); he is also a 'foredoomed, entangled, embarrassed agent'. This combination of qualities provides the *raison d'être* of the story.

because it helps them to safeguard artistic detachment while depicting highly subjective personal impressions. It also tends to cut out the distracting side-winds of imaginative inspiration. Above all, it makes simpler the suspension of disbelief by appearing to get rid of all commentary by the author. Jane Austen dexterously conveys Emma Woodhouse's conceited, self-centred personality without a single direct comment from herself as narrator:

> Harriet's attachment to herself was very amiable; and her inclination for good company, and power of appreciating what was elegant and clever, shewed that there was no want of taste, though strength of understanding must not be expected. Altogether she was quite convinced of Harriet Smith's being exactly the young friend she wanted—exactly the something which her home required. . . .[1]

With equal skill, she manages at the same time to convey to her readers rather more of the general situation than Emma herself is able to see. Jane Austen's treatment of her heroine's subjective commentary is an early instance of the method which James employs in *The Ambassadors*, where we view the situation from Strether's angle of vision but are also made aware of contingencies for which he does not allow. She anticipates, also, James's tendency to concentrate third-person narrative on a single view-point. How different all this is from Fielding! Of Partridge in *Tom Jones* Fielding says blandly,

> Though I called him poor Partridge in the last paragraph, I would have the reader rather impute that epithet to the compassion in my temper than conceive it to be any declaration of his innocence. Whether he was innocent or not will perhaps appear hereafter; but if the historic Muse hath entrusted me with any secrets, I will by no means be guilty of discovering them till she shall give me leave. . . .[2]

It is an obtrusive authorship of this kind—noticeable again in the puppet-master of *Vanity Fair* and in the novels of Anthony Trollope—which the 'oblique view' tries to do away with. In theory, novelists of many different kinds argue that the writer should remain as much as possible off-stage. Maupassant thinks it wrong for the novelist to say 'I', 'me',[3] but so do

[1] *Emma*, Chapter iv. [2] *Tom Jones*, Book II, Chapter iv.
[3] See below, p. 272.

writers like Scott and Dickens who care less for aesthetic principle but do mind about the convincingness of their stories. 'When I have made the people to play out the play, it is, as it were, their business to do it, and not mine', says Dickens.[1] In practice, however, these omniscient narrators often take their readers into their confidence about their characters, usually, says Mr. Forster, with unfortunate results.

It is dangerous, it generally leads to a drop in the temperature, to intellectual and emotional laxity, and worse still to facetiousness . . . with all due respect to Fielding and Thackeray it is devastating, it is bar-parlour chattiness, and nothing has been more harmful to novels of the past.[2]

However, Mr. Forster does not think it so dangerous for the novelist to take the reader into his confidence 'about the universe' and 'to generalize about the conditions under which he thinks life is carried on'. By altogether cutting out his own interpolations and directing attention to the inner feelings of his chosen characters—feelings which a Jamesian fastidiousness will confine to the central situation—the author seeks to withdraw from the field of action in order to heighten the actuality of the conflicts which he presents. 'Anything seemed to me better—better for the process and effect of representation,' declares Henry James, 'than the mere muffled majesty of irresponsible "authorship".' He goes on,

I catch myself . . . shaking it off and withdrawing the pretence of it while I get down into the arena and do my best to live and breathe and rub shoulders and converse with the persons engaged in the struggle.[3]

There is no question that the method can bring about a tremendous heightening of dramatic effect. In *The Portrait of a Lady* (1881), the sense that an impenetrable darkness has descended on Isobel Archer after her marriage to Gilbert Osmund —a darkness temporarily muffling her perceptions while it dims her vivacity and ruthlessly corrects her youthful imprudence— is heightened by the sudden cessation of her own hitherto more or less continuous subjective commentary. Her 'point of view' is replaced by that of the good little Edward Rosier, with

[1] See below, p. 270.   [2] See below, p. 273.   [3] See below, p. 266.

whom we begin to move slowly towards the now remote figure of Madame Osmund, sharing his timid speculations and the thoughts which circle more and more closely around her, until at last she is once more met face to face by us, a dignified figure in black, now two years married and playing hostess to her husband's guests.[1] The sense of 'adventure' which James talks about in his Preface is increased by this delayed re-entry—four chapters have elapsed—into her now greatly altered 'point of view'; much of the effect of Isobel's momentous vigil late into the night depends on the skilful management of this technique.[2] Even more telling in its emotional impact is Flaubert's dramatization of Charles Bovary's consciousness as prelude and coda for his rendering of Emma Bovary's subjective commentary on her *ennui*, her delusive happiness and her final despair.

And yet it is in this kind of writing, paradoxically enough, that the author's temperament and sensibility may be felt with even more vividness than in the freer style of the omniscient narrator. 'Pure' novelists like James or Conrad or Flaubert are often compulsive artists who recognize that the subjective nature of their themes needs a special discipline—they seem to consider that the 'indirect and oblique view' will help them to 'cut the umbilical cord binding them, as authors, to their work'. That the strong, strange flavour of individual idiosyncrasy still clings to their writing is certainly not in itself anything that we need regret. It is filtered through many elements, through the style, through the situation, through the balance and force of contrasts, but most of all through the specially endowed 'centre of consciousness'. In James's shorter works, the observer is quite simply 'the impersonal author's concrete deputy or delegate' and the subjective commentary on the situation is the result of some 'charmed painter's or poet's . . . close and sensitive contact with it'.[3] Later, the observer becomes some other 'entangled, embarrassed agent', like the Prince, or Merton Densher, or Strether. These may not be artists, but they share the artist's perceptive awareness, and what gives their analysis its distinction is its identity with James's own sensi-

[1] See *The Portrait of a Lady*, Chapter xxxvi.

[2] Op. cit., Chapter xl. See also James's Preface, Macmillan edn., Vol. VI.

[3] See Henry James, Preface to *The Golden Bowl*, Macmillan edn., Vol. XXXIV, and below, p. 266.

bility. Conrad attempts to resolve his artistic difficulties by creating a permanently involved spectator, Marlow, who broods over a wide landscape of treachery and violence where creatures endowed with qualities remote from his own imaginative insight and artistic detachment are made to act and feel. But such as these are, it is Marlow who sees them, and as Marlow sees them so does Conrad. Marlow, more exclusively even than the Jamesian narrator, is 'the impersonal author's deputy or delegate'. What in the end saves both these novelists from the dangers of over-powering idiosyncrasy is their talent for—to *negative capability?* use Keats's phrase—'filling some other Body'. Strether and Kate Croy, for example, could not be identified with any novelist other than James, but to identify them with each other would be absurd. Strether remains a prim, elderly, unselfish, conscience-stricken and perplexed New Englander, while Kate Croy is a handsome, bold, clever, ruthlessly self-regarding 'displaced person'. Each is instinct with the vitality which has its source in the genuine novelist's gift for 'going over to his characters' as Flaubert puts it.[1] (Flaubert, indeed, seems to have developed this power of projection to the point of experiencing on behalf of his heroine some of the physical symptoms of arsenical poisoning.[2])

In this century the oblique method, with its 'dramatized consciousness', has been modified by the experimental writers of the 1920's and 1930's into what is known, after William James, as the 'stream of consciousness' method. Now that the stimulus provided by the revolutionary break-up of the old concept of personality has faded, and the first excitement is over of translating the discoveries of depth psychology into terms of art, this variant of the oblique method seems to have become almost as extinct as the epistolary narrative. Sartre's use of it in his *Les Chemins de la Liberté* (begun in 1945) gives that novel-cycle a curiously—and unintentionally—dated air, and certainly adds to its diffuseness. More recently there has been a tendency to return to the closely-knit, densely allusive methods of Conrad and James (a newer taste still is for serio-comic satire in the picaresque manner). If the stream of consciousness method is to survive at all, it may do so vestigially in, perhaps, the disciplined interior monologue of the surefooted technician.

[1] See below, p. 271.   [2] See Part II above, p. 155.

(Mr. Graham Greene, for example, uses it as one among many other devices to portray the character of the priest in *The Power and the Glory* and to underline predominant themes like the betrayals of *It's a Battlefield* or the spiritual dilemmas of *The Heart of the Matter*. Greene becomes more Jamesian, however, in *The End of the Affair*.) The method deserves credit for the additional flexibility and deeper insight into hidden movements of the mind and the emotions which it has brought to the novel, rather than for any intrinsic structural value. It must be remembered that Virginia Woolf, the most sensitive and influential exponent of the method, wrote her manifestoes about the 'enormous elaborations of the realistic novel' [1] less in reaction against the generation of James and Conrad than against the younger and more popular English realists, Arnold Bennett, John Galsworthy and H. G. Wells, who were generally more interested in stirring the social conscience of their readers than in portraying movements of the individual sensibility.

The English novel would have been poorer, unquestionably, without the meditations of *To the Lighthouse* or *Mrs. Dalloway*, whose heroines reach towards infinity while the clothes are mended and the dinner is cooked, or the rich flood of associations which compose our experience of Joyce's Leopold and Molly Bloom, or the elegiac cadences—and the wit—of Anna Livia's ebbing consciousness at the close of *Finnegans Wake*. But the method exceeds every other in its risk of 'terrible fluidity' and its natural threat to balance, proportion and composure. Dorothy Richardson's *Pilgrimage* (1914–38) is perhaps too often quoted scathingly in a context like this, but its undoubted merits are vitiated by an alarming diffuseness and an uncritical subjectivity. Virginia Woolf tries to save herself from these dangers by tethering her material more or less arbitrarily to some element which will help to create an illusion of order—beams flashing intermittently from a lighthouse, a village pageant, waves beating on the shore—and by directing her sensibility to the creation of a handful of realizable characters. That these are almost always drawn from autobiographical experience—the Ramsays are her parents, Jacob is her brother, figures

[1] See 'Modern Fiction', *The Common Reader, First Series* (1925), and 'Mr. Bennett and Mrs. Brown' (1924); reprinted in *The Captain's Death Bed* (1950).

in *The Waves* embody various aspects of her own personality—
is a characteristic of writers who tend to choose this form. Their
art is obedient to the rhythms of personal emotion rather than
disciplined by their grasp of external experience. Joyce is an ✳
exception. His technique is at the service of a wider vision. In
The Dubliners, in *A Portrait of the Artist as a Young Man*, in much
of *Ulysses*, and indeed in the range of human sympathy communicated throughout *Finnegans Wake*, he displays the genuine
novelist's gift of realizing diverse experience outside his own immediate modes of thinking and feeling and of adding to its
authenticity by solidity of detail—he has in particular an infallible ear for the tones of voice and rhythms of speech which
distinguish individuals as well as social classes. And of course
his working-class Irishry takes him a long way from the parlours
of Bloomsbury.

III   Characterization

NO ONE can miss the emphasis on character in the novelist's
debate about narrative technique. Is character, then, the most
important element in the novel? The figures who inhabit the
world of fiction are such anomalous abstractions that one approaches the whole question of characterization with considerable misgiving. 'Homo Fictus', as Mr. Forster rightly reminds
us, is a totally different species from 'Homo Sapiens'.[1] He is
deprived of a great many ordinary human characteristics because these are not relevant to the novelist's design. His function is to act in unison with other narrative elements as a
vehicle for the expression of the author's personal vision of life.
Thus he is capable of wide individual variations, such as the
difference between 'characters of manners' and 'characters of
nature', terms which Johnson used when he tried to distinguish
the art of Fielding and Richardson.[2] 'I believe that all novels . . .
deal with character', says Virginia Woolf, and adds

it is to express character—not to preach doctrines, sing songs, or
celebrate the glories of the British Empire, that the form of the

---

[1] See *Aspects of the Novel*, Chapter iii.
[2] See Boswell's *Life of Johnson*, Oxford ed. (1924), Vol. I, p. 367, and
below, pp. 275-7.

novel, so clumsy, verbose and undramatic, so rich, elastic and alive, has been evolved.[1]

But she immediately goes on to show that the expression of character can mean almost anything:

You see one thing in character, and I another. You say it means this, and I that. And when it comes to writing, each makes a further selection on principles of his own.[2]

A modern English critic of the French novel has said,

a character is a verbal construction which has no existence outside the book. It is a vehicle for the novelist's sensibility and its significance lies in its relations with the author's other constructions. A novel is essentially a verbal pattern in which the different 'characters' are strands, and the reader's experience is the impact of the complete pattern on his sensibility.[3]

This carries some flavour of critical dogmas which have spent a good deal of their force in the last two decades, but it usefully draws attention to the inter-dependence of the various elements in a novel.

It is almost certainly their impatience with the ordinary reader's failure to understand the nature of 'Homo Fictus' which makes novelists react with such violence to the suggestion that their characters are portraits from the life. 'Let us have as little as possible about its "being" Mr. This or Mrs. That', requests James.

If it adjusts itself with the least truth to its new life it can't possibly be either . . . if it persists as the impression not artistically dealt with, it shames the honour offered it and can only be spoken of as having ceased to be a thing of fact, and yet not become a thing of truth.[4]

'We only suffer reality to *suggest*, never to *dictate*', says Charlotte Brontë, angrily repudiating the charge that the characters in *Shirley* are direct representations of real people, '. . . the heroines are abstractions, and the heroes also'.[5] '*There is not a single portrait in Adam Bede*, as I have said before . . .', writes George Eliot,

---

[1] See below, p. 290. [2] Ibid.
[3] See Martin Turnell, *The Novel in France* (1950), p. 6.
[4] See below, p. 284. [5] See below, p. 280.

exasperation underscoring her statement. 'No one who is not an artist knows how experience is wrought up in writing in any form of poetry.'[1] 'Nor do I paint *portraits*: that isn't my way', explains George Sand, exasperated in this case by the suggestion that she has put a living Empress into one of her novels. 'I *invent*. The public, who don't know what invention consists of, try to find originals everywhere. They deceive themselves and debase the art.'[2] Flaubert has an entertaining letter about people whom he had never met claiming to be the originals of Emma and Charles Bovary.[3] As long ago as *Joseph Andrews*, we find Fielding warning his readers that his Parson Adams is not to be taken for a portrait of any person in actual life.[4]

These assertions are supported by the accounts which novelists give us of the way in which their experience is 'wrought up'. How typical, we feel, that Stendhal should turn his gaze on some average human being who devotes his talents to the 'pursuit of pleasure' and then ask, 'What would he do if he had more intelligence?'[5] Dickens, we learn, scribbled over his manuscript in order to make Harold Skimpole as '*un*like' Leigh Hunt as possible—in vain, it appears, so far as Leigh Hunt himself was concerned.[6] Wilkie Collins assembled Count Fosco from 'a man who loved canaries', 'boys who loved white mice', and the sudden inspiration that a fat villain would be less commonplace than a thin one.[7] Stevenson performed 'psychical surgery' on a 'valued friend'—'a common way of "making character"', he says—and out sprang Long John Silver.[8] The 'beautiful genius', Turgenev, was haunted, as we have seen, by '*disponibles*', figures who appeared to him out of the blue and haunted him until he invented situations and relationships favourable to 'the complications they would be most likely to produce and feel'.[9]

Obviously, then, the novelist 'takes the infection' through his contact with actual people. Bazarov of *Fathers and Sons* is a long way from the expert on anthrax encountered by chance on a railway platform,[10] but it was this direct experience of a figure

[1] See below, p. 280. [2] Ibid. [3] See below, p. 282.
[4] See below, p. 279. [5] Ibid. [6] See below, p. 281.
[7] See below, pp. 282-3. [8] See below, p. 283.
[9] See Part II above, p. 119, and below, pp. 286-7.
[10] See Avrahm Yarmolinsky, *Turgenev, The Man, His Art, and His Age* (1926), pp. 190-1.

strikingly representative of new tendencies in the contemporary Russian scene which provided Turgenev with the first inspiration for his Nihilist hero. An over-simple response to biographical information of this kind virtually reduces all novels to *romans à clef*—a kind particularly rare in England, where Peacock is something of a sport—but the confusion about 'portraits' in fiction can come about, of course, through the novelist's own failure to adjust his original experience of a man or woman to its new imaginative context in a work of art. The failure seems to associate itself most frequently with the inclusive, comprehensive writer who is more likely than the careful, exclusive craftsman to crowd his novel with a good deal of undigested material. It is particularly noticeable when this comprehensive novelist is the 'bardic' kind whose personal experience seems apocalyptic: as in D. H. Lawrence, for example, whose original experiences are felt with exceptional intensity and consequently stick out like sore thumbs all over his work. Most of the characters in Lawrence's novels are indeed 'portraits' of people who affected him strongly—so strongly that they sometimes acquire the distended proportions of caricature. These figures—his wife, John Middleton Murry, Philip Heseltine and of course himself —appear again and again with variations of emphasis brought about by shifts in his own emotional attitude. They are still present in one of his more 'organic' novels, *Women in Love*, where they are called Ursula Brangwen, Gerald Crich, Philip Halliday and Birkin. To place Dostoevsky with Lawrence on a similar charge is not an arbitrary juxtaposition. Although it is recognized at once that Dostoevsky has far greater resources to draw upon, it remains obvious that Dostoevsky's art is as subjective as Lawrence's. His spiteful portrait of Turgenev as Karmazinov in *The Possessed*, for instance, reminds us of Lawrence's resentful portrayals of people who angered and irritated him—Heseltine as Halliday in *Women in Love*, for example, or Lady Otteline Morrell as Hermione Roddice in the same novel, or the people who offered him hospitality in Italy and were satirized for their pains in *Aaron's Rod* as Sir William and Lady Franks. An attempt has been made in portrayals of this nature to externalize experience—but primarily for therapeutic rather than aesthetic reasons, with the result that the figures remain in that intermediate state where, still blurred by the writer's emotions, they have ceased to be things 'of fact' and yet not become things 'of truth'.

Novelists of all kinds may suffer a similar failure of adjustment, especially when the experience 'wrought up' is still very close and has perhaps influenced the whole course of a life. In depicting Maggie Tulliver's childhood George Eliot successfully—some flaws aside—translates her own youthful behaviour into the terms of her art, but when she attempts the same thing for the emotional and moral conflicts of adolescence and young womanhood the imperfect 'distancing' betrays itself in sentimentality. The tendency is one of her 'spots of commonness' and it is perhaps an almost inevitable accompaniment of romantic introspection. Such introspection may display an emotionalism bordering at times on hysteria—it can be detected, for example, in the unsteady tones of Jane Eyre and Lucy Snowe, or of George Sand's romantic heroines, as well as in the wishful fantasy of Corvo's Hadrian VII or Lawrence's Lily and Ramon. And yet slight—very slight—signs of this lack of detachment occur even in Jane Austen, whose finely-modulated accents take on a momentary shrillness when Elizabeth Bennet, with somewhat *voulu* gaiety, resigns the pathway at Netherfield to Mrs. Hurst, Miss Bingley and Darcy, retiring to the superior enjoyments of a solitary 'ramble',[1] or when Fanny Price relaxes her self-control (now that it is safe at last to do so) and zestfully assists Edmund to carry out a lugubrious post-mortem on Mary Crawford's character.[2] But it is the total effect of a work which counts, and only when a whole novel is thrown off balance is one really justified in asserting that an extremely personal and subjective experience has chosen the wrong medium for its expression.

In the final impression left by a novel the part played by the novelist's technique of character-creation is certainly very important. His views on the methods which serve him best are of a piece with the kind of response which his work usually creates; so we find that the man with a lively talent for re-creating the surface-textures of life recommends an approach very different from any of those preferred by the analyst of thought and feeling. The difference makes itself felt at the

[1] See *Pride and Prejudice*, Chapter x.
[2] See *Mansfield Park*, Chapter xlvii.

outset of the novel's history. 'Words and actions' are 'the only ways by which we come to any knowledge of what passes in the minds of others', writes Henry Fielding,[1] but his sister, Sarah, an admirer of Richardson and herself a novelist, believes that 'the motives to actions, and the inward turns of the mind' are 'more necessary to be known that the actions themselves'.[2] Richardson himself, delighted no doubt to add the sister of his great rival to his list of disciples, distinguishes the writings of the two Fieldings in a commendatory letter to her:

His was but as the knowledge of the outside of a clock-work machine, while yours was that of all the finer springs and movements of the inside . . .[3]

Did he filch the metaphor from Johnson? Boswell tells us that when Johnson compared the achievement of Richardson and Fielding, he

used this expression 'that there was as great difference between them, as between a man who knew how a watch was made, and a man who could tell the hour by looking on the dial-plate.' This was a short and figurative state of his distinction between drawing characters of nature and characters only of manners.[4]

Johnson's comments on these writers have an important place in the critical debate about their relative merits which continues intermittently even to-day. If we lay aside his personal bias, his characteristic acumen isolates for notice precisely two of the four categories into which—in the last analysis—it has seemed to me that all novelists are divided.[5] Boswell's comments on Johnson's statement altogether miss the point,[6] and it is perhaps Scott who first goes into the question with some thoroughness and intelligence, his discussion adding usefully to the considerable merits of his 'Biographical Memoirs'.[7] For example, in recognizing that the reader will 'laugh with Fielding' and 'weep with Richardson' Scott is acknowledging a real difference be' tween the effects of two types of characterization.[8] A 'dial-plate-novelist like Fielding creates out of the collections of mannerisms

---

[1] See below, p. 275.   [2] Ibid.   [3] Ibid.
[4] Boswell's *Life of Johnson*, loc. cit., and see below, p. 276.
[5] See above, pp. 165–6.   [6] Boswell, loc. cit.
[7] See below, pp. 275–6.   [8] Ibid.

and idiosyncrasies which he calls his 'characters' an illusion of vivid and vigorous comic life, an illusion strengthened in Fielding's case by the adroit variations of ironic tone in the author's personal commentary. Dickens also finds a substitute for the detailed analysis of personality in the comic hyperbole and startling visual imagery with which he induces a galvanic life in his figures. For all 'the wonderful feeling of human depth' which the method releases, it is, as Mr. Forster says, 'a conjuring trick',[1] and that is why, when Dickens creates figures which he intends to be taken seriously—Quilp, let us say, or Bradley Headstone—we respond to the vibrations of the author's own tremendous vitality but miss the deeper springs of creative life from which Dostoevsky's Smerdyakov or Balzac's Père Goriot derive their tragic fullness of stature. 'We must admit', writes Mr. Forster, 'that flat people are not in themselves as big achievements as round ones, and also that they are best when they are comic.' Walter Bagehot, in an essay which is still one of the best assessments of Dickens, recognizes this too. He admits the charm and appeal of Dickens's 'exaggerations pretending to comport themselves as human beings, caricatures acting as if they were characters', but adds,

it is essential to remember, that however great may be and is the charm of such exaggerated personifications, the best specimens of them are immensely less excellent, belong to an altogether lower range of intellectual achievements, than the real depiction of actual living men . . . Who could compare the genius, marvellous as must be its fertility, which was needful to create a Falstaff with that shown in the higher productions of the same mind in Hamlet, Ophelia and Lear? We feel instantaneously the difference between the aggregating incident which makes up from the externalities of life other accidents analogous to itself, and the central idea of a real character which cannot show itself wholly in any accidents, but . . . which unfolds itself gradually in wide spheres of action, and yet, as with those we know best in life, leaves something hardly to be understood . . .[2]

Mrs. Slipslop, Parson Trulliber, Mrs. Gamp, Mr. Pickwick: these are unbeatable on their own ground. But with Quilp or

[1] See *Aspects of the Novel*, Chapter iv.
[2] Walter Bagehot, 'Charles Dickens' (1858); reprinted in *Literary Studies* (1878).

Mr. Dombey or Eugene Wrayburn or Bradley Headstone or Miss Havisham we are moving towards subterranean areas of experience where the 'inner-workings' novelist is more at home. The 'flat' character belongs by nature to the surfaces of experience, where life can still remain laughable; a serious 'flat' character is, in fact, very nearly a contradiction in terms. Novelists who belong to the tradition inaugurated by Richardson and culminating in Conrad and Henry James show that to explore beneath the surface appearance of things is to draw near to the central areas of tragic experience.

It is obvious that both methods provide amply for the expression of personal idiosyncrasy, but on balance the 'dial-plate' novelist seems to run fewer risks of disequilibrium and monotony. Comedy, with its insulating and distancing properties, encourages the sort of ruthless prodigality we find in Dickens when he decides to 'throw another handful of characters on the fire' in order to keep his narrative blazing. This may explain the tendency, which still persists to-day, to look beyond careful historians of the complicated hidden self to these 'dial-plate' writers for the true creators of 'characters'. But in fact it is the 'inner-workings' novelist who is the more interested in what makes 'character': his real concern, in short, is with what we call personality. It is worth remembering that he will make use of a good many theatrical 'dial-plate' figures himself—to set off his own characters, perhaps, or to establish a milieu, provide the necessary *ficelles* for his narrative, or suggest a kind of choric commentary on the action. These figures are recognized by the shorthand—the gestures, mannerisms, peculiarities of clothing or feature—which makes them easily manœuvrable whenever they are needed. A host of examples comes to mind: the figures surrounding Pamela or Clarissa—Mrs. Jewkes, the Swiss Guard, the fashionable ladies quizzing the virtuous servant-girl, the Hogarthian brothel-dwellers; George Eliot's 'Middlemarchers', assembled at street-corner and tavern, their muddled judgments far removed from the inner realities of conflict at the heart of the novel; the ardent figures gesticulating with revolutionary or amatory passion round Stendhal's Julien Sorel or his Sanséverina; James's Colonel Assingham (in *The Golden Bowl*) jerking his neatly-shod foot, one of the few actions available to this patient listener. These are all 'extras', their two-dimensional nature disguised by their creators' talent for selecting the necessary animating detail; and when they appear they provide some useful easing of tension which lessens the dangerous effects of too unremitting an analysis of inner motive and feeling.

It is very rarely, on the other hand, that we find the 'dial-plate' writer of fiction varying his approach by emulating the analysis of the 'inner-workings' novelist. The nearest he comes to it is suggested by E. M. Forster when he talks of the 'flat' character who sometimes seems to be 'ready for extended life'.[1] The impression is not, however, the result of any attempt to explain actions in terms of psychological cause and effect but is again a measure of the novelist's resourcefulness in the selection of the most telling external detail.

For these reasons, then, the description of the 'dial-plate' novel as 'the novel of character' is understandable but misleading. Robert Louis Stevenson accepts the description in his essay, 'A Humble Remonstrance',[2] but his own analysis is enough to show its inadequacy. He sees that the relationship between incident and character can be sufficiently anomalous in this kind of fiction for it to be thought of as simply 'the novel of adventure'. Its characters, he says, are 'statically shown':

As they enter, so may they go out; they must be consistent, but they need not grow.[3]

At this point his argument is directed usefully to the fundamental differences in structure which further separate the 'dial-plate' writer from the novelist concerned to show 'all the finer springs and movements of the inside'. Mr. Edwin Muir adopts Stevenson's definitions and uses them as the basis of his own study, *The Structure of the Novel* (1946). Thus he takes as an example of 'the novel of character' Thackeray's *Vanity Fair* and contrasts it with *Pride and Prejudice* as an example of what Stevenson calls 'the dramatic novel'. He draws attention to the self-contained episodes in Thackeray and shows that in Jane Austen, on the other hand, incidents are governed by the conflict of personality and move forward as part of a reasonable progression. So the account of Becky Sharp's first meeting with Pitt

---

[1] *Aspects of the Novel*, Chapter iv, and below, pp. 288-9.
[2] See Part I above, p. 83. [3] Ibid.

Crawley is seen to be deft and amusing primarily as a sketch in its own right; whereas the first encounter between Darcy and Elizabeth gains in effect by belonging to a dynamic of events depending on the interplay and development of character.[1] However, we are once more up against the problem of terms. 'Dramatic' as a description begs as many questions as 'the novel of character': we already have the phrase 'dramatized consciousness', which we associate with the 'oblique and indirect view' of Jamesian narrative, and now we find that 'the dramatic novel' can include, by this definition, both *Pride and Prejudice*, which is social comedy, and *Wuthering Heights*, which has certain affinities with poetic tragedy. Seen in this light the term 'dramatic' is a description of creative method rather than an indication of literary 'kind'. It tells us to expect a particularly close and interdependent relationship between 'character' and 'plot', but it does not hint that different conceptions of cause and effect can separate an Emily Brontë from a Jane Austen as finally as concentration on 'Words and Actions' instead of on 'the finer springs and workings of the inside' separates Fielding from Richardson or Dickens from Henry James. It is here that we feel the need of terms like Mr. Forster's 'prophecy' or 'song',[2] or Stevenson's 'impersonal utterance of passion',[3] and so feel justified in including the category which I described at the beginning of this chapter: the novel of the 'prophet' who may seem to be as prodigal with his material as the comprehensive, episodic, 'dial-plate' novelist but in fact imposes order and coherence upon it by the force of poetic imagination.

Perhaps it is in this kind of art that the paradoxes of character-creation in the novel become most apparent. We know that the novelist's figures are abstractions whose principal function it is to complete a structural or verbal pattern: character 'must somehow form part of the pattern, or lay the design of the book', notes Arnold Bennett after a conversation with T. S. Eliot 'about character in fiction'.[4] We feel the truth of this most acutely in the great symbolic figures of fiction— Captain Ahab, perhaps, or the Karamazov brothers, or Heathcliff, who are obviously no more detachable from their context

[1] Op. cit., Chapter ii. [2] See *Aspects of the Novel*, Chapter vii.
[3] See Part I above, p. 84. [4] See below, p. 290.

than Lear or Ophelia. They have a stature transcending our normal experience and at certain moments voice 'the impersonal utterance of passion'. Mr. Forster cites Mitya's telling of his 'good dream',[1] and we can add Catherine Linton's threnody for the birds whose feathers fill the pillows of her sick-bed or Ahab's improvisations as he hurries in the whale's 'infallible wake', conscious that the bright day provides 'food for thought, had Ahab time to think, but Ahab never thinks; he only feels, feels, feels, *that's* tingling enough for mortal man'.[2] In these moments, 'Homo Fictus' is seen for what he really is: a single if important element in the imaginative statement made by the whole novel. Yet his 'song' would not capture us if it were to drown the illusion of his human individuality. We have seen, in the discussion of narrative technique, that one of the novelist's essential gifts is his power to inhabit 'some other body'.[3] His characters may be unmistakably a part of his 'design': we can never transfer them to the world of another writer, nor can we mistake their family resemblance. But equally they are rarely to be mistaken for each other and they always inhabit a world of realized particulars. Catherine's wasted fingers pluck nervously at the feathers and feel their texture; the wind lifts Ahab's hair; beneath Mitya as he sleeps is the large chest with its rug covering and when he wakes he feels beneath his head the pillow which someone has placed there on an impulse of rough human kindness.

In the end we recognize the true novelist by the strength with which his realization of the actual world and of human individuality triumphs over his abstract speculations, his oddities and opinions, his puritan concern with the *utile*. 'Never present ideas except as a function of temperament and character', writes André Gide,[4] and the greatest didactic novelists, the finest preachers and teachers, from Fielding and Richardson to Forster, Camus and Mauriac, are those who find their originating impulse in their capacity literally to 'embody' or 'incorporate' ideas. We can always distinguish a novelist's 'moral fable' from the abstract thinker's. *Jonathan Wild* (1742) and *Hard Times* (1854) are novelists' fables; *Rasselas* (1759) is not.

[1] See *Aspects of the Novel*, Chapter vii.
[2] See *Wuthering Heights*, Chapter xii, and *Moby Dick*, Chapter cxxxiv.
[3] See above, p. 195.   [4] See Part I above, p. 104.

All are genuine expressions of what James calls 'felt life', but the first two are vivid with a sense of place and character, while the third does not really evoke this sense at all although it remains deeply moving. The most brilliant modern philosophical novel, *La Peste* (1947) by Albert Camus, again illustrates the novelist's traditional belief that in his own literary medium a set of ideas must be demonstrated through the experience and suffering of ordinary human beings. One writer, George Eliot, in whom as a 'sage' the creative artist is often at war with the moralist and teacher (and sometimes defeated by them), perhaps communicates her recognition of the dangers incurred by the novelist-philosopher when she describes her reluctance to

adopt any formula which does not get itself clothed for me in some human figure and individual experience; and perhaps that is a sign that if I help others to see at all it must be through that medium of art.[1]

Her characters are certainly made to fit into the pattern of her own moral universe: but she elicits belief in this universe in direct proportion to the humanity with which these characters are invested.

doesn't all authors?

IV   Dialogue

DIALOGUE, as one of the novelist's aids to characterization, certainly deserves a section to itself as one of the most exacting techniques of fiction. In order to convey the sense of individual identity, the 'dial-plate' novelist, as we have said, relies heavily on descriptions of appearance, on idiosyncratic gestures, clothes, actions, habits, mannerisms; while the 'inner-workings' novelist likes to record and analyse hidden movements of feeling and thought. Both, however, get many of their best effects through dialogue, an element which imports into the novel something of the dramatist's discipline and objectivity. It requires enormous patience and skill to 'get right' because its authenticity depends, as it does in the theatre, on a nice adjustment of the

---

[1] See her letter to Dr. Joseph Frank Payne (25 January 1876), *The George Eliot Letters* (1956), Vol. VI.

'real' and the stylized. Trollope describes how it must

steer between absolute accuracy of language—which would give to
. . . conversation an air of pedantry, and the slovenly inaccuracy
of ordinary talkers,—which if closely followed would offend by an
appearance of grimace . . .[1]

Flaubert's month-by-month account of his difficulties with
Emma's commonplace exchanges is heart-rending. '*Bovary* is
driving me mad!' he says at one stage:

I have to make up a conversation between my young woman and a
priest, a vulgar, stupid conversation, and because the matter is
commonplace the language must be appropriate.[2]

Four months later, in the middle of composing his famous scene
at the *comices agricoles* he writes,

To use dialogue as a means of portrayal, and yet not allow it to
become less vivid or precise, to give it distinction while it continues
to deal with commonplaces, all this is a colossal task, and I know of
no one who has managed to bring it off in a book.[3]

Half a century after this we find James complaining that even
yet no one has managed to 'bring it off' in England:

. . . really constructive dialogue, dialogue organic and dramatic,
speaking for itself, representing and embodying substance and form,
is among us an uncanny and abhorrent thing, not to be dealt with
on any terms . . .

and he has a more or less justifiable smack at the English
theatre for failing to remedy this state of affairs.[4]

And yet without becoming as rhythmically subtle and suggestive as James's, the bread and butter dialogue of a sound
craftsman like Trollope manages to be both natural and sinewy
—unusually so, for a Victorian—and at times extremely funny.
Mr. Cheesacre, well primed with cherry-brandy, proposes to
Arabella Greenow in *Can You Forgive Her?* (1864–5):

'Mr. Cheesacre, don't make a fool of yourself. Get up,' said she.
'Never, till you have told me that you will be mine!'
'Then you'll remain there for ever, which will be inconvenient.
I won't have you take hold of my hand, Mr. Cheesacre. I tell you

---

[1] See below, p. 295. [2] See below, p. 293.
[3] See below, p. 294. [4] See below, pp. 295–7.

to have done.' Whereupon his grasp upon her hand was released; but he made no attempt to rise.

'I never saw a man look so much like a fool in my life,' said she. 'If you don't get up, I'll push you over. There; don't you hear? There's somebody coming.'

But Cheesacre, whose senses were less acute than the lady's, did not hear. 'I'll never get up,' said he, 'till you have bid me hope.'

'Bid you play the fiddle. Get away from my knees, at any rate. There;—he'll be in the room now before——'

Cheesacre now did hear a sound of steps, and the door was opened while he made his first futile attempt to get back to a standing position. The door was opened, and Captain Bellfield entered. 'I beg ten thousand pardons,' said he; 'but as I did not see Jeannette, I ventured to come in. May I venture to congratulate my friend Cheesacre on his success?'

In the meantime Cheesacre had risen; but he had done so slowly, and with evident difficulty. 'I'll trouble you to leave the room, Captain Bellfield,' said he. 'I'm particularly engaged with Mrs. Greenow, as any gentleman might have seen.'

'There wasn't the slightest difficulty in seeing it, old fellow,' said the Captain. 'Shall I wish you joy?' [1]

This lies, in its comedy and economy of effect, half-way between two stylizations: the imaginative verbal caricature of 'dial-plate' novelists and the carefully allusive dialogue of the analytical writer. It is more natural than, say, Dickens's handling of Guppy's comic proposal to Esther Summerson in *Bleak House*, [2] but less sensitively handled than the even funnier interchanges in *What Maisie Knew* (some of these are the most hilarious things in fiction, and not less so because of the fine line separating the comedy from tears).

What neither James nor Trollope possesses, however, is Dickens's brilliant conversational fantasy. This depends on the verbal inventiveness which is the gift finally separating his genius from that of almost all other novelists (Joyce, perhaps, apart). On examination, Dickens's characters are found to exist very largely through their speech. Jingle, Chadband, Pecksniff, Micawber, above all Mrs. Gamp, live through the words which are put into their mouths. They do not converse so much as utter long monologues, fanciful, baroque, but surprisingly in-

[1] See *Can You Forgive Her?*, Chapter xlviii.
[2] See *Bleak House*, Chapter ix.

dividual. Mrs. Gamp would no more invent a Fiery Serpent on a Steeple[1] (though Mrs. Prig is a 'serpiant' at the end[2]) than Pecksniff would invent a Mrs. Harris and talk about this *alter ego* in a series of inspired malapropisms. Mrs. Gamp is a formidable continuer of the tradition which comes down through Sheridan from Fielding's Mrs. Slipslop, and this is how she explains with a lip-smacking relish for her own startling prose her present widowed and childless state;

'... As a good friend of mine has frequent made remark to me, which her name, my love, is Harris, Mrs. Harris through the square and up the steps a turnin' round by the tobacker shop, "Oh Sairey, Sairey, little do we know wot lays afore us!" "Mrs. Harris, ma'am," I says, "not much, it's true, but more than you suppoge. Our calcilations, ma'am," I says, "respectin wot the number of a family will be, comes most times within one, and oftener than you would suppoge, exact." "Sairey," says Mrs. Harris, in a awful way, "Tell me wot is my individgle number." "No, Mrs. Harris," I says to her, "ex-cuge me, if you please. My own," I says, "has fallen out of three-pair backs, and had damp doorsteps settled on their lungs, and one was turned up smilin' in a bedstead, unbeknown. Therefore, ma'am," I says, "seek not to proticipate, but take 'em as they come and as they go." "Mine," said Mrs. Gamp, "mine is all gone, my dear young chick. And as to husbands, there's a wooden leg gone like-ways home to its account, which in its constancy of walkin' into wine vaults, and never comin' out again 'till fetched by force, was quite as weak as flesh, if not weaker." ' [3]

This 'dialogue' is rich in throw-away detail, like the contents of Mrs. Harris's pocket described on another occasion as containing

two cramp-bones, a bit o' ginger, and a grater like a blessed infant's shoe, in tin, with a little heel to put the nut-meg in: as many times I've seen and said and used for caudle when required, within the month.[4]

It is a splendid method for satire, as Dickens demonstrates with the Transcendental Literary Ladies and the Mother of the Gracchi in the same novel.[5] This verbal ingenuity secures

---

[1] See Lord David Cecil, 'Charles Dickens', *Early Victorian Novelists* (1934).
[2] See *Martin Chuzzlewit*, Chapter xlix.
[3] Op. cit., Chapter xl.   [4] Op. cit., Chapter xlvi.
[5] Chapter xxxiv.

Dickens our forgiveness for the quite terrible things he can per-
petrate in sentimental or moral dialogue: Bella Harmon explaining to her husband that they are to have a child, for
example, or the conversations—if they can be called such—
between David and Dora Copperfield, or the death-bed utterances of the virtuous characters, especially when, as often happens, it is a child who is to expire.

In the case of James or Flaubert, dialogue serves the altogether different intention of the 'pure' artist. It displays as much
as possible 'the motives to actions, and the inward turns of the
mind' and at the same time seeks to bring out the novel's
important underlying themes. There is no place in this economy
for the Mother of the Gracchi or for a nut-meg grater with a
peculiar shape, nor is there even room for the delighted elaboration of a particular dialect which we find in Hardy, George
Eliot and even Emily Brontë. A prodigal, creative zest is behind the Yorkshire idioms of old Joseph's death-and-hellfire
monologues in *Wuthering Heights,* the rustic deliberations of the
members of the Mellstock choir in Hardy's *The Woodlanders,* and
Mrs. Poyser's vigorous Midland repartee in George Eliot's *The
Mill on the Floss* (George Eliot also gets in some neat satirical
touches by means of dialogue—as with Mr. Brooke's dismissal
of science, in *Middlemarch,* because 'it leads to everything' [1]).
But the self-conscious deliberation of the 'pure' artist has its
compensations. James's dialogue is a variety of verbal fencing,
allusive and beautifully wrought even if it is, especially in the
late novels, sometimes over-mannered. He shares with Miss
Compton-Burnett the gift of sharply differentiating his characters' conversation without much varying their vocabulary and
syntax. It is impossible to mistake the identity of his speakers
because none of them think alike or feel alike. His dialogue is,
like hers, 'organic and dramatic' in that it expresses the dis-
turbing impact the characters have on each other once they
emerge from their private self-communings and seek some form
of mutual comprehension. But to a greater degree even than
hers, it suggests that the various tensions and misunderstand-
ings set up in conversation will profoundly affect their subsequent behaviour. Miss Compton-Burnett's novels are written
exclusively in dialogue[2]—a few 'stage-directions' are inter-

[1] Book I, Chapter ii.   [2] See below, pp. 297–8.

spersed here and there—and so dispense altogether with the element which is essential to the full effect of James's dialogue. His novels proceed from 'preparation' to 'scene'. In the 'preparation', on which James lavishes all the skill of his peculiar analytical insight, we are taken into the subterranean world of his characters' inner life and are made to assist in the various processes which guide their feelings and thoughts. Consequently, when we arrive at the 'scene' itself—which corresponds more or less to the dramatist's *scene à faire*—we are in a position to savour the full irony of conversational hesitations, suppressions, wilful distortions and unwitting misapprehensions, and to appreciate the nature of the fresh developments which these will precipitate. The gnomic effect of this densely allusive dialogue appears in the exchange between Maggie Verver and Fanny Assingham concerning the adultery of Maggie's husband with Maggie's young step-mother, Charlotte:

> ' . . . . . I can bear anything.'
> 'Oh "bear"!' Mrs. Assingham fluted.
> 'For love,' said the Princess.
> Fanny hesitated. 'Of your father.'
> 'For love,' Maggie repeated.
> It kept her friend watching. 'Of your husband?'
> 'For love,' Maggie said again.[1]

The cadences are emotionally expressive, as they are again in the taut, nervous dialogue between Maggie and her husband near the close of the story, when Maggie's 'mildness'—a devastating weapon—is seen to have made her victory over Charlotte complete.[2] Or there is the final conversation between Kate Croy and Martin Densher—Milly Theale's money and Milly Theale's memory lying between them—which closes the book with the words,

> 'I'll marry you, mind you, in an hour.'
> 'As we were?'
> 'As we were.'
> But she turned to the door, and her headshake was now the end.
> 'We shall never be again as we were.' [3]

---

[1] *The Golden Bowl*, Book Fourth, Chapter vi.
[2] Op. cit., Book Sixth, Chapter iii.
[3] *The Wings of the Dove*, Book X, Chapter xxxviii.

Although this evocative quality has been rare in more recent writing, the mastery of good, lively, authentic dialogue is one of the real achievements of modern fiction. Mr. E. M. Forster is one of the earliest novelists to employ a dialogue which is simpler and more natural than James's although remaining at the same time allusive and schooled by the artist's central themes. Mr. Forster's ear for certain kinds of idiom is unerring: he gets the slightly dated slang used by Aziz in *A Passage to India* exactly right, and he is equally happy in handling the delightful interchanges between Gino and his Italian friends in *Where Angels Fear to Tread*, Mrs. Honeychurch's comfortable English middle-class fluency in *A Room with a View*, and the clichés of the insensitive Pembrokes in *The Longest Journey*. Any failures occur when there is some uncertainty in the characterization itself (Mr. Emerson in *A Room with a View*, Stephen Wonham in *The Longest Journey*, Leonard Bast and Jacky in *Howards End*). A later novelist, Mr. Graham Greene, with an infallible ear for an even wider range of idiom (it serves him well in the theatre), represents at its best the present-day skill in contriving dialogue which is at once natural, lively, supple and functional. Mr. Greene is able to catch the speech rhythms, the individual turns of phrase, used by all sorts of people, from the Commissioner of Police to the gangster, the neurotic suburban housewife to the shady ex-public-schoolboy, lawyer or confidence-trickster, the bus-driver to the whiskey-priest on the run, the down-at-heel waitress from the slum to the successful secretary and woman of the world. Even at a more popular level the technical achievement in differentiating the idioms of a complicated society while furthering theme and action by rapid conversational interchange is quite remarkable. The gift may not serve a profound or 'significant' vision, but it has its own value as testimony in novels like Balchin's *The Small Back Room* (1943) or Chandler's *The Big Sleep* (1939).

V Background

IT IS OBVIOUS in a discussion of the novel that, with due regard to Mr. Forster's warnings,[1] one cannot avoid talking of

[1] See *Aspects of the Novel*, Chapter i.

its 'development'. It is a form which has sought continually the coherence and integration of a 'pure' art, often coming very near to achieving these even though its survival depends on the credibility and solidity of the world which it portrays. The artistic self-consciousness which compels the novelist to make 'things of truth' from 'things of fact' by adjusting them to their new context has gradually seen to it that the background and setting of his 'scene' shall be as integral to his design as his plot, his characters, his dialogue and his narrative technique. As he reduces what Mr. Liddell calls 'the vicious distinction between "style" and "subject-matter" ',[1] the novelist no longer regards setting and background primarily as opportunities for the display of his descriptive powers in fine writing. Fielding seems to be uttering a playful warning about the ludicrous aspects of this kind of self-indulgence when he describes Mr. Allworthy's 'noble' house in *Tom Jones*.[2] The passage reveals an interestingly early taste for the Gothic, which seems to be quite genuine in spite of the fun. The place has an 'air of grandeur in it that struck you with awe, and rivalled the beauties of the best Grecian architecture', a view of 'an old ruined abbey, grown over with ivy' and grounds owing their pleasing effect 'less to art than Nature'.[3] But Mr. Allworthy is contemplating the whole scene from the top of what Jane Austen would call 'a considerable eminence' (from such a point of vantage Elizabeth Bennet first sees Pemberley[4]) and Fielding heads his account, 'The Reader's Neck Brought into Danger by a Description.'

Fielding's setting here, however, has no genuine imaginative relevance to his novel. Such relevance is encouraged in England only when certain effects of the cult of sensibility begin to make themselves felt in the novel. For Henry Mackenzie's unfortunate hero in *The Man of Feeling* particular settings evoke particular emotions: that Harley should be reminded, as he broods over a scene near his old home, of a painting by Salvator Rosa is the author's way of emphasizing this fact and simultaneously of suggesting the nature of Harley's present mood.[5] By the time of Mrs. Radcliffe's novels and, a little later, of Scott's, the

---

[1] See *A Treatise on the Novel*, Chapter vi.
[2] See *Tom Jones*, Book I, Chapter iv.   [3] Loc. cit.
[4] See *Pride and Prejudice*, Chapter xliii.
[5] See *The Man of Feeling*, Chapter xxxiv.

'reader's neck' is indeed in constant peril from the vertiginous slopes and crumbling towers now brought to the foreground of the novelist's composition. They are in this position because they have a special function to perform by drawing out human feeling for the mysterious and the strange, the 'awe' which Fielding and Jane Austen would rather place at a comic distance. This feeling persists and when it is experienced by the questioning temperament of the imaginative Victorian a new meaning is added to such settings:

The moors in *Wuthering Heights* and Egdon Heath in *The Return of the Native* are . . . immensities which make numinous the human dramas that occur beside them. In such contexts Romanticism first intensifies human feeling and then sets the passionate avowals against a background which reduces them.[1]

In a still later art, where all the weight shifts to the operations of the individual consciousness, the scene acquires significance through the personal emotion of the chosen observer. Adam Verver, brooding alone in the moonlight at Fawns, suddenly makes up his mind to propose to Charlotte Stant:

Just then the autumn night seemed to clear to a view in which the whole place, everything round him, the wide terrace where he stood, the others, with their steps, below, the gardens, the park, the lake, the circling woods, lay there as under some strange midnight sun. It all met him during these instants as a vast expanse of *discovery*, a world that looked, so lighted, extraordinarily new. . . [2]

As far as 'background' is concerned, then, the novelist more and more, in Miss Compton-Burnett's words, 'carries the thing into the human world'.[3] To some extent, the novelist's social conscience has helped this tendency. Zola[4] and Balzac seek to show how environment shapes a man's life and helps to make him what he is, and they dramatize the interplay of character and setting with a wealth of observation and detail in order to emphasize the social implications of their portraits of life. But there is little doubt that in practice the novelist's attention to his setting expresses more often than not the delight which he feels

[1] See Kenneth Allot, Introduction to *Victorian Prose, 1830–1880* (1956), ed. Kenneth and Miriam Allott, pp. xxxviii–ix.
[2] Henry James, *The Golden Bowl*, Book Second, Chapter v.
[3] See below, p. 307. [4] See below, pp. 302–3.

in the imaginative reconstruction of what the real world offers him. We sense this in Scott's account of transposing Melrose into something fresh and new,[1] in Trollope's description of his gradual mastery of 'the horizons and landscapes of a partly real, partly dream-country',[2] in Stevenson's boyish map-making,[3] in Hardy's creation of Wessex.[4] George Eliot, whose novels so conscientiously analyse the clash of character and circumstance in small country towns, grants that she lavishes too much time and space on visualizing the medium in which her characters move[5] (in *Romola* the effect in the end is, alas, to destroy all sense of vitality). A loving pleasure in evoking the atmosphere of place breathes through Flaubert's wonderfully subtle description of Yonville l'Abbaye and is sensed again in Turgenev's delicate, lyrical touch with the vast, sad landscapes of Russia.

Mr. Liddell claims that

there are only two ways of looking at the background in a novel. If it is looked at objectively, it must be seen only in so far as it explains the action, like the scenery in a play. The piling up of details for their own sake is tedious and irrelevant.

The subjective view of the background is only legitimate when it is the view of one of the characters; there is no excuse for the author's subjective view, except perhaps when he enters into the story as Chorus, in the capacity of Time and Fate. Dickens is present in such a capacity when he evokes the rain in Lincolnshire, the fog of the Law Courts, or other of his symbolic atmospheres.[6]

There is little to add to Mr. Liddell's excellent general discussion of the whole subject of background in the novel, except perhaps to say that good novelists can get away with conveying a good many of their own feelings for a place by skilfully handling their characters' subjective commentary. This is one of the advantages of the 'oblique and indirect view', and French novelists have been particularly good at making use of it. Anyone who has read Flaubert or Proust or François Mauriac is left with an extraordinarily vivid sense of what it means to these writers to breathe and smell and feel the atmosphere of such places as Yonville, Balbec or the small towns of the Landes.

---

[1] See below, pp. 299–300. [2] See below, p. 301.
[3] See below, pp. 303–4. [4] See below, pp. 301–2.
[5] See below, p. 301. [6] See Robert Liddell, loc. cit., p. 127.

Lawrence displays this power in a novel like *Kangaroo,* where, for once, his keen feeling for place is made to serve the human situations which he is attempting to explore. (Of course, his magnificent travel sketches are another matter.) One might add further to Mr. Liddell's comments by saying that 'background' is naturally closer to 'character' than one might think. Mr. Liddell believes that

Fiction is the delineation of character in action, and the landscape in the background is merely incidental.[1]

Obviously this is not quite all the truth when applied to Hardy or Emily Brontë, although it is certainly true of Jane Austen (whom Mr. Liddell admirably discusses in this context). What is true is that 'background' in the novel is, like 'character', part of a verbal pattern. Like 'character', it requires of the novelist a firm, clear sense of the actual world and at the same time the power to select and conventionalize those parts of it which most strongly appeal to his imagination for the purpose of serving and strengthening the effect of his design. Background is an abstraction like every other element in the novel, but again like all the other elements it is only really successful when it is 'carried into the human world'.

VI *Style*

THE NOVELIST's difficulties with dialogue remind us more sharply than his other problems that style plays a peculiarly important part in his success or failure, but it is obvious that of the other activities explored in this chapter there is not one that could even begin to be carried out without some feeling for the possibilities of language. Everything in a novel is part of a diversified verbal pattern: only by mastering the range and flexibility of style which this pattern demands can the novelist finally convince us that his concern lies with something other than the abstract and the ideal. It must be said at once that this does not mean that in order to be a good novelist it is necessary to be an accurate stylist. Most modern critics of the novel have come to realize this. 'The genre itself works by exhaustive presentation rather than elegant concentration', says Mr. Ian Watt, finding

[1] Loc. cit., p. 11.

that 'incorrect' writers like Richardson or Defoe achieve a greater immediacy than Fielding, whose 'stylistic virtues tend to interfere with his technique as a novelist, because a patent selectiveness of vision destroys our belief in the reality of report, or at least diverts our attention from the content of the report to the skill of the reporter'.[1] Hardy's books, Mr. Robert Liddell recognizes, may 'contain great writing' but this does not make them great novels: 'The admirers of his novels admit freely—they cannot avoid it—his failure over plot and character as we generally understand these things when we speak of fiction.' Lord David Cecil was able to remind us in *The Early Victorian Novelists* of the specific novelist's gifts displayed by Dickens, Charlotte Brontë and George Eliot without finding that these writers were in any way masters of meticulous prose. Then there is the obvious question of translation:

If 'the way in which words are used' is the only and final criterion, then English readers who do not know Russian have no right to praise the novels of Tolstoy or Dostoevsky, but only to praise the minds of Louise and Aylmer Maude, or of Constance Garnett. Yet there is a sufficiently respectable consensus of English opinion that Tolstoy and Dostoevsky are indeed great novelists to have evidential value.

This is how Mr. Liddell deals with the limitations of 'Practical Criticism'—the analysis of significant passages to test the qualities of a writer's mind and sensibility—as a principal method of evaluating a novel.[2]

And yet it is still true that if the novelist is to work by 'exhaustive presentation' and at the same time keep within the limits of his design, he needs an especially wide command of language and some sense of the power of words.

The web, then, or the pattern; a web at once sensuous and logical, an elegant and pregnant texture: that is style, that is the foundation of the art of literature.[3]

The words are Stevenson's, who is a novelist, it is true, with something of the dandy in his style of writing. A web 'at once sensuous and logical', a texture 'elegant and pregnant', these

---

[1] *The Rise of the Novel*, pp. 29–30.
[2] *A Treatise on the Novel*, pp. 24–5.   [3] See below, p. 319.

may seem to be more in his line and James's than in Dickens's or George Eliot's. George Sand expresses the impatience of some comprehensive, discursive novelists by telling Flaubert that 'the well-made sentence' is 'something' but not by any means the whole of art—

it's a quarter at most, and when the other three quarters are beautiful, people will overlook the one that isn't.[1]

Her arguments, even in the original French, are a little muddled but one sees what she is trying to say. A sound entertainer like Trollope explains the minimum demands of style in his clearer, more straightforward manner by explaining that if a novelist

be confused, tedious, harsh, or unharmonious readers will certainly reject him . . . He may indeed be pleasant without being correct, —as I think can be proved by the works of more than one distinguished novelist. But he must be intelligible,—intelligible without trouble; and he must be harmonious.[2]

His advice to the would-be novelist emphasizes strongly the discipline and self-criticism which a satisfactory style exacts, whether it is to be 'an elegant and pregnant texture', or simply workmanlike, intelligible, and free from clichés and grammatical mistakes. An impetuous talent like that of George Sand may rebel against the anguished searching for the right word which keeps Flaubert awake night after night, but too often, particularly in the early Romantic novels, her own 'welter of helpless verbiage' (James uses the phrase in describing the 'fluid puddings' of certain novelists[3]) illustrates the danger of abandoning the pursuit of clarity and exactness.

George Sand's attitude, so untypical of the French novelist generally, is a characteristically rebellious response to the sometimes crippling preoccupation with stylistic correctness which distinguishes the French novel from *La Princesse de Clèves* onwards. But this long tradition of discipline has its compensating virtues. They are, indeed, discoverable in George Sand herself when she is at her best: she is

one of the few French writers who keep us closely and truly intimate with rural nature. She gives us the wild-flowers by their actual

---

[1] See below, p. 314.   [2] See below, p. 315.
[3] See below, p. 235.

220

names,—snowdrop, primrose, columbine, iris, scabious. Nowhere
has she touched her native Berry and its little-known landscape, its
campagnes ignorées, with a lovelier charm than in *Valentine*. . . .

This is part of Matthew Arnold's tribute to her on her death,
and he goes on to give what is virtually an English rendering
of the passage which he finds so moving.[1] A feeling of responsibility for truth in handling words characterizes almost every
pronouncement on style made by French novelists. 'I know of
only one rule,' says Stendhal, 'style cannot be too *clear*, too
simple.'[2] If Flaubert dreams of 'a beautiful style . . . as rhythmical as verse', he also dreams that it will be 'as precise as
science'.[3] The 'grand style' is achieved through 'logic and
clarity', adds Zola, and he may be thinking of George Sand,
as well as of the exuberance which produced *Salammbô* and made
his own descriptions so lavish, when he complains 'we are rotten
with lyricism'.[4] Whatever it is that one wishes to say, writes
Maupassant in his commemorative essay on Flaubert, 'there is
only one word to express it, one verb to set it in motion and
only one adjective to describe it': makeshifts will not do.[5] It
is not perhaps a less exacting sense of form which gives the corresponding remarks of English novelists a different emphasis so
much as the different qualities of their own language. English
is less 'exact' than French and its ambiguities are often put to
the service of irony, metaphor and symbol with resulting emotional overtones and densities of connotation which are beyond
the range of many French writers. The translator, in particular,
notices these differences and M. D'Albert-Durade, for one, seems
to have been nonplussed by difficulties in translating into French
those many *'intermédiaires entre le style commun et le style élégant'*
which diversify the writing of even a comparatively unsubtle
stylist like George Eliot.[6] But it is a sense of the potential vigour
and the variety of English which makes Wilkie Collins, for
example, reject Addison—how refreshingly!—as 'neat but trivial, not in the least vigorous or dramatic; but the very reverse'.[7]
He chooses to read Byron's letters instead: 'the best English I

---

[1] See Matthew Arnold, 'George Sand' (1877); reprinted in *Mixed Essays*
(1879).
[2] See below, p. 312. [3] See below, pp. 312–13.
[4] See below, pp. 316–17. [5] See below, p. 317.
[6] See below, p. 314. [7] See below, p. 315.

know of—perfectly simple and clear, bright and strong'.[1] A similar feeling lies behind Hardy's assertion that it is better not to have 'too much style': the secret of vitality lies in being 'a little careless, or rather seeming to be, here and there', otherwise one's style

is like worn half-pence—all the fresh images rounded off by rubbing, and no crispness or movement at all.[2]

But this ease and freshness needs endless patience to achieve. Conrad writes of the art which conceals art,

it is only through an unremitting never-discouraged care for the shape and ring of sentences that an approach can be made to plasticity, to colour, and that the light of magic suggestiveness may be brought to play for an evanescent instant over the commonplace surface of words.[3]

His letter to Sir Hugh Clifford summarizes the whole subject:

. . . words, groups of words, words standing alone, are symbols of life, have the power in their sound or their aspect to present the very thing you wish to hold up before the mental vision of your readers. The things 'as they are' exist in words; therefore words should be handled with care lest the picture, the image of truth abiding in facts should become distorted—or blurred.[4]

But the novel's range of tone and emotional temperature makes the task enormously exacting. In the eighteenth century we recognize the high degree of skill which Fielding needs to master those variations of ironic tone which he artfully substitutes for the analytical interpretation of character. He assures us that 'forming an accurate judgment of style' requires more learning and good sense than any other branch of criticism,[5] and then challenges us by manipulating many different kinds of style to suit his themes. When Mr. Wilson tells his life-story in *Joseph Andrews*,

there is a change from the novelist's habitual lightness and wit to the sober, straightforward idiom of the penitent's autobiography (the same form as we find in Defoe's novels, but more 'educated').[6]

---

[1] See below, p. 315.   [2] See below, p. 318.
[3] See below, p. 320.   [4] See below, p. 319.
[5] See below, p. 308.
[6] See Douglas Jefferson, Introduction to *Eighteenth Century Prose, 1700–1780* (1956), p. xx.

Furthermore, Fielding likes to leave the reader guessing and his poised style 'provides beautifully for tactical evasions'.[1] The whole question of Fielding's irony and the nature of its concealments and withdrawals needs more attention than it usually receives. Both his method and Jane Austen's leave us wondering whether the peculiar force of their irony does not after all depend much less on the firmness of their moral beliefs than on the vividness with which they recognize the existence of ambiguity, contradiction and anomaly.

The wit and politeness which colour with refinement even the crudest scenes of Fielding and thereby add to their comic effect, are quite alien to the style of his great contemporary, Richardson. 'We do not find in his writings', says Richardson's biographer, Mrs. Barbauld, 'the ease and elegance of good company, or the polished period of a finished author'.[2] But she admits that we find in their place an attractive immediacy and realism. The scope and vigour of his prose have lately received some deserved recognition from Mr. Allen, who quotes part of the famous brothel scene,[3] Mr. Jefferson, who illustrates the peculiar excellences of his epistolary manner,[4] and Dr. Kettle, who reminds us of the splendid impressionism in the scene where Clarissa is subjected to 'a refined and subtle torture' by her sister Arabella:

What! silent still? But, Clary, won't you have a velvet suit? It would cut a great figure in a country church, you know: and the weather may bear it for a month yet to come. Crimson velvet, suppose! Such a fine complexion as yours, how it would be set off by it! . . . and do you sigh, love? Well then, as it will be a solemn wedding, what think you of *black* velvet, child? Silent still, Clary! Black velvet, so fair as you are, with those charming eyes, gleaming through a wintry cloud, like an April sun! Does not Lovelace tell you they are charming eyes! How lovely will you appear to every one! What! silent still, love! But about your laces, Clary! [5]

The whole scene suggests what Mrs. Barbauld means when she says that Richardson has 'the accuracy and finish of a Dutch

---

[1] Ibid.   [2] See below, p. 308.

[3] See Walter Allen, *The English Novel* (1954), pp. 45–6.

[4] See Douglas Jefferson, op. cit., pp. xxii–iii, 171, 220.

[5] *Clarissa* (Everyman ed.), Vol. I, letter xliv; see also Arnold Kettle, *An Introduction to the English Novel* (1951), Vol. I, Chapter iv.

painter with the fine ideas of an Italian one'.[1] But besides following the 'throb, throb, throb' of emotions—the phrase occurs in one of Anna Howe's letters[2]—Richardson has the 'awful directness' which Mr. Jefferson further illustrates with Clarissa's descriptions of Mr. Solmes 'sitting asquat' or 'hemming up for a speech and beginning to set his splay feet . . .', and with the Hogarthian scene at Mrs. Sinclair's death-bed.[3]

In fact, the divergences of style between Fielding and Richardson correspond with those which separate Dickens and Thackeray a century later. For the Victorians, Thackeray is the 'correct' writer, capable of composing 'the polished period of the finished author', while Dickens is one of the 'incorrect' writers whom Trollope has in mind when discussing his contemporaries.[4] Mrs. Barbauld's comment on Richardson's style as 'blemished with little flippancies of expression, new coined words, and sentences involved and ill-constructed',[5] anticipates Trollope's comments on Dickens's prose.[6] But by the time we reach the Victorians we find that the educated 'correctness' which serves the clear-cut social attitudes of Fielding, Goldsmith and Jane Austen is no longer usual, and that individual differences are almost too varied and numerous to disentangle. It is true that the 'awful directness' which characterizes the earnest, moralizing art of the bourgeois novelist—who has no real interest in 'distancing' refinements—is a quality which helps to place as Victorians novelists as different from each other as Dickens and Thackeray, Trollope and George Eliot. It appears in their close fidelity to the world of appearances and in their sermonizing interpolations (the modern reader flinches as the ominous phrases appear: 'But let the gentle-hearted reader . . .', 'Look back, good friend, at your own youth . . .', 'Do we not all at some time . . . ?'). But a whole new range of tone accompanies the novel's widening themes and the strong feelings which they arouse. 'The modification of style by emotion' is demonstrated by Emily Brontë whose final sentence in *Wuther-*

---

[1] See below, p. 309.
[2] See *Clarissa* (Everyman ed.), Vol. I, letter x.
[3] Douglas Jefferson, op. cit., pp. xxii–xxiii.
[4] See Anthony Trollope, *An Autobiography* (1883), Chapter xiii.
[5] See below, p. 308.
[6] See Anthony Trollope, *An Autobiography*, loc. cit.

ing Heights, as it is pointed out elsewhere, 'brings one into the presence of an imaginative effect seemingly beyond the powers of any English novelist of the eighteenth century':

I lingered among them, under that benign sky; watched the moth, fluttering among the heath, and hare-bells; listened to the soft wind breathing through the grass, and wondered how any one could ever imagine unquiet slumbers, for the sleepers in that quiet earth.[1]

At the same time, the new insights of the analytical writer demand the 'sensitive control of tone and inflection' which distinguishes George Eliot's writing at its best and also prepares us for the subtle 'web', at once 'logical' and 'sensuous', spun by Henry James's introspective art. The emotions released by this insight often find expression in metaphor and image. In George Eliot, the background of scientific knowledge (G. H. Lewes's work was constantly at hand) sometimes gives peculiar force and directness to her imagery. She describes the red decorations hung out in the streets of Rome as breaking out 'like a disease of the retina', and talks of 'the roar on the other side of silence' which would kill us if our perceptions were acute enough 'to hear the grass grow' or the squirrel's heart beating.[2] In James, of course, the whole quality, 'the magic suggestiveness', of his later work derives to a great extent from the use which he makes of extended metaphor. As with everything else in his art, these have their place in a closely-worked design. When the Prince in *The Golden Bowl* sees Charlotte Stant as a long, delicate but strongly-wrought purse filled with gold pieces,[3] the image is playing a part in the rich pattern made by James's interrelated themes of money, art and love.

To-day, the considered use of image and metaphor is still one of the noticeable techniques of English fiction. But James's disciplined use of compulsive images is rare, and so are the 'written' effects of Conrad's style, the extreme sensitivity to the musically rhythmical movements of prose which we find in Virginia Woolf, and the inventive energy of Joyce, whose use of language was one of the really invigorating contributions to

---

[1] Kenneth Allott, Introduction to *Victorian Prose, 1830–1880* (1956), ed. Kenneth and Miriam Allott, pp. xix–xx.

[2] See *Middlemarch*, Book II, Chapter xx.

[3] See *The Golden Boul*, Book First, Chapter iii.

the twentieth-century English novel. As Mr. Forster explains in his lecture, *The Development of English Prose Between 1918 and 1939* (1945), the break-up of accepted social patterns in the period between the two wars brought 'freshness and informality and new usages and democratic good manners into literature', but it also brought 'vulgarity and flatness'. Mr. Forster himself, together with certain other writers of more or less his own generation—his list omits his own name but includes Lytton Strachey, Virginia Woolf, James Joyce, D. H. Lawrence and T. E. Lawrence—wanted 'to create something better than the bloodshed and dullness which have been creeping together over the world'.[1] But their peculiarly sensitive and individual expressiveness is an esoteric tendency. Mr. Forster's own easy, unbuttoned style is deceptive. Its civilized simplicity should help it to wear well, but it is the expression of a highly sophisticated personality, complex and subtly ironical, and as such many of its qualities may be lost sight of to-day. Almost alone among contemporary novelists, Mr. Evelyn Waugh deliberately cultivates with similar meticulousness but intentionally different effect a correct style penetrated by robust satirical irony. It is his gesture of rebellion against the vulgarity and flatness of which Mr. Forster speaks. Apart from Mr. Waugh and, perhaps, the mannered experiments of Mr. Henry Green in such novels as *Loving* (1945), *Back* (1946) and *Concluding* (1948), the contemporary novelist gives us the impression that he would rather confine himself to the minimal qualities of a good style. His writing is not often distinguished by an unusually subtle feeling for words, it is hardly ever worked into 'an elegant and pregnant texture', it is never robustly inventive in the Joycean manner, and its sentence-structure is often loose, pedestrian and commonplace. But it has learned to move with a democratic freedom and pace, to cut out a great deal of helpless verbiage, and, above all, to make the most of the ordinary idioms of everyday talk. The opening chapter of Mr. L. P. Hartley's *The Shrimp and the Anemone* (1944) illustrates admirably both the strengths and some of the limitations of the modern English novelist's use of prose.

[1] P. 15. See also below, p. 322.

TEXT

I Structural Problems

UNITY AND COHERENCE

EPIC REGULARITY

. . . here is a regular story, which, though possibly it is not pursued
with that epic regularity which would give it the name of an action,
comes nearer to that perfection than the loose unconnected adventures in Don Quixote; of which you may transverse the order as you
please, without any injury to the whole.

> *Henry Fielding. Review of Charlotte Lennox's* The Female
> Quixote (*1752*), The Covent Garden Journal (*March
> 1752*).

NOTHING FOREIGN TO THE DESIGN

First, then, we warn thee not too hastily to condemn any of the
incidents in this our history as impertinent and foreign to our main
design, because thou dost not immediately conceive in what manner
such incident may conduce to that design. This work may, indeed,
be considered as a great creation of our own; and for a little reptile
of a critic to presume to find fault with any of its parts, without
knowing the manner in which the whole is connected, and before
he comes to the final catastrophe, is a most presumptuous absurdity.

> *Henry Fielding.* The History of Tom Jones, A Foundling
> (*1749*), Book X, Chapter i.

PLOT UNIFORM AND NARRATIVE UNBROKEN

A novel may be considered as a dilated comedy; its plot therefore should be uniform, and its narrative unbroken: episode and

digression are sparingly, if at all, to be admitted; the adventures of *the Man of the Hill*, in the Foundling, is an excrescence that offends against the grace and symmetry of the plot: whatever makes a pause in the main business, and keeps the chief characters too long out of sight, must be a defect.

Richard Cumberland. Henry (*1795*), *Book the Sixth, Chapter i.*

DIGRESSIONS ARE THE SUNSHINE OF READING

. . . in this long digression which I was accidentally led into, as in all my digressions (one only excepted) there is a master-stroke of digressive skill, the merit of which has all along, I fear, been over-looked by my reader,—not for want of penetration in him,—but because it is an excellence seldom looked for, or expected indeed, in a digression; and it is this:—That tho' my digressions are all fair, as you observe,—and that I fly off from what I am about, as far, and as often too, as any writer in *Great Britain*; yet I constantly take care to order affairs so that my main business does not stand still in my absence.

I was just going, for example, to have given you the great outlines of my uncle *Toby's* most whimsical character;—when my aunt *Dinah* and the coachman came across us, and led us a vagary some millions of miles into the very heart of the planetary system: Not-withstanding all this, you perceive that the drawing of my uncle *Toby's* character went on gently all the time;—not the great contours of it,—that was impossible,—but some familiar strokes and faint designations of it, were here and there touch'd on, as we went along, so that you are much better acquainted with my uncle *Toby* now than you was before.

By this contrivance the machinery of my work is of a species by itself; two contrary motions are introduced into it, and reconciled, which were thought to be at variance with each other. In a word, my work is digressive, and it is progressive too,—and at the same time . . .

Digressions, incontestably, are the sunshine;—they are the life, the soul of reading!—take them out of this book, for instance,—you might as well take the book along with them;—one cold eternal winter would reign in every page of it; restore them to the writer;—he steps forth like a bridegroom,—bids All-hail; brings in variety, and forbids the appetite to fail.

All the dexterity is in the good cookery and management of them, so as not to be only for the advantage of the reader, but also of the author, whose distress in this matter, is truly pitiable: For, if he begins a digression,—from that moment, I observe, his whole work stands stock still;—and if he goes on with his main work,—then there is an end of his digression.

—This is vile work.—For which reason, from the beginning of this, you see, I have constructed the main work and the adventitious parts of it with such intersections, and have so complicated and involved the digressive and progressive movements, one wheel within another, that the whole machine, in general, has been kept a-going;—and what's more, it shall be kept a-going these forty years, if it pleases the fountain of health to bless me so long with life and good spirits.

> *Laurence Sterne*. The Life and Opinions of Tristram Shandy Gentleman (*1759*), *Book I, Chapter xxii.*

NO DETACHED EPISODES

There is not in any of Richardson's works, one of those detached episodes, thrown in like make-weights, to increase the bulk of the volume, which are so common in other works: such is the story of *The Man of the Hill* in Tom Jones. If his works are laboured into length, at least his prolixity is all bestowed upon the subject, and increases the effect of the story. Flashes of humour, and transient touches of sensibility, shew, indeed, genius; but patient and per-severing labour alone can finish a plan, and make every part bear properly on the main subject.

> *Anna Laetitia Barbauld.* 'A biographical account of Samuel Richardson', The Correspondence of Samuel Richardson (*1804*), *Vol. I.*

DEFENDING QUIRKS AND QUIDDITIES

Captain. And the story is, I hope, natural and probable; commencing strikingly, proceeding naturally, ending happily—like the course of a famed river, which gushes from the mouth of some obscure river and romantic grotto—then gliding on, never pausing, never precipitating its course, visiting, as it were, by natural instinct, whatever worthy subjects of interest are presented by the country through which it passes—widening and deepening in interest as it flows on; and at length arriving at the final catastrophe as at some mighty haven, where ships of all kinds strike sail and yard?

Author. Hey! hey! what the deuce is all this? Why, 'tis Ercles' vein, and it would require some one much more like Hercules than I, to produce a story which should gush, and glide, and never pause, and visit, and widen, and deepen, and all the rest on't. I should be chin-deep in the grave, man, before I had done with my task; and, in the meanwhile, all the quirks and quiddities which I might have devised for my reader's amusement, would lie rotting in my gizzard, like Sancho's suppressed witticisms, when he was under his master's displeasure.—There never was a novel written on this plan while the world stood.

Captain. Pardon me—Tom Jones.

Author. True, and perhaps Amelia also. Fielding had high notions of the dignity of an art which he may be considered as having founded. He challenges a comparison between the Novel and the Epic. Smollett, Le Sage, and others, emancipating themselves from the strictness of the rules he has laid down, have written rather a history of the miscellaneous adventures which befall an individual in the course of life, than the plot of a regular and connected epopeia, where every step brings us a point nearer to the final catastrophe. These great masters have been satisfied if they amused the reader upon the road; though the conclusion only arrived because the tale must have an end—just as the traveller alights at the inn, because it is evening.

Captain. A very commodious mode of travelling, for the author at least. In short, sir, you are of opinion with Bayes—'What the devil does the plot signify, except to bring in fine things?'

Author. Grant that I were so, and that I should write with sense and spirit a few scenes unlaboured and loosely put together, but which had sufficient interest in them to amuse in one corner the pain of body; in another to relieve anxiety of mind; in a third place, to unwrinkle a brow bent with the furrows of daily toil; in another, to fill the place of bad thoughts, or to suggest better; in yet another to induce an idler to study the history of his country; in all, save where the perusal interrupted the discharge of serious duties, to furnish harmless amusement,—might not the author of such a work, however inartificially executed, plead for his errors and negligences the excuse of the slave, who, about to be punished for having spread the false report of a victory, saved himself by exclaiming—'Am I to blame, O Athenians, who have given you one happy day?'

> *Sir Walter Scott. Introductory Epistle to*
> The Fortunes of Nigel (*1822*).

THE 'MAN OF THE HILL' IN TROUBLE AGAIN

The attention of the reader is never diverted or puzzled by unnecessary digressions, or recalled to the main story by abrupt and startling recurrences; he glides down the narrative like a boat on the surface of some broad navigable stream, which only winds enough to gratify the voyager with the varied beauty of its banks. One exception to this praise, otherwise so well merited, occurs in the story of the Old Man of the Hill; an episode, which, in compliance with a custom introduced by Cervantes, and followed by Le Sage, Fielding has thrust into the middle of his narrative, as he had formerly introduced the History of Leonora, equally unnecessarily and artificially, into that of *Joseph Andrews*.

> *Sir Walter Scott.* 'Henry Fielding', Lives of the Novelists (*1827*),

CIRCULATING THE BLOOD OF THE BOOK
THROUGH THE INSERTED STORY

I don't see the practicability of making the History of a Self-Tormenter, with which I took great pains, a written narrative. But I do see the possibility of making it a chapter by itself, which might enable me to dispense with the necessity of the turned commas. Do you think that would be better? I have no doubt that a great part of Fielding's reason for the introduced story, and Smollett's also, was, that it is sometimes really impossible to present, in a full book, the idea it contains (which yet it may be on all counts desirable to present), without supposing the reader to be possessed of almost as much romantic allowance as would put him on a level with the writer. In Miss Wade I had an idea, which I thought a new one, of making the introduced story so fit into surroundings impossible of separation from the main story, as to make the blood of the book circulate through both. But I can only suppose, from what you say, that I have not exactly succeeded in this.

> *Charles Dickens. Letter to John Forster (1856). See John Forster.*
> The Life of Charles Dickens (*1874*), *Vol. III, Chapter vi.*

STRIVING FOR UNITY

. . . My god, this novel makes me break out in a cold sweat! Do you know how much I've written in five months, since the end of August? Sixty-five pages! Each paragraph is good in itself and there are some pages that are perfect, I feel certain. But just because of this, *it isn't getting on.* It's a series of well-turned, ordered paragraphs which do not flow on from each other. I shall have to unscrew them, loosen the joints, as one does with the masts of a ship when one wants the sails to take more wind . . .

> *Gustave Flaubert. Letter to Louise Colet (29–30 January 1853),*
> Correspondance (*1900*).

... I should like to write books where one has nothing to do but write sentences (if one can say such a thing) just as in order to live one need only breathe air. What irks me is the trickiness of planning, the combining of effects, all the inner contrivances which yet belong to Art, since the effect of the style depends on them exclusively.

> *Gustave Flaubert. Letter to Louise Colet (25–6 June 1853),*
> Correspondance (*1900*)

... A good subject for a novel is the kind that comes all of a piece, in a single jet. It is the mother-idea from which all the others flow. One isn't in the least free to write just anything. One doesn't choose one's subject. This is something that neither the public nor the critic understands. Here lies the secret of a masterpiece, in the compatibility of the subject and the author's temperament.

> *Gustave Flaubert. Letter to Madame Roger des Genettes (1861?),*
> Correspondance (*1903*).

I've just read *Pickwick* by Dickens. Do you know it? Some bits are magnificent; but what a defective structure! All English writers are like that. Walter Scott apart, they lack composition. This is intolerable for us Latins.

> *Gustave Flaubert. Letter to George Sand (12 July 1872),*
> Correspondance (*1903*).

TWO MAJOR FAULTS

Yes, that was and ever is my greatest torment—I never can control my material. Whenever I write a novel, I crowd it up with a lot of separate stories and episodes; therefore the whole lacks proportion and harmony. You have seen this astonishingly well; how frightfully I have always suffered from it, for I have always been aware that it was so. And I have made another great mistake besides: without calculating my powers, I have allowed myself to be transported by poetic enthusiasm, and have undertaken an idea to which my strength was not equal. (N.B. The force of poetic enthusiasm is, to be sure, as for example with Victor Hugo, always stronger than the artistic force. Even in Pushkin one detects this disproportion.) But *I* destroy myself thereby.

> *Feodor Dostoevsky. Letter to Nikolay Nikolayevitch Strachov*
> (*23 April 1871*), *Letters (1914), transl. Ethel Colburn*
> *Mayne.*

EPISODES DISTRACT ATTENTION

There should be no episodes in a novel. Every sentence, every word, through all those pages, should tend to the telling of the story. Such episodes distract the attention of the reader, and always do so disagreeably. Who has not felt this to be the case even with 'The Curious Impertinent' and with the history of 'The Man of the Hill'? And if it be so with Cervantes and Fielding, who can hope to succeed? Though the novel which you have to write must be long, let it be all one. And this exclusion of episodes should be carried down to the smallest details. Every sentence and every word used should tend to the telling of the story. 'But,' the young novelist will say, 'with so many pages before me to be filled, how shall I succeed if I thus confine myself;—how am I to know beforehand what space this story of mine will require? There must be the three volumes, or the certain number of magazine pages which I have contracted to supply. If I may not be discursive should occasion require, how shall I complete my task? The painter suits the size of his canvas to his subject, and must I in my art stretch my subject to my canvas?' This undoubtedly must be done by the novelist; and if he will learn his business, may be done without injury to his effect. He may not paint different pictures on the same canvas, which he will do if he allow himself to wander away to matters outside his own story; but by studying proportion in his work, he may teach himself so to tell his story that it shall naturally fall into the required length. Though his story should be all one, yet it may have many parts. Though the plot itself may require but few characters, it may be so enlarged as to find its full development in many. There may be subsidiary plots, which shall all tend to the elucidation of the main story, and which will take their place as part of one and the same work,—as there may be many figures on a canvas which shall not to the spectator seem to form themselves into separate pictures.

Anthony Trollope. An Autobiography (*1883*), *Chapter xii.*

THE ARTIST MUST SUPPRESS MUCH AND OMIT MORE

. . . the artist has one main and necessary resource which he must, in every case and upon any theory, employ. He must, that is, suppress much and omit more. He must omit what is tedious or irrelevant, and suppress what is tedious and necessary. But such facts as, in regard to the main design, subserve a variety of purposes, he will perforce and eagerly retain. And it is the mark of the very highest order of creative art to be woven exclusively of such. There, any fact that is registered is contrived a double or a treble debt to pay, and is at once an ornament in its place, and a pillar in the main design. Nothing would find room in such a picture that did not serve, at once, to complete the composition, to accentuate the scheme of colour, to distinguish the planes of distance, and to strike the note of the selected sentiment; nothing would be allowed in such a story that did not, at the same time, expedite the progress of the fable, build up the characters, and strike home the moral or the philosophical design. But this is unattainable. As a rule, so far from building the fabric of our works exclusively with these, we are thrown into a rapture if we think we can muster a dozen or a score of them, to be the plums of our confection. And hence, in order that the canvas may be filled or the story proceed from point to point, other details must be admitted. They must be admitted, alas! upon a doubtful title; many without marriage robes. Thus any work of art, as it proceeds towards completion, too often—I had almost written always—loses in force and poignancy of main design. Our little air is swamped and dwarfed among hardly relevant orchestration; our little passionate story drowns in a deep sea of descriptive eloquence or slipshod talk.

> *Robert Louis Stevenson. 'A Note on Realism', (1883); reprinted in* The Art of Writing *(1919).*

THE NOVEL ALL ONE AND CONTINUOUS

I cannot imagine composition existing in a series of blocks, nor conceive, in any novel worth discussing at all, of a passage of description that is not in its intention narrative, a passage of dialogue that is not in its intention descriptive, a touch of truth of any sort that does not partake of the nature of incident, and an incident that derives its interest from any other source than the general and only source of the success of a work of art—that of being illustrative. A novel is a living thing, all one and continuous, like every other organism, and in proportion as it lives will it be found, I think, that in each of the parts there is something of each of the other parts. The critic who over the close texture of a finished work will pretend to trace a geography of items will mark some frontiers as artificial, I fear, as any that have been known to history.

> *Henry James. 'The Art of Fiction' (1884); reprinted in* Partial Portraits *(1888).*

FOCUS

(5 July 1900) . . . The most important thing in a work of art is that it should have a kind of focus, i.e. there should be some place where all the rays meet or from which they issue. And this focus must not be able to be completely explained in words. This indeed is one of the significant facts about a true work of art—that its content in its entirety can be expressed only by itself.

> Leo Tolstoy. Talks with Tolstoy (*1922*), *ed. A. B. Goldenveizer, transl. S. S. Koteliansky and Virginia Woolf* (*1923*).

FORM *IS* SUBSTANCE

Don't let anyone persuade you—there are plenty of ignorant and fatuous duffers to try to do it—that strenuous selection and comparison are not the very essence of art, and that Form *is* [not] substance to that degree that there is absolutely no substance without it. Form alone *takes*, and holds and preserves, substance—saves it from the welter of helpless verbiage that we swim in as in a sea of tasteless tepid pudding, and that makes one ashamed of an art capable of such degradations. Tolstoi and Dostoevsky are fluid puddings, though not tasteless, because the amount of their own minds and souls in solution in the broth gives it savour and flavour, thanks to the strong, rank quality of their genius and their experience. But there are all sorts of things to be said of them, and in particular that we see how great a vice is their lack of composition, their defiance of economy and architecture, directly they are emulated and imitated; *then*, as subjects of emulation, models, they quite give themselves away. There is nothing so deplorable as a work of art with a *leak* in its interest; and there is no such leak of interest as through commonness of form. Its opposite, the *found* (because the sought-for) form is the absolute citadel and tabernacle of interest.

> *Henry James. Letter to Hugh Walpole* (*19 May 1912*), Selected Letters (*1956*).

ON APPEARING TO DIGRESS

The first thing that you have to consider when writing a novel is your story, and then your story—and then your story! If you wish to feel more dignified you may call it your 'subject.' Any digression will make a *longueur*, a patch over which the mind will progress heavily. You may have the most wonderful scene from real life that you might introduce into your book. But if it does not make your subject progress it will divert the attention of the reader. A good novel needs all the attention the reader can give it. And then some more.

Of course, you must appear to digress. That is the art which conceals your Art. The reader, you should premise, will always dislike you and your book. He thinks it an insult that you should dare to claim his attention, and if lunch is announced or there is a ring at the bell he will welcome the digression. So you will provide him with what he thinks are digressions—with occasions on which he thinks he may let his attention relax. . . . But really not one single thread must ever escape your purpose.

Ford Madox Ford. It Was the Nightingale (*1934*),
Part II, Chapter ii.

MASTERY OF PERSPECTIVE

. . . if there is one gift more essential to a novelist than another it is the power of combination—the single vision. The success of the masterpieces seem to lie not so much in their freedom from faults— indeed we tolerate the grossest errors in them all—but in the immense persuasiveness of a mind which has completely mastered its perspective.

Virginia Woolf. 'The Novels of E. M. Forster',
The Death of the Moth (*1942*).

NO SUPERFLUITIES

I should like to strip the novel of every element that does not specifically belong to the novel. Just as photography in the past freed painting from its concern for a certain sort of accuracy, so the phonograph will eventually no doubt rid the novel of the kind of dialogue which is drawn from the life and which realists take so much pride in. Outward events, accidents, traumatisms, belong to the cinema. The novel should leave them to it. Even the description of the characters does not seem to me properly to belong to the *genre*. No; this does not seem to me the business of the *pure* novel (and in art, as in everything else, purity is the only thing I care about). No more than it is the business of the drama. And don't let it be argued that the dramatist does not describe his characters because the spectator is intended to see them transposed alive on the stage; for how often on the stage an actor irritates and baffles us because he is so unlike the person our own imagination had figured better without him. The novelist does not as a rule rely sufficiently on the reader's imagination.

> André Gide. Les Faux Monnayeurs, *Part I, Chapter viii* (*1925*), transl. Dorothy Bussy (*1952*).

He [i.e. Paul Claudel] speaks with the greatest respect of Thomas Hardy and Joseph Conrad, and with the greatest scorn of English writers in general 'who have never learned that the rule of "nothing unessential" is the first condition of art'.

> André Gide. The Journals of André Gide, Vol. I: 1889–1913; transl. Justin O'Brien (1948).

The novel requires a certain slowness of progress that allows the reader to live with the characters and become accustomed to them. If they do things and make remarks that, knowing them, we might just as well have been able to invent for them, this does not matter; and we are even amused to recognize them in such things and not to be surprised. When I wanted to tell of them only what is disconcerting, and leave to the reader the duty of filling out their characters with everything that did not particularly distinguish them, I was probably not well advised. It may seem that I did not know how to make them come alive because I so readily gave them up as soon as their outline was sufficiently sketched, and when portraying them more fully and following them at greater length told nothing more about them. This is because I have always been bothered in the work of others by all that is not essential and that the alert reader's imagination can supply for itself. A concern for the lightest possible baggage has always tormented me, and I do not like to let time make that abstract of the essentials which I can just as well achieve at once. Allow only the indispensable to subsist was the rule I imposed on myself—nowhere more difficult and dangerous to apply than for the novel. This amounts to counting too much on that collaboration which the reader will supply only when the writer has already been able to secure it.

> André Gide. The Journals of André Gide, Vol. III: 1928–1939, transl. Justin O'Brien (1949).

PATTERN AND RHYTHM

That then is the disadvantage of a rigid pattern. It may externalize the atmosphere, spring naturally from the plot, but it shuts the doors on life and leaves the novelist doing exercises, generally in the drawing-room. Beauty has arrived, but in too tyrannous a guise. In plays—the plays of Racine, for instance—she may be justified, because beauty can be a great empress on the stage, and reconcile us to the loss of the men we knew. But in the novel, her tyranny as it grows powerful grows petty, and generates regrets which sometimes take the form of books like *Boon*. To put it in other words, the novel is not capable of as much artistic development as the drama: its humanity or the grossness of its material (use whichever phrase you like) hinder it. To most readers of fiction the sensation from a pattern is not intense enough to justify the sacrifices that made it, and their verdict is 'Beautifully done, but not worth doing.'

Still this is not the end of our quest. We will not give up the hope of beauty yet. Cannot it be introduced into fiction by some other method than pattern? Let us edge rather nervously towards the idea of 'rhythm'.

Rhythm is sometimes quite easy. Beethoven's Fifth Symphony, for instance, starts with the rhythm 'diddy dum,' which we can all hear and tap to. But the symphony as a whole has also a rhythm—due mainly to the relation between its movements—which some people can hear but no one can tap to. This second sort of rhythm is difficult, and whether it is substantially the same as the first sort only a musician could tell us. What a literary man wants to say though is that the first kind of rhythm, the diddy dum, can be found in certain novels and may give them beauty. And the other rhythm, the difficult one—the rhythm of the Fifth Symphony as a whole—I cannot quote you any parallels for that in fiction, yet it may be present.

Rhythm in the easy sense is illustrated by the work of Marcel Proust . . .

We are not obliged to agree with Proust's musical descriptions (they are too pictorial for my own taste), but what we must admire is his use of rhythm in literature, and his use of something which is akin by nature to the effect it has to produce—namely a musical phrase. Heard by various people—first by Swann, then by the hero—the phrase of Vinteuil is not tethered: it is not a banner such as we find George Meredith using—a double blossomed cherry tree to accompany Clara Middleton, a yacht in smooth waters for Cecilia Halkett. A banner can only reappear, rhythm can develop, and the little phrase has a life of its own, unconnected with the lives of its auditors, as with the life of the man who composed it. It is almost an actor, but not quite, and that 'not quite' means that its power has gone towards stitching Proust's book together from the inside, and towards the establishment of beauty and the ravishing of the reader's memory. There are times when the little phrase—from its gloomy inception, through the sonata, into the sextet—means everything to the reader. There are times when it means nothing and is forgotten, and this seem to me the function of rhythm in fiction; not to be there all the time like a pattern, but by its lovely waxing and waning to fill us with surprise and freshness and hope.

Done badly, rhythm is most boring, it hardens into a symbol and instead of carrying us on it trips us up. With exasperation we find that Galsworthy's spaniel John, or whatever it is, lies under the feet again; and even Meredith's cherry trees and yachts, graceful as they are, only open the windows into poetry. I doubt that it can be achieved by the writers who plan their books beforehand, it has to depend on a local impulse when the right interval is reached. But the effect can be exquisite, it can be obtained without mutilating the characters, and it lessens our need of an external form.

That must suffice on the subject of easy rhythm in fiction: which may be defined as repetition plus variation, and which can be illustrated by examples. Now for the more difficult question. Is there any effect in novels comparable to the effect of the Fifth Symphony as a whole, where, when the orchestra stops, we hear something that has never actually been played? The opening movement, the andante, and the trio-scherzo-trio-finale-trio-finale that composes the third block, all enter the mind at once, and extend one another into a common entity. This common entity, this new thing, is the symphony as a whole, and it has been achieved mainly (though not entirely) by the relation between the three big blocks of sound which the orchestra has been playing. I am calling this relation 'rhythmic'. If the correct musical term is something else, that does not matter; what we have now to ask ourselves is whether there is any analogy to it in fiction.

I cannot find any analogy. Yet there may be one; in music fiction is likely to find its nearest parallel.

The position of the drama is different. The drama may look towards the pictorial arts, it may allow Aristotle to discipline it, for it is not so deeply committed to the claims of human beings. Human beings have their great chance in the novel. They say to the novelist: 'Recreate us if you like, but we must come in,' and the novelist's problem, as we have seen all along, is to give them a good run and to achieve something else at the same time. Whither shall he turn? not indeed for help, but for analogy. Music, though it does not employ human beings, though it is governed by intricate laws, nevertheless does offer in its final expression a type of beauty which fiction might achieve in its own way. Expansion. That is the idea the novelist must cling to. Not completion. Not rounding off but opening out. When the symphony is over we feel that the notes and tunes composing it have been liberated, they have found in the rhythm of the whole their individual freedom. Cannot the novel be like that? Is not there something of it in *War and Peace*? . . . Such an untidy book. Yet, as we read it, do not great chords begin to sound behind us, and when we have finished does not every item—even the catalogue of strategies—lead a larger existence than was possible at the time?

> *E. M. Forster.* Aspects of the Novel (*1927*), *Chapter viii.*

SYMPHONIC EFFECT

. . . If ever the effect of a symphony were achieved in a novel it will be in that scene [i.e. the *comices agricoles*]. It must sound out through the whole concourse, one must hear, all at the same time, the bellowing of bulls, the sighs of love and the words of the officials. The sun shines on all this, and gusts of wind flutter the great hats. But the most difficult passages of *Saint Antoine* were child's play in comparison. I can only reach my dramatic effect by the interplay of dialogue and contrast of character.

> *Gustave Flaubert. Letter to Louise Colet* (*12 October 1853*), Correspondance (*1900*).

THE ART OF FUGUE

'What I should like to do is something like the art of fugue writing. And I can't see why what was possible in music should be impossible in literature . . .'

> *André Gide.* Les Faux Monnayeurs (*1925*), *Part II, Chapter iii, transl. Dorothy Bussy* (*1952*).

THE MUSICALIZATION OF FICTION

The musicalization of fiction. Not in the symbolist way, by subordinating sense to sound. (*Pleuvent les bleus baisers des astres tactiturnes.* Mere glossolalia.) But on a large scale, in the construction. Meditate on Beethoven. The changes of moods, the abrupt transitions. (Majesty alternating with a joke, for example, in the first movement of the B flat major quartet. Comedy suddenly hinting at prodigious and tragic solemnities in the scherzo of the C sharp minor quartet.) More interesting still the modulations, not merely from one key to another, but from mood to mood. A theme is stated, then developed, pushed out of shape, imperceptibly deformed, until, though still recognizably the same, it has become quite different. In sets of variations the process is carried a step further. Those incredible Diabelli variations, for example. The whole range of thought and feeling, yet all in organic relation to a ridiculous little waltz tune. Get this into a novel. How? The abrupt transitions are easy enough. All you need is a sufficiency of characters and parallel, contrapuntal plots. While Jones is murdering a wife, Smith is wheeling the perambulator in the park. You alternate the themes. More interesting, the modulations and variations are also more difficult. A novelist modulates by reduplicating situations and characters. He shows several people falling in love, or dying, or praying in different ways —dissimilars solving the same problem. Or, *vice versa*, similar people confronted with dissimilar problems. In this way you can modulate through all the aspects of your theme, you can write variations in any number of different moods.

Aldous Huxley. Point Counter Point (*1928*), *Chapter xxii.*

PLOT AND STORY

THE NOVELIST MUST HAVE A STORY TO TELL

I have from the first felt sure that the writer, when he sits down to commence his novel, should do so, not because he has to tell a story, but because he has a story to tell. The novelist's first novel will generally have sprung from the right cause. Some series of events, or some development of character, will have presented itself to his imagination,—and this he feels so strongly that he thinks he can present his picture in strong and agreeable language to others. He sits down and tells his story because he has a story to tell; as you, my friend, when you have heard something which has at once tickled your fancy or moved your pathos, will hurry to tell it to the first person you meet. But when that first novel has been received graciously by the public and has made for itself a success, then the writer, naturally feeling that the writing of novels is within his grasp, looks about for something to tell in another. He cudgels his brains, not always successfully, and sits down to write, not because he has something which he burns to tell, but because he feels it to be incumbent on him to be telling something. As you, my friend, if you are very successful in the telling of that first story, will become ambitious of further story-telling, and will look out for anecdotes,—in the narration of which you will not improbably sometimes distress your audience.

Anthony Trollope. Autobiography (*1883*), *Chapter xii.*

NO STORY AT ALL IS BEST

. . . what I should like to do is to write a book about nothing, a book with no reference to anything outside itself, which would stand on its own by the inner strength of its style, just as the earth holds itself without support in space, a book which would have hardly any subject, or at any rate one that is barely perceptible, if that were possible. The best works are those with least matter; the nearer the expression approaches thought, the more the word is silenced by it and disappears, then the more beautiful the work becomes. I think the future of Art lies this way. I see it growing more and more spiritualized as it develops, from Egyptian pylons to Gothic spires, from the twenty thousand verses of the Indian poets to Byron's single jets. Form as it grows skilful becomes attenuated; it abandons all liturgy, rule, metric; it abandons the epic for the novel, verse for prose; it no longer recognizes orthodoxy and is as free as the imagination that produces it. This emancipation from materialism is found everywhere and all governments follow it, from eastern despotism to the socialism of the future.

That is why there are neither good nor bad subjects, and one could almost lay it down as an axiom that, from the point of view of pure Art, there are none at all, style being itself alone an absolute way of looking at things.

Gustave Flaubert. Letter to Louise Colet (16 January 1852), Correspondance (*1900*).

WRITING A STORY FOR PUBLICATION IN WEEKLY PARTS

Having gone through your M.S. . . . I write these few following words about it. Firstly, with a limited reference to its unsuitability to these pages. Secondly, with a more enlarged reference to the merits of the story itself.

If you will take any part of it and cut it up (in fancy) into the small portions into which it would have to be divided here for only a month's supply, you will (I think) at once discover the impossibility of publishing it in weekly parts. The scheme of the chapters, the manner of introducing the people, the progress of the interest, the places in which the principal places fall, are all hopelessly against it.

It would seem as though the story were never coming, and hardly ever moving. There must be a special design to overcome that specially trying mode of publication, and I cannot better express the difficulty and labour of it than by asking you to turn over any two weekly numbers of *A Tale of Two Cities*, or *Great Expectations*, or Bulwer's story, or Wilkie Collins', or Reade's, or *At the Bar*, and notice how patiently and expressly the thing has to be planned for presentation in these fragments, and yet for afterwards fusing together as an uninterrupted whole . . .

. . . As a mere piece of mechanical workmanship, I think all your chapters should be shorter; that is to say, that they should be sub-divided. Also, when you change from narrative to dialogue, or *vice versâ*, you should make the transition more carefully. Also, taking the pains to sit down and recall the principal landmarks in your story, you should make them far more elaborate and conspicuous than the rest. Even with these changes I do not believe that the story would attract the attention due to it, if it were published even in such monthly portions as the space of 'Fraser' would admit of. Even so brightened, it would not, to the best of my judgement, express itself piecemeal. It seems to me to be so constituted as to require to be read 'off the reel.' As a book in two volumes I think it would have good claims to success. But I suppose the polishing I have hinted at (not a meretricious adornment, but positively necessary to good work and good art) to have been first thoroughly administered.

> *Charles Dickens. Letter to Mrs. Brookfield (20 February 1866),* Letters *(1880).*

A STORY SHOULD BE AN ORGANISM

Probably few of the general body denominated the reading public consider, in their hurried perusal of novel after novel, that, to a masterpiece in story there appertains a beauty of shape, no less than to a masterpiece in pictorial or plastic art, capable of giving to the trained mind an equal pleasure. To recognize this quality clearly when present, the construction of the plot, or fable, as it used to be called, is to be more particularly observed . . . in a reading for sentiments and opinions, than in a reading merely to discover the fates of the chief characters. For however real the persons, however profound, witty, or humorous the observations, as soon as the book comes to be regarded as an exemplification of the art of story-telling,

243

the story naturally takes the first place, and the example is not noteworthy as such unless the telling be artistically carried on.

The distinguishing feature of a well rounded tale has been defined in various ways, but the general reader need not be burdened with many definitions. Briefly, a story should be an organism. To use the words applied to the epic by Addison, whose artistic feeling in this kind was of the subtlest, 'nothing should go before it, be intermixed with it, or follow after it, that is not related to it.' Tested by such considerations as these there are obviously many volumes of fiction remarkable, and even great, in their character-drawing, their feeling, their philosophy, which are quite second-rate in their structural quality as narratives. Instances will occur to everyone's mind; but instead of dwelling upon these it is more interesting to name some which most nearly fulfill the conditions. Their fewness is remarkable and bears out the opinion expressed earlier in this essay, that the art of novel-writing is as yet in its tentative stage only. Among them *Tom Jones* is usually pointed out as a near approach to perfection in this as in some other characteristics; though, speaking for myself, I do not perceive its great superiority in artistic form over some other novels of lower reputation. The *Bride of Lammermoor* is an almost perfect specimen of form, which is the more remarkable in that Scott, as a rule, depends more upon episode, dialogue and description, for exciting interest, than upon the well-knit interdependence of parts. And the first thirty pages of *Vanity Fair* may be instanced as well-nigh complete in artistic presentation, along with their other magnificent qualities.

Herein lies Richardson's real if only claim to be placed on a level with Fielding: the artist spirit that he everywhere displays in the structural parts of his work. . . .

I have dwelt the more particularly upon this species of excellence, not because I consider it to rank in quality beside truth of feeling and action, but because it is one which so few non-professional readers enjoy and appreciate without some kind of preliminary direction. It is usually the latest to be discerned by the novel consumer, and it is often never discerned by him or her at all. Every intelligent reader with a little experience of life can perceive truth to nature in some degree; but a great reduction must be made for those who can trace in narrative the quality which makes the Apollo and the Aphrodite a charm in marble.

> *Thomas Hardy.* '*The profitable reading of fiction*' (*1888*);
> *reprinted in* Life and Art (*1925*).

STORY THE SPOILED CHILD OF ART

There is always, of course, for the story-teller, the irresistible determinant and the incalculable advantage of his interest in the story *as such*; it is ever, obviously, overwhelmingly, the prime and precious thing (as other than this I have never been able to see it); as to which what makes for it, with whatever headlong energy, may be said to pale before the energy with which it simply makes for itself. It rejoices, none the less, at its best, to seem to offer itself in a light, to seem to know, and with the very last knowledge, what it's about —liable as it yet is at moments to be caught by us with its tongue in its cheek and absolutely no warrant but its splendid impudence. Let us grant then that the impudence is always there—there, so to speak, for grace and effect and *allure*; there, above all, because the Story is just the spoiled child of art, and because, as we are always disappointed when the pampered don't 'play up', we like it, to that extent, to look all its character. It probably does so, in truth, even when we most flatter ourselves that we negotiate with it by treaty.

> *Henry James. Preface to* The Ambassadors *(1903), first printed in the New York edition of the* Novels and Stories *(1907–17), Vol. XXI.*

A STORY MUST CONVEY A SENSE OF INEVITABILITY

Before everything a story must convey a sense of inevitability: that which happens in it must seem to be the only thing that could have happened. Of course a character may cry: 'If I had then acted differently how different everything would now be.' The problem of the author is to make his then action the only action that character could have taken.

> *Ford Madox Ford.* Joseph Conrad, A Personal Remembrance *(1924), Part III, Section ii.*

OH DEAR YES—THE NOVEL TELLS A STORY

... Yes—oh dear yes—the novel tells a story. That is the fundamental aspect without which it could not exist. That is the highest factor common to all novels, and I wish that it was not so, that it could be something different—melody, or the perception of the truth, not this low atavistic form.

For the more we look at the story (the story that is a story, mind), the more we disentangle it from the finer growths that it supports, the less we shall find to admire. It runs like a backbone—or may I say a tape-worm, for its beginning and end are arbitrary. It is immensely old—goes back to neolithic times, perhaps to palaeo-lithic. Neanderthal man listened to stories, if one may judge by the shape of his skull. The primitive audience was an audience of shock-heads, gaping round the camp-fire, fatigued with contending against the mammoth or the woolly rhinoceros, and only kept awake by suspense. What would happen next? The novelist droned on, and as soon as the audience guessed what happened next, they either fell asleep or killed him. We can estimate the dangers incurred when we think of the career of Scheherazade in somewhat later time. Scheherazade avoided her fate because she knew how to wield the weapon of suspense—the only literary tool that has any effect upon tyrants and savages. Great novelist though she was,—exquisite in her descriptions, tolerant in her judgments, ingenious in her in-cidents, advanced in her morality, vivid in her delineation of character, expert in her knowledge of three Oriental capitals—it was yet on none of these gifts that she relied when trying to save her life from her intolerable husband. They were but incidental. She only survived because she managed to keep the king wondering what would happen next. Each time she saw the sun rising she stopped in the middle of a sentence, and left him gaping. 'At this moment Scheherazade saw the morning appearing, and, discreet, was silent.' This uninteresting little phrase is the backbone of the *One Thousand and One Nights*, the tape-worm by which they are tied together and the life of a most accomplished princess was preserved.

We are all like Scheherazade's husband, in that we want to know what happens next. That is universal and that is why the backbone of a novel has to be a story. Some of us want to know nothing else —there is nothing in us but primeval curiosity, and consequently our other literary judgments are ludicrous. And now the story can be defined. It is a narrative of events arranged in their time sequence —dinner coming after breakfast, Tuesday after Monday, decay after death, and so on. Qua story, it can have only one merit: that of making the audience want to know what happens next. And conversely it can only have one fault: that of making the audience not want to know what happens next. These are the only two criticisms that can be made on the story that is a story. It is the lowest and simplest of literary organisms. Yet it is the highest factor common to all the very complicated organisms known as novels.

When we isolate the story like this from the nobler aspects through which it moves, and hold it out on the forceps—wriggling and inter-minable, the naked worm of time—it presents an appearance that is both unlovely and dull. But we have much to learn from it. . . .

E. M. Forster. Aspects of the Novel (*1927*), *Chapter ii.*

DOING AWAY WITH PLOT

With regard to novels, I should like to see one undertaken without any plot at all. I do not mean that it should have no story; but I should like some writer of luxuriant fancy to begin with a certain set of characters—one family for instance—without any preconceived design further than one or two incidents and dialogues, which would naturally suggest fresh matter, and so proceed in this way, throwing in incident and characters profusely, but avoiding all stage tricks and strong situations, till some death or marriage should afford a natural conclusion to the book.

> *Mary Russell Mitford. Letter to Sir William Elford (13 May 1815),*
> Letters (*1925*).

PLOT THE MOST INSIGNIFICANT PART OF A TALE

Doctor Thorne has, I believe, been the most popular book that I have written . . . The plot of *Dr. Thorne* is good, and I am led therefore to suppose that a good plot,—which, to my own feeling, is the most insignificant part of a tale,—is that which will most raise it or most condemn it in the popular judgment. The plots of *Tom Jones* and of *Ivanhoe* are almost perfect, and they are probably the most popular novels of the schools of the last and of this century; but to me the delicacy of Amelia, and the rugged strength of Burley and Meg Merrilies, say more for the power of those great novelists than the gift of construction shown in the two works I have named. A novel should give a picture of common life enlivened by humour and sweetened by pathos. To make that picture worthy of attention, the canvas should be crowded with real portraits, not of individuals known to the world or to the author, but of created personages impregnated with traits of character which are known. To my thinking, the plot is but the vehicle for all this; and when you have the vehicle without the passengers, a story of mystery in which the agents never spring to life, you have but a wooden show. There must, however be a story. You must provide a vehicle of some sort.

> *Anthony Trollope.* An Autobiography (*1883*), *Chapter vii.*

CONVENTIONAL PLOT A VULGAR COERCION

. . . the vulgar coercion of conventional plot, which is become hardly of higher influence on imaginative representation than a detailed 'order' for a picture sent by a rich grocer to an eminent painter— allotting a certain portion of the canvas to a rural scene, another to a fashionable group, with a request for a murder in the middle distance, and a little comedy to relieve it.

George Eliot. '*Leaves from a Notebook: Historic imagination*', The Impressions of Theophrastus Such (*1879*).

SURPRISING PROPERTIES OF PLOT

Let us define a plot. We have defined a story as a narrative of events arranged in their time sequence. A plot is also a narrative of events, the emphasis falling on causality. 'The king died and then the queen died,' is a story. 'The king died, and then the queen died of grief' is a plot. The time-sequence is preserved, but the sense of causality overshadows it. Or again: 'The queen died, no one knew why, until it was discovered that it was through grief at the death of the king.' This is a plot with a mystery in it, a form capable of high development. It suspends the time-sequence, it moves as far away from the story as its limitations will allow. Consider the death of the queen. If it is in a story we say 'and then?' If it is in a plot we ask 'why?' That is the fundamental difference between these two aspects of the novel. A plot cannot be told to a gaping audience of cave men or to a tyrannical sultan or to their modern descendant the movie-public. They can only be kept awake by 'and then—and then'—they can only supply curiosity. But a plot demands intelligence and memory also. . . .

Memory and intelligence are closely connected, for unless we remember we cannot understand. If by the time the queen dies we have forgotten the existence of the king we shall never make out what killed her. The plot-maker expects us to remember, we expect him to leave no loose ends. Every action or word in a plot ought to count; it ought to be economical and spare; even when complicated it should be organic and free from dead matter, it may be difficult or easy, it may and should contain mysteries, but it ought not to mislead. And over it, as it unfolds, will hover the memory of the reader (that dull glow of the mind of which intelligence is the bright advancing edge) and will constantly rearrange and reconsider, seeing new clues, new chains of cause and effect, and the final sense (if the plot has been a fine one) will not be of clues or chains, but of something aesthetically compact, something which might have been shown by the novelist straight away, only if he had shown it straight away it would never have become beautiful. We come up against beauty here—for the first time in our enquiry: beauty at which a novelist should never aim, though he fails if he does not achieve it. I will conduct beauty to her proper place later on. Meanwhile please accept her as part of a completed plot. She looks a little surprised at being there, but beauty ought to look a little surprised: it is the emotion that best suits her face, as Botticelli knew when he painted her risen from the waves, between the winds and the flowers . . .

E. M. Forster. Aspects of the Novel (*1927*), *Chapter v.*

PLOT THE SUPPORT OF A NOVEL

I never see why murder and perversion of justice are not normal subjects for a plot, or why they are particularly Elizabethan or Victorian, as some reviewers seem to think. But I think it is better for a novel to have a plot. Otherwise it has no shape, and incidents that have no part in a formal whole seem to have less significance. I always wish that Katherine Mansfield's 'At the Bay' was cast in a formal mould. And a plot gives rise to secondary scenes, that bring out personality, and give scope for revealing character. If the plot were taken out of a book, a good deal of what may seem unconnected with it, would have to go. A plot is like the bones of a person, not interesting like expression or signs of experience, but the support of the whole . . .

. . . As regards plots I find real life no help at all. Real life seems to have no plots. And as I think a plot desirable and almost necessary, I have this extra grudge against life. But I think there are signs that strange things happen, though they do not emerge. I believe it would go ill with many of us, if we were faced with a strong temptation, and I suspect that with some of us it does go ill.

Ivy Compton-Burnett. 'A Conversation Between I. Compton-Burnett and M. Jourdain', Orion (*1945*).

BEGINNINGS AND ENDINGS

(i)

. . . I know not of any essential difference between this [i.e. the epistolary method], and any other way of writing novels, save only, that by making use of letters, the writer is freed from the regular beginnings and conclusions of stories, with some other formalities, in which the reader of taste finds no less ease and advantage, than the author himself.

Henry Fielding. Preface to Sarah Fielding's Familiar Letters . . . (*1747*).

(ii)

. . . Beginning with the breaking up of a large party of guests at a country house: house left lonely with the shrunken family in it: guests spoken of, and introduced to the reader that way.—OR, beginning with a house abandoned by a family fallen into reduced circumstances. Their old furniture there, and numberless tokens of their old comforts. Inscriptions under the bells downstairs—'Mr. John's Room,' 'Miss Caroline's Room.' Great gardens trimly kept to attract a tenant: but no one in them. A landscape without figures. Billiard room: table covered up, like a body. Great stables without horses, and great coach-houses without carriages. Grass growing in the chinks of the stone-paving, this bright cold winter day. *Downhills*.

. . . Open a story by bringing two strongly contrasted places and strongly contrasted sets of people, into the connexion necessary for the story, by means of an electric message. Describe the message— *be* the message—flashing along through space, over the earth, and under the sea.

> *Charles Dickens. John Forster*, The Life of Charles Dickens *(1874), Vol. III, Chapter xii.*

(iii)

Beginnings are always troublesome 'ἥμισυ παντός' [1] as Bulwer would say (I like to follow great models). Even Macaulay's few pages of *introduction* to his '*Introduction*' in the English History are the worst bit of writing in the book.

> *George Eliot. Letter to Sarah Hennell, August 15, 1859,* The George Eliot Letters *(1954)*

Conclusions are the weak point of most authors, but some of the fault lies in the very nature of a conclusion, which is at best a negation.

> *George Eliot. Letter to John Blackwood, May 1, 1857,* The George Eliot Letters *(1954).*

(iv)

(9 April 1888) . . . My instinct tells me that at the end of a novel or a story I must artfully concentrate for the reader an impression

---

[1] Hesiod, *Work and Days*, 40: πλέον ἥμισυ παντός.

of the entire work, and therefore must casually mention something about those whom I have already presented. Perhaps I am in error.

> *Anton Chekhov*. Letters on Literature (*1924*), *ed.*
> *Louis S. Friedland.*

(v)

The disadvantage of the dramatic opening is that after the dramatic passage is done you have to go back to getting your characters in, a proceeding that the reader is apt to dislike. The danger with the reflective opening is that the reader is apt to miss being gripped at once by the story. Openings are therefore of necessity always affairs of compromise.

> *Ford Madox Ford*. Joseph Conrad, A Personal Remembrance
> (*1924*), *Part III, Section i.*

(vi)

X. maintains that a good novelist, before he begins to write his book, ought to know how it is going to finish. As for me, who let mine flow where it will, I consider that life never presents us with anything which may not be looked upon as a fresh starting point, no less than as a termination. 'Might be continued'—these are the words with which I should like to finish my *Coiners*.

> *André Gide*. Les Faux Monnayeurs (*1925*), *Part III, Chapter xiii;*
> *transl. Dorothy Bussy (1952).*

THE TIME-FACTOR

FIELDING SETS THE PACE

Though we have properly enough entitled this our work, a history, and not a life, nor an apology for a life, as is more in fashion; yet we intend in it rather to pursue the method of those writers who profess to disclose the revolutions of countries, than to imitate the painful and voluminous historian, who, to preserve the regularity of his series, thinks himself obliged to fill up as much paper with the detail of months and years in which nothing remarkable happened, as he employs upon those noble eras when the greatest scenes have been transacted on the human stage.

Such histories as these do, in reality, very much resemble a newspaper, which consists of just the same number of words, whether there be any news in it or not. They may likewise be compared to

a stage-coach, which performs constantly the same course, empty
as well as full. The writer, indeed, seems to think himself obliged to
keep even pace with time, whose amanuensis he is; and, like his
master, travels as slowly through centuries of monkish dullness,
when the world seems to have been asleep . . .

Now it is our purpose, in the ensuing pages, to pursue a contrary
method. When any extraordinary scene presents itself (as we trust
will often be the case), we shall spare no pains nor paper to open it
at large to our readers; but if whole years should pass without
producing anything worthy his notice, we shall not be afraid of a
chasm in our history, but shall hasten on to matters of consequence,
and leave such periods of time totally unobserved. . . .

My reader then is not to be surprised, if, in the course of this
work, he shall find some chapters very short, and others altogether
as long; some that contain only the time of a single day, and others
that comprise years; in a word, if my history sometimes seems to
stand still, and sometimes to fly. For all which I shall not look on
myself as accountable to any court of critical jurisdiction whatever;
for as I am, in reality, the founder of a new province of writing,
so I am at liberty to make what laws I please therein. And these
laws, my readers, whom I consider as my subjects, are bound to
believe in and to obey; with which that they may readily and
cheerfully comply, I do hereby assure them that I shall principally
regard their ease and advantage in all such institutions. . . .

Henry Fielding. Tom Jones (*1749*), *Book II, Chapter i.*

FORESHORTENING: THE PROBLEM ALWAYS THERE AND ALWAYS FORMIDABLE

To re-read *Roderick Hudson* was to find one remark so promptly
and so urgently prescribed that I could at once only take it as
pointing almost too stern a moral. It stared me in the face that the
time-scheme of the story is quite inadequate, and positively to that
degree that the fault but just fails to wreck it . . . I felt too, all the
while, how many more adventures and complications my young
man would have had to know, how much more experience it would
have taken, in short, either to make him go under or to make him
triumph. The greater complexity, the superior truth, was all more
or less present to me; only the question was, too dreadfully, how to
make it present to the reader? How boil down so many facts in the
alembic, so that the distilled result, the reproduced appearance,
should have intensity, lucidity, brevity, beauty, all the merits
required for my effect? How, when it was already so difficult, as I

found, to proceed even as I *was* proceeding? It didn't help, alas, it only maddened, to remember that Balzac would have known how, and would have yet asked no additional credit for it. All the difficulty I could dodge still struck me, at any rate, as leaving more than enough; and yet I was already consciously in presence here, of the most interesting question the artist has to consider. To give the image and sense of certain things while keeping them subordinate to his plan, keeping them in relation to matters more immediate and apparent, to give all the sense, in a word, without all the substance, or all the surface, and so to summarise and foreshorten, so to make values both rich and sharp, that the mere procession of items and profiles is not only, for the occasion, superseded, but is, for essential quality, almost 'compromised'—such a case of delicacy proposes itself at every turn to the painter of life who wishes both to treat his chosen subject and to confine his necessary picture. It is only by doing such things that art becomes exquisite, and it is only by becoming exquisite that it keeps clear of becoming vulgar, repudiates the coarse industries that masquerade in its name. This eternal time-question is accordingly, for the novelist, always there and always formidable; always insisting on the *effect* of the great lapse and passage, of the 'dark backward and abysm', by the terms of truth, and on the effect of compression, of composition and form, by the terms of literary arrangement. It is really a business to terrify all but the stoutest hearts into abject omission and mutilation, though the terror would indeed be more general were the general consciousness of the difficulty greater. It is not by consciousness of difficulty, in truth, that the story-teller is mostly ridden; so prodigious a number of stories would otherwise scarce get themselves (shall it be called?) 'told'. None was ever very well told, I think, under the law of mere elimination—inordinately as that device appears in many quarters to be depended on.

Henry James. Preface to Roderick Hudson (*1876*), *first printed in the New York edition of the* Novels and Stories (*1907–17*), *Vol. I.*

ALLEGIANCE TO 'TIME BY THE CLOCK'

. . . daily life, whatever it may be really, is practically composed of two lives—the life in time and the life by values—and our conduct reveals a double allegiance. 'I only saw her for five minutes, but it was worth it.' There you have both allegiances in a single sentence. And what the story does is to narrate the life in time. And what the entire novel does—if it is a good novel—is to include the life by values as well; using devices hereafter to be examined. It, also, pays a double allegiance. But in it, in the novel, the allegiance to time is imperative: no novel could be written without it. Whereas in daily life the allegiance may not be necessary: we do not know, and the experience of certain mystics suggests, indeed, that it is not necessary, and that we are quite mistaken in supposing that Monday is followed by Tuesday, or death by decay. It is always possible for you or me in daily life to deny that time exists and act accordingly even if we become unintelligible and are sent by our fellow citizens to what they choose to call a lunatic asylum. But it is never possible for a novelist to deny time inside the fabric of his novel: he must cling however lightly to the thread of his story, he must touch the interminable tapeworm, otherwise he becomes unintelligible, which, in his case, is a blunder.

I am trying not to be philosophic about time, for it is (experts assure us) a most dangerous hobby for an outsider, far more fatal than place; and quite eminent metaphysicians have been dethroned through referring to it improperly. I am only trying to explain that as I lecture now I hear that clock ticking or do not hear it ticking, I retain or lose the time sense; whereas in a novel there is always a clock. The author may dislike his clock. Emily Brontë in *Wuthering Heights* tried to hide hers. Sterne, in *Tristram Shandy*, turned his upside down. Marcel Proust, still more ingenious, kept altering the hands, so that his hero was at the same period entertaining a mistress to supper and playing ball with his nurse in the park. All these devices are legitimate, but none of them contravene our thesis: the basis of a novel is a story, and a story is a narrative of events arranged in a time sequence.

E. M. Forster. Aspects of the Novel (*1927*), *Chapter ii.*

THE PRESENTNESS OF THE PAST

. . . It was all settled at the moment when, unable to await the morning to press my lips upon my mother's face, I had taken my resolution, I had jumped out of bed and had stood in my nightshirt by the window through which the moonlight shone, until I heard M. Swann go away. My parents had accompanied him, I had heard the door open, the sound of bell and closing door. At that very moment, in the Prince de Guermantes' mansion, I heard the sound of my parents' footsteps and the metallic, shrill, fresh echo of the little bell which announced M. Swann's departure and the coming of my mother up the stairs; I heard it now, its very self, though its peal rang out in the far distant past. Then thinking of all the events which intervened between the instant when I had heard it and the Guermantes' reception I was terrified to think that it was indeed that bell which rang within me still, without my being able to abate its shrill sound, since, no longer remembering how the clanging used to stop, in order to learn, I had to listen to it and I was compelled to close my ears to the conversations of the masks around me. To get to hear it close I had again to plunge into myself. So that ringing must always be there, and with it, between it and the present, all that indefinable past unrolled itself which I did not know I had within me. When it rang I already existed and since, in order that I should hear it still, there could be no discontinuity, I could have had no instant of repose or of non-existence, of non-thinking, of non-consciousness, since that former instant clung to me, for I could recover it, return to it, merely by plunging more deeply into myself. It was that notion of the embodiment of Time, the inseparableness of us from the past that I had now the intention of bringing strongly into relief in my work. And it is because they thus contain the past that human bodies can so much hurt those who love them, because they contain so many memories, so many joys and desires effaced within them but so cruel for him who contemplates and prolongs in the order of time the beloved body of which he is jealous, jealous to the point of wishing its destruction. For after death Time leaves the body and memories—indifferent and pale—are obliterated in her who exists no longer and soon will be in him they still torture, memories which perish with the desire of the living body . . .

The day on which I heard the distant, far-away sound of the bell in the Combray garden was a land-mark in that enormous dimension which I did not know I possessed. I was giddy at seeing so many years below and in me as though I were leagues high. . . . If at least, time enough were allotted to me to accomplish my work, I would not fail to mark it with the seal of Time, the idea of which imposed itself upon me with so much force to-day, and I would therein describe men, if need be, as monsters occupying a place in Time infinitely more important than the restricted one reserved for them in space, a place, on the contrary, prolonged immeasurably since, simultaneously touching widely separated years and the distant periods they have lived through—between which so many days have ranged themselves—they stand like giants immersed in Time.

Marcel Proust. Time Regained (*1927*), *Chapter iii,* transl. *Stephen Hudson* (*1931*).

II Narrative Technique

EPISTOLARY METHOD IMPROPER

. . . sure no one will contend, that the epistolary style is in general the most proper to a novelist, or that it hath been used by the best writers of this kind . . .

> Henry Fielding. Preface to Sarah Fielding's Familiar Letters . . . (*1747*).

LETTERS MUCH MORE LIVELY AND AFFECTING

. . . *Much more* lively and affecting . . . must be the style of those who write in the height of a *present* distress, the mind tortured by the pangs of uncertainty (the events then hidden in the womb of fate); than the dry, narrative unanimated style of a person relating difficulties and danger surmounted, can be . . . the relater perfectly at ease; and if himself unmoved by his own story, not likely greatly to affect the reader.

> Samuel Richardson. Preface to Clarissa, The History of a Young Lady . . . (*1747–8*).

Some have wished that the story had been told in the usual narrative way of telling stories designed to amuse and divert, and not in letters written by the respective persons whose history is given in them. The author thinks he ought not to prescribe the taste of others; but imagined himself at liberty to follow his own. He perhaps mistrusted his talents for the narrative kind of writing. He had the good fortune to succeed in the epistolary way once before. A story in which so many persons were concerned, either principally or collaterally, and of characters and dispositions so various, carried on with tolerable connection and perspicuity, in a series of letters from different persons without the aid of digressions and episodes foreign to the principal end and design, he thought had *novelty* to be pleaded for it: and that, in the present age, he supposed would not be a slight recommendation.

> *Samuel Richardson. Post-script to* Clarissa, The History of a Young Lady . . . (*1747–8*).

ANOTHER VAGARY

At present, nothing is talked of, nothing admired, but what I cannot help calling a very insipid and tedious performance: it is a kind of novel, called *The Life and Opinions of Tristram Shandy*; the great humour of which consists in the whole narration always going backwards. I can conceive a man saying that it would be droll to write a book in that manner, but have no notion of his persevering in executing it.

> *Horace Walpole. Letter to Sir David Dalrymple (4 April 1760),* Correspondence with Sir David Dalrymple (*1952*).

LETTERS FOR THE AUTHOR, OMNISCIENT NARRATIVE FOR THE READER

A novel may be carried on in a series of letters or in regular detail; both methods have their partisans, and in numbers they seem pretty equally divided; which of the two is the more popular, I cannot take upon myself to say; but I should guess that letters give the writer most amusement and relief, not only from their greater diversity of style, but from the respite which their intermissions afford him. These advantages however have a counterpoise, for his course becomes more circuitous and subject to embarrassment than when he takes the narrative wholly into his own hands; without great management and address in keeping his dates progressive, and distinctly methodized, his reader is exposed to be called back and puzzled; and as the characters who conduct the correspondence must be kept asunder, the scene is oftentimes distracted, where we wish it to be entire, or else the intercourse of letters is made glaringly unnatural and pedantic by compressing the distances from which they are dated, and putting two people to the ridiculous necessity of writing long narrations to each other, when conversation was within their reach.

For myself, having now made experiment of both methods, I should prefer the vehicle of letters: this however must be acknowledged, that all conversations, where the speakers are brought upon the scene, are far more natural when delivered at first hand, than when retailed by a correspondent; for we know that such sort of narratives do not commonly pass by the post, and the letter, both in style and substance, appears extremely stiff, tedious, and pedantic. Upon the whole, I should conjecture that the writer is best accommodated by the one, and the reader most gratified by the other: I hope I am right in my conjecture as to the reader's preference of the method I am now pursuing, else I have chosen it for myself, and gained no credit by the sacrifice.

Richard Cumberland. Henry (*1795*), *Book Third, Chapter i.*

THREE WAYS OF TELLING A STORY

There are three modes of carrying on a story: the narrative or epic as it may be called; in this the author relates himself the whole adventure; this is the manner of Cervantes in his Don Quixote, and of Fielding in his Tom Jones. It is the most common way. The author, like the muse, is supposed to know every thing; he can reveal the secret springs of actions, and let us into events in his own time and manner. He can be concise, or diffuse, according as the different parts of his story require it. He can indulge, as Fielding has done, in digressions, and thus deliver sentiments and display knowledge which would not properly belong to any of the characters. But his narration will not be lively, except he frequently drops himself, and runs into dialogue: all good writers therefore have thrown as much as possible of the dramatic into their narrative. Mad. d'Arblay has done this so successfully, that we have as clear an idea, not only of the sentiments, but the manner of expression of her different personages, as if we took it from the scenes in a play.

Another mode is that of memoirs; where the subject of the adventures relates his own story. Smollet, in his *Roderic Random*, and Goldsmith, in his *Vicar of Wakefield*, have adopted this mode; it confines the author's stile, which should be suited, though it is not always, to the supposed talents and capacity of the imaginary narrator. It has the advantage of the warmth and interest a person may be supposed to feel in his own affairs; and he can more gracefully dwell upon minute circumstances which have affected him. It has a greater air of truth, as it seems to account for the communication to the public. The author, it is true, knows every thing, but when the secret recesses of the heart are to be laid open, we can hear no one with so much pleasure as the person himself. Marivaux, whose productions partly followed, and partly were contemporary with those of Richardson, has put the history of Marianne into

258

her own mouth, and we are amused to hear her dwell on little touches which are almost too trivial to be noticed by any body but herself.

But what the hero cannot say, the author cannot tell, nor can it be rendered probable, that a very circumstantial narrative should be given by a person, perhaps at the close of a long life, of conversations that have happened at the beginning of it. The author has all along two characters to support, for he has to consider how his hero felt at the time of the events to be related, and how it is natural he should feel them at the time he is relating them; at a period, perhaps, when curiosity is extinguished, passion cooled, and when, at any rate, the suspense which rendered them interesting is over. This seems, therefore, the least perfect mode of any.

A third way remains, that of *epistolary correspondence*, carried on between the characters of the novel. This is the form made use of by Richardson and many others after, none, I believe, before him. He seems to have been led to it by circumstances in his early youth, which will be hereafter related. This method unites, in a good measure, the advantages of the other two; it gives the feelings of the moment as the writers felt them *at* the moment. It allows a pleasing variety of stile, if the author has sufficient command of pen to assume it. It makes the whole work dramatic, since all the characters speak in their own persons. It accounts for breaks in the story, by the omission or loss of letters. It is incompatible with a rapid stile, but gives room for the graceful introduction of remark and sentiment, or any kind, almost, of digressive matter. But, on the other hand, it is highly fictitious; it is the most natural and the least probable way of telling a story. That letters should be written at all times, and upon every occasion in life, that those letters should be preserved, and altogether form a connected story, it requires much art to render specious. It introduces the inconvenience so much felt in dramatic writing, for want of a narrator; the necessity of having an insipid confidant to tell the circumstances that an author cannot relate in any other way. It obliges a man to tell of himself, what perhaps no man would tell; and sometimes to repeat compliments which modesty would lead him to suppress: and when a long conversation is repeated, supposes a memory more exact than is generally found. Artificial as it therefore is, still as it enables an author to assume, in a lively manner, the hopes and fears, and passions, and to imitate the peculiar way of thinking of his characters, it became fashionable, and has been adopted by many both at home and abroad, especially by the French writers; their language, perhaps, being particularly suited to the epistolary stile, and Rousseau himself, in his *Nouvelle Héloise*, has followed the steps of our countryman.

> Anna Laetitia Barbauld. '*A Biographical Account of Samuel Richardson*', The Correspondence of Samuel Richardson (*1804*), Vol. I.

EPISTOLARY FORM AN ANTIQUATED AFFAIR

I am of the opinion that the epistolary form is an antiquated affair. It is all right when the gist of the matter is in the letters themselves (e.g., in the case of a district policeman who loves letter-writing), but as a literary form it is no good in many respects: it puts the author into a frame,—that is its main weakness.

> Anton Chekhov. Letter to *N. A. Leikin (4 March 1886)*, Letters on Literature (*1924*), ed. Louis S. Friedland.

ADVANTAGES OF THE LETTER-SYSTEM

The advantages of the letter-system of telling a story (passing over the disadvantages) are that, hearing what one side has to say, you are led constantly to the imagination of what the other side must be feeling, and at last are anxious to know if the other side does really feel what you imagine.

> Thomas Hardy. Notebook entry (*April 1878*) from The Early Life of Thomas Hardy, 1840–91 (*1928*), Chapter ix.

PERILS OF FIRST-PERSON NARRATIVE

. . . it is always dangerous to write from the point of 'I'. The reader is unconsciously taught to feel that the writer is glorifying himself, and rebels against the self-praise. Or otherwise the 'I' is pretentiously humble, and offends from exactly the other point of view. In telling a tale it is, I think, always well to sink the personal pronoun. The old way, 'Once upon a time,' with slight modifications is the best way of telling a story.

> Anthony Trollope. Letter to Kate Field (*24 May 1868*), Letters (*1951*)

THE TERRIBLE FLUIDITY OF SELF-REVELATION

Had I meanwhile, made him (Strether) at once hero and historian, endowed him with the romantic privilege of the 'first person'—the darkest abyss of romance this, inveterately, when

enjoyed on the grand scale—variety, and many other queer matters
as well, might have been smuggled in by a back door. Suffice it, to
be brief, that the first person, in the long piece, is a form foredoomed
to looseness, and that looseness, never much my affair, had never
been so little so as on this particular occasion. All of which reflexions
flocked to the standard from the moment—a very early one—the
question of how to keep my form amusing while sticking close to
my central figure and constantly taking its pattern from him had to
be faced . . . I couldn't, save by implication, make other persons tell
each other about him—blest resource, blest necessity, of the drama,
which reaches its effects of unity, all remarkably, by paths absolutely
opposite to the paths of the novel: with other persons, save as they
were primarily *his* persons (not he primarily but one of theirs),
I had simply nothing to do. I had relations for him none the less,
by the mercy of Providence, quite as much as if my exhibition *was*
to be a muddle; if I could only by implication and a show of consequence make other persons tell each other about him, I could at
least make him tell *them* whatever in the world he must; and could
so, by the same token—which was a further luxury thrown in—see
straight into the deep differences between what that could do for me,
or at all events for *him*, and the large ease of 'autobiography.' It may
be asked why, if one so keeps to one's hero, one shouldn't make a
single mouthful of 'method,' shouldn't throw the reins on his neck
and, letting them flap there as free as in *Gil Blas* or in *David
Copperfield*, equip him with the double privilege of subject and
object—a course that has at least the merit of brushing away questions at a sweep. The answer to which is, I think, that one makes
that surrender only if one is prepared *not* to make certain precious
discriminations.

The 'first person' then, so employed, is addressed by the author
directly to ourselves, his possible readers, whom he has to reckon
with, at the best, by our English tradition, so loosely and vaguely
after all, so little respectfully, on so scant a presumption of exposure
to criticism. Strether, on the other hand, encaged and provided
for as *The Ambassadors* encages and provides, has to keep in view
proprieties much stiffer and more salutary than any our straight and
credulous gape are likely to bring home to him, has <u>exhibitional
conditions</u> to meet, in a word, that forbid the terrible *fluidity* of self-
revelation.

> Henry James. Preface to The Ambassadors (*1903*),
> first printed in the New York edition of the Novels
> and Stories (*1907–17*), Vol. XXI.

261   *questions of formality*

THE NARRATOR'S INTERPOLATIONS IN THE HISTORICAL NOVEL

I want to spare you the criticisms that crushed *Salammbô*, a powerful and beautiful work but without any real interest for anyone except artists and scholars . . . before you undertake a new *Golden Ass* I should like you to make the *Coq d'or* a work of the same colouring. It was decided that an apocryphal Apuleius or Lucian, one of their friends perhaps, should have travelled in India or Persia, and have heard from the lips of a Bousikof of those days the traditional story of Atlantis, and that he should explain in a few words the figures and the legends in his own way and from his own point of view.

Example: 'You ask me, my dear Lucian, what I think about the Gauls, and whether I believe in their existence. In fact, to some extent I do believe in it, for such and such a reason.'

These interpolations by the narrator will do very well. They will bring the reader back from the depths of a fantastic antiquity to the sense of a real antiquity that he knows. They will indicate habits of mind in the narrator's own times . . . All this will set the reader on his feet. He will say to himself: 'Here is where I start from, and there is where they are taking me. I am quite agreeable, provided they remind me from time to time where I was before.'

Otherwise, he will say that they are taking him too far away, that he is lost in a fog, and either that the people of so long ago aren't sufficiently different from those of the present, or else that they are too much so and that he cannot really judge them; and when the reader feels too greatly disorientated he will abandon you.

So, he wants to be able to say to himself all the time: 'Well, what quaint customs and incredible habits these are! But it must all have been like that, they prove it. The man telling me all this I know quite well since he's a friend of my old friend Apuleius, and he explains that things must have been like that. So I believe him, and, from the moment that I believe a little, I am beguiled.'

There are my reasons, matter of fact and prosaic; but one has to keep all this in mind when addressing the public that reads novels. Otherwise, one must write works of pure scholarship; another public altogether.

George Sand. Letter to Maurice Sand (20 June 1865), Correspondance *(1892).*

MANY GOOD WAYS OF TELLING A STORY

What is the best way of telling a story? Since the standard must be the interest of the audience, there must be several or many good ways rather than one best. For we get interested in the stories life presents to us through divers orders and modes of presentation. Very commonly our first awakening to a desire of knowing a man's past or future comes from our seeing him as a stranger in some unusual or pathetic or humorous situation, or manifesting some remarkable characteristics. We make inquiries in consequence, or we become observant and attentive whenever opportunities of knowing more may present themselves without our search. You have seen a refined face among the prisoners picking tow in gaol; you afterwards see the same unforgettable face in a pulpit: he must be of dull fibre who would not care to know more about a life which showed such contrasts, though he might gather his knowledge in a fragmentary and unchronological way.

Again, we have heard much, or at least something not quite common, about a man whom we have never seen, and hence we look round with curiosity when we are told that he is present; whatever he says or does before us is charged with a meaning due to our previous hearsay knowledge about him, gathered either from dialogue of which he was expressly and emphatically the subject, or from incidental remark, or from general report either in or out of print.

These indirect ways of arriving at knowledge are always the most stirring even in relation to impersonal subjects. To see a chemical experiment gives an attractiveness to a definition of chemistry, and fills it with a significance it would never have had without the pleasant shock of an unusual sequence such as the transformation of a solid into gas, and *vice versâ*: To see a word for the first time either as substantive or adjective in a connection where we care about knowing its complete meaning, is the way to vivify its meaning in our recollection. Curiosity becomes the more eager from the incompleteness of the first information. Moreover, it is in this way that memory works in its incidental revival of events: some salient experience appears in inward vision, and in consequence the antecedent facts are retraced from what is regarded as the beginning of the episode in which that experience made a more or less strikingly memorable part. 'Ah! I remember addressing the mob from the hustings at Westminster—you wouldn't have thought that I could ever have been in such a position. Well, how I came there was in this way.—'; and then follows a retrospective narration.

The modes of telling a story founded in these processes of outward and inward life derive their effectiveness from the superior mastery of images and pictures in grasping the attention—or, one might say with more fundamental accuracy, from the fact that our earliest, strongest impressions, our most intimate convictions, are simply images added to more or less of sensation. These are the primitive instruments of thought. Hence it is not surprising that early poetry took this way—telling a daring deed, a glorious achievement, without caring for what went before. The desire for orderly narration is a later, more reflective birth. The presence of the Jack in the box affects every child: it is the more reflective lad, the miniature philosopher, who wants to know how he got there.

The only stories life presents to us in an orderly way are those of our autobiography, or the career of our companions from our childhood upwards, or perhaps of our own children. But it is a great art to make a connected strictly relevant narrative of such careers as we can count from the beginning. In these cases the sequence of associations is almost sure to overmaster the sense of proportion. Such narratives *ab ovo* are summer's-day stories for happy loungers; not the cup of self-forgetting excitement to the busy who can snatch an hour of entertainment.

But the simple opening of a story with a date and necessary account of places and people, passing on quietly towards the more rousing elements of narrative and dramatic presentation, without need of retrospect, has its advantages which have to be measured by the nature of the story. Spirited narrative, without more than a touch of dialogue here and there, may be made eminently interesting, and is suited to the novelette. Examples of its charm are seen in the short tales in which the French have a mastery never reached by the English, who usually demand coarser flavours than are given by that delightful gaiety which is well described by La Fontaine as not anything that provokes fits of laughter, but a certain charm, an agreeable mode of handling which lends attractiveness to all subjects even the most serious. And it is this sort of gaiety which plays around the best French novelettes. But the opening chapters of *The Vicar of Wakefield* are as fine as anything that can be done in this way.

Why should a story not be told in the most irregular fashion that an author's idiosyncrasy may prompt, provided that he gives us what we enjoy? The objection to Sterne's wild way of telling *Tristram Shandy* lies more solidly in the quality of the interrupting matter than in the fact of interruption. The dear public would do well to reflect that they are often bored from the want of flexibility in their own minds. They are like the topers of 'one liquor.'

George Eliot. 'Leaves from a Note-book: storytelling',
The Impressions of Theophrastus Such (*1878*).

FORM AS VARIED AS CONTENT

(28 July 1900) . . . I think that every great artist necessarily creates his own form also. If the content of works of art can be infinitely varied, so also can their form. Once Turgenev and I came back from the theatre in Paris and discussed this. He completely agreed with me. We recalled all that is best in Russian literature and it seemed that in these works the form was perfectly original. Omitting Pushkin, let us take Gogol's *Dead Souls*. What is it? Neither a novel nor a story. It is something perfectly original. Then there is the *Memoirs of a Sportsman*, the best book Turgenev ever wrote; then Dostoevsky's *House of the Dead*, and then, sinner that I am, my *Childhood*; Herzen's *Past and Thoughts*; Lermontov's *Hero of our Time* . . .

> Leo Tolstoi. Talks with Tolstoi (*1922*), ed. A. B. Goldenveizer, transl. S. S. Koteliansky and Virginia Woolf (*1923*).

A CERTAIN INDIRECT AND OBLIQUE VIEW

(i)

Among many matters thrown into relief by a refreshed acquaintance with *The Golden Bowl* what perhaps most stands out for me is the still marked inveteracy of a certain indirect and oblique view of my presented action; unless indeed I make up my mind to call this mode of treatment, on the contrary, any superficial appearance notwithstanding, the very straightest and closest possible. I have already betrayed, as an accepted habit, and even to extravagance commented on, my preference for dealing with my subject-matter, for 'seeing my story,' through the opportunity and the sensibility of some more or less detached, some not strictly involved, though thoroughly interested and intelligent witness or reporter, some person who contributes to the case mainly a certain amount of criticism and interpretation of it. Again and again, on review, the shorter things in especial that I have gathered into this Series have ranged themselves not as my own impersonal account of the affair in hand, but as my account of somebody's impression of it—the terms of this person's access to it and estimate of it contributing thus by some fine little law to intensification of interest. The somebody is often, among my shorter tales I recognize, but an unnamed, unintroduced and (save by right of intrinsic wit) unwarranted participant, the impersonal author's concrete deputy or delegate, a convenient substitute or apologist for the creative power otherwise so veiled and disembodied. My instinct appears repeatedly to have been that to arrive at the facts retailed and the figures introduced by the given help of some other conscious and confessed agent is essentially to find the whole business—that is, as I say, its effective interest—enriched *by the way*. I have in other words constantly inclined to the idea of the particular attaching case *plus* some near individual view of it; that nearness quite having thus to become an imagined observer's, a projected, charmed painter's or poet's—however avowed the 'minor' quality in the latter—close and sensitive contact with it. Anything, in short, I now reflect, must have seemed to me better—better for the process and the effect of representation, my irrepressible ideal—than the mere muffled majesty of irresponsible 'authorship' . . .

I am aware of having glanced a good deal already in the direction of this embarrassed truth—which I give for what it is worth; but I feel it come home to me afresh on recognizing that the manner in which it betrays itself may be one of the liveliest sources of amusement in *The Golden Bowl*. It's not that the muffled majesty of authorship doesn't here *ostensibly* reign; but I catch myself again shaking it off and disavowing the pretence of it while I get down into the arena and do my best to live and breathe and rub shoulders and converse with the persons engaged in the struggle that provides for the others in the circling tiers the entertainment of the great game. There is no other participant, of course, than each of the real, the deeply involved and immersed and more or less bleeding participants; but . . . the whole thing remains subject to the register, ever so closely kept, of the consciousness of but two of the characters. The Prince, in the first half of the book, virtually sees and knows and makes out, virtually represents to himself everything that concerns us—very nearly (though he doesn't speak in the first person) after the fashion of other reporters and critics of other situations. Having a consciousness highly susceptible of registration, he thus makes us see the things that may most interest us reflected in it as in the clean glass held up to so many of the 'short stories' of our long list; and yet after all never a whit to the prejudice of his being just as consistently a foredoomed, entangled, embarrassed agent in the general imbroglio, actor in the offered play. The function of the Princess, in the remainder, matches exactly with his; the register of *her* consciousness is as closely kept—as closely, say, not only as his own, but as that (to cite examples) either of the intelligent but quite unindividualized witness of the destruction of *The Aspern Papers*, or of the all-noting heroine of *The Spoils of Poynton*, highly individualized *though* highly intelligent; the Princess, in fine, in addition to feeling everything she has to, and to playing her part just in that proportion, duplicates, as it were, her value and becomes a compositional resource, and of the finest order, as well as a value intrinsic. So it is that the admirably-endowed pair, between them, as I retrace their fortune and my own method, point again for me the moral of the endless interest, endless worth for 'delight', of the compositional contribution. Their chronicle strikes me as quite of the stuff to keep us from forgetting that absolutely *no* refinement of ingenuity or of precaution need be dreamed of as wasted in that most exquisite of all good cause the appeal to variety, the appeal to a high refine- · ment and a handsome wholeness of effect.

> *Henry James. Preface to* The Golden Bowl *(1904);*
> *first printed in the New York edition of the* Novels
> and Stories *(1907–17),* Vol. XXIII.

(ii)

Saturday, December 21th [1913],—I am now reading *The Way of All Flesh*. It stands it. There is very little wrong with this book, even technically. But the trick of reading a piece of the narrative to the hero himself and then writing down what the hero's comment on it was, is a mistake—especially when it is repeated.

(24 January 1914) . . . I finished Conrad's *Chance* in the middle of the night. It is very fine. The best chapters are 'The Governess' and the last one. The Tea Party chapter, and 'On the Pavement' chapter are too long. The indirect narrative is successfully managed on the whole, even to fourth hand narrative, but here and there recounted dialogue and gesture is so minute as to be unconvincing.

> *Arnold Bennett.* The Journals *(1931).*

(iii)

My own impression is that what he[1] really meant was that my manner of telling, perfectly devoid of familiarity as between author and reader, aimed essentially at the intimacy of a personal com- munication, without any thought for other effects. As a matter of fact, the thought for effects is there all the same (often at the cost of mere directness of narrative), and can be detected in

---

[1] i.e. a critic 'in a long article in the Seccolo'.

my unconventional grouping and perspective, which are purely temperamental and wherein all my 'art' consists.

Joseph Conrad. Letter to Richard Curle (14 July 1923),
Life and Letters (1927), ed. G. Jean-Aubry.

'BOUNCING' MORE IMPORTANT THAN THE 'POINT OF VIEW'

. . . 'The whole intricate question of method, in the craft of fiction,' says Mr. Percy Lubbock, 'I take to be governed by the question of the *point of view*—the question of the relation in which the narrator stands to the story'. And his book *The Craft of Fiction* examines various points of view with genius and insight. The novelist, he says, can either describe the characters from outside, as an impartial or partial onlooker; or he can assume omniscience and describe them from within; or he can place himself in the position of one of them and affect to be in the dark as to the motives of the rest; or there are certain intermediate attitudes.

Those who follow him will lay a sure foundation for the aesthetics of fiction—a foundation which I cannot for a moment promise. This is a ramshackly survey and for me the whole intricate question of method resolves itself not into formulae but into the power of the writer to bounce the reader into accepting what he says—a power which Mr. Lubbock admits and admires, but locates at the edge of the problem instead of at the centre. I should put it plumb in the centre. Look how Dickens bounces us in *Bleak House*. Chapter I of *Bleak House* is omniscient. Dickens takes us into the Court of Chancery and rapidly explains all the people there. In Chapter II he is partially omniscient. We still use his eyes, but for some unexplained reason they begin to grow weak: he can explain Sir Leicester Dedlock to us, part of Lady Dedlock but not all, and nothing of Mr. Tulkinghorn. In Chapter III he is even more reprehensible: he goes straight across into the dramatic method and inhabits a young lady, Esther Summerson. 'I have a great deal of difficulty in beginning to write my portion of these pages, for I know I am not clever', pipes up Esther, and continues in this strain with consistency and competence, so long as she is allowed to hold the pen. At any moment the author of her being may snatch it from her, and run about taking notes himself, leaving her seated goodness knows where, and employed we do not care how. Logically, *Bleak House* is all to pieces, but Dickens bounces us, so that we do not mind the shiftings of the view point.

Critics are more apt to object than readers. Zealous for the novel's eminence, they are a little too apt to look out for problems that shall be peculiar to it, and differentiate it from the drama; they feel it ought to have its own technical troubles before it can be accepted as an independent art; and since the problem of a point of view certainly is peculiar to the novel they have rather over-stressed it. I do not myself think it is so important as a proper mixture of characters—a problem which the dramatist is up against also. And the novelist must bounce us; that is imperative. . . .

A novelist can shift his view point if it comes off, and it came off with Dickens and Tolstoy. Indeed this power to expand and contract perception (of which the shifting view point is a symptom), this right to intermittent knowledge:—I find it one of the great advantages of the novel-form, and it has a parallel in our perception of life. We are stupider at some times than others; we can enter into people's minds occasionally but not always, because our own minds get tired; and this intermittence lends in the long run variety and colour to the experiences we receive. A quantity of novelists, English novelists especially, have behaved like this to the people in their books: played fast and loose with them, and I cannot see why they should be censured.

E. M. Forster. Aspects of the Novel (*1927*), *Chapter iv.*

EXIT AUTHOR?

(i)

In all histories, whether true or fictitious, the author cannot too carefully refrain from speaking in his own person . . . and this is yet another reason to be added to those already given, why political discussions should never be admitted in a novel, as they are sure to be set down to the author's account, let him assign them as he will.

Richard Cumberland. Henry (1795), *Book the Sixth, Chapter i.*

(ii)

. . . Fielding pauses to explain the principles of his art, and to congratulate himself and his readers on the felicity with which he conducts his narrative, or makes his characters evolve themselves in its progress. These appeals to the reader's judgment, admirable as they are, have sometimes the fault of being diffuse, and always to the great disadvantage, that they remind us we are perusing a work of fiction; and that the beings with whom we have been conversant during the perusal, are but a sort of evanescent phantoms, conjured up by a magician for our own amusement. Smollett seldom holds communication with his readers in his own person. He manages his delightful puppet-show without thrusting his head beyond the curtain, like Gines de Passamonte, to explain what he is doing; and hence, besides that our attention to the story remains unbroken, we are sure that the author, fully confident in the abundance of his materials, has no occasion to eke them out with extrinsic matter.

Sir Walter Scott. 'Tobias Smollett', Lives of the Novelists (*1827*).

(iii)

But let the gentle-hearted reader be under no apprehension whatsoever. It is not destined that Eleanor shall marry Mr. Slope or Bertie Stanhope. And here, perhaps, it may be allowed to the novelist to explain his views on a very important point in the art of telling tales. He ventures to reprobate that system which goes so far to violate all proper confidence between the author and his readers, by maintaining nearly to the end of the third volume a mystery as to the fate of their favourite personage. Nay, more, and worse than this is too frequently done. Have not often the profoundest efforts of genius been used to baffle the aspirations of the reader, to raise false hopes and false fears, and to give rise to expectations which are never to be realized? Are not promises all but made of delightful horrors, in lieu of which the writer produces nothing but most commonplace realities in his final chapter? And is there not a species of deceit in this to which the honesty of the present age should lend no countenance? . . .

Our doctrine is, that the author and the reader should move along together in full confidence with each other . . .

Anthony Trollope. Barchester Towers (*1857*) *Chapter xv.*

(iv)

. . . It strikes me that you constantly hurry your narrative (and yet without getting on) *by telling it, in a sort of impetuous breathless way, in your own person, when the people should tell it and act it for themselves.* My notion always is, that when I have made the people to play out the play, it is, as it were, their own business to do it, and not mine. Then, unless you really have led up to a great situation, like Basil's death, you are bound in art to make more of it. Such a scene should form a chapter of itself. Impressed upon the reader's memory, it would go far to make the fortune of the book. Suppose yourself telling that affecting incident in a letter to a friend. Wouldn't you describe how you went through the life and stir of the streets and roads to the sick-room? Wouldn't you say what kind of room it was, what time of day it was, whether it was sunlight, starlight, or moonlight? Wouldn't you have a strong impression on your mind of how you were received, when you first met the look of the dying man, what strange contrasts were about you and struck you? I don't want you, in a novel, to present *yourself* to tell such things, but I want the things to be there. You make no more of the situation than the index might, or a descriptive playbill might in giving a summary of the tragedy under representation.

> *Charles Dickens. Letter to Mrs. Brookfield*
> (*20 February 1866*), Letters (*1880*).

(v)

I expressed myself badly in telling you that 'one must not write with one's heart.' What I meant was: One mustn't bring one's own personality on to the scene. I believe that great Art is scientific and impersonal. We must, by an effort of the mind, go over to our characters, as it were, not make them come over to us.

> *Gustave Flaubert. Letter to George Sand (15–16 December 1866),*
> Correspondance (*1929*).

. . . there is nothing 'true' in *Madame Bovary*. It is a story of *pure invention*; I have put none of my own feelings into it, nor anything of my own life. The illusion [of truth], on the contrary (if there is any), comes from the very objectivity of the work. It is one of my principles that one must not write oneself into one's work. The artist must be in his work as God is in creation, invisible yet all-powerful; we must sense him everywhere but never see him.

Then again, Art should rise above personal feeling and emotional susceptibilities! It is time we gave it, through rigid systematization, the exactness of the physical sciences! The chief difficulty for me, however, still remains style, form, that indefinable Beauty arising from the very conception which, as Plato says, is the very splendour of Truth.

> *Gustave Flaubert. Letter to Mademoiselle Leroyer de Chantepie,*
> (*19 February 1857*), Correspondance (*1903*).

(vi)

M. Flaubert is, then, first and foremost an artist; that is, an objective writer. I defy anyone, after having read all his works, to make out what he is in private life, what he thinks or what he says in his everyday conversation. One knows what Dickens must have thought, what Balzac must have thought. They appear all the time in their books; but what do you imagine La Bruyère to have been, or the great Cervantes to have said? Flaubert never wrote the words *I, me*. He never talks to the audience in the middle of a book, or greets it at the end, like an actor on the stage, and he never writes prefaces. He is the showman of human puppets who must speak through his mouth while he refrains from the right to think through theirs; and there is to be no detecting the strings or recognizing the voice.

> *Guy de Maupassant. 'Gustave Flaubert' (1876); reprinted in* Chroniques, Etudes, Corre- spondance *(1938), ed. René Dumesnil.*

(vii)

Certain accomplished novelists have a habit of giving themselves away which must often bring tears to the eyes of people who take their fiction seriously. I was lately struck, in reading over the pages of Anthony Trollope, with his want of discretion in this particular. In a digression, a parenthesis or an aside, he concedes to the reader that he and his trusting friend are only 'making believe'. He admits that the events he narrates have not really happened, and that he can give his narrative any turn the reader may like best. Such a betrayal of a sacred office seems to me, I confess, a terrible crime; it is what I mean by the attitude of apology, and it shocks me every whit as much in Trollope as it would have shocked me in Gibbon or Macaulay. It implies that the novelist is less occupied in looking for the truth than the historian, and in doing so it deprives him at a stroke of all his standing-room. To represent and illustrate the past, the actions of men, is the task of either writer, and the only difference that I can see is, in proportion as he succeeds, to the honour of the novelist, consisting as it does in his having more difficulty in collect- ing his evidence, which is so far from being purely literary.

> *Henry James. 'The Art of Fiction' (1884); reprinted in* Partial Portraits *(1888).*

(viii)

. . . the object of the novelist is to keep the reader entirely oblivious of the fact that the author exists—even of the fact that he is reading a book. This is of course not possible to the bitter end, but a reader *can* be rendered very engrossed, and the nearer you can come to making him entirely insensitive to his surroundings, the more you will have succeeded.

> *Ford Madox Ford.* Joseph Conrad: A Personal Remembrance (*1924*), *Part III, Section ii.*

(ix)

. . . may the writer take the reader into his confidence about his characters? . . . better not. It is dangerous, it generally leads to a drop in the temperature, to intellectual and emotional laxity, and worse still to facetiousness, and to a friendly invitation to see how the figures hook up behind. 'Doesn't A look nice—she always was my favourite', 'Let's think of why B does that—perhaps there's more in him than meets the eye—yes, see—he has a heart of gold—having given you this peep at it I'll pop it back—I don't think he's noticed'. 'And C—he always was the mystery man.' Intimacy is gained but at the expense of illusion and nobility. It is like standing a man a drink so that he may not criticize your opinions. With all respect to Fielding and Thackeray it is devastating, it is bar-parlour chattiness, and nothing has been more harmful to the novels of the past. To take your reader into your confidence about the universe is a different thing. It is not dangerous for a novelist to draw back from his characters, as Hardy and Conrad do, and to generalize about the conditions under which he thinks life is carried on. It is confidences about the individual people that do harm, and beckon the reader away from the people to an examination of the novelist's mind. Not much is ever found in it at such a moment, for it is never in the creative state: the mere process of saying 'come along, let's have a chat' has cooled it down.

> *E. M. Forster.* Aspects of the Novel (*1927*), *Chapter iv.*

(x)

It is appropriate, in opposition to the manner of Meredith and James, to let the reader get the advantage over me—to go about it in such a way as to allow him to think he is more intelligent, more moral, more perspicacious than the author, and that he is discovering many things in the characters, and many truths in the course of the narrative, in spite of the author and, so to speak, behind the author's back.

André Gide. Logbook of The Coiners *(1927), p. 85, transl. Justin O'Brien.*

(xi)

The novelist can assume the god-like creative privilege and simply elect to consider the events of the story in their various aspects—emotional, scientific, economic, religious, metaphysical, etc. He will modulate from one to the other—as from the aesthetic to the psychico-chemical aspect of things, from the religious to the physiological or financial. But perhaps this is a too tyrannical imposition of the author's will. Some people would think so. But need the author be so retiring? I think we're a bit too squeamish about these personal appearances nowadays.

Put a novelist into the novel. He justifies aesthetic generalizations, which may be interesting—at least to me. He also justifies experiment. Specimens of his work may illustrate other possible or impossible ways of telling a story. And if you have him telling parts of the same story as you are, you can make a variation on the theme. But why draw the line at one novelist inside your novel? Why not a second inside his? And a third inside the novel of the second? And so on to infinity, like those advertisements of Quaker Oats where there's a quaker holding a box of oats, on which is a picture of another quaker holding another box of oats, on which etc., etc. At about the tenth remove you might have a novelist telling your story in algebraic symbols or in terms of variations in blood-pressure, pulse, secretion of ductless glands and reaction times.

Aldous Huxley. Point Counter Point *(1928), Chapter xxii.*

III Characterization

THE DIAL-PLATE OR THE INNER WORKINGS?

(i)

The only ways by which we can come at any knowledge of what passes in the minds of others, are their words and actions, the latter of which hath by the wiser part of mankind been chiefly depended on, as the surer and more infallible guide.

Henry Fielding. The Champion (*11 December 1739*).

(ii)

The motives to actions, and the inward turns of the mind, seem in our opinion more necessary to be known than the actions themselves; and much rather would we choose that our readers should clearly understand what our principal actors think, than what they do.

Sarah Fielding. Preface to The Cry (*1754*).

(iii)

I have just gone through your two vols. of Letters. Have re-perused them with great pleasure, and found many new beauties in them. What a knowledge of the human heart! Well might a critical judge of writing say, as he did to me, that your late brother's knowledge of it was not (fine writer as he was) comparable to yours. His was but as the knowledge of the outside of a clock-work machine, while yours was that of all the finer springs and movements of the inside.

Samuel Richardson. Letter to Sarah Fielding (7 December 1756), Correspondence (*1804*).

(iv)

Richardson was well qualified to be the discoverer of a new style of writing, for he was a cautious, deep, and minute examinator of the human heart, and, like Cooke or Parry, left neither head, bay nor inlet behind him, until he had traced its soundings, and laid it down in his chart, with all its minute sinuosities, its depths, and its shallows. Hence the high, and comparatively considered, perhaps the undue superiority assigned by Johnson to Richardson over Fielding, against whom the Doctor seems to have entertained some prejudice. In one passage he asserts, that 'there is more knowledge of the human heart in one letter of Richardson's than in all *Tom Jones*'. And in another, he thus explains the proposition: 'There is all the difference in the world between characters of nature and characters of manners, and there is this difference between the characters of Fielding and those of Richardson. Characters of manners are very entertaining; but they are to be understood by a more superficial observer than characters of nature, where a man must dive into the recesses of the human heart'. Again, in comparing these two distinguished authors, the critic uses this illustration,— 'that there was as great a difference between them, as between a man who knew how a watch was made, and a man who could tell the hour by looking at the dial-plate'. Dissenting as we do from the conclusions to be deduced from Dr. Johnson's simile, we would rather so modify it as to describe both authors as excellent mechanics; the time-pieces of Richardson showing a great deal of the internal work by which the index is regulated; while those of Fielding merely point to the hour of the day, being all that most men desire to know. Or, to take a more manageable comparison, the analogy betwixt the writings of Fielding and Richardson resembles that which free, bold and true sketches bear to paintings that have been very minutely laboured, and which, amid their excellence, still exhibit some of the heaviness that almost always attends the highest degree of finishing. This, indeed, is admitted by Johnson himself, in his reply to the observation of the Honourable Thomas Erskine, that Richardson was tedious.—'Why, sir, if you were to read Richardson for the story, your impatience would be so much fretted, that you would hang yourself. But you must read him for the sentiment'. Were we to translate the controversy into plain language, it might be summed up in pronouncing the works of Richardson the more instructive, and the more deeply affecting, those of Fielding the more amusing; and that a reader might select the one or the other for his studies, according to Tony Lumpkin's phrase, as he felt himself 'in a concatenation accordingly';—with this difference, however, that he who would laugh with Fielding, may open *Tom Jones* at a venture; but he who would weep with Richardson must be content to read through many pages, until his mind is in the mood fittest to appreciate the pathetic scenes introduced by a succession of minute and highly laboured details. This no doubt frequently occasions a suspension of the narrative, in order to afford time for the minute delineation of character. 'Richardson himself has explained his principle', as is well observed by Mr. D'Israeli. 'If', he tells us, 'I give speeches and conversations, I ought to give them justly, for the humours and persons of characters cannot be known, unless I repeat what they say, and their manner of saying it'. This process of miniature painting, has, however, its bounds; and many readers will be disposed to acquiesce in the remark of D'Alembert,—'La Nature est bonne à imiter, mais non pas jusqu'à l'ennui.'

> *Sir Walter Scott.* '*Samuel Richardson*', Lives
> of the Novelists (*1827*).

NO PICTURES OF PERFECTION

(i)

. . . we must admonish thee, my worthy friend (for, perhaps, thy heart may be better than thy head), not to condemn a character as a bad one because it is not perfectly a good one. If thou dost delight in these models of perfection, there are books enow written to gratify thy taste; but, as we have not, in the course of our conversation, ever happened to meet with any such person, we have not chosen to introduce any such here. To say the truth, I a little question whether mere man ever arrived at this consummate degree of excellence, as well as whether there hath ever existed a monster bad enough to verify that

> . . . nulla virtute redemptum
> A vitiis. . . .[1]

Henry Fielding. The History of Tom Jones, a Foundling (*1749*), *Book X, Chapter i.*

(ii)

I do not aim to draw a perfect character, for after a pretty long acquaintance with mankind I have never met with any one example of the sort: How then shall I describe what I have not seen? On the contrary, if I wish to form a character, like this of Henry, in which virtue predominates, or like that of Blackford, where the opposite

---

[1] His vices are not allayed with a single virtue.

qualities prevail, I have nature before me in both cases: but if in the former instance I will not suffer a single shade to fall on my canvas, and in the latter do not let one hint of light appear, what do I present to the spectator, but a confused and shapeless mass, here too glaring, and there too opaque, to preserve any outline that can give to view the form and fashion of a man?—The brightest side of human nature is not without a spot, the darkest side is not without a spark.

> *Richard Cumberland.* Henry (*1795*),
> Book the Fourth, Chapter i.

(iii)

. . . pictures of perfection as you know make me sick and wicked . . . You may perhaps like the Heroine,[1] as she is almost too good for me . . .

> *Jane Austen. Letter to Cassandra Austen* (*23 March 1817*),
> Letters (*1932*)

(iv)

I want to see man as he really is. He is neither good nor bad. But he is something else besides . . . being both good and bad, he possesses an inner force which drives him to be very bad and a bit good, or else very good and a bit bad.

> *George Sand. Letter to Gustave Flaubert* (*18–19 December 1875*),
> Correspondance (*1892*).

(v)

. . . we are for the most part an abominably foolish and selfish people 'desperately wicked' and all eager after vanities. Everybody is you see in that book [i.e. *Vanity Fair*],—for instance if I had made Amelia a higher order of woman there would have been no vanity in Dobbin's falling in love with her, whereas the impression at present is that he is a fool for his pains, that he has married a sweet little thing and in fact has found out his error, rather a sweet and tender one however, *quia multum amavit*. I want to leave everybody dissatisfied and unhappy at the end of the story—we ought all to be with our own and all other stories. Good God, don't I see (in that may-be cracked and warped looking glass in which I am always looking) my own weaknesses, wickednesses, lusts, follies, short-

---

[1] Anne Elliot in *Persuasion* (1818).

comings? in company let us hope with better qualities about which we will pretermit discourse. We must lift up our voices about these and howl to a congregation of fools: so much at least has been my endeavour. You have all of you taken my misanthropy to task—I wish I could myself: but take the world by a certain standard (you know what I mean) and who dares talk of having any virtue at all?

> *William Makepeace Thackeray. Letter to Robert Bell*
> *(3 September 1848)*, Letters *(1945)*.

NO PORTRAITS

(i)

And here I solemnly protest I have no intention to vilify or asperse anyone; for though everything is copied from the book of nature, and scarce a character or action produced which I have not taken from my own observations and experience; yet I have used the utmost care to obscure the persons by such different circumstances, degrees, and colours, that it will be impossible to guess at them with any degree of certainty; and if it ever happens otherwise, it is only where the failure characterized is so minute, that it is a foible only which the party himself may laugh at as well as any other.

As to the character of Adams, as it is the most glaring in the whole, so I conceive it is not to be found in any book now extant. It is designed a character of perfect simplicity; and as the goodness of his heart will recommend him to the good-natured, so I hope it will excuse me to the gentlemen of his cloth; for whom, while they are worthy of their sacred order, no man can possibly have a greater respect. They will therefore excuse me, notwithstanding the low adventures in which he is engaged, that I have made him a clergyman: since no other office could have given him so many opportunities of displaying his worthy inclinations.

> *Henry Fielding. 'Author's Preface'*, The History of the
> Adventures of Joseph Andrews . . . *(1742)*.

(ii)

I take a being whom I have known, and say to myself: with the same habits, contracted in the art of going every morning 'in pursuit of pleasure', what would he do if he had more intelligence?

> *Stendhal. Letter to Balzac (30 October 1840), first draft,*
> Selected Letters *(1952), transl. Norman Cameron.*

(iii)

You are not to suppose any of the characters in *Shirley* intended as literal portraits. It would not suit the rules of art, nor of my own feelings, to write in that style. We only suffer reality to *suggest*, never to *dictate*. The heroines are abstractions, and the heroes also. Qualities I have seen, loved and admired, are here and there put in as decorative gems, to be preserved in that setting.

> *Charlotte Brontë. Letter to Ellen Nussey (16 November 1849)*
> *from Mrs. Gaskell's* Life *(1857).*

(iv)

There is not a single portrait in Adam Bede, as I have said before . . . I could never have written Adam Bede if I had not learned something of my father's early experience: but no one who knew my father could call Adam a portrait of him—and the course of Adam's life is entirely different from my father's. Again, Dinah and Seth are *not* my aunt and uncle. I knew my aunt and uncle and they were Methodists—my aunt a preacher, and I loved them: so far only they resembled Seth and Dinah. The whole course of the story in Adam Bede—the descriptions of scenery and houses—the characters —the dialogue—*everything* is a combination from widely sundered elements of experience . . . But no one who is not an artist knows how experience is wrought up in writing any form of poetry.

> *George Eliot. Letter to Charles Bray (19 September 1859),*
> The George Eliot Letters *(1954).*

(v)

I don't write satire; I don't even know what it is. Nor do I paint *portraits*: that isn't my way. I *invent*. The public, who don't know what invention consists of, try to find originals everywhere. They deceive themselves and debase the art.

> *George Sand. Letter to Gustave Flaubert (19 March 1870).*
> Correspondance *(1892).*

(vi)

(To 'Mr. Haines', 1837) . . . In my next number of *Oliver Twist* I must have a magistrate; and casting about for a magistrate whose harshness and insolence would render him a fit subject to be *shown up*, I have as a necessary consequence stumbled upon Mr. Laing of Hatton-garden celebrity. I know the man's character perfectly well; but as it would be necessary to describe his personal appearance also, I ought to have seen him, which (fortunately or unfortunately as the case may be) I have never done. In this dilemma it occurred to me that perhaps I might under your auspices be smuggled into the Hatton-garden office for a few moments some morning. If you can further my object I shall really be very greatly obliged to you.

> *Charles Dickens. John Forster*, The Life of Charles Dickens
> (*1874*), *Vol. III, Chapter i.*

(To Leigh Hunt, concerning Harold Skimpole in *Bleak House*)
. . . As it has given you so much pain, I take it at its worst and say I am deeply sorry, and that I feel I did wrong in doing it. I should otherwise have taken it at its best, and ridden off upon what I strongly feel to be the truth, that there is nothing in it that *should* have given you pain. Every one in writing must speak from points of his experience, and so I of mine with you: but when I have felt it was going too close I stopped myself, and the most blotted parts of my M.S. are those in which I have been striving hard to make the impression I was writing from, *un*like you. The diary-writing I took from Haydon, not from you. I now first learn from yourself that you ever set anything to music, and I could not have copied *that* from you. The character is not you, for there are traits in it common to fifty thousand people besides, and I did not fancy you would ever recognize it. Under similar disguises my own mother and father are in my books, and you might as well see your likeness in Micawber.

> *Charles Dickens. John Forster*, The Life of Charles Dickens
> (*1874*), *Vol. III, Chapter i.*

(vii)

. . . there is nothing 'true' in *Madame Bovary*. It is a story of *pure invention*; I have but none of my own feelings into it, nor anything of my own life. The illusion [of truth], on the contrary (if there is any), comes from the very objectivity of the work.[1]

> *Gustave Flaubert. Letter to Mademoiselle Leroyer de Chantepie*,
> (*19 February 1857*), Correspondance (*1903*).

[1] See also above, p. 271.

The public, I repeat, see allusions where none exist. When I'd finished *Madame Bovary*, I was asked several times, 'Was it Madame XXX whom you intended to portray?' And I received several letters from perfect strangers, one of them from a gentleman in Reims who congratulated me on having *avenged him!* (for a faithless woman).

All the chemists in the Seine-Inférieure recognized themselves in Homais and wanted to come and slap me in the face; but best of all (I discovered this five years later) at that time in Africa there was an army doctor's wife called Madame Bovaries who resembled Madame Bovary, a name which I'd invented by altering Bouvaret.

The first words of our friend Maury in discussing *L'Education Sentimentale* were: 'Did you know X . . ., an Italian mathematics master? Your Sénécal is his portrait, physically and morally! Everything is there, down to the cut of his hair!' Others claim that in Arnoux I wanted to portray Bernard-Latte (the former editor) whom I'd never seen, etc.

All this is to tell you, chère Madame, that the public is mistaken in attributing intentions to us that we don't possess.

> Gustave Flaubert. Letter to Madame Hortense Cornu
> (*20 March 1870*), Correspondance (*1903*).

(viii)

. . . I thought the crime too ingenious for an English villain, so I pitched upon a foreigner. You know that I have lived a great deal abroad, and have had many opportunities of observing foreign people. It seems that I did so to some purpose, for after *The Woman in White* appeared, I received a large number of letters from abroad accusing me of gross personal caricature or rather too accurate portraiture. The writers were in a great rage at having their personal weaknesses applied to a scoundrel and held up to derision. I need not tell you that Fosco is not modelled on any one or any half dozen persons. His character grew on me,—a great danger to a novelist by the way. I know a man who loved canaries, and I had known boys who loved white mice, and I thought the mice running about Fosco while he meditated on his schemes would have a fine effect. You ask me why I made him fat; his greatest beauty in the opinion of the majority of competent judges. You give me good reasons for making him fat: that fat men are malevolent and ruthless, and that the first Napoleon was a fat man, together with the chemical demonstration that fatty substances when heated above a certain temperature develop an acid known as butyric acid. I knew all this, but none of these considerations influenced me. I had begun to write my story, when it struck me that my villain would be common-place, and I made him fat in opposition to the recognized type of villain. His theories concerning the vulgar clap-trap that murder will out, are my own.

Wilkie Collins. Interview in The World (*26 December 1877*).

(ix)

And then I had an idea for John Silver from which I promised myself funds of entertainment; to take an admired friend of mine (whom the reader very likely knows and admires as much as I do), to deprive him of all his finer qualities and higher graces of tempera-ment, to leave him with nothing but his strength, his courage, his quickness, and his magnificent geniality, and to try to express these in terms of the culture of a raw tarpaulin. Such psychical surgery is, I think, a common way of 'making character'; perhaps it is, indeed, the only way. We can put in the quaint figure that spoke a hundred words with us yesterday by the wayside; but do we know him? Our friend, with his infinite variety and flexibility, we know —but can we put him in? Upon the first, we must engraft secondary and imaginary qualities, possibly all wrong; from the second, knife in hand, we must cut away and deduct the needless arborescence of his nature, but the trunk and the few branches that remain we may at least be fairly sure of.

Robert Louis Stevenson. 'My first book' (1894); reprinted in The Art of Writing (*1919*)

(x)

What I should, for that matter, like most to go into here, space serving, is the so interesting question—for the most part, it strikes me, too confusedly treated—of the story-teller's 'real person' or actual contemporary transplanted and exhibited. But this pursuit would take us far, such radical revision do the common laxities of the case, as generally handled, seem to call for . . . We can surely account for nothing in the novelist's work that hasn't passed through the crucible of his imagination, hasn't, in that perpetually simmer-ing cauldron, his intellectual *pot-au-feu*, been reduced to savoury fusion. We here figure the morsel, of course, not as boiled to nothing, but as exposed, in return for the taste it gives out, to a new and richer saturation. In this state it is in due course picked out and served . . . Its final savour has been constituted, but its prime identity destroyed—which is what was to be demonstrated.

Thus it becomes different and, thanks to a rare alchemy, a better thing. Therefore let us have here as little as possible about its 'being' Mr. This or Mrs. That. If it adjusts itself with the least truth to its new life it can't possibly be either. If it gracelessly refers itself to either, if it persists as the impression not artistically dealt with, it shames the honour offered it and can only be spoken of as having ceased to be a thing of fact, and yet not become a thing of truth.

> *Henry James. Preface to* The Lesson of the Master, *first printed in the New York edition of the* Novels and Stories *(1907–17), Vol. XV.*

(xi)

I may make the note that I never in my life, as far as I can remember, used a character from actual life for the purposes of fiction—or never without concealing their attributes very carefully. This is not so much because I wish to avoid hurting people's feelings as because it is, artistically, a very dangerous practice. It is even fatal.

> *Ford Madox Ford.* It was the Nightingale *(1934), Part Two, Chapter ii.*

(xii)

I think that actual life supplies a writer with characters much less than is thought. Of course there must be a beginning to every conception, but so much change seems to take place in it at once, that almost anything comes to serve the purpose—a face of a stranger, a face seen in a portrait, almost a face in the fire. And people in life hardly seem definite enough to appear in print. They are not good or bad enough, or clever or stupid enough, or comic or pitiful enough. They would have to be presented by means of detailed description, and would not come through in talk. I think that the reason why a person is often angered by a supposed portrait of himself, is that the author leaves in some recognizable attributes, while the conception has altered so much that the subject is justified in thinking there is no resemblance. And I believe that we know much less of each other than we think, that it would be a great shock to find oneself suddenly behind another person's eyes. The things we think we know about each other, we may often imagine and read in. I think this is another reason why a supposed portrait gives offence. It is really far from the truth.

In cases where a supposed portrait of some living person has caused trouble, I have thought that the explanation lies in these things, and that the author's disclaimer of any intention of portraiture is in the main sincere and just.

> Ivy Compton-Burnett. 'A Conversation Between I. Compton-Burnett and M. Jourdain', Orion (1945).

THE NOVELIST'S CHARACTERS MUST BE REAL TO HIM

But the novelist has other aims than the elucidation of his plot. He desires to make his readers so intimately acquainted with his characters that the creations of his brain should be to them speaking, moving, living, human creatures. This he can never do unless he knows those fictitious personages himself, and he can never know them well unless he can live with them in the full reality of established intimacy. They must be with him as he lies down to sleep, and as he wakes from his dreams. He must learn to hate them and to love them. He must know of them whether they be cold-blooded or passionate, whether true or false, and how far true, and how far false. The depth and the breadth, and the narrowness and the shallowness of each should be clear to him. And as, here in our outer world, we know that men and women change,—become worse or better as temptation or conscience may guide them,—so should these creations of his change, and every change should be noted by him. On the last day of each month recorded, every person in his novel should be a month older than on the first. If the would-be novelist have aptitudes that way, all this will come to him without much struggling;—but if it do not come, I think he can only make novels of wood.

It is so that I have lived with my characters, and thence has come whatever success I have attained. There is a gallery of them, and of all in that gallery I may say that I know the tone of voice, and the colour of the hair, every flame of the eye, and the very clothes they wear. Of each man I could assert whether he would have said these or the other words; of every woman, whether she would then have smiled or so have frowned. When I shall feel that this intimacy ceases, then I shall know that the old horse should be turned out to grass. That I shall feel it when I ought to feel it, I will by no means say. I do not know that I am at all wiser than Gil Blas' canon; but I do know that the power indicated is one without which the teller of tales cannot tell them to any good effect.

> Anthony Trollope. Autobiography (1883), Chapter xii.

THE NOVELIST HAUNTED BY HIS CHARACTERS

... I admit that outwardly I resembled sufficiently a man who could make a second officer for a steamer chartered by a French company. I showed no sign of being haunted by the fate of Nina and by the murmurs of tropical forests; and even my intimate intercourse with Almayer (a person of weak character) had not put a visible mark upon my features. For many years he and the world of his story had been the companions of my imagination without, I hope, impairing my ability to deal with the realities of sea life. I had had the man and his surroundings with me ever since my return from the eastern waters, some four years before the day of which I speak.

It was in the front sitting-room of furnished apartments in a Pimlico square that they first began to live again with a vividness and poignancy quite foreign to our former real intercourse. I had been treating myself to a long stay on shore, and in the necessity of occupying my mornings, Almayer (that old acquaintance) came nobly to the rescue. Before long, as was only proper, his wife and daughter joined him round my table, and then the rest of that Pantai band came full of words and gestures. Unknown to my respectable landlady, it was my practice directly after my breakfast to hold animated receptions of Malays, Arabs and half-castes. They did not clamour aloud for my attention. They came with silent and irresistible appeal—and the appeal, I affirm here, was not to my self-love or my vanity. It seems now to have had a moral character, for why should the memory of these beings, seen in their obscure sun-bathed existence, demand to express itself in the shape of a novel, except on the ground of that mysterious fellowship which unites in a community of hopes and fears all the dwellers on this earth.

Joseph Conrad. A Personal Record (*1912*), *Chapter i.*

L'IMAGE EN DISPONIBILITÉ

I have always fondly remembered a remark that I heard fall years ago from the lips of Ivan Turgenieff in regard to his own experience of the usual origin of the fictive picture. It began for him almost always with the vision of some person or persons, who hovered before him, soliciting him, as the active or passive figure, interesting him and appealing to him just as they were and by what they were. He saw them, in that fashion, as *disponibles*, saw them subject to the chances, the complications of existence, and saw them vividly, but then had to find for them the right relations, those that would most bring them out; to imagine, to invent and select and piece together the situations most useful and favourable to the sense of the creatures themselves, the complications they would be most likely to produce and feel.

'To arrive at these things is to arrive at my "story"', he said, 'and that's the way I look for it. The result is that I'm often accused of not having "story" enough. I seem to myself to have as much as I need—to show my people, to exhibit their relations with each other; for that is all my measure. If I watch them long enough I see them come together, I see them *placed*, I see them engaged in this or that act and in this or that difficulty. How they look and move and speak and behave, always in the setting I have found for them, is my account of them—of which I dare say, alas, *que cela manque souvent d'architecture*. But I would rather, I think, have too little architecture than too much—when there's a danger of its interfering with my measure of the truth. The French of course like more of it than I give—having by their own genius such a hand for it; and indeed one must give all one can. As for the origin of one's wind-blown germs themselves, who shall say, as you ask, where *they* come from? We have to go too far back, too far behind, to say . . .'

So this beautiful genius, and I recall with comfort the gratitude I drew from his reference to the intensity of suggestion that may reside in the stray figure, the unattached character, the *image en disponibilité*. It gave me higher warrant than I seemed then to have met for just that blest habit of one's own imagination, the trick of investing some conceived or encountered individual, some brace or group of individuals, with the germinal property and authority. I was myself so much more antecedently conscious of my figures than of their setting—a too preliminary, a preferential interest in which struck me as in general such a putting of the cart before the horse. I might envy, though I couldn't emulate, the imaginative writer so constituted as to see his fable first and to make out its agents afterwards: I could think so little of any fable that didn't need its agents positively to launch it; I could think so little of any situation that didn't depend for its interest on the nature of the persons situated, and thereby on their way of taking it.

Henry James. Preface to The Portrait of a Lady (*1881*); *first printed in the New York edition of the* Novels and Stories (*1907–17*), *Vol. III.*

'FLAT' AND 'ROUND' CHARACTERS

We may divide characters into flat and round.

Flat characters were called 'humours' in the seventeenth century, and are sometimes called types, and sometimes caricatures. In their purest form, they are constructed round a single idea or quality: when there is more than one factor in them, we get the beginning of the curve towards the round. The really flat character can be expressed in one sentence such as 'I never will desert Mr. Micawber.' There is Mrs. Micawber—she says she won't desert Mr. Micawber, she doesn't, and there she is . . .

One great advantage of flat characters is that they are easily recognized whenever they come in—recognized by the reader's emotional eye, not by the visual eye which merely notes the recurrence of a proper name. In Russian novels, where they so seldom occur, they would be a decided help. It is a convenience for an author when he can strike with his full force at once, and flat characters are very useful to him, since they never need reintroducing, never run away, have not to be watched for development, and provide their own atmosphere—little luminous disks of a pre-arranged size, pushed hither and thither like counters across the void or between the stars; most satisfactory.

A second advantage is that they are easily remembered by the reader afterwards. They remain in his mind as unalterable for the reason that they are not changed by circumstances; they moved through circumstances, which gives them in retrospect a comforting quality, and preserves them when the book that produced them may decay. The Countess in *Evan Harrington* furnishes a good little example here. Let us compare our memories of her with our memories of Becky Sharp. We do not remember what the Countess did or what she passed through. What is clear is her figure and the formula that surrounds it, namely, 'Proud as we are of dear Papa, we must conceal his memory'. All her rich humour proceeds from this. She is a flat character. Becky Sharp is round. She, too, is on the make, but she cannot be summed up in a single phrase, and we remember her in connection with the great scenes through which she passed and as modified by those scenes—that is to say, we do not remember her so easily because she waxes and wanes and has facets like a human being. . . .

As for the round characters proper, they have already been defined by implication and no more need be said. All I need do is to give some examples of people in books who seem to me round so that the definition can be tested afterwards:

All the principal characters in *War and Peace,* all the Dostoevsky characters, and some of the Proust—for example, the old family servant, the Duchess of Guermantes, M. de Charlus, and Saint-Loup; Madame Bovary—who, like Moll Flanders, has her book for herself, and can expand and secrete unchecked; some people in Thackeray—for instance, Becky and Beatrix; some in Fielding— Parson Adams, Tom Jones; and some in Charlotte Brontë, most particularly Lucy Snowe. (And many more, this is not a catalogue.) The test of a round character is whether it is capable of surprising in a convincing way. If it never surprises, it is flat. If it does not convince, it is flat pretending to be round. It has the incalculability of life about it—life within the pages of a book. And by using it sometimes alone more often in combination with the other kind, the novelist achieves his task of acclimatization, and harmonizes the human race with the other aspects of his work.

E. M. Forster. Aspects of the Novel (*1927*), *Chapter iv.*

ABANDONING THE 'OLD STABLE EGO'

. . . Somehow—that which is physic—non-human in humanity, is more interesting to me than the old-fashioned human element— which causes one to conceive a character in a certain moral scheme and make him consistent. The certain moral scheme is what I object to. In Turgenev, and in Tolstoy, and in Dostoevsky, the moral scheme into which all the characters fit—and it is nearly the same scheme—is, whatever the extraordinariness of the characters them-selves, dull, old, dead. When Marinetti writes: 'it is the solidity of a blade of steel that is interesting by itself, that is, the incomprehend-ing and inhuman alliance of its molecules in resistance to, let us say, a bullet. The heat of a piece of wood or iron is in fact more passion-ate, for us, than the laughter or tears of a woman'—then I know what he means. He is stupid, as an artist, for contrasting the heat of the iron and the laugh of the woman. Because what is interesting in the laugh of the woman is the same as the binding of the mole-cules of steel or their action in heat: it is the inhuman will, call it physiology, or like Marinetti, physiology of matter, that fascinates me. I don't so much care what the woman *feels*—in the ordinary usage of the word. That presumes an *ego* to feel with. I only care for what the woman *is*—what she is—inhumanly, physiologically, materially—according to the use of the word . . . You mustn't look in my novel for the old stable *ego* of the character. There is another *ego*, according to whose action the individual is unrecognizable, and passes through, as it were, allotropic states which it needs a deeper

sense than any we've been used to exercise, to discover are states
of the same single radically unchanged element. (Like as diamond
and coal are the same pure single element of carbon. The ordinary
novel would trace the history of the diamond—but I say, 'Diamond,
what! This is carbon'. And my diamond might be coal or soot, and
my theme is carbon.)

D. H. Lawrence. Letter to Edward Garnett
(5 June 1914), Letters *(1932)*.

ALL NOVELS DEAL WITH CHARACTER

I believe that all novels . . . deal with character, and that it is to
express character—not to preach doctrines, sing songs, or celebrate
the glories of the British Empire, that the form of the novel, so
clumsy, verbose, and undramatic, so rich, elastic, and alive, has
been evolved. To express character, I have said; but you will at once
reflect that the very widest interpretation can be put upon those
words . . . besides age and country there is the writer's temperament
to be considered. You see one thing in character, and I another.
You say it means this, and I that. And when it comes to writing,
each makes a further selection on principles of his own.

Virginia Woolf. 'Mr. Bennett and Mrs. Brown' (1924),
first printed in The Captain's Death Bed *(1950)*.

A CHARACTER HAS TO BE CONVENTIONALIZED

(11 September 1931) . . . I was thinking about what T. S. Eliot
and I had said about character in fiction. A character has to be
conventionalized. It must somehow form part of the pattern, or lay
the design of the book. Hence it must be conventionalized. You can't
put the whole of a character into a book, unless the book were of
inordinate length and the reader of inordinate patience. You must
select traits. You must take many traits for granted, and refer to
them, in a way to show that they are conventionalized. If you wanted
to get at a total truth you'd only get a confused picture. Question:
Does a novelist want his characters to remain in the mind of the
reader? Some novelists don't. But I do, for one. Dickens's characters
remain in the mind. They may perhaps be too conventionalized, too
simplified. Same for Thackeray—Dobbin and Amelia. But they
remain in the mind. No novelist can always be creating absolutely
new, or fresh, characters. Balzac used the same frame of conventionalization over and over again. His titled amorous dames many
of them of the same pattern. So did Shakespeare. So did Scott.

CHARACTERIZATION

This implies a form of conventionalization. Then half-critics say, when they observe the necessary conventionalization, that there is no character-drawing at all. The thing is to produce an impression on the reader—the best you can, the truest you can: but some impression. The newest despisers of form and conventionalization produce no impression at all.

Arnold Bennett. The Journals of Arnold Bennett (*1931*).

AUTHENTICITY

If I spoiled the portrait of old La Pérouse it was because I clung too closely to reality; I neither knew nor was able to lose sight of my model. The narrative of that first visit will have to be done over. La Pérouse will not come to life nor shall I really visualize him until he completely displaces his original. Nothing so far has given me so much trouble. The difficult thing is inventing when you are encumbered by memory . . .

The poor novelist constructs his characters, he controls them and makes them speak. The true novelist listens to them and watches them function; he eavesdrops on them even before he knows them. It is only according to what he hears them say that he begins to understand *who* they are.

I have put 'watches them function' second—because for me, speech tells me more than action. I think I should lose less if I went blind than if I became deaf. Nevertheless I do *see* my characters—not so much in their details as in their general effect, and even more in their actions, their gait, the rhythm of their movements. I do not worry if the lenses of my glasses fail to show them completely 'in focus'; whereas I perceive the least inflections of their voices with the greatest sharpness.

I wrote the first dialogue between Olivier and Bernard and the scenes between Passavant and Vincent without having the slightest idea what I was going to do with those characters, or even who they were. They thrust themselves upon me, despite me . . .

André Gide. Logbook of The Coiners (*1927*), *pp. 38, 44, transl. Justin O'Brien*.

Inconsistency. Characters in a novel or a play who act all the way through exactly as one expects them to . . . This consistency of theirs, which is held up to our admiration, is on the contrary the very thing which makes us recognize that they are artificially composed.

André Gide. Les Faux Monnayeurs (*1925*), *Part III, Chapter xiii, transl. Dorothy Bussy (1952)*.

IV Dialogue

STRONG LANGUAGE

That the delicate reader may not be offended at the unmeaning oaths which proceed from the mouths of some persons in these memoirs, I beg leave to premise, that I imagined nothing could more effectually expose the absurdity of such miserable expletives, than a natural and verbal representation of the discourse in which they occur.

Tobias Smollett. Preface to The Adventures of Roderick Random (*1748*).

FLAUBERT DESCRIBES HIS DIFFICULTIES TO LOUISE COLET

Yet how can one produce well-written dialogue about trivialities? But it has to be done . . .

(13 September 1852.)

How exasperated I am by my *Bovary* . . . I've never in my life written anything more difficult than these conversations full of trivialities. This scene at the inn may take me three months for all I know. I could weep sometimes, I feel so helpless . . .

(19 September 1852.)

Things have been going well for two or three days now. I'm writing a conversation between a young man and a young woman on literature, the sea, mountains, music—all the poetic subjects. It could be taken seriously but it is meant to have a clearly ludicrous effect. This will be the first time, I think, that anyone will see a book making fun of its heroine and leading man. The irony doesn't lessen the pathos; on the contrary it adds to it.

In Part 3, which will be full of farce, I want the reader to cry.

(9 October 1852.)

Bovary is driving me mad! I'm coming to the conclusion that it *can't be written*. I have to make up a conversation between my young woman and a priest, a vulgar, stupid conversation, and because the matter is so commonplace the language must be appropriate. I understand the *feeling*, but the ideas and words escape me.

(10 April 1853.)

At last I'm beginning to see my way a bit more clearly in this blessed dialogue with the priest. But honestly there are times when I could be almost *physically* sick, the stuff's so low. This is the situation I want to present: my young woman, in an access of religious feeling, goes to church; she finds the priest at the door and in a conversation (the subject not decided) he shows himself to be so stupid, empty, inept, crass, that she comes away disgusted, her religious mood dispersed. And my priest is a very good fellow, excellent even. But he only thinks about bodily ills (the sufferings of the poor, lack of food and warmth) and doesn't sense moral back-slidings or vague mystical longings; he is very chaste and practises his religious duties. This should take six or seven pages at the most, without intruded *comment* or *analysis* (all straight dialogue). More-over, since I think it low to write dialogue with dashes instead of 'he said, he answered', you can see that the repetition of the same phrases isn't easy to avoid.

(13–14 April 1853.)

This evening I've just sketched out the whole of my great scene at the agricultural show. It will be very long—thirty pages at least. In the course of describing this 'rustic-municipal' festival with all its side-issues (and *all* the minor characters of the book appear, talking and acting) I must keep up, in the foreground, the interminable conversation of a gentleman making up to a lady. In the middle of all this I also have a councillor's pompous speech and, at the end (when everything's over), a newspaper article by my chemist, who writes up the show in a fine philosophical, poetical and progressive style. You can see that all this is no light task. I'm sure of my colouring and of many of the effects; but it's the very devil to stop it being too long!

(15 July 1853.)

I had a real triumph to-day. You know that yesterday we had the *pleasure* of seeing M. Saint-Arnaud here. Well, this morning in the *Journal de Rouen* I found a sentence in the mayor's address to him

293

which was the very sentence I had written *word for word* the day before in *Bovary* (in the prefect's speech at the agricultural show). Not only were the words and the idea the same, but the very assonances were identical. I don't deny that this sort of thing gives me real pleasure.

(22 July 1853.)

Here I am, almost in the middle of my agricultural show (I've written fifteen pages this month, though they aren't finished). Is it any good? I just don't know. How difficult it is to write dialogue, especially when one wants it to possess its own *character*. To use dialogue as a means of portrayal and yet not allow it to become less vivid or precise, to give it distinction while it continues to deal with commonplaces, all this is a colossal task, and I know of no one who has managed to bring it off in a book. Dialogue should be written in the style of comedy, narrative in that of the epic . . .

You say that you are sometimes astonished at my letters, and find them well-written. There's a nice bit of malice! I write as I think in them, but what a difference there is when it comes to thinking in the way that other people may think and then making them talk! For example, I've just now been displaying, in the course of a conversation that is carried on through rain and sunshine, a certain character who has to be a good fellow and at the same time a bit vulgar and pretentious! And yet through all this the reader must nevertheless recognize that he *drives home his argument*.

(30 September 1853.)

Gustave Flaubert. Correspondance (*1903*).

RELEVANT, NATURAL, SHORT

There is no portion of a novelist's work in which this fault of episodes is so common as in the dialogue. It is so easy to make any two persons talk on any casual subject with which the writer presumes himself to be conversant! Literature, philosophy, politics, or sport, may thus be handled in a loosely discursive style; and the writer, while indulging himself and filling his pages, is apt to think that he is pleasing his reader. I think he can make no greater mistake. The dialogue is generally the most agreeable part of a novel; but it is so only so long as it tends in some way to the telling of the main story. It need not seem to be confined to that, but it should always have a tendency in that direction. The unconscious critical acumen of a reader is both just and severe. When a long dialogue on extraneous matter reaches his mind, he at once feels that he is being cheated into taking something which he did not bargain to accept when he took up that novel. He does not at that moment require politics or philosophy, but he wants his story. He will not perhaps be able to say in so many words that at some certain point the dialogue has deviated from the story; but when it does so he will feel it, and the feeling will be unpleasant. Let the intending novel-writer, if he doubt this, read one of Bulwer's novels, —in which there is very much to charm,—and then ask himself whether he has not been offended by devious conversations.

And this dialogue, on which the modern novelist in consulting the taste of his probable readers must depend much, has to be constrained also by other rules. The writer may tell much of his story in conversations, but he may do so by putting such words into the mouths of his personages as personages so situated would probably use. He is not allowed, for the sake of his tale, to make his characters give utterance to long speeches, such as are not customarily heard from men and women. The ordinary talk of ordinary people is carried on in short sharp expressive sentences, which very frequently are never completed,—the language of which even among educated people is often incorrect. The novel-writer in constructing his dialogue must so steer between absolute accuracy of language—which would give to his conversation an air of pedantry, and the slovenly inaccuracy of ordinary talkers,—which if closely followed would offend by an appearance of grimace,— as to produce upon the ear of his readers a sense of reality. If he be quite real he will seem to attempt to be funny. If he be quite correct he will seem to be unreal. And above all, let the speeches be short. No character should utter much above a dozen words at a breath,—unless the writer can justify to himself a longer flood of speech by the speciality of the occasion.

Anthony Trollope. An Autobiography (*1883*), *Chapter xii.*

ORGANIC AND DRAMATIC

. . . My idea was to be treated with light irony—it would be light and ironical or it would be nothing; so that I asked myself, naturally, what might be the least solemn form to give it, among recognized and familiar forms. The question thus at once arose: What form so familiar, so recognized among alert readers, as that in which the ingenious and inexhaustible, the charming philosophic 'Gyp' casts most of her social studies? Gyp had long struck me as mistress, in her levity, of one of the happiest of forms—the only objection to my use of which was a certain extraordinary benightedness on the part of the Anglo-Saxon reader. One had noted this reader as perverse and inconsequent in respect to the absorption of 'dialogue'—observed the 'public for fiction' consume it, in certain connexions, on the scale and with the smack of lips that mark the consumption of bread-and-jam by a children's school-feast, consume it even at the theatre, so far as our theatre ever vouchsafes it, and yet as flagrantly reject it when served, so to speak, *au naturel*. One had seen good solid slices of fiction, well endued, one might have surely thought, with this easiest of lubrications, deplored by editor and publisher as positively not, for the general gullet as known to *them*, made adequately 'slick'. ' "Dialogue," always "dialogue"!' I had seemed from far back to hear them mostly cry: 'We can't have too much of it, we can't have enough of it, and no excess of it, in the form of no matter what savourless dilution, or what boneless dispersion, ever began to injure a book so much as even the very scantest claim put in for form and substance'. This wisdom had always been in one's ears; but it had at the same time been equally in one's eyes that really constructive dialogue, dialogue organic and dramatic, speaking for itself, representing and embodying substance and form, is among us an uncanny and abhorrent thing, not to be dealt with on any terms. A comedy or a tragedy may run for a thousand nights without prompting twenty persons in London or in New York to desire that view of its text which is so desired in Paris, as soon as a play begins to loom at all large, that the number of copies of the printed piece on circulation far exceeds at last the number of performances. But as with the printed piece our own public, infatuated as it may be with the theatre, refuses all commerce—though indeed this can't but be, without cynicism, very much through the infirmity the piece, *if* printed, would reveal—so the same horror seems to attach to any typographic hint of the proscribed playbook or any insidious plea for it. The immense oddity resides in the almost exclusively typographic order of the offence. An English, an American Gyp would typographically offend, and that would be the end of her. *There* gloomed at me my warning, as well as shone at me my provocation, in respect to the example of this delightful writer. I might emulate her since I presumptuously would, but dishonour would await me if, proposing to treat the different faces of my subject in the most completely instituted colloquial form, I should evoke the figure and affirm the presence of participants by the repeated and prefixed name rather than by the recurrent and *af*fixed 'said he' and 'said she'. All I have space to go into here—much as the funny fact I refer to might seem to invite us to dance hand in hand round it—is that I was at any rate duly admonished, that I took my measures accordingly, and that the manner in which I took them has lived again for me ever so arrestingly, so amusingly, on re-examination of the book.

> *Henry James. Preface to* The Awkward Age (*1899*);
> *first printed in the New York edition of the* Novels *and*
> Stories (*1907–17*), *Vol. IX.*

FURTHER PROBLEMS

The rendering in fact of speeches gave Conrad and the writer more trouble than any other department of the novel whatever. It introduced at once the whole immense subject of under what convention the novel is to be written. For whether you tell it direct and as an author—which is the more difficult way—or whether you put it into the mouth of a character—which is easier by far but much more cumbersome—the question of reporting or rendering speeches has to be faced. To pretend that any character or any author writing directly can remember whole speeches with all their words for a matter of twenty-four hours, let alone twenty-four years, is absurd. The most that the normal person carries away of a conversation after even a couple of hours is just a salient or characteristic phrase or two, and a mannerism of the speaker . . .

One unalterable rule that we had for the rendering of conversations—for genuine conversations that are an exchange of thought, not interrogatories or statements of fact—was that no speech of one character could ever answer the speech that goes before it. This is almost invariably the case in real life where few people listen, because they are always preparing their own next speeches . . .

. . . on the whole, the indirect, interrupted method of handling interviews is invaluable for giving a sense of the complexity, the tantalization, the shimmering, the haze, that life is . . .

> *Ford Madox Ford.* Joseph Conrad, A Personal
> Remembrance (*1924*), *Part III, Section ii.*

STYLIZATION

I. C. B. I do not see why exposition and description are a necessary part of a novel. They are not of a play, and both deal with imaginary human beings and their lives. I have been told that I ought to write plays, but cannot see myself making the transition. I read plays with especial pleasure, and in reading novels I am disappointed if a scene is carried through in the voice of the author rather than the voices of the characters. I think that I simply follow my natural bent . . .

M. J. I have heard your dialogue criticized as 'highly artificial' or stylized. One reviewer, I remember, said that it was impossible to 'conceive of any human being giving tongue to every emotion, foible, and reason with the precision, clarity and wit possessed by all Miss Compton-Burnett's characters, be they parlourmaids, children, parents or spinster aunts'. It seems odd to object to precision, clarity and wit, and the same objection would lie against the dialogue of Congreve and Sheridan.

I. C. B. I think that my writing does not seem to me as 'stylized' as it apparently is, though I do not attempt to make my characters use the words of actual life. I cannot tell you why I write as I do, as I do not know. I have even tried not to do it, but find myself falling back into my own way. It seems to me that the servants in my books talk quite differently from the educated people, and the children from the adults, but the difference may remain in my own mind and not be conveyed to the reader. I think people's style, like the way they speak and move, comes from themselves and cannot be explained. . . . I cannot tell why my people talk sometimes according to conventional style, and sometimes in the manner of real speech, if this is the case. It is simply the result of an effort to give the impression I want to give.

Ivy Compton-Burnett. 'A Conversation Between I. Compton-Burnett and M. Jourdain', Orion *(1945).*

V Background

Indeed, the country around Melrose, if possessing less of romantic beauty than some other scenes in Scotland, is connected with so many associations of a fanciful nature, in which the imagination takes delight, as might well induce one even less attached to the spot than the author, to accommodate, after a general manner, the imaginary scenes he was framing to the localities to which he was partial. But it would be a misapprehension to suppose, that, because Melrose may in general pass for Kennaquhair, or because it agrees with scenes of the Monastery in the circumstances of the drawbridge, the mill-dam, and other points of resemblance, that therefore an accurate or perfect local similitude is to be found in all the particulars of the picture. It was not the purpose of the author to present a landscape copied from nature, but a piece of composition, in which a real scene, with which he is familiar, had afforded him some leading outlines. Thus the resemblance of the imaginary Glendearg with the resemblance of the real vale of the Allen, is far from being minute, nor did the author aim at indentifying them. This must appear plain to all who know the actual character of the Glen of Allen, and have taken the trouble to read the account of the imaginary Glendearg. The stream in the latter case is described as wandering down a romantic little valley, shifting itself, after the fashion of such a brook, from one side to the other, as it can most easily find its passage, and touching nothing in its progress that gives token of cultivation. It rises near a solitary tower, the abode of a supposed church vassal, and the scene of several incidents in the Romance.

The real Allen, on the contrary, after traversing the romantic ravine called the Nameless Dean, thrown off from side to side alternately, like a billiard ball repelled by the sides of the table on which it has been played, and in that part of its course resembling the stream which pours down Glendearg, may be traced upwards into a more open country, where the banks retreat further from each other, and the vale exhibits a good deal of dry ground, which has not been neglected by the active cultivators of the district. It arrives, too, at a sort of termination, striking in itself, but totally irreconcilable with the nature of the Romance. Instead of a single peel-house, or border tower of defence, such as Dame Glendinning is supposed to have inhabited, the head of the Allen, about five miles above its junction with the Tweed, shows three ruins of Border houses, belonging to different proprietors, and each from the desire of mutual support so natural to troublesome times, situated at the extremity of the property of which it is the principal messuage . . .

All these ruins, so strangely huddled together in a very solitary spot, have recollections and traditions of their own, but none of them bear the most distant resemblance to the descriptions in the Romance of the Monastery; and as the author could hardly have erred so grossly regarding a spot within a morning's ride of his own house, the inference is, that no resemblance was intended.

Sir Walter Scott. Introduction to The Monastery (*1820*).

THE SETTING OF 'WUTHERING HEIGHTS'

. . . It is rustic all through. It is moorish, and wild, and knotty as a root of heath. Nor was it natural that it should be otherwise; the author being herself a native and nursling of the moors. Doubtless, had her lot been cast in a town, her writings, if she had written at all, would have possessed another character. Even had chance or taste led her to choose a similar subject, she would have treated it otherwise. Had Ellis Bell been a lady or gentleman accustomed to what is called 'the world', her view of a remote and unclaimed region, as well as of the dwellers therein, would have differed greatly from that actually taken by the home-bred country girl. Doubtless it would have been wider—more comprehensive: whether it would have been more original or more truthful is not so certain. As far as the scenery and locality are concerned, it could scarcely have been so sympathetic: Ellis Bell did not describe as one whose eye and taste alone found pleasure in the prospect; her native hills were far more to her than a spectacle; they were what she lived in, and by, as much as the wild birds, their tenants, or as the heather, their produce. Her descriptions, then, of natural scenery, are what they should be, and all they should be.

Charlotte Brontë. Preface to the 1850 edition of
Wuthering Heights (*1847*).

TOO MUCH BACKGROUND

. . . It is the habit of my imagination to strive after as full a vision of the medium in which a character moves as of the character itself. The psychological causes which prompted me to give such details of Florentine life and history as I have given, are precisely the same as those which determined me in giving the details of English Village life in *Silas Marner*, or the 'Dodson' life, out of which were developed the destinies of poor Tom and Maggie. But you have correctly pointed out the reason why my tendency to excess in this effort after artistic vision makes the impression of a fault in *Romola* much more perceptibly than in my previous books.

> *George Eliot. Letter to R. H. Hutton (8 August 1863), from* George Eliot's Life as related in her Letters and Journals (*1884*), *ed. J. W. Cross.*

A NEW ENGLISH COUNTY

Of *Framley Parsonage* I need only further say, that as I wrote it I became more closely acquainted than ever with the new shire which I had added to the English counties. I had it all in my mind, —its roads and railways, its towns and parishes, its members of Parliament, and the different hunts which rode over it. I knew all the great lords and their castles, the squires and their parks, the rectors and their churches. This was the fourth novel of which I had placed the scene in Barsetshire, and as I wrote it I made a map of the dear county. Throughout these stories there has been no name given to a fictitious site which does not represent to me a spot of which I know all the accessories, as though I had lived and wandered there.

> *Anthony Trollope.* An Autobiography (*1883*), *Chapter viii.*

WESSEX

. . . it was in the chapters of *Far from the Madding Crowd*, as they appeared month by month in a popular magazine, that I first ventured to adopt the word 'Wessex' from the pages of early English history, and give it a fictitious significance as the existing name of the district once included in that extinct kingdom. The series of novels I projected being mainly of the kind called local, they seemed to require a territorial definition of some sort to lend unity to their scene. Finding that the area of a single county did not afford a canvas large enough for this purpose, and that there were objections

to an invented name, I disinterred the old one. The region desig-
nated was known but vaguely, and I was often asked even by
educated people where it lay. However, the press and the public
were kind enough to welcome the fanciful plan, and willingly joined
me in the anchronism of imagining a Wessex population living under
Queen Victoria;—a modern Wessex of railways, the penny post,
mowing and reaping machines, union workhouses, lucifer matches,
labourers who could read and write, and National school children.
But I believe I am correct in stating that, until the existence of this
contemporaneous Wessex in place of the usual counties was announced in the present story, in 1874, it had never been heard of in
fiction and current speech, if at all, and that the expression, 'a
Wessex peasant', or 'a Wessex custom', would therefore have been
taken to refer to nothing later in date than the Norman Conquest . . .

Since then the appellation which I had thought to reserve to the
horizons and landscapes of a partly real, partly dream-country, has
become more and more popular as a practical provincial definition;
and the dream-country has, by degrees, solidified into a utilitarian
region which people can go to, take a house in, and write to the
papers from. But I ask all good and idealistic readers to forget this,
and to refuse steadfastly to believe that there are any inhabitants of
a Victorian Wessex outside these volumes in which their lives and
conversations are detailed.

> *Thomas Hardy. Preface to* Far *from the Madding Crowd*
> (*1874*).

THE SCIENTIFIC IMPORTANCE OF BACKGROUND

I also attach considerable importance to environment. Here we
should touch on Darwinian theory; but this is intended only as a
general study of the experimental method as applied to the novel
and I should lose my way if I were to go into detail. I shall only
say a few words about settings. We've just seen the great importance
that Claude Bernard attaches to the study of 'intra-organic' environment, an element which has to be taken into account if one wishes
to discover the determinism of events in living beings. Well now, in
the study of a family, or group of living beings, I believe that the
social environment has a similar capital importance. Some day in the
future physiology will doubtless be able to explain the mechanism of
thought and emotion. We shall know how the individual 'machinery'
works, how a man thinks, loves, and swings from rationality through
passion to madness; but these phenomena . . . do not appear in
isolation from what is going on around them, that is to say in a

vacuum. Man is not alone but exists in society, in a social environment, and so far as we novelists are concerned, this environment is constantly modifying events. That is just where our real task lies, in studying the interaction of society on the individual and of the individual on society. For the physiologist, environment—whether external or internal—is purely chemical and physical, which makes it easy for him to determine its laws. On the other hand, we are in no position to prove that the *social* environment is only chemical and physical. It is that, certainly, or at any rate it is made with all its variations by a group of living beings who are themselves entirely subject to the physical and chemical laws that govern dead and living matter. Once we grasp this, we see that social environment will be affected by our manipulation of all those human phenomena we learn to control. And in this direction lies all that constitutes the experimental novel: mastery of the mechanism of human events: demonstration of the way in which intellectual and sensory processes, as explained to us by physiology, are conditioned by heredity and environment; and finally portrayal of the human being in the environment which he himself has made and alters daily, and in the midst of which he in his turn undergoes continual transformation. And thus it is that we look to physiology for guidance, taking the isolated individual from the physiologist's hands in order to carry research further by solving scientifically the problem of how men behave once they become members of a society.

Emile Zola. '*Le Roman Expérimental*', *Chapter ii*,
Le Roman Expérimental (*1880*).

MAP AND ALMANACK

It is, perhaps, not often that a map figures so largely in a tale, yet it is always important. The author must know his countryside, whether real or imaginary, like his hand; the distances, the points of the compass, the place of the sun's rising, the behaviour of the moon, should all be beyond cavil. And how troublesome the moon is! I have come to grief over the moon in *Prince Otto*, and so soon as that was pointed out to me, adopted a precaution which I recommend to other men—I never write now without an almanack. With an almanack, and the map of the country, and the plan of every house, either actually plotted on paper or already and immediately apprehended in the mind, a man may hope to avoid some of the grossest possible blunders. With the map before him, he will scarce allow the sun to set in the east, as it does in *The Antiquary*. With the almanack at hand, he will scarce allow two horsemen, journeying on the most urgent affair, to employ six days, from three of the Monday morning till late in the Saturday night, upon a journey of, say, ninety or a hundred miles, and before the week is out, and still on the same nags, to cover fifty in one day, as may be read at length in the inimitable novel of *Rob Roy*. And it is certainly well, though far from necessary, to avoid such 'croppers'. But it is my contention —my superstition, if you like—that who is faithful to his map, and consults it, and draws from it his inspiration, daily and hourly, gains positive support, and not mere negat've immunity from accident. The tale has a root there; it grows in that soil; it has a spine of its own behind the words. Better if the country be real, and he has walked every foot of it and knows every milestone. But even with imaginary places, he will do well in the beginning to provide a map; as he studies it, relations will appear that he had not thought upon; he will discover obvious, though unsuspected, shortcuts and footprints for his messengers; and even when a map is not all the plot, as it was in *Treasure Island*, it will be found to be a mine of suggestion.

Robert Louis Stevenson. 'My First Book' (1894); reprinted in The Art of Writing (*1919*).

THE SELECTION OF TELLING DETAIL

In my opinion descriptions of nature should be very brief and have an incidental character. Commonplaces like: 'The setting sun, bathing in the waves of the darkening sea, flooded with purple and gold', etc . . . 'The swallows, flying over the surface of the water, chirped merrily'—such commonplaces should be finished with. In descriptions of Nature one has to snatch at small details, grouping them in such a manner that after reading them one can obtain the picture on closing one's eyes.

For instance, you will get a moonlight night if you write that on the dam of the mill a fragment of broken bottle flashed like a small bright star, and there rolled by, like a ball, the black shadow of a dog, or a wolf—and so on. Nature appears animated if you do not disdain to use comparisons of its phenomena with those of human actions, etc.

The same, too, in the sphere of psychology.

Anton Chekhov. Letter to his brother (10 May 1886), Life and Letters (*1925*), *transl. and ed. S. S. Koteliansky and Philip Tomlinson.*

HENRY JAMES FOLLOWS THE WRONG MASTER

Pathetic . . . the manner in which the evocation, so far as attempted, of the small New England town of my first two chapters [of *Roderick Hudson*] fails of intensity . . . To name a place, in fiction, is to pretend in some degree to represent it—and I speak here of course but of the use of existing names, the only ones that carry weight—so at least I supposed; but obviously I was wrong, since my effort lay, so superficially, and could only lie, in the local *type*, as to which I had my handful of impressions. The particular local case was another matter, and I was to see again, after long years, the case into which, all recklessly, the opening passages of *Roderick Hudson* put their foot . . . But one nestled, technically, in those days, and with yearning, in the great shadow of Balzac; his august example, little as the secret might ever be guessed, towered for me over the scene; so that what was clearer than anything else was how, if it was a question of Saumur, of Limoges, of Guérande, he 'did' Saumur, did Limoges, did Guérande. I remember how, in my feebler fashion, I yearned over the preliminary presentation of my small square patch of the American scene, and yet was not sufficiently on my guard to see how easily his high practice might be delusive for my case. Balzac talked of Nemours and Provins: therefore why shouldn't one, with fond fatuity, talk of almost the only small American *ville de province* of which one had happened to lay up, long before, a pleased vision? The reason was plain; one was not in the least, in one's prudence, emulating his systematic closeness. It didn't confuse the question either that he would verily, after all, addressed as he was to a due density in his material, have found little enough in Northampton, Mass. to tackle. He tackled no group of appearances, no presented face of the so-called organism (conspicuity thus attending it), *but* to make something of it. To name it simply and not in some degree tackle it would have seemed to him an act reflecting on his general course the deepest dishonour. Therefore it was that, as the moral of these many remarks, I 'named', under his contagion, when I was really most conscious of not being held to it; and therefore it was, above all, that for all the effect of representation I was to achieve, I might have let the occasion pass. A 'fancy' indication would have served my turn—except that I should so have failed perhaps of a pretext for my present insistence.

Henry James. Preface to Roderick Hudson *(1876), first printed in the New York edition of the* Novels and Stories *(1907–17), Vol. I.*

PURSUING THE GUERMANTES' WAY

. . . And with Mme. de Guermantes, was transformed simultaneously her dwelling, itself also the offspring of that name, fertilised from year to year by some word or other that came to my ears and modulated the tone of my musings; that dwelling of hers reflected them in its very stones, which had turned to mirrors, like the surface of a cloud or of a lake. A dungeon keep without mass, no more indeed than a band of orange light from the summit of which the lord and his lady dealt out life and death to their vassals, had given place—right at the end of the 'Guermantes way' along which on so many summer afternoons, I retraced with my parents the course of the Vivonne—to that land of bubbling streams where the Duchess taught me to fish for trout and to know the names of the flowers whose red and purple clusters adorned the walls of the neighbouring gardens; then it had been the ancient heritage, famous in song and story, from which the proud race of Guermantes, like a carved and mellow tower that traverses the ages, had risen already over France when the sky was still empty at those points where, later, were to rise Notre Dame of Paris and Notre Dame of Chartres, when on the summit of the hill of Laon the nave of its cathedral had not yet been poised, like the Ark of the Deluge on the summit of Mount Ararat, crowded with Patriarchs and Judges anxiously leaning from its windows to see whether the wrath of God were yet appeased, carrying with it the types of the vegetation that was to multiply on the earth, brimming over with animals which have escaped even by the towers, where oxen grazing calmly upon the roof look down over the plains of Champagne; when the traveller who left Beauvais at the close of the day did not yet see, following him and turning with his road, outspread against the gilded screen of the western sky, the black, ribbed wings of the cathedral. It was, this 'Guermantes', like the scene of a novel, an imaginary landscape which I could with difficulty picture to myself and longed all the more to discover, set in the midst of real lands and roads which all of a sudden would become alive with heraldic details, within a few miles of a railway station; I recalled the names of the places round it as if they had been situated at the foot of Parnassus or of Helicon, and they seemed precious to me, as the physical conditions—in the realm of topographical science—required for the production of an unaccountable phenomenon. I saw again the escutcheons blazoned beneath the windows of Cambray church; their quarters filled, century after century, with all the lordships which, by marriage or conquest, this illustrious house had brought flying to it from all the corners of Germany, Italy and France; vast territories in the North, strong cities in the South, assembled there to group themselves in Guermantes, and, losing their material quality, to inscribe allegorically their dungeon vert, or castle triple-towered argent upon its azure field.

> *Marcel Proust.* The Guermantes Way (*1920*), *Chapter I, transl. C. K. Scott Moncrieff* (*1925*).

BACKGROUND REDUCED TO A MINIMUM

M. J. There is little attention to external things and almost no descriptive writing in your novels, and that is a breach with tradition. Even Jane Austen has an aside about the 'worth' of Lyme, Charmouth and Pinhay, 'with its green chasms between romantic rocks'. And there is much more description in later novels, such as Thomas Hardy's. In *The Return of the Native*, the great Egdon Heath has to be reckoned with as a protagonist. Now you cut out all this. The Gavestons' house in *A Family and a Fortune* is spoken of as old and beautiful, but its date and style are not mentioned.

I. C. B. I should have thought that my actual characters were described enough to help people to imagine them. However detailed such description is, I am sure that everyone forms his own conceptions, that are different from everyone else's, including the author's. As regards such things as landscape and scenery, I never feel inclined to describe them; indeed I tend to miss such writing out, when I am reading, which may be a sign that I am not fitted for it. I make an exception of Thomas Hardy, but surely his presentation of natural features almost as characters puts him on a plane of his own, and almost carries the thing into the human world. In the case of Jane Austen, I hurry through her words about Lyme and its surroundings, in order to return to her people.

It might be better to give more account of people's homes and intimate background, but I hardly see why the date and style of the Gavestons' house should be given, as I did not think of them as giving their attention to it, and as a house of a different date and style would have done for them equally well. It would be something to them that it was old and beautiful, but it would be enough.

> *Ivy Compton-Burnett.* 'A Conversation Between I. Compton-Burnett and M. Jourdain', Orion (*1945*).

VI Style

THE JUDGMENT OF STYLE

. . . there is no branch of criticism in which learning as well as good sense, is more required than to the forming an accurate judgment of style, though there is none, I believe, in which every trifling reader is more ready to give his decision.

> Henry Fielding. *Preface to Sarah Fielding's* Familiar Letters . . . (*1747*).

RICHARDSON'S STYLE

The style of Richardson, which it remains to take notice of, was not in proportion to his other excellencies of composition. He wrote with facility; expressions, as well as thoughts, flowing readily to his pen; but we do not find in his writings, either the ease and elegance of good company, or the polished period of a finished author. They are not only overloaded with a redundance of complimentary expression, which gives a stiffness to the dialogue, particularly in his Grandison, where he has most attempted to give a picture of genteel life, but they are blemished with little flippancies of expression, new coined words, and sentences involved and ill-constructed. One of his correspondents, a Mr. Read, after giving him high and just praise, thus expresses himself: 'But is there not here and there a nursery phrase, an ill-invented uncouth compound; a parenthesis, which interrupts, not assists, the sense? If I am wrong, impute it to the rudeness of a college-man, who has had too little commerce with the world, to be a judge of its language'. If this was considered to be the case when Richardson wrote, it is a still greater impediment to his fame at present, when we are become more fastidious with regard to style, in proportion as good writing is become more common; that degree, I mean, of good writing, which a habit of the pen will always give. The style of Richardson, however, has the property of setting before the reader, in the most lively manner, every circumstance of what he means to describe. He has the accuracy and finish of a Dutch painter, with the fine ideas of an Italian one. He is content to produce effects by the patient labour of minuteness. Had he turned his thoughts to an observation of rural nature, instead of human manners, he would have been as accurate a describer as Cowper: how circumstantial is the following description of a bird new caught! 'Hast thou not observed how, at first, refusing all sustenance, it beats and bruises itself against its wires, till it makes its gay plumage fly about, and overspread its well-secured cage. Now it gets out its head, sticking only at its beautiful shoulders; then, with difficulty, drawing back its head, it gasps for breath, and erectly perched, with meditating eyes, first surveys, and then attempts, its wired canopy. As it gets breath, with renewed rage, it beats and bruises again its pretty head and sides, bites the wires, and pecks at the fingers of its delighted tamer; till, at last, finding its efforts ineffectual, quite tired and breathless, it lays itself down, and pants at the bottom of the cage, seeming to bemoan its cruel fate, and forfeited liberty. And, after a few days, its struggles to escape still diminishing, as it finds it to no purpose to attempt it, its new habitation becomes familiar, and it hops about from perch to perch, and every day sings a song to amuse itself, and reward its keeper.'

> *Anna Laetitia Barbauld. 'A biographical account of Samuel Richardson', The Correspondence of Samuel Richardson (1804), Vol. I.*

THE VOICE OF TRUE FEELING IN EPISTOLARY NARRATIVE

N. What an epistolary style! how strained! what exclamations! what affectation! what emphasis to express nothing but commonplaces! what big words for little ideas! hardly any sense or precision; no subtlety, power or depth. The language perpetually high-flown, the ideas perpetually uninspired. If your characters really do belong to the natural world, you have to admit that their style is anything but natural.

R. I agree that from where you stand it may seem so.

N. Do you think that the public is likely to see it differently? and isn't it my opinion that you want?

R. It is to know it more fully that I'm answering you. I see that you would prefer letters written with an eye to publication.

N. The desire seems reasonable enough for letters that one intends to print.

R. So we are never to see human beings in books other than as they wish to appear?

N. The author as he wishes to appear; the people whom he portrays as they are. But even that merit is wanting here. Not a single vigorously defined portrait, not one sufficiently distinctive character, no concrete observation, no knowledge of the world. What are we to learn from a tiny circle of two or three lovers or friends who are always exclusively preoccupied with themselves?

R. We learn to love human beings. In great societies we only learn to hate people.

Your judgment is severe; that of the public, then, will be even more so. Without taxing it with injustice, I want in my turn to tell you how I look on these letters—less to excuse the faults which you blame them for than to discover their cause.

In retirement people acquire ways of seeing and feeling different from those in their dealings with the world; emotions, altered likewise, are likewise differently expressed: the imagination is constantly engaged by the same unchanging objects and so is more vividly affected by them. These few impressions recur again and again, mingling themselves with every idea and giving it that eccentric, rather monotonous style that we notice in the conversation of the recluse. Does it follow from this that his language is forcefully energetic? Not at all; it is merely out of the ordinary. It is only in society that one learns to talk energetically. First, because one must always talk differently from all the others and also better than them; and second, since people are obliged to keep on saying things they don't mean and expressing feelings they don't possess, they try to give what they say an expressive persuasiveness which will make up for lack of inner conviction. Do you believe that people who are genuinely moved speak in the vital, powerful, colourful way that you admire in your plays and novels? No; genuine emotion is completely self-absorbed and expresses itself copiously rather than forcefully: it doesn't even intend to be persuasive—it has no suspicion that anyone would doubt its truth. When it says what it feels it is less to communicate this feeling than to relieve it. People portray love more vividly in the big cities: do they feel it more intensely there than in villages?

N. This implies that poverty of language signifies strength of feeling.

R. Sometimes, at any rate, it shows its genuineness. Read a love-letter composed in his study by some author, some fine wit, who wants to scintillate: however little real fire he has in his head, his pen, as they say, scorches the paper; the warmth goes no further: you will be charmed, possibly even moved—but by an

ephemeral, sterile emotion which leaves you only words to remember. On the other hand, a letter genuinely inspired by love,
a letter written by a truly passionate lover, will be slip-shod,
diffuse, long-winded, disorganized and full of repetitions. His
heart, filled and overflowing with emotion, says the same thing
over and over again and never finishes saying it, like a living
spring which flows ceaselessly without exhausting itself. Nothing
outstanding, nothing remarkable; there are no resounding words
or turns of phrase or sentences. And yet our heart softens, we are
touched without knowing why. If we are not impressed by the
strength of the feeling we are moved by its sincerity . . .

To come back to our letters. If you read them as the work of
an author who is anxious to please or who prides himself on his
writing they are execrable. Take them, however, for what they are
and judge them according to their kind. Two or three simple, but
sensitive, young people keep up among themselves a correspondence about their heart's deepest interests; they have no intention
of dazzling each other; they know and like each other so much
that there is no place for self-conceit among them. As youngsters
are they likely to think things out like grown men and women?
As foreigners, are they likely to write correctly? As solitaries, are
they likely to know the ways of the world and of society? Full of
the one feeling that absorbs them, they are filled with ecstasy
and imagine that they are philosophizing. Do you expect them to
observe, to judge, to reflect? They don't know how to do any of
these things: they know how to love; they relate everything to
their passion. Is the importance which they attach to their extravagant notions any less entertaining than all the wit that they
might display? . . .

> *Jean-Jacques Rousseau. Preface (1762) to* La Nouvelle
> Héloise *(1760)*.

JANE AUSTEN BECOMES SELF-CONSCIOUS

. . I wish the knowledge of my being exposed to her discerning
Criticism,[1] may not hurt my stile, by inducing too great a solicitude.
I begin already to weigh my words and sentences more than I did,
and am looking about for a sentiment, an illustration or a metaphor
in every corner of the room. Could my ideas flow as fast as the rain
in the Store Closet it would be charming.

> *Jane Austen. Letter to Cassandra Austen, January 24, 1809,*
> Letters *(1932)*.

[1] The reference is to Fanny Knight.

CLEAR AND SIMPLE

. . . I agree with all you say, except about style. Pray do not think that this is overweening conceit. I know of only one rule: style cannot be too *clear*, too *simple* . . . Ever since 1802 I have thought M. de Chateaubriand's 'fine style' ridiculous. It seems to me to give expression to a number of falsehoods . . .

I read very little. When I read for pleasure, I pick up the *Mémoires* of Marshal Gouvion Saint-Cyr. He is my Homer. I often read Ariosto. There are only two books that give me a sense of 'good writing': Fénelon's *Dialogues des Morts*, and Montesquieu.

I detest the style of M. Villemain, for example, which seems to me adapted only to the polite utterance of insults.

The essence of my trouble is that the style of Jean-Jacques Rousseau, M. Villemain or Mme Sand seems to me to say many things that *should not be said*, and often tells many actual falsehoods. There, the big word has slipped out.

Often I ponder a quarter of an hour whether to place an adjective before or after its noun. I seek (1) to be truthful, (2) clear in my accounts of what happens in a human heart.

I think that since a year ago I have realized that one must sometimes give the reader a rest by describing landscape, clothes, etc.

> Stendhal. *Letter to Balzac (30 October 1840), first draft,* Selected Letters, *transl. Norman Cameron (1952).*

Whilst writing the Chartreuse, in order to acquire the correct tone I occasionally read a few pages of the *Code Civil* . . . If I am not clear, all 'my world' is annihilated. I want to describe what happens in the depth of the souls of Mosca, the Duchess and Clélia. 'Tis a region scarcely penetrable by the gaze of the newly rich, of people like the Latinist Director of the Mint, M. le comte Roy, M. Lafitte, etc., etc.,—the gaze of grocers, good paterfamilias, etc., etc., . . .

If to the obscurity of the subject, I add the stylish obscurities of M. Villemain, Mme Sand, etc. (supposing that I had the rare privilege of writing like these coryphées of the grand style)—if to the fundamental difficulty I add the obscurities of this much vaunted style—absolutely nobody will understand the Duchess's struggle against Ernest IV.

> Stendhal. *Second draft of the same letter, ibid.*

FLAUBERT ON THE ART OF WRITING

. . . I've imagined a style for myself—a beautiful style that someone will write some day, in ten years' time maybe, or in ten centuries.

It will be as rhythmical as verse and as precise as science, with the booming rise and fall of a cello and plumes of fire; it will be a style which penetrates the idea for you like a dagger-thrust and from which at last thought is sent sailing over smooth surfaces as a boat glides rapidly before a good wind. Prose was born yesterday—this is what we must tell ourselves. Poetry is pre-eminently the medium of past literatures. All the metrical combinations have been tried but nothing like this can be said of prose.

> *Gustave Flaubert. Letter to Louis Colet (24 April 1852),* Correspondance (*1900*).

. . . I'm re-reading some Boileau now, or rather all of Boileau, and making numerous pencil marks in the margin. It seems to me genuinely strong. One never tires of anything that is well written. Style is life! Indeed it is the life-blood of thought! Boileau was a little river, narrow and not very deep, but beautifully clear and well embanked. That's why his waters never run dry. Nothing of what he wants to say is lost. But how much Art he needed for this, with such scant material too. For the next two or three years, I am going to re-read carefully, in this way, *all* the French classics and annotate them, a task which will come in useful for my *Prefaces* (my work of literary criticism) . . . I shall try to show why aesthetic criticism has remained so far behind historical and scientific criticism: it *had no foundation*. The knowledge everyone lacked was *analysis of style*, the understanding of how a phrase is constructed and articulated. People study lifeless models or translations, following teachers who are dolts incapable of wielding the scientific instrument they teach—I mean the pen—and life is missing, and love—love, the divine secret which does not give itself away—and soul, without which nothing can be understood.

> *Gustave Flaubert. Letter to Louise Colet (7 September 1853),* Correspondance (*1900*).

. . . You say that I pay too much attention to form. Alas! it is like body and soul: form and content to me are one; I don't know what either is without the other. The finer the idea, be sure, the finer-sounding the sentence. The exactness of the thought makes for (and is itself) that of the word.

If I can't make anything out just now, if everything I write is empty and flat, this is because I am not shaken with the emotions of my chief characters . . . 'If you have faith you will move mountains' is also the principle of the Beautiful. It can be translated more prosaically: 'If you know exactly what you want to say, you will say it well'.

> Gustave Flaubert. Letter to Mademoiselle Leroyer de Chantepie, (*12 December 1857*), Correspondance (*1903*).

... This care for external beauty which you reproach me with is a *method* with me. When I find that my sentences contain ugly assonance or repetition then I'm sure I am floundering in falsities. By dint of looking, I discover the right expression, which is by the same token the only one that is at the same time possible and also harmonious.

> Gustave Flaubert. Letter to George Sand (*between 10 and 14 March 1876*), Correspondance (*1899*).

A PROTEST

... you seek for nothing more than the well-made sentence, it is something—but only something—it isn't the whole of art, it isn't even the half of it, it's a quarter at most, and, when the other three quarters are beautiful, people will overlook the one that isn't.

> George Sand. Letter to Gustave Flaubert (*9 March 1876*), Correspondance (*1892*).

THE FAMILIAR STYLE

I can well imagine that you find *The Mill* more difficult to render than *Adam*. But would it be inadmissible to represent in French, at least in some degree, those 'intermédiaires entre le style commun et le style elegant' to which you refer? It seems to me that I have discerned such shades very strikingly rendered in Balzac, and occasionally in George Sand. Balzac, I think, dares to be thoroughly colloquial, in spite of French strait-lacing. Even in English this daring is far from being general. The writers who dare to be thoroughly familiar are Shakespeare, Fielding, Scott (where he is expressing the popular life with which he is familiar), and indeed every other writer of fiction of the first class. Even in his loftiest tragedies—in Hamlet, for example—Shakespeare is intensely colloquial. One hears the very accent of living men.

> George Eliot. Letter to François D'Albert Durade (*29 January 1861*), Letters (*1954*).

BYRON A MODEL

. . . I don't attempt the style of Addison because I hardly think it worth while. Addison was a neat but trivial writer, not in the least vigorous or dramatic; but the very reverse—analytical and painfully minute. His style bears about as much resemblance to good strong nervous English as silver filigree does to a bronze statue. Lord Byron's letters are the best English I know of—perfectly simple and clear, bright and strong . . . I think so much of sound that, when I do not like the look of a sentence, I read it aloud, and alter it till I can read it easier.

Wilkie Collins. Interview in The World (*26 December 1877*).

HOW TO BE INTELLIGIBLE AND HARMONIOUS

The language in which the novelist is to put forth his story, the colours with which he is to paint his picture, must of course be to him a matter of much consideration. Let him have all other possible gifts,—imagination, observation, erudition, and industry,—they will avail him nothing for his purpose, unless he can put forth his work in pleasant words. If he be confused, tedious, harsh, or un-harmonious, readers will certainly reject him. The reading of a volume of history or on science may represent itself as a duty; and though the duty may by a bad style be made very disagreeable, the conscientious reader will perhaps perform it. But the novelist will be assisted by no such feeling. Any reader may reject his work without the burden of a sin. It is the first necessity of his position that he make himself pleasant. To do this, much more is necessary than to write correctly. He may indeed be pleasant without being correct,—as I think can be proved by the works of more than one distinguished novelist. But he must be intelligible,—intelligible without trouble; and he must be harmonious.

Any writer who has read even a little will know what is meant by the word intelligible. It is not sufficient that there be a meaning which may be hammered out of the sentence, but that the language should be so pellucid that the meaning should be rendered without an effort to the reader;—and not only some proportion of the mean-ing, but the very sense, no more and no less, which the writer has intended to put into his words. What Macaulay says should be remembered by all writers: 'How little the all-important art of making meaning pellucid is studied now! Hardly any popular author except myself thinks of it'. The language used should be as ready and as efficient a conductor of the mind of the writer to the mind of the reader as is the electric spark which passes from one battery to another battery. In all written matter the spark should carry everything; but in matters recondite the recipient will search to see that he misses nothing, and that he takes nothing away too much. The novelist cannot expect that any such search will be made. A young writer, who will acknowledge the truth of what I am saying, will often feel himself tempted by the difficulties of language to tell himself that some one little doubtful passage, some single collocation of words, which is not quite what it ought to be, will not matter. I know well what a stumbling-block such a passage may be. But he should leave none such behind him as he goes on. The habit of writing clearly soon comes to the writer who is a severe critic to himself.

As to that harmonious expression which I think is required, I shall find it more difficult to express my meaning. It will be granted, I think, by readers that a style may be rough, and yet both forcible and intelligible; but it will seldom come to pass that a novel written in a rough style will be popular,—and less often that a novelist who habitually uses such a style will become so. The harmony which is required must come from the practice of the ear. There are few ears naturally so dull that they cannot, if time be allowed them, decide whether a sentence, when read, be or be not harmonious. And the sense of such harmony grows on the ear, when the intelligence has once informed itself as to what is, and what is not harmonious . . . But, in order that familiarity may serve him in his business, [the writer] must so train his ear that he shall be able to weigh the rhythm of every word as it falls from his pen. This, when it has been done for a time, even for a short time, will become so habitual to him that he will have appreciated the metrical duration of every syllable before it shall have dared to show itself upon paper. The art of the orator is the same. He knows beforehand how each sound which he is about to utter will affect the force of his climax. If a writer will do so he will charm his readers, though his readers will probably not know how they have been charmed.

Anthony Trollope. Autobiography (*1883*), *Chapter xii.*

NATURALISM AND THE GRAND STYLE

. . . For the writer, genius is not to be found only in the feeling, in the *a priori* idea, it is also in the form and style. But the question of method and the question of rhetoric are separate. And naturalism, I say it again, consists solely in the experimental method, in observation and experience as applied to literature. Rhetoric, for the moment, has no place here. Let us first establish the method—which must become universal—then accept in literature all those kinds of rhetoric that emerge; let us regard them as an expression of the writer's literary temperament.

If you want my plain opinion, it is that an exaggerated importance is attached to form now-a-days. It would take a long time to discuss this subject. Fundamentally, I consider that method itself achieves form, that a language is nothing other than a logic, a natural and scientific construction. He who writes best is not the man who wanders wildly among theories, but the man who goes straight to the heart of truths. We are in fact rotten with lyricism; we believe, quite wrongly, that the grand style is the product of some sublime terror always on the verge of pitching over into frenzy; the grand style is achieved through logic and clarity.

> *Emile Zola. 'Le Roman Expérimental', Chapter v,*
> Le Roman Expérimental (*1880*).

EXACTNESS

Whatever you want to say, there is only one word to express it, one verb to set it in motion and only one adjective to describe it. And so you must hunt for this word, this verb and this adjective until you find them and never be content with any approximations, never fall back on verbal trickery and clownishness, however apt, in order to evade the difficulty.

It is possible to convey and demonstrate the most subtle notions by following this quotation from Boileau:

A word in its place is a symbol of strength

In order to catch the various shades of thought there is no need of the eccentric vocabulary, complicated, elaborate and exotic, which they impose on us now-a-days under the guise of artistic style; but it is necessary to distinguish with extreme clarity all the shifts in value which a word undergoes according to the place it occupies. Let us have fewer nouns, verbs and adjectives whose sense it is almost impossible to grasp, but more varied phrases, diversified in construction, ingeniously broken up, full of resonance and cunning rhythms. Let us try to make ourselves excellent stylists rather than collectors of uncommon terms.

It is, indeed, more difficult to handle a sentence to one's liking, to make it say everything, even what it doesn't put into words, to invest it with implications, with intentions concealed and not formulated, than to invent new expressions or to re-discover, in the depths

317

of old volumes, all those whose usage and meaning we have forgotten and which are virtually dead words for us.

Guy de Maupassant. 'Le Roman,' introduction to Pierre et Jean (*1888*).

ON NOT HAVING TOO MUCH STYLE

Read again Addison, Macaulay, Newman, Sterne, Defoe, Lamb, Gibbon, Burke, *Times* leaders, etc., in a study of style. Am more and more confirmed in an idea I have long held, as a matter of common sense, long before I thought of any old aphorism bearing on the subject: 'Ars est celare artem'. The whole secret of a living style and the difference between it and a dead style, lies in not having too much style—being in fact a little careless, or rather seeming to be, here and there. It brings wonderful life into the writing:

A sweet disorder in the dress . . .
A careless shoe-string, in whose tie
I see a wild civility,
Do more bewitch me than when art
Is too precise in every part.

Otherwise your style is like worn half-pence—all the fresh images rounded off by rubbing, and no crispness at all.

It is, of course, simply a carrying into prose the knowledge I have acquired in poetry—that inexact rhymes and rhythms now and then are far more pleasing than correct ones.

Thomas Hardy. Notebook entry (March 1875) from The Early Life of Thomas Hardy, 1840–1891 (*1928*), Chapter vii.

AN ELEGANT AND PREGNANT TEXTURE

Style is synthetic; and the artist, seeking, so to speak, a peg to plait about, takes up at once two or more elements or two or more views of the subject in hand; combines, implicates, and contrasts them; and while, in one sense, he was merely seeking an occasion for the necessary knot, he will be found, in the other, to have greatly enriched the meaning, or to have transacted the work of two sentences in the space of one. In the change from the successive shallow statements of the old chronicler to the dense and luminous flow of highly synthetic narrative, there is implied a vast amount of both philosophy and wit. The philosophy we clearly see, recognizing in the synthetic writer a far more deep and stimulating view of life, and a far keener sense of the generation and affinity of events. The wit we might imagine to be lost; but it is not so, for it is just that wit, these perpetual nice contrivances, these difficulties overcome, this double purpose attained, these two oranges kept simultaneously dancing in the air, that, consciously or not, afford the reader his delight. Nay, and this wit, so little recognized, is the necessary organ of that philosophy which we so much admire. That style is therefore the most perfect, not, as fools say, which is the most natural, for the most natural is the disjointed babble of the chronicler; but which attains the highest degree of elegant and pregnant implication unobtrusively; or if obtrusively, then with the greatest gain to sense and vigour. Even the derangement of the phrases from their (so-called) natural order is luminous for the mind; and it is by the means of such designed reversal that the elements of a judgment may be most pertinently marshalled, or the stages of a complicated action most perspicuously bound into one.

The web, then, or the pattern; a web at once sensuous and logical, an elegant and pregnant texture: that is style, that is the foundation of the art of literature.

> *Robert Louis Stevenson. 'On some technical Elements of Style in Literature' (1885); reprinted in* The Art of Writing *(1919).*

THE CRAFT OF WRITING

You do not leave enough to the imagination. I do not mean as to facts—the facts cannot be too explicitly stated; I am alluding simply to the phrasing. True, a man who knows so much (without taking into account the manner in which his knowledge was acquired) may well spare himself the trouble of meditating over the words, only that words, groups of words, words standing alone, are symbols of life, have the power in their sound or their aspect to present the very thing you wish to hold up before the mental vision of your readers. The things 'as they are' exist in words; therefore words should be handled with care lest the picture, the image of truth abiding in facts, should become distorted—or blurred.

These are the considerations for a mere craftsman—you may say; and you may also conceivably say that I have nothing else to trouble my head about. However the *whole* of the truth lies in the presentation; therefore the expression should be studied in the interest of veracity. This is the only morality of *art* apart from *subject*.

I have travelled a good way from my original remark—not enough left to the imagination in the phrasing. I beg leave to illustrate my meaning from extracts. . . . 'When the whole horror

319

of his position forced itself with an agony of apprehension upon his frightened mind, Pa'Tûa for a space lost his reason.' . . . In this sentence the reader is borne down by the full expression. The words: *with an agony of apprehension* completely destroy the effect—therefore interfere with the truth of the statement. The word *frightened* is fatal. It seems as if it had been written without any thought at all. It takes away all sense of reality—for if you read the sentence *in its place on the page* you will see that the word '*frightened*' (or indeed any word of that sort) is inadequate to express the true state of that man's mind. No word is adequate. The imagination of the reader should be left free to arouse his feeling.

'. . . When the whole horror of his position forced itself upon his mind, Pa'Tûa for a space lost his reason . . .' This is truth; this it is which, thus stated, carries conviction because it is a *picture* of a mental state. And look how finely it goes on with a perfectly legitimate effect . . . 'He screamed aloud, and the hollow of the rocks took up his cries' . . . It is magnificent! It is suggestive. It is truth effectively stated. But 'and hurled them back to him mockingly' is nothing at all. It is a phrase anybody can write to fit any sort of situation; it is the sort of thing I write twenty times a day and (with the fear of overtaking fate behind me) spend half my nights in taking out of my work—upon which depends the daily bread of the house (literally—from day to day); not to mention (I dare hardly think of it) the future of my child, of those nearest and dearest to me, between whom and the bleakest want there is only my pen—as long as life lasts. And I can sell all I write—as much as I can.

This is said to make it manifest that I practise the faith which I take the liberty to preach . . .

> *Joseph Conrad. Letter to Sir Hugh Clifford (9 October 1899),*
> Life and Letters *(1927), ed. G. Jean-Aubry.*

. . . it is only through an unremitting never-discouraged care for the shape and ring of sentences that an approach can be made to plasticity, to colour, and that the light of magic suggestiveness may be brought to play for an evanescent instant over the commonplace surface of words: of the old, old words, worn thin, defaced by ages of careless usage.

The sincere endeavour to accomplish that creative task, to go as far on that road as his strength will carry him, to go undeterred by faltering, weariness, or reproach, is the only valid justification for the worker in prose. And if his conscience is clear, his answer to those who, in the fullness of a wisdom which looks for immediate profit, demand specifically to be edified, consoled, amused; who demand to be promptly improved, or encouraged, or frightened, or shocked, or charmed, must run thus: My task which I am trying to achieve is, by the power of the written word to make you hear, to make you feel—it is, before all, to make you *see*. That—and no more, and it is everything. If I succeed, you shall find there according to your deserts: encouragement, consolation, fear, charm—all you demand—and, perhaps, also that glimpse of truth for which you have forgotten to ask.

Joseph Conrad. Preface to The Nigger of the Narcissus *(1897)*.

FRESH, USUAL WORDS

A style interests when it carries the reader along: it is then a good style. A style ceases to interest when by reason of disjointed sentences, over-used words, monotonous or jog-trot cadences, it fatigues the reader's mind. Too startling words, however apt, *too* just images, too great displays of cleverness are apt in the long run to be as fatiguing as the most over-used words or the most jog-trot cadences. That a face resembles a Dutch clock has been too often said; to say that it resembles a ham is inexact and conveys nothing; to say that it has the mournfulness of an old squashed-in meat tin, cast away on a waste building lot, would be smart—but too much of that sort of thing would become a nuisance. To say that a face was cramoisy is undesirable: few people nowadays know what the word means. Its employment will make the reader marvel at the writer's erudition: in this marvelling he ceases to consider the story and an impression of vagueness or length is produced on his mind. A succession of impressions of vagueness and length render a book in the end unbearable.

There are, of course, pieces of writing intended to convey the sense of the author's cleverness, knowledge of obsolete words or power of inventing similes: with such exercises Conrad and the writer never concerned themselves . . .

We used to say that a passage of good style began with a fresh, usual word, and continued with fresh usual words to the end: there was nothing more to it. When we felt that we had really got hold of the reader, with a great deal of caution we would introduce a word not common to a very limited vernacular, but that only very occasionally. Very occasionally indeed: practically never. Yet it is in that way that a language grows and keeps alive. People get tired of hearing the same words over and over again . . . It is again a matter for compromise.

Our chief masters in style were Flaubert and Maupassant: Flaubert in the greater degree, Maupassant in the less . . . We stood as it were on those hills and thence regarded the world.

Ford Madox Ford. Joseph Conrad, A Personal Remembrance (*1924*), *Part III, Chapter ii.*

THOUGHT CHARGED WITH EMOTION

The great secret of Stendhal, his great shrewdness, consisted in writing *at once*. His thought charged with emotion remains as lively, as fresh in colour as the newly developed butterfly that the collector has surprised as it was coming out of the cocoon. Whence that element of alertness and spontaneity, of incongruity, of suddenness and nakedness, that always delights us anew in his style. It would seem that his thought does not take time to put on its shoes before beginning to run. This ought to serve as a good example; or rather: I ought to follow his good example more often. One is lost when one hesitates. The work of translating, for this, does a disservice. Dealing with someone else's thought, it is important to warm it, to clothe it, and one goes seeking the best words, the best turn of expression; one becomes convinced that there are twenty ways of saying anything whatever and that one of them is preferable to all the others. One gets into that bad habit of dissociating form from content, the emotion and the expression of the emotion from the thought, which ought to remain inseparable.

André Gide. The Journals of André Gide, Vol. III: 1928–1939, *transl. Justin O'Brien* (*1949*).

EFFECTS OF THE LONG WEEK-END (1918–1939)

To sum up my remarks. Our period: a long week-end between two wars. Economic and psychological changes already in existence intensifying. Writers are intimidated by the economic changes but stimulated by the psychological. Prose, because it is a medium for daily life as well as for literature, is particularly sensitive to what is going on, and two tendencies can be noted: the popular, which absorbs what is passing, and secondly, the esoteric, which rejects it, and tries to create something more valuable than monotony and bloodshed. The best work of the period has this esoteric tendency . . .

E. M. Forster. The Development of English Prose between 1918 and 1939 (*1945*).

ACKNOWLEDGEMENTS

THE compiler and the publishers are grateful to the following publishers and literary executors for permission to include copyright material:

Edward Arnold (Publishers) Ltd. for extracts from *Aspects of the Novel* and *Two Cheers for Democracy* by E. M. Forster; Mrs. Janice Biala for extracts from *Joseph Conrad: A Personal Remembrance* by Ford Madox Ford; W. A. Aspenwall Bradley (Paris) for extracts from *It was the Nightingale* by Ford Madox Ford; Cassell & Company Ltd. for extracts from *The Coiners* and *The Logbook of the Coiners* by André Gide; Chatto & Windus Ltd. for extracts from *Letters* by Feodor Dostoevsky, translated by Ethel Colburn Mayne, and for extracts from *Guermantes Way* and *Time Regained* by Marcel Proust, translated by C. K. Scott-Moncrieff and Stephen Hudson; Chilton Company (New York) for extracts from *Life and Art* by Thomas Hardy; Editions Louis Conard (Paris) for extracts from *Correspondance* by Gustave Flaubert; J. M. Dent & Sons Ltd. for extracts from *A Personal Record, Notes on Life and Letters* and *Prefaces* by Joseph Conrad, and for extracts from *Life and Letters* by Joseph Conrad, edited by G. Jean-Aubry; John Farquharson Ltd. for extracts from *Letters, The Ambassadors, Portrait of a Lady, The Spoils of Poynton, Roderick Hudson, The American, The Awkward Age, The Lesson of the Master, The Golden Bowl, The Altar of the Dead* and *Partial Portraits* by Henry James; Librairie Gallimard (Paris) for extracts from *To the Happy Few* by Stendhal, translated by Norman Cameron, Librairie Gallimard, all rights reserved; Harcourt Brace & Company Inc. (New York) for extracts from *Aspects of the Novel* by E. M. Forster, copyright, 1927, by Harcourt, Brace and Company, Inc. (renewed, 1954, by E. M. Forster, and used by permission of the publishers), and for extracts from *Two Cheers for Democracy* by E. M. Forster, copyright, 1947, by E. M. Forster (also used by permission of the publishers); the trustees of the Hardy Estate for extracts from *Life and Art* by Thomas Hardy; Harvard University Press (Cambridge, U.S.A.) for extracts from *Dr. Grimshawa's Secret* by

Nathaniel Hawthorne; William Heinemann Ltd. for extracts from *Life and Letters* by Joseph Conrad, edited by G. Jean-Aubry; David Higham Associates Ltd. for extracts from *Joseph Conrad: A Personal Remembrance* by Ford Madox Ford; Alfred A. Knopf Inc. (New York) for extracts from *Journals of André Gide*, by André Gide, translated by Justin O'Brien (Volume I, copyright 1947 by Alfred A. Knopf Inc., Volume III, copyright 1949 by Alfred A. Knopf Inc.), and for extracts from *The Counterfeiters* by André Gide, translated by Dorothy Bussy, copyright 1927, 1951, by Alfred A. Knopf Inc.; The Estate of the late Mrs. Frieda Lawrence for extracts from *The Letters of D. H. Lawrence* and *Phoenix* by D. H. Lawrence; Macdonald & Co. (Publishers) Ltd. for extracts from *To the Happy Few* by Stendhal, translated by Norman Cameron; Macmillan & Co. Ltd. for extracts from *Far from the Madding Crowd, Early Life* and *Later Years* by Thomas Hardy; Oxford University Press Inc. (New York) for extracts from *The Notebooks of Henry James* by Henry James, edited by F. O. Matthiessen and Kenneth B. Murdock, reprinted by permission of Oxford University Press Inc.; Laurence Pollinger Ltd. for extracts from *The Letters of D. H. Lawrence* and *Phoenix* by D. H. Lawrence; Random House Inc. (New York) for extracts from *Guermantes' Way* and *Time Regained* by Marcel Proust, copyright Random House Inc.; Mr. Denys Kilham Roberts for extracts from 'A Conversation Between I. Compton-Burnett and M. Jourdain', *Orion* (1945); Martin Secker & Warburg Ltd. for extracts from *Journals* by André Gide; Sheed & Ward Inc. (New York) for extracts from *God and Mammon* by François Mauriac, published by Sheed & Ward Inc., New York; Sheed & Ward Ltd. also for extracts from *God and Mammon* by François Mauriac; The Viking Press Inc. (New York) for extracts from *Phoenix* and *Letters* by D. H. Lawrence and for extracts from *Journals* by Arnold Bennett; The Owner of the Copyright for extracts from *Journals* by Arnold Bennett; Mr. Leonard Woolf for extracts from *A Writer's Diary* by Virginia Woolf.

INDEX OF AUTHORS AND TITLES
IN THE INTRODUCTIONS

INDEX TO THE TEXT